WORK WITH YOUTH IN DIVIDED AND CONTESTED SOCIETIES

Work with Youth in Divided and Contested Societies

Edited by

Doug Magnuson
School of Child & Youth Care
University of Victoria
Victoria, Canada

and

Michael Baizerman
School of Social Work
University of Minnesota
St. Paul, U.S.A.

SENSE PUBLISHERS
ROTTERDAM / TAIPEI

A C.I.P. record for this book is available from the Library of Congress.

ISBN 90-8790-023-6 (paperback)
ISBN 90-8790-024-4 (hardback)

Published by: Sense Publishers,
P.O. Box 21858, 3001 AW Rotterdam, The Netherlands
http://www.sensepublishers.com

Printed on acid-free paper

CONTENTS

CONTENTS

RESEARCH, THEORY, AND YOUTH

PROGRAMS AND ORGANIZATIONS

STORIES AND BIOGRAPHIES

CONTENTS

PREFACE

I agreed to write this preface for two reasons: Young people have long been my interest and concern, and I created Peace People after a particular young student had been hurt in sectarian conflict, and because the man who headed the youth programme of the Peace People, Paul Smyth, asked me. What we began then, in 1976, he continues in his work with Public Achievement, one of the three sponsors of the annual meetings called Youthworkers in Contested Spaces. The first three were held here in Northern Ireland, at a reconciliation space, appropriately so.

Of course, as is said, "Young people are our future." But equally important, they are our present too, and without recognition of their presence among us we will never come to invite their active participation in engaging how we go about often sustaining division and conflict. In this, young people are often active, carrying on – too often under direct threat and duress – the tensions rife within their own and the larger community: They embody both the ongoing quality of these conflicts *and* the possibility of containing or ending it.

For young people to become active, positive contributors to diminishing, controlling and preventing these tensions, divisions, and conflicts, there must be adults available who give their lives to engaging with youth in this positive work, working with them to prevent their own recruitment into paramilitaries and other formal and informal groups playing negative roles in violence and conflict; working together with young people to create alternate, non-violent, just, and equitable ways and paths for and through adolescence and into adulthood; work with young people to create alternate visions of a peaceful, just, equitable, and fair community and society, and work with youth and others to realize these visions in buildings, programmes, and activities.

Youthwork, as I understand this ethos and set of practices, is the society's announcement that young people have communal value, now. It is a statement that they, the young people, are noticed, valued, and needed by the whole community.

When youthwork is exemplary and conditions are supportive, it may be possible also to engage adults in peacemaking and peace-sustaining. Together across age, youth, worker and young person are foundational for the work of transforming divided and contested places into spaces of civic vitality where all the people of a community and society can meet, talk, laugh together, sit alone, and, in these ways, carry-on everyday life.

Youthwork in Contested Spaces is about working in the everyday with young people to create and sustain civic and private life, without the extra tensions and conflict of divided and contested neighborhoods, communities, and nations; it is about civility, decency, caring and helping, being available, and being responsible – all the simple, ordinary and possible ways we could live together *with* our differences.

Work with youth matters. And when it is grounded in skills and a clear moral stance against and a clear moral stance for, it can teach that individuals, groups, and communities can, should, indeed, must work at living together for our collective and individual betterment where age, sex, race, ethnicity, language capacity, place, and sexual orientation are not allowed to keep us apart; indeed, where we come together in common cause *because* we find each other so necessary to our common fate and to individual lives.

Without good youthwork, the task will be that much more difficult. With good youthwork it is possible.

Mairead Corrigan Maguire
Nobel Laureate
The Peace People

ACKNOWLEDGEMENTS

The authors and editors are grateful to the participants and organizers of the Youth Work in Contested Spaces initiative, a partnership between Public Achievement in Northern Ireland, The Youth Council for Northern Ireland, and the University of Ulster's Community Youth Work team. It was funded by the Office of the First and Deputy First Minister of Northern Ireland, through the European Special Support Programme for Peace and Reconciliation (Peace II).

The editors thank Paul Smyth, of Public Achievement Northern Ireland, for inviting us into this project and for educating us about "this work" and his work.

We thank all of the authors for their diligence and patience and for sharing their wisdom.

We thank Elisse Magnuson for editorial assistance and proofreading.

To the young people and youthworkers whose everyday lives in their divided and contested communities embody the realities that this book is about.

They address us and call us. In our response we tell who we are.
They are waiting.

MICHAEL BAIZERMAN

INTRODUCTION

A question invites and structures reflection and inquiry, drawing the reader toward a perspective, a stance, an insight, a space unfilled: A question opens a world. A response may close it, and when the response is an answer, it does close the question. A good answer invites other questions. Everyday and professional thinking and reflection, disciplined science, and creative art are all animated in some way by the interrogatory. Rarely this orientation to thinking and to reflection discloses one of our deepest human qualities – our orientation to ourselves and our world through wondering, for we embody "primordial wonderment" (Boelen, n.d.).

In some religious, social, and scholarly worlds, questions are basic orientations to belief, understanding, and search. To many in everyday life, questions drive them crazy! Typically, people want "answers," not questions. They want to "get on with it" and not spend so much time "analyzing." "Don't be so theoretical!", they say, often seeming to mean, "Don't be so abstract and conceptual." "Just decide!", some say, stop "making it more complex" even, and stop looking for subtleties, exceptions, contingencies, even patterns: Stop questioning! Stop interrogating! Stop trying to figure it out; "Act!"

Too often youthworkers talk like this, pushing for concrete, specific action, now when others might want to wait, question, analyze, discuss, reflect – seemingly endlessly. Youthworkers are persons of action, living and working co-presently with young people right here, right now. "Save the questions for later!" some say: First act, then analyze. They are partly right; life indeed is lived now, here, this instant, and the next. So too is youthwork. But, we claim, good youthwork lives also and simultaneously in the worker's wondering, analyzing, questioning, in reflexivity in the moment and reflection and evaluation in the following moment.

We advocate a craft orientation to youthwork grounded in both situational and ongoing inquiry, structured in the shape of questions and given purpose and meaning by the work-to-be-done and the work-being-done-now. And we propose that such a questioning orientation be elemental to the act of reading. Reading this book, on this view, is to be actively engaged in a trialogue among you, this book and your youthwork world.

Interrogate yourself and what you read. Invite the text to question you and your practice. It is in this spirit and with this substance that each of the sections is given an introduction, and this is followed by a set of questions designed to invite angles for reading, thinking, and youthwork. The queries are about practice,

Doug Magnuson and Michael Baizerman (eds), Work with Youth in Divided and Contested Societies, 1–2.

theory, research, and policy. In the final chapter, these are brought together into a deeper analysis of what was learned about youthworkers in contested spaces.

Always the deeper answer for those who ask a necessary, good, right, and important question.

Michael Baizerman
University of Minnesota

DOUG MAGNUSON

THE PERILS, PROMISE, AND PRACTICE OF YOUTHWORK IN CONFLICT SOCIETIES

We are the children of an epoch,
the epoch is political.

Everything of yours, ours, theirs,
daytime affairs, night-time affairs,
are political affairs.

Like it or not,
your genes have a political past,
your skin has a political hue,
and your eyes a political aspect.

What you speak about has resonance,
What you hush has a voice
more or less political.

Even walking through field or forest
you take political steps
on a political basis.

Apolitical verses are also political, and the moon above
is shining a thing no longer moonly.
To be or not to be, that is the question.
What kind of question? answer, my dear.
A political question.

> From *Children of an Epoch*, Wislawa
> Szymborska, trans. Walter Whipple available
> http://www.mission.net/poland/warsaw/
> literature/poems/epoch.htm

Doug Magnuson and Michael Baizerman (eds), Work with Youth in Divided and Contested Societies, 3–12.

For societies in conflict and emerging from conflict, youthwork is a moral and existential necessity, since youth are both vulnerable to and contributors to violence and trouble. For youthworkers in the rest of the world, work with youth in conflict societies is morally and existentially compelling because of the anguish present in some youth stories and the fragile balance between hope and desperation. This is demonstrated even here at the University of Victoria, in Canada and located on an island in the Pacific Ocean, where we may be as far away from this type of political conflict as possible, yet there are, presently, eight undergraduate and graduate students with youthwork experience in Africa, Eastern Europe, and Northern Ireland. What these students learn there is important and valuable for youthwork professions in the developed world: the political re-enchantment of everyday life.

This enchantment is contrasted with Radiohead's tone poem inversion of Szymborska:

> Fitter, happier, more productive,
> Comfortable,
> Not drinking too much,
> Regular exercise at the gym,
> (3 days a week),
> getting on better with your associate employee
> contemporaries,
> at ease,
> eating well (no more microwave dinners and saturated
> fats),
> a patient better driver,
> a safer car
> (baby smiling in back seat),
> sleeping well
> (no bad dreams),
> no paranoia...

This might be an appropriate satire of North American and, increasingly, European youth development: its instrumentalism, scientism, and dullness.

Still, in Western Europe and North America, there is on occasion a manifest event to remind us that political conflict—even ethnic conflict--is not so far away. The aftermath of Hurricane Katrina from 2005 in the state of Louisiana, U.S., the riots in Los Angeles in 1992, riots in France in the fall of 2005, and the controversy over the publication of racist cartoons by European newspapers in the fall of 2005 and early 2006 suggest that our own conflicts are less resolved than temporarily suppressed. Youthworkers in conflict societies may be more prepared for the modern world than the rest of us, and they can teach us to re-populate our work with politics.

A COMPARISON OF YOUTHWORK LITERATURES

What is remarkably similar in the literature and practice of work in conflict societies and the literature about youthwork in North America and Europe is the content of ideological and practice debates. For example, Boyden and de Berry (2004) suggest that the agenda of practice in conflict societies move away from child and youth as victim—from a medical model of treatment—and away from purely intrapsychic processes. This is a good set-up for youthwork, which has a history of objecting to these. Eyber and Ager (2004) claim that post-traumatic stress disorder (PTSD) is a Western concept, socially constructed, that has been imported into other cultural contexts where it does not apply, an argument that parallels youthwork's objection to the Diagnostic and Statistical Manual of Mental Disorders. Mann (2004) argues that Western concepts of parental attachment are imported with harmful result to non-Western cultures. Newman (2005) argues that Western notions of childhood interfere with effective policy about war-affected children. All of these are important conversations.

In this volume, however, there is a different--albeit related--set of ideological issues. The classic explanation of these is by Kohlberg and Mayer (1972), who distinguished between three different ideological traditions in the pedagogy of work with youth: the romanticist, cultural transmission, and developmental. Youthwork's historical origins in Europe began as a romanticist impulse. Pestalozzi, following Rousseau, organized schools for youth where education was conceived as an organic impulse that begins with the child's interests and attractions. Imposing education and values on children is seen here as a form of oppression. A second strand of the romanticist impulse is found in the work of Jorczak (Lifton, 1988) who, of necessity and under difficult conditions, organized orphans into communities.

Their work has contemporary parallels, as in the streetwork in Brazil described by de Oliveira (2000) and in the trauma work described by (although not advocated by) Boyden and de Berry (2004), both of which assume the innocence of children and the necessity to restore organic conditions of growth. In recent work, these assumptions, especially the assumption of innocence and of trauma, have taken a beating on cultural difference grounds and on the grounds that children are both victims and contributors to violence.

The cultural transmission model is also seen in contemporary work, especially in the literature of conflict resolution. Shapiro (2004) says that, in Romania, "People were free to deal with their differences but, after living in a closed society for 45 years, they had few skills to do so" (p. 70). Shapiro designed a conflict management program to teach youth these skills, because "to develop future leaders, adolescents became the target population..." (p. 70). Conflict management, conflict resolution, and mediation training have also been widely used in Northern Ireland. The view of young people here is that they need preparation for the coming world, and the youthwork task is to teach the needed skills and values. This model assumes that conflict is a consequence of "not knowing better," a lack of skills, and largely individually controlled. In some situations it may also assume a lack of a particular kind of enculturation.

In comparison, Bigirindavyi (2004) says that ethnic violence is a "communal interaction. . . . an effort to achieve security. . . . an expression of purpose, control, and power. . . . a means to a better future.. ." (pp. 84-85). Others, such as Kemper (in this volume), point out that conflict and violence can become their own reward in the intoxicating aromas of battle, power, money, and sex.

These youth are the ultimate participants in globalization, in ways that theorists of the left do not often imagine. They participate in a marketplace of ideas, arms, sex, and power in service to the demands of the marketplace—local or not—and the voyeurism of political ideology. War and conflict give them entrée and equal access to the world: attention and with it power, a ladder of opportunity, and it is immediate. In this volume, Lancaster describes well the deep-seated justifications and motivations for joining a militia. Against these motivations, new skills are a weak force.

A third line of work with youth is developmental, in a sense that attaches development to politics and to moral commitment. In Britain and the U.S., this work has its origin in the pragmatic pedagogies of Dewey (1916) and Jane Addams (Elshtain, 2002). Development is a consequence of recognizing the conditions of one's life, how it is connected to others, and testing plans and solutions against experience, and youth grow and develop through role-taking, perspective taking, including empathy, and--most importantly--through the implementation and accomplishment of justice.

It is this third branch of youthwork that is widely assumed by the authors in this volume. In contrast to relief and therapeutic work, Kemper proposes a model of building a "peace constituency" of young people who chart for themselves alternatives to violence and victimhood. In Belgrade, Ognjenovic, Skoc, and Ivackovic describe how youth organized into clubs gain sanctuary from the ethnic conflicts around them but also plan projects for themselves that transform their daily lives. In this he shows how politics and applied development are attached. Kresoja tells the story of the Novi Sad youth branch of the Helsinki Committee in a project promoting the memory of victims of Srebrenica. The Women's Commission for Refugees conducted a research study in which youth trained as researchers designed instruments and conducted surveys and interviews.

All of these use, at least, common youthwork practices such as "planned uncertainty" (Malekoff, 1977) and a future orientation rather than a past-oriented therapeutic orientation. As Bryderup (2004) says, "The principle of inclusion is thus assumed to turn the relationship between the individual and society upside down, ascribing society the task of creating a space for the individual's own projects, thus preventing marginalisation...Such a shift in perspective might give rise to a relational view of children's and youngster's difficulties or special needs" (p. 346).

Still, while youthwork in conflict societies resembles professional work elsewhere in form and content, the conditions under which it is performed are extraordinary and what makes it unique is simply the courage required to do it. The bold statements of the Helsinki Committee Youth Group in Novi Sad, under threat from fellow Serbs and being denied protection by the police, the persistent work of the KOSOVO youth network which has no financial support, and refugee youth doing research are unlikely to happen in the developed world. When our students return from these countries, they return changed, including being unable to understand the petty concerns of workers and youth here in Canada when others have such compelling and consequential needs.

Youthwork in conflict societies stretches and challenges us by showing us the political nature of all work with youth, the limits and possibilities of work where youth are alienated from their families, processes of reflexive identity management and negotiation under extreme conditions, the necessity of respect for the challenges of multi-culturalism, exemplars of moral commitment, the importance of interdependence, what can and should be done when youth are "immigrants" in and alienated from their own culture, and the power of enculturation.

YOUTH AS "IMMIGRANTS"

Mead (1970), Keniston (1975), Bronfenbrenner (1974), Erikson (1950), Coleman (n.d.), and Lewin (1951) call our attention to the status of young people, whether "immigrants" (Mead), "alienated" (Bronfenbrenner, Lewin), "not children but not certain to become adults" (Keniston), or "lacking a guide to adulthood" (Coleman). For each of these authors, traditional processes of enculturation are not effective or even useful as a guide to young people. The reasons for this are theorized to be that the conditions of modern life are different in important respects for younger generations, and so the accumulated wisdom of elders is less useful.

For youth in conflict societies, the circumstances of this immigrant status are extreme and extenuated, with the added condition that the pressures of enculturation are stronger, even as tradition is more conflicted as a guide. McEvoy-Levy (this volume) describes how well girls' speech reproduces the troubles of Northern Ireland, and ethnic prejudices in other parts of the world carry on for generation after generation. Whereas youthworkers in the developed world can take the status of youth and youth culture for granted, in conflict societies this immigrant status is an existential and moral challenge, because youth may face stark choices. Choosing to be different than their elders may be a moral claim but dangerous to their lives and a threat to their future. There is pressure to maintain traditions, to maintain the "Other" as enemy, and to fear change.

Work with youth under these conditions will teach the rest of us about what it truly means to be a generalist and about staying power under difficult conditions. Deconstructing and reconstructing a culture, one-on-one and group-by-group, takes real time and real opportunities. The power of enculturation in conflict societies should give us pause, given that it seems on the surface to be self-destructive. But perhaps too much has been made of generational difference in the developed world as well. The social and moral role of work with youth as challenge to enculturation and as a moral claim probably needs to be rethought.

There is a further historical and ideological issue in this work; Kett (1977) believed that prior to industralization, most youth organizations were youth-led but, as adult anxiety about youth increased, most were gradually co-opted by adults. In conflict societies, a similar dynamic may occur, as in Mokwena's description of how youth movements against apartheid in South Africa have moved toward institutionalization and away from charisma. In Serbia, protests against the regime of Milosevic started with young people, and in this volume there is an excellent description by Gashi of the drama of being a protester, including the terror of being captured by police and the thrill of taking a stand. Youth are leaders in all conflict societies, unless the conflict has become more ritualized, as in the case in Northern Ireland, where there is a large "conflict industry" largely controlled by adults.

In the Western world, youth participation, youth leadership, and participatory research are values that threaten to become platitudes because, it seems, what we really mean is careful parceling out of resources, decision-making power, and access. In conflict societies, it is likely that Western aid organizations are reproducing this careful control by adults rather than promoting democracy. This is bound to fail to attract youth in societies where, in other places, youth are deciding the future. Across the globe, work with youth in conflict societies challenges us to be more innovative and more honest about these issues.

MULTICULTURALISM, DIVERSITY, AND THE NEGOTIATION OF IDENTITY

There are many examples of how this work may be cutting edge and an exemplar of how traditional cultural values, ethnic and religious ideologies, transcendent moral ideals, and globalization come together. Youth participation, the latest in a long line of North American youthwork fashions, is almost completely apolitical and even acultural, a technique available to all ideologies and cultures without much controversy. In contrast, in places like Kosovo, much of South America, and the Middle East, youth participation is a global ideal raised as a challenge to local culture, even as it is being adapted to local conditions. Tala Weiss of Jordan is helping to organize a network of Arab youth in the region, including the participation of young women. In Kosovo, the Kosovo Youth Network advocates for youth-led organizations, and in Northern Ireland, Public Achievement models a process of involving youth in decision-making about their own lives, within and across religious boundaries. In Chile, youth group membership implies political ideology.

A further example of the role of global ideals and of the limitations of North American thinking about globalization is from my experience at the University of Northern Iowa. I supervised an M.A. project of a student from Ghana, who was interested in the United Nations Convention on the Rights of the Child (UNCRC) and its implications for youthwork. During his presentation, another faculty member whose expertise was diversity suggested that the UNCRC was a colonial framework imposed on the developing world by the industrialized West.

Before the student could respond, his wife spoke up, saying that if it had not been for universal, international standards—Western or not—she would not have been able to go to school, she would have been married off at a young age, and she would not have been allowed to work. She had no interest in raising her own children with the values of her childhood village.

Similarly, this work with youth implies something about the common experience of young people in contested and conflicted societies, including the aspiration to transcend local identities that are based on hostility or violence, the experience of following in their parents' footsteps or striking out on their own, and staying in one's own community or leaving for a place of sanctuary and new opportunity. For these youth, when they have a choice, are drawing on global ideals and lifestyle possibilities and, once they do so, it is very hard to return to local cultures and values.

Yet universal ideals have to be locally appropriated, and these ideals cannot and should not be confused with Western interventions, models, and techniques. It is the latter that Boyden (2004) rightly objects to. The local aspirations--embodiments of universal ideals--do not have to embody Western economic, familial, religious, or practice values and models. Furthermore, it is possible that Western models of multi-culturalism may be getting in the way as much as other kinds of Western practices, in that it represents a careless relativism that refuses to judge injustice and harm or it reveals itself as little more than sentiment and reverse prejudice. Youthworkers in conflict societies are less cautious, out of necessity and urgency.

What is needed, at least in the English language literature, is a discussion of what these local appropriations in other cultures can teach the rest of the world about how universal moral values are instantiated in particular cases of injustice, about community development, and about education—formal and informal. More can be done to learn to set aside aid and intervention models, capitalizing on local understandings of community restoration, resolution, and justice, cultural senses of time and value, and local definitions of growth and change. These are urgent issues, because the cultural and organizational incompetence of Western bureaucracies causes trouble, as Epstein (2005) pointed out in her article about AIDS programs in Africa.

Of equally serious concern for local values, culture, and infrastructure is the threat of emigration once the door is opened to live elsewhere. Even a recently peaceful country like Poland is losing much of a generation to Western Europe and the rest of Central Europe, a loss of expertise and energy. In short, youth and youthworkers in conflict societies experience many of the same limits and opportunities of multi-culturalism and identity negotiation, albeit under more stressful conditions, as youth and youthworkers everywhere.

What has yet to be discussed well is how those local cultures and values can be rescued against the threat of both factionalism of the traditional culture and also the threat of abandonment by the younger generation. Escape from the former does not have to mean a rush toward Western materialism and Western youth culture.

What is also needed in this regard is some careful sorting out of the conditions of the work in places where the roots of the conflict are ethnic and religious as compared to places where economic globalization uproots local communities, as in parts of Nigeria, the Congo, and Latin America.

EVALUATING AND CONCEPTUALIZING THE WORK

Lederach (1997) argues that peace-building, of which reconciliation is a core value and practice, is rooted in building trust, a "process-structure," and in "creating a platform from which it is possible to respond creatively to evolving situations" (p. 131). Youthwork in the Western world does relationship-building. But we also know that relationship-building, while comforting to youth and to us, is not enough either for rescuing youth from trouble or for contributing to social change, whether in conflict societies or not. For these the skills, vision, and resources necessary are more formidable and require locating and creating transcendent, superordinate goals and interests across conflict divides. With due and sincere respect to the wisdom of Lederach and others, there is a considerable gap between ideas about how this work is done and empirical research studying the work.

Careful descriptive work would be a good beginning: how, where, and when workers spend their time working. Under what circumstances is the work focused on individuals or on groups? What kind of supervision is provided and what is the relationship of this supervision to practices in organized youthwork? What interpersonal, managerial, organizational, and leadership skills are demonstrated, and to what effect?

It is important to study the conditions under which this work can be effective, or not. For example, Lancaster (this volume) suggests that we might question effectiveness when there is ongoing violence. This is a challenge to much of this work that assumes a goal of violence reduction. But, certainly, Lancaster's viewpoint is supported by Kemper's (this volume) and Bigirindavyi's (2004) sobering descriptions of the difficulty of creating alternatives to soldiering or joining the militia. On the post-conflict side of the spectrum, Mokwena's (this volume) history of South African youthwork may suggest that the work has to evolve after the urgency of the conflict ends.

There are many terms used for which some rich description of practice would be helpful, for example, inclusion, diversity, reconciliation, repatriation, leadership, participation, civic engagement, integration, and single-identity work. Finally, there is a sophisticated literature in conflict resolution, especially in the literature having to do with of international relations and with business negotiations. It does not appear that these ideas, except in general terms, are used with young people.

IN THIS VOLUME

An expertise about relief work and intervention in the midst of armed conflict requires one kind of expertise and a unique set of resources, represented in part by Lorey (2001). This volume has little to say about those kinds of interventions and crises. They require particular kinds of wisdom, experience, and cleverness, say, to figure out what to do about the complexities of conflict and war in the Congo or Burundi.

But the authors here have long experience in conflict societies where violence, rioting, harassment, and threats are ongoing problems but also where some kind of longer-term development and work is possible, and this work is made dynamic under the uncertain terrain of working out political, economic, religious, or ethnic conflicts. Most of these authors have personal experience of participation in conflict, some in opposition to each other, and all have experienced loss. Like youthworkers everywhere, their commitment to the work is intertwined with their personal stories. For this reason, this volume includes numerous personal biographies.

The aim is to provide a flavor of the work and an introduction to its practice. While there is plenty of literature about children as victims of war and violence and literature about charity and relief work in these areas, the perspective of this volume is on the complex world of work with youth as participants and at the intersection of "social need, social inquiry, and social action," as Jane Addams once described her educational aims in the poor immigrant communities of Chicago.

Every book leaves something out, intentionally or not, and what is missing from this volume are contributions from Latin America, especially, and many places in Africa. This is due mainly to our own ignorance about the work there and also to the challenges of collecting writing across cultures and from practitioners for whom writing takes time away from the urgencies of day-to-day life in conflict societies. These omissions will need to be corrected.

Doug Magnuson
University of Victoria

REFERENCES

Bigirindavyi, J. P. (2004). Youth intervention for peace project: Burundi case study. *New Directions for Youth Development, 102*, 81-94.

Boyden, J., & de Berry, J. (2004). *Children and youth on the front line: Ethnography, armed conflict, and displacement.* New York: Berghahn Books.

Bronfenbrenner, U. (1974). The origins of alienation. *Scientific American, 23*(1), 53-61.

Bryderup, I. M. (2004). The educational principles of social education and special education for children and youngsters in care: A Danish study. *Young: Nordic Journal of Youth Research, 12*(4), 337-355.

Coleman, J. S. (n.d.) *Innovations in the structure of education.* Baltimore: Johns Hopkins University. (ERIC Document Reproduction Service No. ED 015159).

de Oliveira, W. (2000). *Working with children on the streets of Brazil: Politics and practice.* New York: Haworth.

Dewey, J. (1916). *Democracy and education.* New York: MacMillan.

Elshtain, J. B. (2002). *Jane Addams Reader.* New York: Basic Books.

Eyber, C., & Ager, A. (2004). Researching young people's experience of war: participatory methods and the trauma discourse in Angola. In J. Boyden & J. de Berry (Eds.), *Children and Youth on the Front Line* (pp. 189-208). New York: Oxford.

Erikson, E. (1950). *Childhood and society.* New York: W. W. Norton.

Epstein, H. (2005, November 3). The lost children of AIDS. *New York Review of Books, 52*(17). Downloaded November 5, 2005, from http://www.nybooks.com/articles/18399

Keniston, K. (1975). Prologue: youth as a stage of life. In R. J. Havighurst & P. H. Dreyer (Eds.), *Youth: The seventy-fourth yearbook of the National Society for the Study of Education.* Chicago: University of Chicago Press.

Kett, J. (1977). *Rites of passage: Adolescence in America 1790 to the present.* New York: Basic Books.

Kohlberg, L., & Mayer, R. (1972). Development as the aim of education. *Harvard Educational Review, 42*, 451-496.

Lorey, M. (2001). *Child soldiers. Care and protection of children in emergencies: A field guide.* NP: Save the Children.

Lederach, J. P. (1997). *Building peace: Sustainable reconciliation in divided societies.* Washington, DC: United States Institute of Peace Press.

Lewin, K. (1951). *Field theory in social science.* New York: Harper & Row.

Lifton, B. J. (1988). *The king of children: A biography of Janusz Korczak.* New York: Farrar, Straus, Giroux.

Malekoff, A. (1997). *Group work with adolescents: Principles and practice.* New York: Guilford.

Mann, G. (2004). Separated children: care and support in context. In J. Boyden & J. de Berry (Eds.), *Children and Youth on the Front Line* (pp. 3-22). New York: Oxford.

Mead, M. (1970). *Culture and commitment: A study of the generation gap.* Garden City, NY: Natural History Press.

Newman, J. (2005, March). *Protection through participation: Young people affected by forced migration and political crisis.* Oxford: Refugee Studies Center, University of Oxford.

Shapiro, D. M. (2004). After the fall: A conflict management program to foster open society. *New Directions for Youth Development, 102,* 69-80.

INTRODUCTION TO CONTEXTS AND POLICY

Life is lived in context, in a place and time and among others. Growing-up and living in a contested space – pre-violent, violent, or post-violent – is one such contextual reality, with especially powerful short-to-long-term effects on who one is and how one does life – as child, youth, and adult--and youthworker. The authors in this section think carefully and thoroughly, in different ways, about how to understand the work and its evolution under changing conditions.

Mokwena and Smyth tell the story about the origins of youthwork in South Africa and Northern Ireland, respectively, and the influences of the dramatic movements toward peace in each setting. Kemper and Lancaster tell the story from the point of view of international NGOs, and each is interested in how these NGOs conceive of the work and when and where it should be done. Spanja tells about how European social education has been adapted to the local practice and educational needs in Vukovar, Croatia.

In each of these are interpretations of the context or setting and are opportunities for reflection and comparison. Consider the following questions:

What do these chapters teach us about:
- contested-spaces (pre, current, and post-violent)?
- what it means to be a young person?
- the nature of the organizations hosting (and resisting) work with young people?
- the nature, shape, and practice of work with youth?
- what counts as "context?"

Violence

- Is violence and/or "contested spaces" the only or even the most salient context for being a young person? For doing youthwork? For one's everyday life?
- What power does violence take and what power is it given over the life-world of young people? Of youthwork?
- What are the words used to name violence in your context?
- Who does violence belong to in your context?
- In your context, who can make violence do what they want it to? How did they come to have this power? What sustains this power? What and whom could limit or take away this power?
- If not violence, what? After violence, what?

Policy

- What scholarly and practical theories help interpret and explain the contested spaces you live and work in? The contested spaces in the article you are reading?
- What is your theory about how your contested space came to be, was sustained, and may be controlled or pushed away or transcended? And contested space in general?
- In your context, who are the makers of youth policy and the developers and managers of youth programmes?
- What policy and management choices are foreclosed, forbidden, or too dangerous simply because they would have to be made and carried out in a contested space?

PHIL LANCASTER

CATEGORIES AND ILLUSIONS: CHILD SOLDIERS IN BURUNDI

ABSTRACT

Children in Burundi are employed as scouts or spies, used in local defence militias, and recruited or forced into rebel groups. There may be as many as 14,000 child soldiers. The causes for this have to do with survival imperatives and social decay as a result of civil war, and children suffer. Soldiers also take in homeless and abandoned children, feed hungry children, and care for them. At the same time children suffer from violence, they are protected from violence by their own unit.

Stopping the use of child soldiers proved to be difficult while conflicts continued. Attempts included invoking international conventions, building informal consensus, and rights-based programming. Lacking an effective State to enforce agreements, these were ineffective until a true peace agreement was achieved and enforced. Outside intervention on behalf of child soldiers may not be effective, or even useful, without a political resolution of the conflict.

I always find it difficult to understand a particular child soldier case without first understanding some of the historical context. But tracing the history of a particular conflict is a bit like trying to relate a cup of water dipped out of a stream to a particular source. It may be easy to find the beginning of the stream, but tracing the origins of a single part of it from among all the possible tributaries is much more complicated. Perhaps it is for this reason that historians tread so carefully around the notion of causality.

With due concern to the need to strike a balance between historical accuracy and general understanding, I think we can make some sense of the recent conflict in Burundi by tracing it back to the imposition of a power imbalance during the colonial period. Though Tutsi dominance had a long history before the arrival of the Belgians, the development of a modern state administrative system, complete with a well-equipped national army and police force, allowed political power to be manipulated in new ways. In 1963, shortly after independence, the struggle for control of state administration led to a cycle of interethnic massacres, reprisal killings, and political assassinations that is only now slowly calming. It

Doug Magnuson and Michael Baizerman (eds), Work with Youth in Divided and Contested Societies, 15–26.

boiled over in 1993, when violence increased dramatically in response to the assassination of the first elected Hutu president.

A military coup returned to power Major Pierre Buyoya, an ethnic Tutsi, but generated a crisis that led to the death of approximately 300,000 Burundians. Mutual fear and panic prompted wide scale displacement and led to the emergence of several rebel movements, the crumbling of social order, the growth of armed militias, and a dramatic increase in the number of children involved in the fighting. Since the beginning of the most recent troubles, children have been drawn into the conflict in a number of roles that meet the most common definition of child soldier.[1] That child soldier recruitment has gone on throughout this period despite the coming into force of a set of international conventions and covenants suggests that there is something about the phenomenon of child soldiers in this particular case that might reward careful analysis. That child recruitment continues now even after the deployment of a United Nations Peace Keeping (2004) force ought to make us all take another look at what we think we are achieving.

The scale of the use of child soldiers by all parties to the conflict reached a point such that, sometime in the late 1990s, it sparked general alarm. In late 2001, a paper entitled *Enfants soldats: un defi a lever au Burundi* was circulated within various departments of the Government of Burundi. This paper was surprising both in its candour and for the fact that it was generated within the government and did not, despite the strong position it took against recruitment within government forces, lead to censure of the middle-level bureaucrats who produced it. UNICEF was quick to spot the opportunity the circulation of this paper presented and began exploratory work to develop a project aimed at disarming, demobilising, rehabilitating, and reintegrating (DDRR) children on all sides of the conflict. Despite the apparently broad consensus behind their efforts, they met with mixed results and the problem of child recruitment continues into 2006, despite a peace agreement that has led to the disarmament of all but one of the rebel movements, the *Forces Nationals de Liberations* (FNL) and the deployment of a United Nations Peace Keeping Operation in Burundi (UNOB). The aim of this paper is to describe some of the difficulties encountered in the attempt to protect children from recruitment in Burundi and to explore some of the more troublesome issues that pop out against the background of our collective failures.

HISTORY OF CHILD SOLDIER INTERVENTIONS IN BURUNDI

Despite the lack of reliable data about the number of child soldiers in Burundi, by early 2002 a good deal of anecdotal evidence had been gathered, largely through a determined effort spearheaded by UNICEF, working in collaboration with the

---

[1] The Cape Town Principles list all children with or associated with an armed force in any capacity except that of family dependent.

Burundian Ministry for Human Rights and Social Mobilisation.[2] Child soldiers fell into several rough categories. Those who were employed by the *Forces Armees Burundaises* (FAB or Army) as spies or scouts were given the name *doriya*[3] and included children who had collected around military posts in search of scraps of food or security as well as those who were actually given scouting missions. A second group consisted of those recruited by the government to form local defence militias *(guardiens de la paix)*. This set of children did not generally deploy away from home but were used more as sentries or point guards within their own villages and towns. The third set was composed of children with the rebel groups. No numbers were available while the conflict continued, though estimates in 2002 generally put the figure at about 14,000 for all categories.[4] Though the smaller of the two rebel groups has yet to put down its weapons, UNICEF had, by September 2005, disarmed a total of 3,000 children as part of the peace process that began in 2004. Though the discrepancy between estimate and reality is of interest, this paper, to remain consistent with its aim, examines only two of many possible questions: 1) why these children, whatever their number, could not be rescued prior to the cessation of conflict; and 2) why FNL recruitment cannot be stopped.

In November, 2001, a rebel force attacked Kirambi II school in the Ruyigi district, kidnapping 26 children and two teachers. At Kayanza school, they abducted over one hundred more. Over the course of the following days, the rebels attacked other schools and medical centres where they systematically looted or burnt buildings and forcibly recruited more children to act as porters. As of the end of January, 21 children had escaped or been released and five were still in rebel hands. At the end of February, a report on the experiences and condition of these children was submitted by the NGO, Transcultural Psychosocial Organisation (TPO). According to TPO, boys between the ages of 13-17 had been the prime targets for recruitment in this case. Once captured, they were pressed into immediate service as porters. Over the course of the time they were held captive, the children reported they were subjected to constant verbal and physical abuse, threats, under-nourishment, exhaustion, and were also exposed to all of the risks and terror of combat. Not surprisingly, many of the children exhibited signs of acute psychological trauma.

Though the effects of serving as a child soldier naturally vary according to individual makeup, the circumstances of recruitment and subsequent service and the extreme conditions faced by this particular group of children was, at the time, taken as evidence of the need for immediate action. Though most of these particular children escaped or were released after a short period, the relative vulnerability of all children in the area to similar acts had a fairly strong psychological effect on the entire community.

---

[2] UNICEF Burundi hired me as a consultant to develop their first child soldier project proposal in February, 2002. Before my arrival, political and security conditions had mitigated against any overt action in this regard. It should be noted that the UNICEF Country Representative had been assassinated in 1999 and survivors were justifiably cautious.

[3] This is Kirundi for "one who listens."

[4] Both the government document already cited and the Coalition Report of 2001 gave the same figure. Both used estimates provided by UNICEF that proved, on investigation, to be ungrounded.

Anecdotal testimony collected by UNICEF over the period 2001-2002 from escaped children who had been forced into rebel ranks described a grim set of conditions including:

- violent training methods;
- threats, physical abuse, and harassment;
- acute hunger;
- extreme fatigue as a result of being forced to keep pace with adult soldiers while carrying heavy loads;
- forced cross border movement into Democratic Republic of Congo and Tanzania;
- lack of medical care;
- extreme fear; and
- being forced into combat in which the poorly trained child conscript was sometimes pushed into the front lines ahead of his leaders (UNICEF Burundi Proposal for Demobilisation of Child Soldiers, 2002).

Accounts of conditions faced by *doriya* and child *Guardiens de la paix* painted a slightly less grim picture of conditions. The causes of child recruitment into government forces have been investigated in some depth.[5] Poverty, displacement, loss of parents, hunger, search for status, peer pressure, and desire for revenge were all cited as common causes of voluntary recruitment for all categories of child soldiers (Field interviews, Bujumbura, May 2002). The sad truth was that many children were driven into military service by a combination of survival imperatives and social decay, both of which were a direct result of civil war. While the FAB clearly were selective in the access they allowed me, it was difficult to find solid evidence of intentional abuse or deliberate exposure to risk. Rather, I found many accounts of army subunits taking pity on children who came to them in pitiable condition and who had nowhere else to turn. I also met a number of junior ranking soldiers who admitted to making good use of the cheap labour the children provided.

Later, in 2005, I met one young man whose school fees had been paid by voluntary subscription from the unit he had been associated with. Suffice to say that the conditions of service were not entirely bad for all child soldiers with the government. However, following field studies in the provinces of Ruyigi, Bubanza, and Gitega conducted in 2002 (UNICEF Burundi, 2002), it was clear that there was widespread concern at nearly every level of Burundian society about the effects on individual children and the long term consequences for the country. Yet no action was taken to demobilise the children until a cease fire was signed a year later, no effective means of protecting children from recruitment was found, and no effective action has yet been taken in the case of those children still with the FNL or to provide protection against FNL recruitment in areas where they are active.

WHAT TO DO?

One of the major problems encountered in any attempt to get children out of the middle of active hostilities is that posed by the prevailing security conditions. In

---

[5] In 2002, the Army appointed a full colonel to facilitate development of a process to prevent FAB recruitment. First steps included facilitating a number of interviews with children in their ranks.

the case of inter-ethnic conflict, such as in Burundi, children were vulnerable in part because of their ethnicity. This was a war of massacre and counter massacre in which whole communities were attacked regardless of their combatant status. Indeed, both sides use the term genocide freely when speaking of the actions of the other.[6] Armed groups on both sides targeted each other's civilians. Under such circumstances it is difficult to imagine how one might separate out the children from the general mass of victims. But let us consider the problem of each subset of child soldiers in an attempt to try to tease some tentative conclusions.

The phenomenon of children with the FAB, the *doriya*, arose largely as a result of family separation, the specific nature of guerrilla style combat, and the general vulnerability resulting from political and social anarchy. The Army had an interest in having effective spies as a consequence of a type of warfare that followed no rules. The guerrillas had no logistics capacity other than what they could beg or tax from the civilian population, so they were driven by need to move clandestinely through villages and to disguise their military role until the moment of attack. Children offered an effective form of protection to the military forces of both sides precisely because they are a common sight in Africa and were, consequently, able to pass unnoticed virtually anywhere children gather, which is wherever the action is. By placing children loyal to them in markets or school grounds, the Army was able to monitor rebel movements. The Army could also send children ahead of their own movements to listen to what was happening in village markets and so help indicate the houses that might be sheltering rebels. For their part, the children saw the Army as their best hope of survival. As cycles of panic and flight separated families across the country, a number of children had no other choice but to beg protection from the Army. It must be understood here that as the state was torn apart, the only institution still functioning reasonably effectively was the Army. Consequently, it frequently found itself filling a rather large vacuum.

It is difficult to understand the level of vulnerability if one does not at least grasp the basic elements of life in Burundi. Most Burundians live from the produce of very small farms. Both ethnic groups lived on the small holdings of a few hectares scattered far and wide through mountainous terrain with only foot paths linking them. Lacking castles or fortified towns, the safest place to be during unsettled times was a military position, and the best way to be let in was to provide a service. The army's need for porters, servants, scouts, and spies created space for children needing protection and food. Meaningful intervention to protect children in this context would have entailed developing some other means of both providing protection from physical attack and dissuading the Army from meeting its military needs by taking advantage of children's vulnerability.[7] While the government of Burundi and UNICEF were able to bring the Army into line with respect to

---

[6] On the Gitega road, one finds a monument dedicated to the Tutsi victims of an attempted genocide. Curiously, there are not yet any such monuments to draw attention to the very much larger number of Hutu victims.

[7] Contrast contemporary thinking about using children in war with earlier times: "It was then that Lord Cecil Edward, the chief staff officer, gathered together the boys of Mafeking and made them into a

recruitment, they could do nothing about the security part of the equation until the fighting stopped.

Rebel child soldiers faced parallel conditions amplified by the rebel's lack of logistics and transport capacities lacuna that could be compensated by child recruitment, and the past history of government massacre of whole Hutu communities. Children sometimes saw themselves as part of an ethnic community driven to fight in self-defence against an army with genocidal intentions.[8] The rebel case was, and to some extent continues to be, complicated by the sense of injustice that fuelled the passions that prompted fighting in the first place and, as a consequence, motivated recruitment. During a field mission for UNICEF in October, 2002, I interviewed a number of Hutu refugees living in UNHCR run refugee camps in Tanzania and discovered a set of strongly expressed convictions on the necessity of fighting to win a share of power. As one school teacher I met put it, "If we don't take our state back, we will never be safe at home." This conviction was echoed by a group of young men I met who were counting the days until they could go back across the border.[9] Interestingly, these young men/boys all had army boots lined up for inspection outside their dwelling, all had injuries attended to recently and looked, to my cynical old soldier's eyes, like an infantry section taken out of the line for medical attention and rest. Needless to say, they made good use of the resources provided by the good will of the international community through the offices of UNHCR.[10]

The *Guardiens de la Paix* arose out of the pattern of ethnic distribution and the relative strengths of the opposing forces. Rebels could move easily through the countryside to attack isolated outposts and conduct small raids on larger centres but never had the military strength to take on the FAB in battle. Conversely, the Army had superior military strength but lacked both the mobility and military intelligence capacity to fix rebel forces in place for attack. In practice this meant the government was forced to hunker down in a defensive posture. In order to free up forces for more aggressive operations, the Ministry of the Interior instituted a local defence militia and, *voila*, child soldier *guardiens* began to appear across the country. While it is true that there were probably a number of economic and social factors that played a role in this phenomenon, the problem again can be seen most clearly against the backdrop of prevailing security considerations. Children living in communities vulnerable to rebel attack lived with constant threat. The logic of the situation suggested to many of them that they would be

---

cadet corps....And a jolly smart and useful lot they were....These boys didn't seem to mind the bullets one bit" Lord Baden-Powell, *Scouting for Boys* (Boy Scouts Association of Canada, circa 1964, p. 17).

[8] The argument explaining possible justification for including children as active participants in wars of survival is well made in David M. Rosen, *Armies of the Young: Child Soldiers in War and Terrorism* (London, 2005). Chapter two is of particular relevance.

[9] See Liisa H. Malki, *Purity in Exile: Violence, Memory, and National Cosmology Among Hutu Refugees in Tanzania* (University of Chicago Press, 1995) for a more complete account of the dominant political narrative among Hutu refugees in Tanzania.

[10] This statement may provoke an angry response. At the time of my field mission to Tanzania, UNHCR had held to the line that there was no evidence either of child recruitment or military use of their facilities. While their motivation for holding to this story is easy to understand, the fact that the strength of their denial stopped effective child protection activities is difficult to justify.

less vulnerable if they took an active role in their own defence. In the case of likely attack, many no doubt thought it better to have a weapon than to sit passively waiting for some non-existent force to come to their aid.[11]

Again, the challenge for international intervention in these cases is to come up with a credible security alternative. I leave aside for the moment the likely reaction from the children themselves to the suggestion that they should be protected by adults from their own community rather than the other way around. My own memory of late adolescence leads me to see this as imposing a preference for passivity that many sixteen-year-old boys in any part of the world would automatically reject.

So, in each case, the predominant precondition for ending child recruitment is the provision of security. Civil war brought with it conditions that made appeal to law completely unrealistic, since no agency existed with the power to apply it. We might make all sorts of additional claims about economic or social condition causes of conflict but, it seems intuitively obvious to me at least, that these are secondary to the more important issue of security. Economic or social changes may be part of the eventual solution to the conflict and may be critical to post-conflict stability but are really beside the point where the challenge we have taken on is to protect children from recruitment *while hostilities continue.*

WHAT WORKED AND WHAT DIDN'T

The fact that the FAB and all rebel groups but one stopped using children the moment they entered a peace agreement might be claimed a success but falls short of satisfying the requirement to protect children before hostilities end.[12] The main strategy in the period leading up to full implementation of the Arusha Accord was to invoke international conventions protecting the rights of children and to condemn all parties to the conflict who violated them by recruiting children. Practically, this relied most heavily on advocacy that followed two complementary strategies. The first aimed at achieving a set of formal legislative measures to establish an appropriate legal basis on which to prosecute cases of child recruitment. Though formal changes were indeed made, they had no teeth as long as the government was unable to govern and so failed to achieve any perceivable result.

---

[11] In October 2001, I met a group of frightened Ugandan farmers who had been chased into hiding by their cattle raiding neighbours, the Karamajong. These people did not fight back and could not rely on effective protection from the Ugandan People's Defence Force. They spent most nights during that season huddled with their families and animals in traditional hiding spots that seemed equally well known to their attackers. While those of us raised in well formed states might think their actions consistent with civil order, without the key element of an arbitrating force to protect all citizens from each other, there simply was no civil order. The options were simple: fight or flight. Flight was ineffective.

[12] According to UNICEF progress reports, the FAB have released approximately 600 child soldiers and the FDD, which became the most prominent rebel force and from which the current president was elected, released another 600 since entering a peace accord in 2003. The remainder of the 3000 involved in the current DDR project come from the *guardians de la paix* with a small number from other minor rebel outfits.

The second strategy aimed to build an informal consensus against the practice of child recruitment. This included working closely with the government of Burundi to support a child protection unit within the appropriate government department, establishing and maintaining a close relationship with the FAB for advocacy purposes, and developing a network of social contacts to promote community dialogue on the subject. For a time, it also included an effort to make contact with the main rebel group leadership, though it appears that this initiative was not followed through.[13] This strategy succeeded insofar as it led to a fruitful period of cooperation with the FAB so that child soldiers could be demobilised slightly ahead of general demobilisation but failed to slow recruitment in any way or to bring about demobilisation of any children before the formal end of conflict. One wonders if FAB cooperation did not owe more to strategic thinking about ways to take the moral high ground away from their opponents than to pressure, but I suppose that really does not matter if the result worked to the benefit of children. However, getting FAB cooperation and pledges to stop recruitment was, at best, a limited success. The larger problem remained and still remains. Children are still being recruited by the FNL despite the advocacy and an improved political outlook. The best the humanitarian community, which in this instance includes a fairly robust peacekeeping mission, has so far produced is the establishment of a task force based on Security Council Resolution 1612, which calls for monitoring and reporting of child recruitment and other forms of abuse. Meanwhile, recruitment continues.[14]

For several years since the ratification on the UN Convention of the Rights of the Child (UNCRC), UNICEF and several other UN agencies had been developing a rights-based approach to programming. The fundamental idea is that the CRC proclaims a set of rights that could be used as the basis for all programme activities from traditional water and sanitation programmes to focused child protection programmes. Unfortunately, this approach stumbled into deeper waters than the institutions using it seemed to understand. Where the most difficult child soldier cases are concerned, the approach generated little more than noise. Reaching an understanding of the rights protection problem requires a short digression into philosophy.

The general idea of the concept of a right is that it entails a corresponding obligation on some particular agent or set of agents. Some philosophers make a distinction between positive and negative rights, arguing that they impose different types of obligations (Dworkin, 1977; Nozick, 1974). A negative right, such as the right to non-interference in the pursuit of one's legitimate goals would, by some

---

[13] This may be sour grapes on my part as I was the consultant hired by UNICEF in late 2002 to start the process but, despite having succeeded in opening dialogue with the FNL, the process appears to have been aborted after I handed in my report.

[14] SC Resolution 1612 has prompted the development of a questionnaire to be used in the reporting of ongoing abductions/recruitment in Burundi. While no figures yet exist, the phenomenon of FNL recruitment is widely recognised.

[17] Jan Narveson, for one, argues for a minimal state sufficient to the guaranteeing of property rights and enforcing of contracts *The Libertarian Idea*, Philadelphia: Temple University Press, 1988. Robert Nozik famously described a "night watchman" form of statehood in *Anarchy, State and Utopia* (Basic Books, New York, 1974). Others think there are emotional elements to political life completely missed in the purely rational approaches named here.

distinctions, require only that all persons party to the rights agreement refrain from interfering. There would be no corresponding requirement for enabling action or assistance. Property rights are sometimes held to offer a concrete example of a negative right in that one holds property by the let of others who have obligations corresponding to ones claims of ownership.

However, Holmes and Sunstein (1999) have pointed out that property entails a social contract among all members of the society within which the right is claimed and that these rights impose an architecture of enforcement that must be supported by taxation, which is a positive obligation. A positive right, such as the right to education, would require positive action to meet the entailed obligation that, in this case, would be to provide an educational system. To make a meaningful rights claim in either case suggests that there is some system in place that guarantees obligations of either kind will be respected. This implies a system of adjudication of claims and a complementary system of enforcement animated by some agency endowed with the power to convert word into action.

If one takes as a starting point the current set of commonly accepted basic human rights listed in the Universal Declaration of Human Rights, one is quickly led to the conclusion that the most promising institution capable of meeting the full systemic requirements of a context within which a full set of positive and negative rights can be meaningfully claimed is the state. One need only consider the impossibility of making any sort of rights claim in present day Somalia to see how necessary the agency of state institutions is to the protection of rights in general. We may quibble about how much power the state should have but still agree that some form of collective agency, or some form of state, is required to create a context of rights.[17] However, our particular concern is the right of children to be protected from recruitment into armed conflict, so we need to consider what form of general obligation this right entails and how the agency needed to meet it might be achieved.

Conceptually, the right to be protected from underage recruitment could be easily understood as a matter of law. But in the Burundi case, the legitimacy of the machinery of state had been thrown into question in the most brutal way. When the massacres started, law lost its effective force and the state lost its capacity for effective agency as a result. The fact that enough citizens felt themselves justified in picking up arms against their own state, whatever their reasons, effectively blocked the state's capacity to apply its own laws. It had neither the moral nor the military or physical capacity. Does this mean that rebellion is, or ought to be, against the law?[18] Or does it rather suggest that states ought to be constituted in ways that make it impossible for states' armies to attack their own citizens with impunity?

There are a host of philosophical issues here that are beyond the scope of this work and for which there is a long tradition of discussion within Western culture. Suffice to say for the moment that the issue of law is embedded

---

[18] Aristotle offers an interesting discussion of possible grounds for rebellion in Chapter 5 of his Politics. For a more recent argument, see T.E Gurr, *Why Men Rebel* (Princeton University Press, 1979).

conceptually in notions of political, economic, and social justice that are themselves complicated by linguistic issues that I will not delve into here.[19]

But in the most general sense, political obligations entailed by individual rights claims depend on a capacity for effective agency that is challenged by civil war. Agency requires a combination of will and active capacity. For states, generating political will entails a process through which collective decisions are reached and subsequently respected enough to permit will to be translated into action. The state of Burundi had lost the capacity to act to protect the rights of its citizens precisely at the moment that its collective decision-making process fell prey to ethnic factionalism. Since much of the action in question was directed against its own citizens, this is hardly surprising, though it does raise some interesting historical questions in the context of other states.[20] However, we are left with a niggling doubt about the qualifying conditions of state legitimacy that is interesting.

One way of looking at the problem of child protection is to consider the entailments of relevant international agreements. On this view, a state that has signed and ratified the Convention on the Rights of the Child and its subsequent protocols is required to constitute itself in a certain way just because it has obligations to its children that cannot be met if it loses its legitimacy in the eyes of its own people. From this perspective, any action that undermined state capacity for effective agency on behalf of its children would be wrong, including rebellion or unjust state actions that lead to rebellion. But where does that leave us?

Herodotus tells a story about the chief architect of the Athenian victory in the Battle of the Hellespont, Themisticles. It would seem that the hero saw the victory as an opportunity to extract tribute from the Greek city states that had been saved by the destruction of the Persian fleet, so he sent his agents to collect. According to the story, when they arrived at Andros, they were confronted by outright refusal to pay up. When the Athenians threatened the Andradeans with the twin gods of "Persuasion and Compulsion," the city fathers replied that they were under the dictatorship of the gods "Poverty and Inability" and therefore could not pay no matter how much they might wish to. "For however strong Athens was, she could not turn Andros' 'can't' into 'can'."[21]

Fanciful as this tale might be, it seems to describe quite well the condition of the Burundian government *vis a vis* advocacy aimed at convincing them to stop the use of child soldiers within their borders. Lacking sufficient military force to impose law, the only way they could comply would be to either concede defeat or negotiate a compromise. Given the political context and their fear that loss of political supremacy would expose them to the risk of genocide, their unwillingness

---

[19] I hold back with some difficulty. The debates between communitarian theorists, such as Alasdair MacIntyre or Jurgen Habermas, and those who argue for the possibility of universal notions of rationality, such as John Rawls or Alan Gewirth, seem largely ignored in humanitarian debates. Shlomo Avineri and Avner de-Shalit provide a synopsis in *Communitarianism and Individualism* (Oxford University Press, 1992).

[20] The reasons why the Holocaust did not lead to open rebellion and civil war need thought. Certainly, the claim that Hutu extremists would almost certainly have wiped out all their Tutis victims in Rwanda had it not been for the intervention of the Rwandan Patriotic Army is hard to refute *–despite the presence of UNAMIR.*

[21] Herodotus, *The Histories*, Aubrey de Selincourt (trans.) (Penguin Edition, 1965), p. 561.

to do either is understandable. The situation was similar in the case of those rebel groups who represented a defensive response to what they saw as a threat of genocide. Each side continued to use all means, including child recruitment, to protect itself against the other. Each side justified its recruitment against that of the other, and children on all sides were motivated by their own security concerns to fight in their own defence.

Given that the point I am trying to make cannot be easily made without a great deal more argument, I am left hoping that there might be just enough here to suggest that one of the problems faced in dealing with the child protection issue in Burundi was, and to some extent continues to be, a lack of understanding of what it means to be able to live up to the political obligations entailed by rights claims. That child recruitment went on despite the fact that Burundi had expressed a will to stop it and has continued even after a partial peace agreement has been reached suggests a correlation between the need for peace and the possibility of meaningful child protection.

While the state may have been able to stop its own troops from active recruitment, it had--and continues to have--little power to protect children physically from attack by other armed groups. To meet its obligations, it would have had to either defeat all rebel forces or to protect every community in the country from rebel attack, neither of which it could do. Nor did it have the military power to apply the legal sanctions that might have forced respect for laws against child recruitment. Lacking sufficient military power to dominate politically, the state could only regain its capacity for collective political action through political compromise.

Ultimately, the only thing that worked to protect at least some children from recruitment and to obtain the release of the 3,000 who were eventually identified as belonging to one of the armed groups discussed above was a peace process. Child soldiers were only demobilised once the ink dried on the peace agreement.

ILLUSIONS OF POWER

I have argued that the primary problem in dealing with the challenge of protecting children against recruitment in the Burundi case was, and to some extent continues to be, the lack of an effective agency capable of meeting the security requirements. I argue further that this agency would have to establish itself as an outcome or an effect of governance and that only a well-formed state would be capable of providing it. If my argument holds, then it follows that humanitarian intervention to protect children from recruitment is not going to be adequate to the task in cases where government is no longer possible, that is, in cases of ongoing civil war or rebellion. No matter how much an outside agency might try, the difficulty of protecting children from recruitment into armed forces in cases like that of Burundi will exceed their reach unless they are first able to re-establish the order that is the basis for effective governance and, therefore, of effective agency. No matter what rights are violated, unless the capacity for governance exists, there is simply no way to meet the entailed obligations.

PHIL LANCASTER

Politics is about power. It is about the way power is organised, legitimised, and exercised. As long as the international community accepts the notion of national sovereignty, there is little that can be done to prevent or correct cases of political meltdown in countries where the internal dynamics of power fail to generate consensus adequate to satisfy the rights and obligations formula. That is not to say that there is no hope to be found in either diplomacy or international intervention, but the case of Burundi is typical in that it is one of many that happened in relative obscurity and that took well over ten years to resolve.

Even Nelson Mandela could not bring the conflict to a sudden stop, though it is fairly clear that his personal intervention was instrumental in setting the wheels of the current peace process into motion. Diplomacy takes time. As the cases of Rwanda and Darfur illustrate, international intervention needs both the will to sweep aside issues of sovereignty and the military force to do it effectively. As the case of Iraq illustrates, there may not be sufficient force available and it is no substitute for politics. Suffice to say that there are times and places where the only effective means of protecting children within a context of violent politics is through peace. Either that or some new strategy needs to be developed that can accomplish the task. Until then, strategies based on advocacy, appeals to human rights arguments, or humanitarian imperatives have limited hope. The lesson of Burundi is simply that there are limits to what can be achieved on behalf of children from outside a failing political dynamic.

Phil Lancaster
University of Victoria, Canada

REFERENCES

Dworkin, R. (1977). *Taking rights seriously*. Cambridge, MA: Harvard University Press.
Nozick, R. (1974). *Anarchy, state, and utopia*. New York: Basic Books.
Holmes, S., & Sunstein, C. R. (1999). *The cost of rights: Why liberty depends on taxes*. New York: W.W. Norton & Company.

YVONNE KEMPER

YOUTH IN WAR-TO-PEACE TRANSITIONS: APPROACHES OF INTERNATIONAL ORGANIZATIONS EXECUTIVE SUMMARY AND INTRODUCTION[22]

EXECUTIVE SUMMARY

This study deals with youth in war-to-peace transitions and the response of international organizations to them. While youth's relevance for societal transformation is a long-acknowledged fact, their large numbers and potential roles in conflict have recently caused organizations to consider them a target group for peace and development programs. Reflecting on this process, this study thus assesses the difficulties in conceptualizing the role of youth in peace-building processes, on the one hand, and the concrete efforts of international organizations to integrate them into their policies and programs on the other. For this purpose, it explores four guiding questions: First, what approaches have international organizations developed regarding youth? Second, on which assumptions about youth and their role in violent conflicts are they based? Third, how do the different approaches affect program development and, fourth, are they compatible?

One of the obstacles in targeting youth is finding a common definition. While the United Nations (UN) defines them as people between the ages of 15 and 24, youth are, in reality, a heterogeneous group. According to this study, youth is a transitional state between childhood and adulthood and is highly dependent on the socio-cultural environment. The situation of violent armed conflict exacerbates the problems of finding a common definition, because it forces children to assume adult roles and functions.

Indeed, a large and growing portion of combatants in protracted armed conflicts are youth. Since there is no legal framework for this group, however, demobilization and reintegration programs (DRPs) have largely neglected them in practice. Neither small children nor mature adults, international organizations have been torn between a desire to protect them and allowing for their meaningful

[22] The complete report is available from www.berghof-center.org and from the Berghof Research Center for Constructive Conflict Management, Altensteinstrasse 48a, D-14195, Berlin, Germany. The editors gratefully acknowledge and thank the Berghof Research Center and Yvonne Kemper for permission to reprint excerpts from the full report.

participation. In contrast to armed groups, which regularly offer youth an income, an occupation, status, identity, and the "excitement" of violence, most DRPs fail to appeal to older children and young adults. But the failure to (re)integrate youth into civil structures cannot only put the peace-building process at jeopardy but also deprives these war-affected societies of a potential driving force for peace and development.

In order to explain the various responses of international organizations towards youth in conflict contexts, specifically regarding demobilization and reintegration, this study developed three ideal-typical approaches: (1) a rights-based approach, (2) an economic approach, and (3) a socio-political approach. The rights-based approach is based on the UN Convention on the Rights of the Child and has so far confined the work of international organizations to youth under 18 years of age. The economic approach views youth as decision-makers in the marketplace who respond to supply and demand in pursuit of their interests. The socio-political approach regards youth's self-perception and their relationship to civil society as crucial for the peace-building process. After outlining the basic ideas on a theoretical level, we examine two exemplary demobilization and reintegration programs to determine their practical value for post-conflict peace building.

Accordingly, each approach possesses distinct strengths and weaknesses that are ultimately derived from the different roles they assign to youth in peace and conflict. The strengths of the rights-based approach, therefore, lie in the preventive phase, the advocacy function, and the strengthening of community responsibility. The economic approach, on the other hand, is most effective in the short-term, because it can deliver immediate results to young beneficiaries and lure them away from armed forces. The socio-political approach fosters long-term reconciliation by countering the marginalization of young people through their integration into societal structures; it can best account for youth's gender-related identity, because it is based on their participation. As a result of these different qualities, this study concludes that a holistic approach is needed in order for international organizations to profit from their distinct advantages.

All approaches should converge in their common objective to create an enabling environment for youth in post-conflict situations: protecting them from forced recruitment, giving them a job perspective, furthering their personal development, and asking for their opinion and action. In fact, legal, economic, and socio-political dimensions are all necessary features of war-to-peace transitions. In order to make all three approaches compatible, the challenge is to adapt them to youth. Moreover, international organizations have to share a common perception of youth and to coordinate their policies and programs, putting youth's concerns before the organization's confined interests. By consolidating and systemizing experiences with youth in war-to-peace transitions, this study hopes to contribute to this endeavor.

INTRODUCTION

Adolescence shares many aspects with post-conflict situations: Both are periods of transition marked by struggles, instability, hopes, and fears. In contrast to children, who are covered under the UN Convention on the Rights of the Child (CRC), the "in-between" status of youth has been largely excluded from the agenda of international peace and development efforts. Most conflict-related data simply omit them, making analysis and targeted programming extremely difficult. Youth have entered public debate and discourse mainly as accomplices in crime, suicide bombers, soldiers or, simply, rebels.[23]

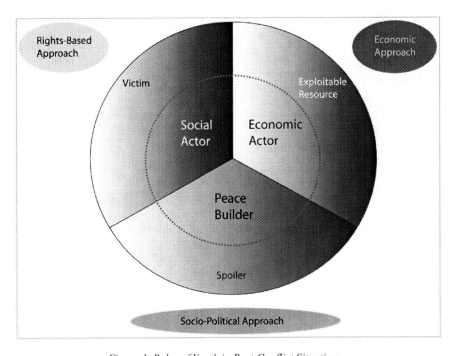

Figure 1. Roles of Youth in Post-Conflict Situations

---

[23] Adolescents also form a high-risk group for sexually transmitted diseases, especially HIV/AIDS, to which many negative connotations are attached.

	Rights-Based Approach	Economic Approach	Socio-Political Approach
Optimal Period	Prevention	Short term	Long term
Objective	Human security	Stability	Reconciliation
Target Group	Children (less than 18 years of age)	Youth (15 to 24 years)	Flexible, responsive to self- perception and socio-cultural concept
Roles of Youth (Characteristics)	Victim (vulnerable, innocent) ↓ Social actor (adaptable, resilient)	Exploitable resource (aggressive, greedy) ↓ Economic actor (resourceful, rational)	Spoiler (frustrated, excluded) ↓ Peace builder (transformable, active)
Instruments	Legal norms and conventions	Economic policies on micro / macro level	Participatory approaches
Typical Programs (Selection)	Reintegration into families; human rights advocacy; psychosocial work; basic education	Socio-economic reintegration; vocational training; income-generating activities; catch-up education	Participatory surveys; support of youth activities, organizations and networks; peace education
Typical Actors (Selection)	Save the Children, UNICEF	ILO, World Bank	GTZ, SFCG, WCWRC, UNDP

Figure 2. Three Approaches toward Youth in War-to-Peace Transitions

Emerging from this problem-based approach that characterizes them by their irresponsible and harmful behavior, several international organizations have recently discovered youth as a target group in peace building. The Women's Commission for Refugee Women and Children (WCRWC) has been one of the leading advocates for putting youth on the international agenda. The United Nations Development Programme (UNDP) and the United Nations International Children's Emergency Fund (UNICEF) are currently in the process of evaluating their youth programs in armed conflict. The World Bank (WB) has just opened an interactive internet discussion on the organization's youth strategy. Despite these efforts, the lack of a framework and the scarcity of program evaluations are daunting.

The following study thus aims to explore both the particular problems in conceptualizing the role of youth in peace-building processes and the responses of international organizations to this new target group. What approaches have international organizations developed towards youth? On which assumptions about youth and their role in violent armed conflicts are they based? How do the different approaches affect program development, and are they compatible? This study has identified three approaches for this purpose (see Figure 1) that underscore programs for youth in post-conflict situations: (1) a rights-based approach based on the framework of the CRC, (2) an economic approach that views youth through the lens of monetary decision-making during war, and (3) a socio-political approach that examines youth *vis-à-vis* its relationship to civil society. Only the rights-based approach has explicitly appeared in organizations' policies and practice.

Although the three approaches overlap in some areas, this study posits that each approach possesses distinct characteristics that can negatively affect the practice of organizations, leading to inconsistencies, gaps, and inefficiencies in the international response towards youth. Conversely, the three approaches can also complement each other if organizations capitalized on the approaches' comparative advantages through their cooperation and coordination. The approaches should thus be understood as a somewhat idealized construct to explain phenomena of youth programs.

This study will employ the term "youth," which includes adolescents and young adults as a distinct phase between childhood and adulthood. According to the UN World Youth Report, this includes persons from 15 to 24 years (World Youth Report, 2003). Rather than limiting this notion to a certain age range, however, this study emphasizes the necessity to define the term according to the functional and socio-cultural context. When appropriate, it employs Newman's (2004) distinction between "child," "adolescent," "youth," and the "young" or "young people." Accordingly, "child" describes individuals who have not yet reached puberty. "Adolescents" refers to youth who are at the transition from puberty to physiological maturity. "Youth" includes older teens up to those in their early mid-twenties. The "young" or "young people" serves as a general category."

This study will focus on the demobilization[25] and reintegration[26] of ex-combatants[27] in order to illustrate some practical implications of applying different approaches towards youth. The general distinction between child and adult combatants, which ultimately results from the legal status conferred to children, also highlights the problems in forcing youth into either of these categories. The

---

[25] Demobilization refers to the process of downsizing or disbanding armed forces (DPKO 1999, p. 15; GTZ/NODEFIC /SNDC/PPC, 2004).

[26] Reintegration programs assist former combatants with the families' economic and social reintegration into civil society. This can include cash assistance, compensation in kind or training, and income-generating measures (DPKO 1999: 15).

[27] For simplification, this study does not differentiate between recruitment and demobilization by armies, paramilitary groups, and civil-defence bodies although there may be considerable differences.

findings of this study are accordingly based on program descriptions and/or evaluations of demobilization and reintegration programs (DRPs) for children and youth. As a result of the absence of youth as a specific target group in most DRPs, this study will apply a broad definition of both youth and DRPs: DRPs for child soldiers will illustrate the rights-based approach, for youth-at-risk the economic approach is used in socio-economic reintegration and training and employment programs, and the socio-political approach is used in participatory programs for war-affected youth.

To collect opinions and information on the three approaches, nine semi-structured background phone or email interviews were conducted, including at least two representatives of each approach. Geoffrey Oyat, program officer at Save the Children in Uganda, and Casey Kelso, International Coordinator at the Coalition to Stop the Use of Child Soldiers, were interviewed for information on the rights-based approach. Irma Specht, director of the consultancy firm Transition International and formerly responsible for the socio-economic reintegration of ex-combatants at the International Labor Organization (ILO), and Maurizia Tovo, Senior Social Protection Specialist and Coordinator of the Orphans and Vulnerable Children at the World Bank, were interviewed for information on the economic approach. Michael Shipler, Program Coordinator of the Youth and Children Programs at Search for Common Ground (SFCG), and Kai Leonhardt, Project Manager of the youth program in Kosovo at the German Development Cooperation Agency (GTZ), were interviewed for information on the socio-political approach. In order to acquire expertise in the fields of DRPs and child psychology, semi-structured interviews were also conducted with Colin Gleichmann, Program Manager at the GTZ and specializing in demobilization and reintegration programs, Vera Chrobok, Researcher at the Bonn International Center for Conversion (BICC) with a focus on underage soldiers, Boia Efraime Jr., psychotherapist at the psychosocial rehabilitation project for former child soldiers in Mozambique, and Jo Boyden, Senior Research Officer at the Refugees Studies Centre at the University of Oxford with an expertise in children and youth living in extreme adversity. In addition to these hands-on insights, this study will utilize secondary literature to reflect the interdisciplinary dimension of this field of study.

DEFINITIONS AND CONCEPTS

Defining "Youth"

International organizations do not offer a common definition of youth, partly as a result of the multifaceted nature of this group. Each agency has therefore adopted a concept in line with their respective missions or mandates, mostly accompanied by an age range. The World Health Organization (WHO) distinguishes between three different categories: adolescents (10 to 19 years old), youth (15 to 24 years old), and young people (10 to 24 years old). Defining age chronologically reflects a research bias towards Western notions of normal childhood that are rooted in biomedical theory[28] and assigns a development stage to a particular age range (Newman, 2004, p. 8). In recent literature, however, child development is increasingly seen as "an active, social process" that is subject to "a process of negotiations between individuals, family members, peer groups. and the wider community in the context of life events and rites of passage" (Mawson, 2004, p. 226). As a result, the definition of "childhood" or "adolescent" must account for the functions of youth in a socio-cultural context, not just a particular age range (Women's Commission for Refugee Women and Children, 2000, p. 10ff).

A functional definition describes adolescence as a temporary stage in life between childhood and adulthood and subject to external circumstances. A visible physical maturation with the advent of puberty does, therefore, not automatically equate with a mental maturation towards adulthood (Wolman, 1998, p. 5ff). The situation of war makes growing up a matter of surviving, often turning a child into the sole caretaker of his or her younger siblings or a relentless warrior. A child thus acquires a *de facto* status of adulthood.[29] A child's performance in the emergency can, however, conceal whether the child has adapted to the growing challenge of surviving or whether this is merely an ad hoc coping mechanism followed by permanent psychological damage. The effect ultimately depends on the predisposition of the individual and the existence of protective factors such as parents or peers (Boyden & Mann, 2001, pp. 4, 10; Wessels, 1998). The socio-cultural environment can inform the understanding about children's resilience.

In fact, the cultural relativity of childhood, adolescence, and adulthood calls for an adaptation of definitions according to socio-cultural context. There exist profound differences between developing and developed countries that put universal definitions into perspective. One must recognize that industrialization and the extension of education have come along with the discovery of adolescence as a distinct life stage in many Western societies, a distinction that has not permeated every society to the same extent (Boyden interview, 2004).[30] The duration a society affords youth for growing up and maturing also depends on political and economic conditions (Newman, 2004, p. 10ff; Tefferi, 2003). In North America and Europe, a chronological categorization of youth between 12 to 13 and 21 to 25 prevails with a focus on the individual rather than the community. In contrast, societies in Africa or the Middle East usually regard it rather as a developmental stage between childhood and adulthood that is largely determined by the community and corresponds to the young person's functions (Sommers, 2001, p. 3ff; World Youth Report, 2003). Adding to the complexity of finding a

---

[28] There is a biomedical component to the adolescent stage because certain functions of the brain develop, especially the ability for abstract thinking (UNICEF, 2002, p. 6f).

[29] This ability to cope with adverse situations is described as a child's "resiliency." In contrast, its susceptibility to suffer damage as a result denotes its "risk" (Boyden & Mann, 2000, pp. 5-7).

[30] Ms. Graça Machel, expert of the UN Secretary-General on the impact of armed conflict on children, nevertheless, claims, "All cultures recognize adolescence as a highly significant period in which young people learn future roles and incorporate the values and norms of their societies" (2001, par. 170). This fact does not contest the necessity of adapting this definition to socio-cultural contexts.

socio-cultural definition, globalization can alter intergenerational relations by imposing a "global" definition of adolescence on societies (World Youth Report, 2003, p. 6).[31]

What happens, however, if the society that is meant to provide orientation is disintegrating? The dependency of adolescence on a protective socio-cultural frame of orientation puts them into an uneasy state of limbo in a crisis setting (Kübler, 2002, p. 10). States may be unable or unwilling to offer education, social services, or basic security that are preconditions for acquiring the economic and social status upon which adulthood is contingent. Many children and adolescents lose their family and community support and network because they are forced to migrate. The usual criteria for reaching adulthood, like financial independence, marriage, initiation rites, the right to vote, or full judicial liability can become illusory in a crisis setting (McIntyre & Wiess, 2002, p. 1). Although some adolescents thus perform some adult functions, like defending their country or earning their own income, political instability and poverty prevent them from reaching adulthood as defined by socio-cultural criteria. Some of them may thus "form regressive groupings, where preadolescent values such as being tough, arrogant, and mischievous prevail" (Wolman, 1998, p. 51). This regression inadvertently feeds into negative stereotypes of adolescents in a given crisis. The situation of armed conflict therefore reaffirms the utility of socio-cultural and functional criteria in grasping the complexity of the youth phenomenon.

Cynically, just as much as the vague notions of youth have discouraged international organizations from targeting this group, government and rebel forces alike have found the expandable definition advantageous for their mobilization efforts. Throughout history, teenagers' feelings of exclusion and drive for independence have been easily manipulated and exploited for military purposes. Further, there are strong political implications in defining childhood and youth: Young activists call themselves children to avoid punishment while authorities call them youth to make them legally culpable (Boyden & Mann, 2001, p. 68). In the end, adolescent groups are likely to choose to join organizations whose understanding of youth offers them "immediate participation in decision-making processes of the adult society" (Wolman, 1998, p. 50). Alas, militaries around the world regularly seem to hold this promise.

DEMOBILIZATION AND REINTEGRATION IN POST-CONFLICT SITUATIONS

With a ceasefire or a peace agreement, an intricate process of rebuilding war-torn societies sets in. Weak political and social structures, power competitions, and insecurity make countries in transition prone to relapse into violent conflict, decreasing people's trust in a viable peace. Rather than rebuilding the pre-war

---

[31] The media and international trade has transferred a global image of "teenage" life associated with certain products and activities, e.g. listening to rock or pop music, having fun, or drinking alcohol. The inability to share in this (costly) lifestyle can prompt a feeling of injustice among young people in poor countries who feel cheated by a system that denies them access to what commercials depict as their identity (World Youth Report, 2003, p. 6).

structures that catalyzed war, peace-building requires forming a new structure out of existing components of civil society. War-to-peace transitions aim to achieve a secure environment, accountable political structures, economic and social revitalization, and promoting societal reconciliation (Ball, 2001, pp. 720-724). Recognizing the importance of all of these tasks, the challenge becomes "to incorporate the longer-term objective of strengthening economic and political governance into short-term rehabilitation and reconstruction efforts" (Ball, 2001, p. 725).

The demobilization and reintegration of former combatants can become a visible and powerful sign of societal transformation. Its overall objective is the conversion of ex-combatants into civilians, usually after a peace agreement. In this, demobilization entails the more short-term process of separating combatants from military service or armed groups whereas reintegration focuses on the more long-term "social and economic inclusion of former combatants into their communities of origin or new communities" (IPA, 2002, p. 2). The chance of their re-recruitment into fighting forces is significant, though. A fragile state of peace can barely accommodate the excessive security demands of former combatants. At the same time, a weak economic system cannot satisfy their usually "unrealistic expectations concerning jobs for people who are normally not even prepared for civilian life" (Ball, 2001, p. 720). The traumas and vengeful mindsets that go along with being a combatant are psychologically damaging, making their reentry into regular society a complex and long-term endeavor. All the same, effective programs ultimately have to persuade ex-combatants that peace pays off for society as a whole and, more importantly, for them as individuals. Otherwise, ex-combatants can jeopardize a frail state of peace.

The key for successful DRPs lies in the integration of short- and long-term goals as part of the overall war-to-peace transition. While progressive disarmament and demobilization are supposed to provide a secure and stable environment initially, the sustainability of demobilization and reintegration ultimately depends on prospects of a more long-term social and economic development (IPA, 2002, p. 5). Before singling out ex-combatants for added benefits, programs should thus always question whether the demobilization assistance promotes the ex-combatants' long-term integration into the community. Reinsertion assistance could otherwise appear as a "reward" for previous violence and send the wrong signal to ex-combatants and their communities alike (IPA, 2002, p. 4). So far, reintegration has only received minor funding and analysis compared to the better-understood military aspects of disarmament and demobilization. In many cases, up to ninety percent of the funding for disarmament, demobilization, and reintegration (DDR) goes to disarmament and demobilization so that there is often no money left for reintegration. Ms. Chrobok (personal communication, 2004) from BICC thus warns that, "The money is thrown out of the window if reintegration fails and former combatants are recruited again." The reason for the neglect of reintegration lies in the anticipated need for a long-term commitment, its dual nature in development and security, the lack of quantifiable results, and the regular omission of reintegration aspects in peacekeeping mandates (IPA, 2002, p. 2).

Reintegration into communities can and should become a focus for responding to children and youth's particular situation. Communities can help to cater to youth's demand for life skills, education, and vocational training, endowing them with a sense of belonging. They can offer alternative ways of making a living and earning respect in society other than military life. Moreover, letting communities apply their own reintegration strategies is often necessary for child soldiers to become reaccepted by their families and communities; their integration also serves as a vital protection against their re-recruitment (Steudtner, 2000). Most DRPs for underage or child soldiers[32] therefore discharge and rapidly reinsert the children into their communities, preferably into their families if they can still be found (United Nations Development program KO, 1999, pp. 87 - 90).[33] These programs regularly operate under adverse conditions: In many contexts, there is no formal demobilization and reintegration process for underage soldiers whatsoever, because they are either not recognized or because the demobilization and reintegration process has not begun (Lorey, 2001, p. 15; Verhey, 2001, p. 6). Their demobilization and reintegration during ongoing conflict often demands nothing less than providing a safe space for a group of the population with no territorial boundaries and frequently at a time when a ceasefire has not yet been agreed upon.

Although underage soldiers have existed for centuries, the changing nature of war has increasingly encapsulated children and youth for three main reasons. First, fighting groups are increasingly neglecting the division between civilian and military targets while engaging in a "total warfare." Second, the proliferation of cheap, small, and easy-to-use weapons enables military units to recruit weak and inexperienced combatants. The most popular weapons, the AK-47 and the M-16, weigh little more than 3 kg each (Millard, 2001, pp. 193-195). For example, in Uganda, they cost only as much as a chicken (Machel, 2001, p. 13). Third, prolonged wars strip societies of their adult generation and require armies to resort to the younger generations as cheap, effective, and obedient fighters. Commanders describe these young soldiers as "easier to condition into fearless killing and unthinking obedience" (McIntyre & Weiss, 2000, p. 16). Older children or young adults are even more useful for the military than younger children due to their greater physical strength and skills (Women's Commission for Refugee Women and Children, 2000). They are also easier to recruit because they lack social protection when they are out of school but not yet married (Newman, 2004, p. 13). What is more, many feel a strong desire to be part of a group again and without family commitments are more willing to engage in risky behavior and the thrill of fighting. During conflict, the breakdown of state and family structures including homes, schools, health systems, and religious institutions removes an

---

[32] This study employs the widely-accepted definition of child soldiers in accordance with the Cape Town Principles, which were adopted on April 30, 1997. According to the document, "child soldier" refers to "any person under 18 years of age who is part of any kind of regular or irregular armed force or armed group in any capacity.... It includes girls recruited for sexual purposes and forced marriage. It does not, therefore, only refer to a child who is carrying or has carried arms."

[33] The Lomé Agreement included provisions for dealing with children and youth for the first time and created the office for children's protector (McIntyre & Thusi, 2003).

important protection so that childhood may seem an unattainable good in the midst of chaos (Machel, 2001, p. 13; Stohl et al. 2001, p. 193).[34]

Most definitions of childhood include persons under the age of 18, but voluntary recruitment is permitted for persons above the age of 15 in the CRC and above the age of 16 in the Optional Protocol.[35] As a result, the legal system leaves room for interpretation concerning the recruitment of persons between the ages of 15 and 18 years. Whereas conscription, abduction, or any threats of force unquestionably constitute cases of forced recruitment, the criteria for voluntary recruitment and their verification are more contentious issues. Most of the young ex-combatants interviewed by Rachel Brett and Irma Specht in *Why Young Soldiers Choose to Fight* defined themselves as volunteers, although they did not meet the cumulative Optional Protocol safeguards that prohibit recruitment below the age of 18 including proof of age, parental consent, a "genuinely voluntary" recruitment, and full information on "the duties involved in such military services" (Brett & Specht, 2004, pp. 114ff.). In many cases, "voluntary" recruitment just constitutes a "reasonable adaptive strategy or practical protection mechanism in situations of extreme danger or deprivation" (West, 2004, p. 185). Most children and youth experts consequently denounce the division between voluntary and forced recruitment as set forth by the CRC and the Optional Protocol. The distinction furnishes the illusion that children have a choice in resisting the mobilization efforts and thus proves an arbitrary categorization given the lack of human security in these countries (Lorey, 2001; Machel, 2001; West, 2000). In situations of protracted conflict, however, insecurity, poverty, and violence become equally persuasive forces (McCallin, 1998; Utas, 2004).

Considering the complexity of causes leading to young people's recruitment, the expectations for reintegration programs must be realistic. Maslen (1997) warns "not to confuse reintegration programmes with the reintegration process....a programme can promote a process but it cannot replace it" (p. 8). With little life experience beyond war, the problems of violently divided societies exacerbate when applied to young people. These reintegration programs can rarely build on prior lives and have to overcome influences and knowledge that young people gained at a significant time of their development. Youth have to re-learn normal cultural and moral values after having passed through a process of "asocialization" (Verhey, 2001, p. 1). If successful, DRPs can contribute to the peace-building process by making the skills and knowledge of ex-combatants accessible to civilian life and by preventing former combatants from turning into "spoilers." On the contrary, failure to complete the demobilization and reintegration process can jeopardize peace as ex-combatants may resort to violence as a familiar way of making a living.

---

[34] On a global level, child soldiers have become an integral part of growing transnational networks of shadow economies in the view of Peter Lock, German professor of political science at the University of Kassel. A neo-liberal system has accordingly excluded the developing world from the regular economies, causing "social polarization within societies and between states and entire regions". Lock therefore stresses the links between globalization, loss of identity, and violence: "Force exerted through an automatic rifle becomes the means of resisting social exclusion" (Lock, 2003). On youth and globalization see World Youth Report (2003, pp. 290-309) and Arvanitakis, (2003).

[35] Many states have made a legally binding declaration on ratification or accession to the Optional Protocol, specifying their minimum voluntary recruitment age as 16, 17, or 18 years.

A RIGHTS–BASED APPROACH: FINDING A LEGAL FRAMEWORK FOR YOUTH

A rights-based approach has so far defined the work of international organizations regarding youth below the age of 18 years. The underlying normative idea of the rights-based approach assumes that children can claim certain individual rights even in adverse situations, transcending border and conflict lines. The moral obligation to protect them derives from a ubiquitous belief that children suffer the most, that they are innocent, and that their welfare lies in the interest of all. As a result, the approach ultimately aims to cover children's basic human needs, thus providing them with human security[36] (Bajpai, 2000; United Nations Development Programme, 1994). The UN Convention on the Rights of the Child (CRC)[37] of 1989 remains the most widely ratified UN document with 191 signatories and "the most comprehensive and specific protection for children" (Machel, 1996). It replaced the former needs-based approach, which defined vulnerability criteria primarily in terms of health, involuntarily favoring younger children (Oyat, personal communication, 2004). Through the CRC emancipated children lose the status as indirect holders of rights as part of their families and became "social actors" with their own set of rights (Millard, 2001, p. 188).

The CRC draws a strict line between children and adults as defined by age. Article 1 affirms that children include "every human being below the age of 18 years unless, under the law applicable to the child, majority is attained earlier." It puts the main responsibility for ensuring children's socio-political and economic rights on the state. Accordingly, states parties have to "take all appropriate legislative, administrative, social and educational measures to protect the child from all forms of physical or mental violence, injury or abuse, neglect or negligent treatment, maltreatment or exploitation" (Art. 19 (1)). The explicit declaration of political will sets an international standard for which governments can be held accountable and indicates a clear course of action. The CRC has, indeed, caused a massive response by the donor community, not least because its legitimacy derives from the victimization of the most vulnerable of society, "our" children. The ultimately protective system that targets governments clashes with children's actual exposure to violence and forces them into a category some of them have already "outgrown."

Images of children as young as four fighting for the Ugandan National Resistance Army in Kampala in 1986, however, challenged the assumption of children's passivity during war, inducing worries of raising "future barbarians" or

---

[36] In 1994 the United Nations Development Programme (UNDP) introduced the concept of "human security" as an alternative to the realist security concept in the Human Development Report. Security thus covered seven basic human needs: economic security, food security, health security, environmental security, personal security, community security, and political security.

[37] The World Youth Report 2003 calls the World Programme of Action for Youth "the key instrument of global youth policy" for 2000 and after. Although the United Nations General Assembly affirmed its commitment towards young people by adopting it in 1995, it refers back to the United Nations Charter as a "normative basis for youth policy." It includes some guidelines for the development, monitoring and evaluation of national youth policies (2003, p. 7ff.) However, compared to the CRC, the Programme has received token attention.

"killing machines" (Verhey, 2001, p. 1). The notion prevailed, nonetheless, that children are not responsible for the wars they are fighting and stressed the importance of protecting them. The 1998 Rome Statute of the International Criminal Court, specifically Art. 8, considered the conscription, enlistment, or use of children below the age of 15 years in hostilities a war crime.[38] The International Labor Organization (ILO) prohibited forced labor[39] recruitment of children below the age of 18 years in June, 1999, making it part of ILO Convention 182 on the Worst Forms of Child Labor, the most widely ratified labor convention. As a result, not only governments but also employers were to be held accountable.

Additionally, the UN adopted the Optional Protocol to the Convention on the Rights of the Child in May, 2000, raising the minimum age for conscription as a form of forced recruitment from 15 to 18 years.[40] The Protocol has been signed by 115 countries and ratified by 66, among them the Democratic Republic of Congo, Sri Lanka, Rwanda, and Uganda, and has guided advocacy efforts (Coalition to Stop the Use of Child Soldiers, 2004). More recently, the Security Council Resolution 1460 announced "the era of application" of the global ban on the use of children as soldiers in January, 2003.

Despite public condemnation and the unambiguous illegality, the current 300,000 child soldiers in more than 60 countries has not decreased but is on the rise (Becker, 2004; Coalition to Stop the Use of Child Soldiers, 2004).[41] Human Rights Watch charges the international community with not taking more concrete countermeasures to punish perpetrators such as cuts in military aid or sanctions (Becker, 2004). The world's failure to decrease the use of child soldiers, however, has also cast doubts on the value of the CRC in practice. The military advantage and costs of foregoing these additional soldiers apparently outweigh benefits of better reputation and legitimacy under current conditions (Harvey, 2000, p. 163). Child soldiers have become a "manifestation of [...the] dynamics of new wars" (Millard, 2001, pp. 187ff). Rather than preventing their recruitment, some child soldiers have thus merely been forced to conceal their age by their commanders as a result of the CRC (Coalition to Stop the Use of Child Soldiers, 2004, p. 5). In the end, the CRC contradicts itself by demanding that governments demobilize and reintegrate their "own" child soldiers (Art. 39), thereby accepting but denouncing the existence of such recruitment practices (Millard, 2001).

The strength of the rights-based approach is also its weakness: Rights cannot be compromised. Save the Children clearly states: "The release or

---

[38] At the same time, there is a fierce debate about the culpability of underage persons (Brett, 2002). Child protection agencies such as UNICEF were disinclined to try underage persons in the Special Court in Sierra Leone because it would undermine their protection efforts. Human rights organizations, on the other hand, wanted to hold them accountable and end impunity (Lorey, 2001, p. 12).

[39] Defined as "work which, by its nature or the circumstances in which it is carried out, is likely to harm the health, safety or morals of children" (Art. 3d).

[40] Those between the ages of 16 and 18 years can still join on a voluntary basis and only the government's armed forces. Many Western countries were responsive to advocacy efforts for raising the minimum age of recruitment as it matched their own plans to downsize their troops ("Kalashnikov Kids," The Economist, 8 July 1999).

[41] DRP for former child soldiers has occurred in six countries up to now, including Colombia, the Democratic Republic of Congo (DRC), Rwanda, Sierra Leone, Somalia, Sudan and Uganda and new programs were planned in Afghanistan, Burundi, Liberia and Sri Lanka; the assistance benefits only a small number of children (Becker, 2004).

demobilization of child soldiers should be based on humanitarian, not political, considerations" (McConnan & Uppard, 2001, p. xix; UNICEF, 2002, p. 36). Discounting the military rationale surely holds great promise for a holistic approach, because it does not distinguish between girls and boys, non-combatant and combatant child, or younger and older children. Reality shows, however, that the legal instruments to protect youth are ineffectual against the social, political, and economic forces enticing them during war. The Optional Protocol does not address some of the root causes for the recruitment of children; economic or personal incentives for joining the army are ignored (McIntyre, 2002). The ILO's Convention 182 describes children as "non-participatory victims." A "gray area of international law" (McIntyre, 2002, p. 1) has accordingly left the task of constructing youth to corrupt regimes and rebels.

The notion of meaningful participation as stipulated in Art. 12 (1) of the CRC, however, somewhat counterbalances the Convention's static and passive image of children. Art. 12 (1) accordingly calls on state parties to "assure to the child who is capable of forming his or her own views the right to express those views freely in all matters affecting the child, the views of the child being given due weight in accordance with the age and maturity of the child for the participation of children." Young people should be able to voice their interests and act on their own behalf. The notion of meaningful participation hence guarantees equal opportunities for all children but also appreciates the individuality of each child, thus implicitly opening space for programs targeting older children.

Yvonne Kemper
Berghof Research Center for Constructive Conflict Management

REFERENCES

Arvanitakis, J. (Ed.). (2003). *Highly affected, rarely considered: The International Youth Parliament Commission's report on the impacts of globalisation on young people.* Oxfam: London
Bajpai, K. (2000, Aug.). *Human security: Concept and measurement* (Joan B. Kroc Institute for International Peace Studies. Columbia International Affairs). NY: Columbia University Press. Retrieved 2 July 2004 from www.cc.Columbia.edu/sec/dlc/ciao/wps/baj01/baj01.html
Ball, N. (2001). The challenge of rebuilding war-torn societies. In A. Chester, F. O. H. Crocker, & A. Pamela. (Eds.), *Turbulent peace. The challenges of managing international conflict* (pp. 719-736). Washington, DC: United States Institute of Peace Press.
Becker, J. (2004). *Children as weapons of war.* Human Rights Watch World Report. www.hrw.org/wr2k4/11htm
Boyden, J., & Mann, G. (2001, Sept). *Children's risk, resilience and coping in extreme situations.* Background paper to the Consultation on Children in Adversity, Oxford, UK.
Brett, R. (2002). Juvenile justice, counter-terrorism and children. *Disarmament Forum, 3,* 29-36.
Brett, R., & Specht, I. (2004). *Young soldiers. why they choose to fight.* Geneva: ILO.
Coalition to Stop the Use of Child Soldiers. (2004). *Child soldiers use 2003: A briefing for the 4th UN Security Council open debate on children and armed conflict.* London: Author.
German Development Cooperation Agency [GTZ]. NODEFIC / SNDC / PPC. (2004). *Disarmament, demobilisation and reintegration: A practical field and classroom guide.* Eschborn: GTZ.
Harvey, R. (2000). Child soldiers: The beginning of the end? *Child Right, 164.* Retrieved 1 July 2004 from www.essex.ac.uk/armedcon/story_id/000036.doc

IPA. (2002, Dec.). *A framework for lasting disarmament, demobilization, and reintegration of former combatants in crisis situation*. IPA-UNDP Workshop. German House, New York: IPA Workshop Report.

Kübler, T. (2002, Nov.). Bewaffnete Jugendgewalt: Herausforderungen und Grenzen der Entwicklungszusammenarbeit. Jugendliche und Kleinwaffen. In *GTZ, Jugendliche und Kleinwaffen – eine gefährliche Kombination* [trans. Armed youth violence: Challenges and limits of development cooperation. In Youth and small weapons – A dangerous combination]. (Documentation of the Expert Talk) pp. 9-13. Eschborn: GTZ.

Lock, P. (2002). The dynamics of shadow globalisation and the diffusion of armed violence as an obstacle to build peace. Text presented at the Hamburg Winterschool on Crisis Prevention and Peace Support, 18 Nov. Retrieved 1 July 2004 from www.peter-lock.de/txt/winterschool.html

Lock, P. (2003). Wer gibt dem kindersoldaten sein mörderisches Handwerkszeug? Gewalt ist der böse Schatten der neoliberalen Globalisierung. [trans. Who gives child soldiers their murderous instruments? Violence is the evil shadow of the neoliberal globalization]. Frankfurter Rundschau 16 Apr. Retrieved 1 July 2004 from www.peter-lock.de/txt/fr.html

Lorey, M. (2001). *Child soldiers. Care and protection of children in emergencies: A field guide*. NP: Save the Children.

Machel, G. (1996). Promotion and protection of the rights of children: Impact of armed conflict on children. Report of Graça Machel, Expert of the Secretary General of the United Nations. New York: United Nations.

Machel, G. (2001). *The impact of war on children: A review of progress since the 1996 report on the impact of armed conflict on children*. London: Hurst & Co.

Mawson, A. (2004). Children, impunity and justice: Some dilemmas from Northern Uganda. In J. Boyden, & J. de Berry (Eds.), *Children and youth on the front line: Ethnography, armed conflict and displacement*. Oxford: Berghahn Books.

McConnan, I., & Uppard, S. (2001, Jan.). *Children not soldiers. Guidelines for working with child soldiers and children associated with fighting forces*. London: The Save the Children Fund. Retrieved 1 July 2004 from http://www.reliefweb.int/library/documents/2002/sc-children-dec01.htm

McIntyre, A., & Weiss, T. (2003). *Exploring small arms demand: a youth perspective*. Institute for Security Studies. ISS Paper 57 (March).

Millard, A. S. (2001). Children in armed conflicts: Transcending legal responses. *Security Dialogue, 32*(2), 178–200.

Newman, J. (2004, March). *Protection through participation. Background paper on the conference, "Voices out of conflict: young people affected by forced migration and political crisis."* Cumberland Lounge.

Sommers, M. (2001). *Youth: Care & protection of children in emergencies. A field guide*. London: Save the Children Federation.

Stohl, R., Aird, S., Barnitz, L., Briggs, J., Catalla, R., Eframe Jr., B., Errante, A., Path, H., Smyth, F. (2001). *Putting children first: Building a framework for international action to address the impact of small arms on children*. (Biting the Bullet 11). London: BASIC, International Alert, Saferworld. Available at http://www.crin.org/docs/resources/publications/BitingtheBullet11.pdf

Tefferi, H. (2003). The reconstruction of adolescence in conflict situations: Experience from Eastern Africa. Paper presented in the *RSC Public Seminar Series: Adolescents, Armed Conflict, and Forced Migration: An International Seminar Series*, 15 Oct.

UNDPKO. (1999, Dec.). *Disarmament, demobilization and reintegration of ex-combatants in a peacekeeping environment: Principles and guidelines. Lessons learned unit*. Retrieved 1 July 2004 from www.un.org/Depts/dpko/lessons/D&R.pdf

Verhey, B. (2001). *The prevention, demobilization and reintegration of child soldiers: Lessons learned from Angola*. Forthcoming Working Paper. Washington, DC: World Bank. Retrieved 1 July 2004 from http://lnweb18.worldbank.org/ESSD/sdvext.nsf/67ByDocName/CaseStudiesThePreventionDemobilizationandReintegrationofChildSoldiers/$FILE/angola+case+-+july+2001+final.pdf

Wessells, M. G. (1998). Children, armed conflict and peace. *Journal of Peace Research 35*(5), 635-646.

West, H. (2004). Girls with guns: Narrating the experience of FRELIMO's female detachment. In J. Boyden, & J. de Berry (Eds.), *Children and youth on the front line: Ethnography, armed conflict and displacement* (pp. 183- 217). Oxford: Berghahn Books.

Wolman, B. B. (1998). *Adolescence. biological and psychological perspectives*. Westport, Connecticut/ London: Contributions in Psychology 35.

YVONNE KEMPER

Women's Commission for Refugee Women and Children. (2000). *Untapped potential: Adolescents affected by armed conflict: A review of programs and policies.* NY: Author.

World Youth Report 2003. *The global situation of young people.* New York: U.N. Department of Economic and Social Affairs.

YVONNE KEMPER

THE SOCIO-POLITICAL APPROACH: YOUTH--A PEACE CONSTITUENCY?[42]

ABSTRACT

A socio-political approach regards youth self-perception and relationship to civil society as crucial for the peace-building process. Rather than defining youth according to norms or assessing their "value" in war economies, this approach demands that international organizations listen to youth voices and support youth in implementing their ideas (Boyden & Mann, 2000; Newman, 2004). Influenced by constructivist theory, it aims to rebuild war-torn societies through and by youth. Compared to the legal and economic aspects, this approach represents the need for youth's socio-political involvement. It is the most recent and untested approach, with rather vague theoretical foundations, partly as a result of the ill-defined concept of civil society itself. It largely describes youth's contribution to peace in terms of (untapped) potentials, contesting that societies have so far not accounted for youth's perspectives and capabilities (Pieck, 2000, p. 33). Organizations have, nevertheless, used it as a framework for programming as the only existing option to conceptualize youth as an agent in the peace-building process.

Grasping the constructed nature of youth allows one to analyze inter-societal relations on a sub-state level. John Paul Lederach's renowned peace-building model can be used to assess the value of youth as a civil society actor in war-to-peace transition. Lederach finds civil conflicts to be more similar to communal than to international conflicts, since human relations provide "the basis for both the conflict and its long-term solution" (Lederach, 1997, pp. 23, 26). His three-leveled peace-building triangle reveals the significance of integrating civil society into peace building.[43] Reconstruction efforts should support "peace constituencies" whose support for the peace process directly challenges the interest of "war constituencies" in continuing the violence (Lederach, 1997; Ropers, 1997,

---

[42] The complete report is available from www.berghof-center.org and from the Berghof Research Center for Constructive Conflict Management, Altensteinstrasse 48a, D-14195, Berlin, Germany. The editors gratefully acknowledge and thank the Berghof Research Center and Yvonne Kemper for permission to reprint excerpts from the full report.

[43] The triangle divides members of a society according to their degree of power and influence from the top to the bottom. The peace process can accordingly profit from the strengths of each level but has to create the spaces that are crucial for utilizing their transformative potential (Lederach, 1997, pp. 21, 35, 37, 108, 111, 117).

Doug Magnuson and Michael Baizerman (eds), Work with Youth in Divided and Contested Societies, 43–46.

pp. 29ff; Ropers, 2002, pp. 117-124). Thania Paffenholz (2002) of the Swiss Peace Foundation defines "peace constituencies" as individuals or groups who have a "long-term interest in peaceful conflict management and are capable of exerting a certain influence on other groups [in order] "to make an active, socially relevant contribution towards the prevention and peaceful resolution of violent conflicts" (Paffenholz, p. 3). Can youth form a peace constituency following this definition?[44] The answer remains ambiguous.

> The long-term interest in peace ultimately depends on youth's ability to remove themselves from the destructive environment around them. Warfare might be the most brutal but also one of the most intense human experiences of higher social status, comradeship, and feelings of superiority which is usually appealing to underprivileged individuals. The psychologist Boia Efraime, Jr., doubts the chances for their full rehabilitation after having worked with child soldiers in Mozambique for years:In some cases, it is not a trauma but rather a different kind of socialization process. These persons have just learned the values of war like "whoever kills stays alive" and see them as normal. We lack a basis for our work. (personal communication, 2004)

The World Health Organization (Krug, Dahlberg, Merci, Zwi, & Lazano, 2002) warns that continual abuse of violence can ultimately create a "general culture of terror" (p. 25) in prolonged conflicts.

In order to overcome this cycle of violence, a new stream of literature[45] in line with the socio-political approach is exploring ways and methods to "promote resilience" rather than "forces to protect from risk" (Boyden & Mann, 2000, pp. 18-20). Accordingly, children often bear the main responsibility in adverse situations and can even mature as a result of the experience as case studies in Northern Ireland indicate (Boyden & Mann, 2000; Cairns, 1998). Rather than protect them as future assets, participatory and child-centered approaches would render them today's actors. Asking youth themselves would thus not only reveal insights about their long-term interest in peace but also indicate their ability to concede to a life without violence. At the moment, their alleged innocence "remove[s them] from the conditions and ideologies that generate violence" (Newman, 2004, p. 13). There are few empirical studies dealing with the motivation and experiences of young fighters. Questions of identity, perceptions, gender, or role in society form the basis for programs following the socio-political approach. The approach thus also gives insights into some of the root causes of the conflict.

The socio-political approach contends that youth's exclusion usually emulates the disintegration of civil society in these conflict-affected countries. Youth are a "seismograph" for the state of a society as a whole (Rudolph, 2000, pp.

---

[44] Fischer and Tumler recognize youth's "potential for societal innovation and reconciliation processes in post-war regions" (transl. Fischer & Tumler, 2000, Sept. 17). Rather than engaging in an extensive theoretical discussion on "peace constituencies," they attest to its practical utility in Bosnia's peace-building process, in which youth programs, organizations, and networks clearly have a role to play.

[45] For reviews of new literature on child and youth psychology and programs see Newman, 2004, and Hart et al. 2004.

1, 4).[46] "Masses of alienated youth in Africa's cities call the idea of "civil society" into question" (Youssef, 2003, p. 33) and testify to the lack of representation even in urban areas where they represent the majority. As a result, civil society has mainly been defined by adults rather than by an "inter-generational learning" process up to now (Rudolph, 2000, p. 5).[47] If the economic approach depicts the "youth bulge" as a threat to stability, the socio-political approach renders the exclusion of a large share of the population as an obstacle for democratization and reconciliation.[48] As an integral part of civil society, they can enforce "a renegotiation of the social contract" (Tulchin & Varat, 2003, p. 2) and thus become a cornerstone for societal transformation. There is an inherent assumption in the socio-political argument that youth can and will transfer their war capacities for peace promotion in the reconstruction phase if provided with the opportunities. This idealized view of youth bears the risk, however, of blending out their negative potential. In the end, the desire to challenge authority and seek independence is, however, typical of adolescence and, as some claim, "can be instrumentalized for any number of ends" (McIntyre & Weiss, 2002, p. 8).

In conclusion, youth should be considered and supported as peace constituencies because they can both promote peace but also endanger it. Their predisposition, which partly reflects their integration into society, would, however, call for different policy and program responses. Since unemployed youth, street children, or ex-combatants are "(potentially) interested in war" and latent spoilers, they would accordingly require indirect promotion by preventing them from engaging in violence (Paffenholz, 2002, pp. 18ff). In contrast, if youth are organized in clubs or groups, they should be directly supported in a way that builds their capacities for crisis prevention (Paffenholz, 2002). Their level of organization and structure along with a willingness to interact with other members of civil society would accordingly qualify them as partners for cooperation. In most post-conflict societies, the conditions for youth organizations have to be created first so that youth can turn from latent spoilers to peace builders. In the end, the socio-political approach has to leave young people the benefit of the doubt to some extent so that they can prove themselves to be viable actors in decision-making processes.

Yvonne Kemper
Berghof Research Center for Constructive Conflict Management

---

[46] Hans-Heiner Rudolph, who heads GTZ's youth programming, claims that the treatment of youth in one's own and partner countries mirrors the state of one's own society (Rudolph, 2000, p. 4).

[47] On a global level, one may argue that the international community indirectly supports the continuation of "gerontocracies" that suppress young people in their "'traditional' social frameworks" and expose them to manipulation and exploitation (McIntyre & Weiss, 2003).

[48] Scholars and international organizations have paid surprisingly little attention so far to exploring what democratization means in countries where young people up to the age of 25 years form a majority of the population.

REFERENCES

Boyden, J., & Jo de Berry. (2004). *Children and youth on the front line: Ethnography, armed conflict and displacement.* Oxford: Berghahn Books.

Boyden, J., & Mann, G. (2000, Sept.). *Children's risk, resilience and coping in extreme situations.* Background paper to the Consultation on Children in Adversity. Oxford.

Cairns, E., & Roe, M. D. (1998). Adolescents and political violence: The case of Northern Ireland. In J. Nurmi (Eds.), *Adolescents: Cultures and conflicts. Growing up in contemporary Europe* (pp. 171 – 198). (Michigan State University series on children, youth, and families 3). New York/London: Garland Publishing.

Krug, E. G., Dahlberg, L. L., Merci, J. A., Zwi, A. B., Lazano, R. (Eds.). (2002). *World report on violence and health.* Geneva: World Health Organization.

Lederach, J. P. (1997). *Building peace: Sustainable reconciliation in divided societies.* Washington, DC: United States Institute of Peace Press.

McIntyre, A., & Weiss, T. (2003). *Exploring small arms demand: A youth perspective.* Institute for Security Studies, ISS Paper 57 (March).

Newman, J. (2004, March). *Protection through participation. Background paper on the conference, "Voices out of conflict: Young people affected by forced migration and political crisis."* Cumberland Lounge.

Paffenholz, T. (2002). *Strengthening peace constituencies.* Eschborn: GTZ.

Pieck, P. (2000, May). Conditions for working with the youth in Africa. In J. Rollin (Ed.), *Youth between political participation, exclusion and instrumentalisation.* (Thematic area "Youth" No. 15) (pp. 33-34). Eschborn: GTZ and Protestant Academy of Bad Böll.

Ropers, N. (1997, Nov.). *Roles and functions of third parties in the constructive management of ethnopolitical conflicts* (Berghof Occasional Paper No. 14). Berlin: Berghof Research Center for Constructive Conflict Management.

Ropers, N. (2002). Civil-society peace constituencies. NGO-involvement in conflict resolution – areas of activity and lessons learned. In G. Baechler (Ed.), *Promoting peace. The role of civilian conflict resolution* (pp. 97-126). Bern: Staempfli Publishers Ltd.

Rudolph, H. H. (2000, May). A proposition on youth between political participation, exclusion, and instrumentalisation. In J. Rollin (Ed.), *Youth between political participation, exclusion, and instrumentalisation* (Thematic area "Youth" No. 15) (pp. 4-5). Eschborn: GTZ and Protestant Academy of Bad Böll.

Tulchin, J. S., & Varat, D. H.. (2003). In B. A. Ruble et al. (Eds.), *Youth explosion in developing world cities. Approaches to reducing poverty and conflict in an urban age* (pp. 1-8). Washington, DC: Woodrow Wilson International Center for Scholars.

Yousef, T. (2003). Youth in the Middle East and North Africa: demography, employment, and conflict. In B. A. Ruble et al. (Ed.), *Comparative urban project youth explosion in developing world cities. Approaches to reducing poverty and conflict in an urban age* (pp. 9-25). Washington, DC: Woodrow Wilson International Center for Scholars.

PAUL SMYTH

THE DEVELOPMENT OF COMMUNITY RELATIONS YOUTHWORK IN NORTHERN IRELAND: 1968 TO 2005

ABSTRACT

From the perspective of a practitioner and activist, community relations youthwork practice over four decades has three phases in the development of this work: Peacekeeping, peacemaking, and democracy building, and each has characteristic strengths and weaknesses. These models still coexist, and there is a need for a deeper critique of practice through ongoing evaluation and research. There is also a need for better-focused resources and an ongoing international conversation about the role of youthwork in violently divided societies.

In this article, I weave together professional and personal narratives, because I cannot relate the story of the development of community-relations youthwork practice without explaining my role within it. So this is the subjective and partial account of a participant, practitioner, and one-time policy-maker of informal educational responses to the challenges of working with young people to counter the effects of living in what remains a divided and contested society. I will look at how youthworkers, managers, and policy makers have responded to the needs of young people in the changing but still contested space called (by some) Northern Ireland.[49]

I explain how forms of youthwork practice have emerged and coexist. I also examine how the State has responded to the challenges the conflict has posed for young people and the communities in which they live. I am not talking about the generality of youthwork in Northern Ireland but about those specific attempts to address the realities of the conflict or ameliorate its effects. In this still divided and contested society, the majority of young people (and former young people)

---

[49] The fact that even the name of the country/province is contested is indicative of the nature of the conflict. Republicans and Nationalists refer to it variously as "the six counties," the "occupied six counties," "the Northern statelet," and the "North of Ireland." Loyalist and Unionists use the term "Ulster" and are generally more comfortable with the official name under UK law: "Northern Ireland" is probably also the most common and widely used name.

Doug Magnuson and Michael Baizerman (eds), Work with Youth in Divided and Contested Societies, 47–60.

have not had the opportunity to mix with those of the other tradition, whether Catholic or Protestant. Much youth provision organised by churches and uniformed youth organisations takes place within traditions and is part of their reproduction.

I take a critical look at these developments and point to considerations for the future of this work in this place and, hopefully, other societies attempting to emerge from prolonged conflict, and the legacies of that conflict.

THE CONTEXT (SEE CHRONOLOGY IN APPENDIX A)

Northern Ireland has been struggling to put behind it a period of prolonged civil conflict that lasted more than 30 years and claimed over 3500 lives. Young people have been both victims and perpetrators of this conflict (Smyth, Fay, Morrisey, & Wondg, 1999; Smyth & Hamilton, 2003). Whilst the scale of the suffering has been significant in terms of the population (currently 1.7 million people), more than half the deaths occurred during the first seven years of the conflict, from 1969 to 1976 and, in large part, the conflict could be characterised as a low-scale civil conflict, punctuated by atrocities perpetuated by Republican, Loyalist, and State forces.

Although I was born in Singapore[50], I moved within a few short months to Belfast where I spent most of my childhood and youth, and I am the son of parents from working-class Loyalist areas of Belfast. I was just past my sixth birthday when "the Troubles" started, and I grew up in their shadow in west and then east Belfast, with two sojourns in England of several months each when I was 13–14 and 17–18 years of age. The first was during the early days of the Peace People movement (1976) and the second during the IRA Hunger Strikes of 1980 to 1981. My schooling was largely within the controlled (almost entirely Protestant) school system, and the communities in which I lived until I left home at 19 were also predominately Protestant.

Whilst the conflict has had a horrendous impact on many individuals and specific communities, for most it had the impact of limiting movements and contacts and narrowing worlds. One of the most potent legacies of the conflict is a stifling culture of apathy: Most people have not cared sufficiently about the problems that have created the conflict and which have resulted from it to change how and where they live, how they vote, and how we live in community together.

THE EARLY DAYS

One of the earliest organised responses to the impact of the divided society on our lives was the founding by the Reverent Ray Davey of the Corrymeela Reconciliation Centre outside Ballycastle on Northern Ireland's beautiful north

---

[50] My father was, at this point and for several years prior, a member of the British Royal Marines, where he rose to the rank of Sergeant before leaving the Army to return to Belfast just after my birth.

Antrim coast. The founding of this Christian community in 1965 predates the recent troubles and was inspired by Davey's vision following his experiences of the Second World War and visits to the Agape community in Italy and the Iona community in Scotland. Davey was the Presbyterian Chaplain at Queen's University in Belfast and catalysed students and others to create and sustain the centre. Early activities included political conferences and activities to bring together families and groups of children and young people from all sections of the community.

As the situation in Northern Ireland worsened, Corrymeela became an important place of retreat and respite but also of creative and courageous thinking and hope. The centre and the community that have developed there have remained central to the development of creative responses to the conflict and have given birth to a number of other initiatives and programmes such as the Understanding Conflict Project and the Mediation Network for Northern Ireland (See www.corrymeela.org; McCreary, 1976; Morrow, 2003).

As the conflict accelerated, many people were deeply concerned about the impact it was having on young people and about the numbers of young people being drawn into riots and, increasingly, into armed paramilitary organisations. Schemes were quickly organised on an ad hoc and localised basis to get young people off the streets (peace-keeping), particularly during the summers when warm weather and long evenings facilitated extensive rioting. More organised schemes developed around this theme of diversionary work (see Appendix A), leading to the formation of organisations such as the Harmony Community Trust with their residential facility at Glebe House in Strangford and the Northern Ireland Children's Holiday Scheme (NICH), also with residential facilities.

The hottest, most violent years of the conflict were from 1969 to 1976. There were a large number of shootings, bombings, riots, and rapid social disintegration. Young people were caught up in this maelstrom, and many in the community sought to divert them into activities that took them away from harm. On August 10, 1976, a young IRA activist was shot by the British army and the car he was driving careened into a group of children leaving their school in West Belfast, killing three of them and led to the largest outpouring of a public desire for peace ever seen during the troubles (McKeown, 1984). The aunt of the dead children, Mairead Corrigan (now Maguire), and a neighbour, Betty Williams (now Perkins), quickly became the figure-heads of a movement dubbed The Peace People, which organised a series of peace rallies inspired by the civil rights leadership of Martin Luther King in the U.S. and the intellectual commitment to non-violence on the part of co-leader and journalist, Ciaran McKeown. Subsequently Corrigan and Williams received the 1977 Nobel Peace Prize in recognition of their courage and contribution to peace building.[51]

---

[51] The reader might like to know that Northern Ireland has the highest number of Nobel Peace Prize winners per capita of any country in the world! John Hume and David Trimble were awarded the prize in 1998 following the signing of the Good Friday Agreement. We also have a fifth living Nobel Laureate in the shape of Seamus Heaney, the poet, who won the prize for literature.

Table 1. Phases of Community Relations Youth Work

Phase	Stages	Characteristics	Examples	Strengths	Weaknesses
I. Peace-Keeping	Diversion	Getting young people off the streets and out of trouble – generally focused on recreation and non-controversial discussion	Summer schemes, 'inter-face' activities, outings and sporting competitions	May help to avoid or reduce conflict – reducing tension and saving resources	Limited long-term benefits, or strategy. Ignores underlying problems
	Cross-Community contact	As above, but involving cross-community contact and discussion	Short term contacts between youth clubs, international camps – particularly in the USA	Young people may utilize the experience to explore issues themselves. Break from tensions in local communities	Failure to address underlying issues, could even reinforce prejudices
II. Peace-Making	Addressing issues together	Facilitated discussion of more difficult issues. Higher level of specific training for staff involved	YMCA peer education and Youth in Government programmes, YFP talks with political parties, Speak Your Piece	Longer-term developmental approach. More likely to change attitudes and behaviours over time	Can create an environment of 'political correctness' without dealing with underlying prejudices
	'Single Identity' work	Exploration of own identity, history and culture	Preparatory work for bringing youth clubs together. Local history and culture projects	Can allow for the development of a deeper understanding of own background in a less threatening environment	Can be an avoidance mechanism, and even reinforce prejudice

PEACE MOVEMENT

My first encounter with this peace movement was during its first summer when I attended a peace rally in my local park on the Woodvale Road in West Belfast. The rally walked the full length of the solidly Protestant Shankill Road, and at its head were a mixture of Protestant and Catholic clergy, holding hands and singing songs of peace. The crowed then flowed into the park, and I ended up towards the back of the proceedings. In spite of hearing almost nothing from the platform, I was taken with the atmosphere of this event, and it was the first time I can consciously remember being in the company of Catholics.

Just over a year later, I was invited by a friend to attend a meeting across town of Youth For Peace, the Peace People's youth section, at their new headquarters, *Fredheim,*[53] on the Lisburn Road. This was the first of many hundreds of similar journeys, for I quickly became an active member of the organisation and went out two or three times a week, selling the organisation's newspaper, *Peace by Peace,* door-to-door in many of Northern Ireland's most polarised and embittered communities. I quickly learnt some door-step debating skills and how to stay safe as part of a team in such situations. This experience was to be the largest single influence on the development of my career and vocation.[54]

The movement brought many thousands of people onto the streets in protests against the ongoing violence and in a plea for peace and reconciliation. Alongside this activity, the leadership attempted to form an organisation and worked on plans to organise within communities around Northern Ireland in an attempt to transform and transcend the sectarianism that was tearing the country apart. Many young people were inspired by this movement and got engaged in its activities. The organisation capitalised on its international profile by organising peace camps in Europe, particularly Norway. Whilst these camps were organised initially as another form of diversionary activity, the organisation quickly realised their potential as opportunities for peace-making and encouraging young people to explore difficult social and political issues. Youth for Peace was sustained over many years through the participants of these camps returning to Northern Ireland with an increased desire to build peace and enjoy new relationships with friends from all sections of our society. I was a participant in one of these camps in 1978 when I went to Kristiansand in the south of Norway. I returned in 1982 as a junior leader after which I took up a one-year volunteer position with the Peace People that turned into three. During this time I ran weekly sessions for Youth for Peace, broadened the age range of the organisation's work, and organised and ran a series of international youth camps and exchanges. The main thrust of the work was to help build relationships between Catholic and Protestant young people and to get them interested in addressing issues related to the conflict. I established contact

---

[53] *Fredheim* means home of peace, and it was given this name as it was purchased through the Norwegian People's Peace Prize, awarded to the Peace People before the awarding of the joint Nobel Peace Prize to Betty and Mairead.

[54] Indeed, it was through the activities of the Peace People that I met my wife, Kim, and became part of a mixed marriage.

with all the main political groupings in Northern Ireland, including Sinn Fein and the Loyalist Paramilitary group the Ulster Defence Association. I took mixed groups of young people on visits to each of these organisations to encourage discussion and debate. At this period we were the only organisation doing this kind of work, though it became more prevalent later in the 1980s.

THE LONG GAME

Whether or not it was in response to the emotional outpouring witnessed in the response to the death of the Maguire children and the subsequent series of peace rallies, the level of violence dropped by around 70% at the end of the summer of 1976, and we never went back to those levels again. What ensued was a long, pernicious, and low-scale war at an average rate of two deaths per week (Smith, 1999), punctuated by a series of atrocities committed by all sides. The election of Margaret Thatcher as Conservative Prime Minister of the United Kingdom in 1979 saw a hardening of attitudes on the part of the British state. In particular, her refusal to respond to issues raised through protests and subsequent hunger strikes in the Maze prison H Blocks gave new impetus to the waning Republican movement, including the development of a parallel political process and electoral success. These events served to further alienate each community from the other.

It was during the 1980s that a small number of youthworkers in a variety of projects began to take their work in a more overtly political direction, such as the example of visits to political organisations by Youth for Peace. Few of the politicians and paramilitary members were used to this kind of engagement. Corrymeela ran a series of political conferences, often involving young people, as did the Glencree Centre for Reconciliation outside Dublin.

During all of these years, there was very little in the way of a public policy response to what was happening to young people in our society. Indeed, the first significant initiative came in 1987 in the form of some curriculum guidance for youthworkers (Department of Education Northern Ireland, 1987). This coincided with initiatives in the schools sector including the introduction of the Education for Mutual Understanding programme (EMU). Subsequent to this initiative there were a number of policy changes that saw a more formal structuring of the Youth Service, including the creation of the Youth Council for Northern Ireland, whose role was to advise the Department of Education and the Youth Service Branches within the five Education and Library Boards.[55]

The Department of Education's policy document made a commitment to "encourage cross-community activity," echoed again in the "Order in Council" that established the Youth Council. By 1992, the Youth Council had created the first set of community-relations guidelines for youthworkers (Youth Council Northern

---

[55] These are roughly the equivalent of school districts within the US and local education authorities in England. Youth Council Northern Ireland and the Education Library Boards (ELBs) are QUANGOS (Quasi-Automomous Non-Governmental Organisations), non-departmental public bodies run by government appointees in the absence of any effective local democratic structures.

Ireland, 1992) with accompanying resources and contacts for groups working in this area.

I returned to college in 1985, though remaining heavily involved with the Peace People in a voluntary capacity. In 1990, I took up post as head of their youth programmes, further developing and consolidating their work, including a small expansion in the staff team. In the main this was about building on the work done on international exchanges and camps to build preparatory and follow-up programmes and more actively pursue the development of political education underpinned by the central commitment to nonviolence that is the ethos of the Peace People. I also registered for a distance learning masters degree in Youth and Community Studies through Brunel University.

The efforts of the Youth Service fared favourably when compared with the parallel efforts in our schools system, at least in terms of the percentages of young people engaged in community relations programmes and cross-community contact activities and the frequency of this contact (JEDI, 2000; Smith & Robinson, 1996; YCNI, 1997). However, other research (Youth Service Partnership Group, 1995) showed that, as in the school system, much of this activity was superficial in nature and failed to adequately address difficult issues related to the conflict.

In late 1995, the University of Ulster School of Education and the Council for Curriculum, Examinations, and Assessment (CCEA) created a partnership with the Youth Council and Channel 4 Schools, known as the Speak Your Piece project. This project was created in direct response to the acknowledgement that, in schools and youth organisations, teachers and youthworkers, in the main, studiously avoided any engagement with political, social, and theological issues related to the conflict. Channel 4 created a television series called Off the Walls that included a mediated exploration by a young studio audience of a series of important themes, a visual essay comparing the conflict in Northern Ireland to that in the Middle East, and a series of drama pieces involving four central characters and their friends.

I joined the staff team of this project in January, 1996, and with my colleagues in the project created support materials and then designed and delivered training for teachers and youthworkers. It was the first project of its kind to do joint training within the Education and Library Board structures for teachers and youthworkers, looking at formal and informal educational approaches to improving community relations and handling controversial social and political issues. One of the key findings of the project was that resistance to addressing issues related to the conflict often stemmed from anxiety on the part of the practitioner. Adults who had not addressed their own feelings about difficult issues, and who had not experienced skilful facilitation of these, were understandably reticent when it came to helping young people to work through the same issues.

THE AGREEMENT AND A CHANGING ENVIRONMENT

During the lifetime of this project, 1995 to 1998, there were significant changes afoot in Northern Ireland. Negotiations had resulted in the signing of the Good Friday Agreement on 10 April, 1998, and this milestone encouraged some rethinking of the role of community relations work given the possibility of a more stable and less violent society.

These changes and the imminent ending of the Speak Your Piece project encouraged me to apply for a new post with the Youth Council for Northern Ireland as Community Relations Officer. During the changeover between these posts, I was part of a study visit to the United States where, amongst other projects, we encountered Public Achievement, an initiative based at the Center for Democracy and Citizenship at the Hubert H. Humphrey Institute, the University of Minnesota. I have documented this story in more detail elsewhere (Smyth, 2000; 2003), but the delegation decided that we should pilot Public Achievement in Northern Ireland. There was unanimous agreement that the model of civic engagement (Boyte & Kari, 1996; Boyte, 1999; Evans & Boyte, 1987), building on the tradition of community relations youthwork, offered an added dimension of the practical and political elements necessary to take the work beyond reconciliation to building democracy.

In the summer of 1998, the Youth Council for Northern Ireland led a coalition of youth service agencies in the creation of the JEDI Initiative. JEDI (Joined in Equity, Diversity, and Interdependence)[56] was funded by the International Fund for Ireland (Community Bridges Programme) and the Department of Education and originally involved a partnership with the University of Ulster School of Education.[57] The twin aims of the project were:

- To develop a coherent strategy for community relations youthwork and education for citizenship within the Northern Ireland youth sector.

- To imbed the inter-related principles of equity, diversity and interdependence into the ethos, policies, and programmes of the organisations which make up the youth sector.

Part of the rationale for this project was the belief that there needed to be a clearer demonstration of commitment from the leadership of the Youth Service and that, as the Speak Your Piece project had demonstrated, there was a need for adults to address for themselves the controversial social and political issues that underpin the conflict as a prerequisite to attempting to work with young people on these issues. Four working groups were established under the themes of training, practice, research and evaluation, and policy development. The initiative produced a number of products including policy change within specific organisations involved in a pilot project, practical resources for practitioners (primarily a document, *Reflections in Practice*, that sought to update and replace the 1992 Community Relations Guidelines), and changes to the youthwork curriculum document, *A Model for Effective Practice*, with a corresponding audit of training and subsequent training courses.

The project has also been a difficult political process. For example, there is a tension between the implementation of the Equity, Diversity, and Interdependence principles and the culture and structures of the Youth Service itself, particularly,

---

[56] www.jedini.com

[57] Internal politics within the project subsequently led the University to pull out of the project.

tensions between the different parts of the statutory youth service (in particular, the Youth Council and the five Education and Library Board Youth Service Departments) and between the statutory and voluntary sectors. Additionally, the project did not make explicit during its lifetime the different models of youthwork being practiced and the assumptions of these models in terms of the types of change they were attempting to effect.[58]

It also failed to clarify what "education for citizenship" meant within the context of youthwork (Deloitte, 2003) and, as this became an increasingly significant theme within formal education, some active resistance to using the terminology developed within some sections of the Youth Service.

Simultaneous to the development of JEDI, the Youth Council was also developing its relationship with the University of Ulster Community Youthwork Team.[59] Initially the two organisations worked on holding an annual youthwork conference at the University primarily aimed at the local youthwork community. It quickly became clear that there was significant potential for internationalising this event, and this realisation led to the creation of the Youthwork in Contested Spaces (YWICS) project that spawned this journal. Public Achievement quickly became a third partner in this project in early 2003, when I left the Youth Council to become the first Director of Public Achievement.

Implicit in the rationale behind the YWICS project is an assumption that Northern Ireland has some kind of *de facto* leadership role within the clarification and promotion of effective practice relating to youthwork in divided and contested societies. Certainly Northern Ireland has a unique combination of an extremely protracted and resolution resistant conflict, very high levels of international goodwill, and the corresponding relative absence of external political interference,[60] and relatively abundant resources committed to finding ways of resolving and transforming the conflict. This combination gives Northern Ireland the potential to be the Beacon of Hope for other parts of the world suffering from prolonged conflict that former US President Bill Clinton described on one of his visits there.

Peacekeeping

Initial responses to the position of youth in relation to the ensuing conflict from a youthwork perspective consisted largely of a peace-keeping approach. As young people were at the forefront of street disturbances and these, in turn, were a recruiting ground for the more serious activities of paramilitary organisations, energies went into diversionary activities. These included taking young people out of their community environments in times of tension to a wide range of

---

[58] For example, the vast majority of participants in youthwork programmes in Northern Ireland are through uniformed organisations (for example Scouts, Guides and "brigades" of various kinds) and church-based youth programmes. Different models of youthwork are practiced in, for example, the Guides, a church hall, a youth club, a programme like Children's Express, or other organisations such as the National Council of YMCAs whose focus is on reconciliation and spiritual development.

[59] Currently this department is the only professional youthwork trainer based in a University in Northern Ireland.

[60] Compared with the Middle East, for example.

international camps and also to centres such as Corrymeela in Northern Ireland or the Glencree Centre outside Dublin. Some of this work was done on a cross-community basis though, in general, issues related to the conflict were avoided in the interests of building friendships. But these relationships were extremely difficult to sustain in the midst of a protracted and violent conflict.

Stage 1. Diversion--getting young people away from the conflict. A range of schemes and projects to literally "get young people off the streets" away from paramilitaries and street conflict. Characterised largely by entertainment, social, and sporting activities, usually with no content related specifically to the conflict.

Stage 2. Cross-community contact–bringing young people together from the two main communities in Northern Ireland. The bulk of this work also involved avoidance of the main issues, concentrating instead on "building relationships."

Peace-Making

The next phase of development could be characterised as peace-making where more conscious attempts were made to address aspects of diversity and the issues underpinning the conflict. This process has included, as in the Speak Your Piece project and the JEDI initiative, for example, conscious efforts to get both those adults who work directly with young people and those responsible for management and policy to consciously address these issues for themselves.

Stage 1. Cross-community contact addressing controversial issues-- bringing mixed groups of young people together with the specific intention of addressing difficult issues and building a commitment to non-violence and reconciliation. Within this model a number of groups and agencies engaged directly with politicians, members of paramilitary organisations, and other players in the conflict from about 1980 onwards.

Stage 2. Single identity work, possibly the most controversial model to emerge. It is argued by some that the approach of working separately within a Protestant or Catholic community is necessary to build confidence ahead of cross-community contact. It is a particularly popular model in some loyalist communities, where it is argued there is a disparity in confidence and understanding of that community's own cultural and political traditions. Critics of the approach argue that single identity work is about maintaining avoidance or reinforcing existing prejudice and/or historical revisionism.

Stage 3. In work underpinned by the EDI principles, particularly under the auspices of the JEDI project, a number of projects were carried out across the voluntary and statutory youth services building a commitment to the principles of equity, diversity, and interdependence at practice and policy levels. The approach argues that organisations must address these interrelated principles in not only its youthwork practice but also in its policies and organisational culture (Eyben, Morrow, & Wilson, 1997). The model calls for a broader appreciation of diversity beyond the Protestant-Catholic axis to look at other issues such as gender, ethnicity, disability, and so on, particularly the categories identified in Section 75 of the Northern Ireland Act[61]. Whilst this is an important development, there is a danger that looking at wider issues of diversity can be a mechanism for ignoring the core conflict and sectarian nature of Northern Irish society and that the focus on diversity becomes an exercise in political correctness rather than a genuine commitment to social change.

Democracy Building

The third stage might be characterised as peace-building, though my preference would be to call it democracy-building work or, in the case of youthwork, what Baizerman (2000) has called "civic youthwork," that is, work that sets out to create democratic space with young people in their own communities, schools, and other public spaces. This work is more overtly political in nature, encouraging people to move beyond narrow definitions of democracy as the workings of the state and party politics, to understand it through other frames such as the principles of equity, diversity, and interdependence as outlined by the Future Ways team, and the use of universal human rights instruments. As Cornel West puts it:

> To focus solely on electoral politics as the site of democratic life is myopic. Such a focus fails to appreciate the crucial role of the underlying moral commitments and visions and fortifications of the soul that empower and inspire a democratic way of living in the world. (West, 2004, p. 15)

Models in this category must attempt to make sense of what it is to be a citizen in what remains a divided and contested society. As with the broader emphasis on diversity under the previous category, there is a danger that in focusing on the broad area of citizenship, an emphasis on the importance of peace building and reconciliation can be lost.

Though these models evolved on a roughly chronological basis, all still exist and are practised in a range of settings and supported by statutory and other funders. For example, during the summer marching season, there tends to be increased levels of tension, particularly in inter-face communities (areas where Protestant and Catholic communities are adjacent and there is a history of serious conflict along the border between these communities). Every year there are schemes developed to help reduce tensions in these areas and divert young people out of harms way. The bulk of work being supported by state and European Union funds would fall into the second (peace-making) category, and there is currently a struggle to get funders to understand the links between community relations and active citizenship.

CONCLUSIONS

One characteristic of all this work is the relative absence of research and thorough evaluation (particularly on a longitudinal basis) to test the efficacy and impact of

---

[61] This refers to Section 75 of the Northern Ireland Act (1998) which outlines a race of categories including (dis)ability, age, gender, sexuality, and ethnic background against which it is prohibited for public bodies to discriminate, with these bodies also having a responsibility to promote "Good Relations" between the main communities here.

the work. As we move forward, the case has to be made for significant resources being made available for research, evaluation, and evaluation capacity-building. This question becomes increasingly important as Northern Ireland becomes a focus for people attempting to develop or refine forms of youthwork in other conflicted societies.

This is particularly important given that, as the Office of the First Minister and Deputy First Minister (2001) suggests, "...the evidence reviewed... does not suggest that significant progress has been made towards a more tolerant or inclusive society ...Despite some positive evidence... the amount of sharing in our society in education, housing, and personal relationships remains limited..."

The issue of resources is more important, particularly as an indication of how seriously as a society we take the challenge of changing the way we engage young people in the process of building a more democratic, vibrant, and pluralist society. As Baizerman (2000) put it, "Consider how young people are being fought over and recruited for criminal careers but far less so for life-long citizen involvement in schools, work settings, sports, and in neighborhoods. What needs to be in place for this to begin?" (p. 1).

In Northern Ireland there still appears to be more energy going into the recruitment of young people into criminality, paramilitary organisations, and sectarian politics and into moral panics around their behaviours than into their engagement as serious contributors to the building of civic space. As Tony Gallagher (2004) put it at a Public Achievement Conference, "Everyone within the system ...says that citizenship education is important, but they won't say how important." The question is, "How seriously does our society take this challenge and, therefore, what order of resources and energies are we prepared to put into getting this right?"

Of course, this is not always an issue of *more* resources. Like most areas of public service in Northern Ireland, the Youth Service is highly bureaucratised, and relatively large proportions of the resources available are soaked up in these bureaucracies. In terms of the issue of evaluation raised above, it may make sense to ring-fence these resources, even if it means in the short-term a reduction in the number of projects and organisations supported. However, given the relatively small amount of resources committed to youthwork (less than one percent of the education budget) a case could be made for additional funding, particularly to support reflective practice underpinned by sound research.

These questions are not only important for Northern Ireland but for that increasing group of places around the world who now look to us for inspiration and leadership as they attempt to address the legacies and realities of their own conflicts. There are few places in the world as well placed to provide this support, particularly in supporting the building of indigenous approaches to a civic focus in youthwork in conflicted societies which, at the same time, encourages the sharing of learning and the development of practice.

Of course, in an increasingly troubled world, there may be lessons for all societies from the issues we have been working on here for so long and the methods we have developed for addressing these issues. The Youth Work in Contested Spaces project, which gave birth to this volume, has demonstrated the importance of collaborative working and networking across a range of societies with recent and/or ongoing experience of violent conflicts. Central to this is a relationship between the practice and research communities in the interest of building better models of practice and theoretical rigour and, ultimately to benefit and enhance the civic lives of young people across the globe.

Paul Smyth
Public Achievement, Northern Ireland

APPENDIX A
CHRONOLOGY

1965: Setting up of the Corrymeela Reconciliation Centre by students from Queen's University working with the University Presbyterian Chaplain, Reverent Ray Davey.

1976: Founding of the Peace People movement including their youth wing, Youth for Peace.

1987: First Department of Education policy document on youth work (the blue book) making a commitment to "encouraging cross-community contact."

1991: Formation of the Youth Council for Northern Ireland.

1992: Community Relations Guidelines (YCNI/DENI)

1995 to 1998: Speak Your Piece initiative, UU, CCEA, Channel 4 and YCNI.

1997: "A Worthwhile Venture?" research (Eyben et al) elicits the principles of "equity, diversity, and interdependence."

1997: "A Model for Effective Practice" Youth Work Curriculum.

1998 (10 April): Signing of the Good Friday Agreement.

1998: PEACE I: first round of the Special European Support Programme for Peace and Reconciliation.

1998: Formation of the JEDI Initiative and JEDI AUDIT

1998; Founding of Public Achievement, Northern Ireland

PEACE II: second round of the Special European Support Programme for Peace and Reconciliation.

2003: Revision and updating of "A Model for Effective Practice."

2003: Initiation of the "Youth Work in Contested Spaces" Initiative

PAUL SMYTH

REFERENCES

Baizerman, M. (2000). Youth: Fact or fiction? Paper presented at Youth: Fact or Fiction? 15 September 2000, Jordanstown: University of Ulster.

Boyte, H., & Kari, N. (1996). *Building America: The democratic promise of public work*. Philadelphia: Temple University Press.

Boyte, H. (1999). Education for democracy in creating the commonwealth, Kettering Foundation.

Cutler, D. (2002). Taking the initiative: Promoting young people's involvement in public decision making in the USA. London: Carnegie Young People's Initiative.

Deloitte & Touche. (2003, December). *Joined in equity, diversity and interdependence, external evaluation of JEDI, Final Report*. Belfast: Youth Council for Northern Ireland.

Department of Education Northern Ireland. (1987). *Policy for the youth service in Northern Ireland*. Bangor, N.I.

Evans, S., & Boyte, H. (1987). Free spaces: The sources of democratic change in America. New York: Harper and Row.

Eyben, K., Morrow, D., & Wilson, D. (1997). A worthwhile venture? Practically investing in equity diversity and interdependence in Northern Ireland. Coleraine, N.I: The Future Ways Programme, University of Ulster.

Joined in Equity, Diversity, and Interdependence. (2000). *An audit of community relations and education for citizenship within youthwork in Northern Ireland*. Belfast: Youth Council for Northern Ireland.

Joined in Equity, Diversity, and Interdependence. (2002). *Reflections on practice*. Belfast: Youth Council for Northern Ireland.

Joined in Equity, Diversity, and Interdependence. (2003). *Windows on practice*. Belfast: Youth Council for Northern Ireland.

McCreary, A. (1976). *Corrymeela: Hill of harmony in Northern Ireland*. New York: Hawthorne Books.

McKeown, C. (1984). *The passion of peace*. Belfast: Blackstaff Press.

Morrow, J. (2003). *On the road to reconciliation: A brief memoir*. New York: Columbia Press.

Office of the First Minister and Deputy First Minister. (2001). *Divisions in society: Northern Ireland today*. Review of Community Relations Policy Working Paper. Available from www.ofmdfmni.gov.uk

Smith, A., & Robinson, A. (1996). *EMU: The initial statutory years*. Coleraine: University of Ulster.

Smyth, M., Fay, M. T., Morrisey, M., & Wong, T. (1999). The cost of the troubles study report on the Northern Ireland survey: The experience and impact of the troubles. Derry: Incore.

Smyth, M., & Hamilton, J. (2003). The human cost of the troubles. In O. Hargie & D. Dickson (Eds.), *Researching the troubles: Social science perspectives on the Northern Ireland conflict* (pp. 15-36). Edinburgh: Mainstream Publishing.

Smyth, P. (2001). From subject to citizen? The role of youthwork in the building of democracy in Northern Ireland. In M. Smyth, & K. Thompson (Eds.), *Working with children and young people in violently divided societies: Papers from South Africa and Northern Ireland*. Derry: Incore.

Smyth, P. (2003). *The diffusion and adaptation of Public Achievement in Northern Ireland: An activist's perspective*. Presentation at the International Civic Education Conference, New Orleans, LA, USA. November 16 to 18.

West, C. (2004). *Democracy matters: Winning the fight against imperialism*. New York: The Penguin Press.

Youth Council for Northern Ireland. (1992). *Community relations guidelines* (Resource Pack).

Youth Council for Northern Ireland. (1998). *Benefits of the youth service: A study of the experiences of 14-18 year old members of registered youth groups in Northern Ireland*. Belfast.

Youth Service Partnership Group. (1995). *Reconciliation and cross-community projects in the Northern Ireland youth service*. Belfast.

STEVE MOKWENA

YOUTH AND NATION BUILDING IN SOUTH AFRICA: FROM YOUTH STRUGGLES TO YOUTH DEVELOPMENT

ABSTRACT

Youth became a part of the political resistance movement in South Africa in the 1940s, and in the 1960s youth found new outlets for these concerns, including black consciousness. When the government tried to force Afrikaans on black school children, youth marched in the streets, and the government used deadly force to suppress it, killing 500 children. This galvanized increasingly organized political movements about education, freedom, rent, transportation, release of political prisoners, and trade unions, and youth were called "The Young Lions." After official recognition of the African National Congress and other organizations, youth movements came under the control of adults and were demobilized, with the result that today only a small number of youth participate in politics. Many youth are alienated from the political process and are marginalized in their communities. In response, the National Youth Commission has attempted to build a consensus about young people, although such consensus is often about the lowest common denominator, and centralization leads to problems of gate-keeping, centralization, and becoming distant from the front-lines.

The process of building a free, equal, and democratic South Africa is exciting and challenging. Key among the manifold challenges is the challenge of creating appropriate and effective mechanisms for ensuring that young people continue to play an active and constructive role in rebuilding a new society. The creation of the National Youth Commission (NYC) in 1996 represents a political commitment to involving young people centrally in developing solutions and in meeting the challenges that they face growing up in South Africa today. Building on the objective of welding together a nation, the NYC is an attempt to bring together young people from different sections of the political spectrum. This article is a reflection on South Africa's attempts to provide a mechanism for sustaining youth participation in the political process. This discussion is divided into three parts. The next section deals with the rise of youth as a dominant political force. It is followed by a discussion of the changing political role of young people in the 1990s and the development of a youth policy and youth structure. Our aim is to highlight the challenges and opportunities for young people's continued role in the political process in the post-apartheid period.

Doug Magnuson and Michael Baizerman (eds), Work with Youth in Divided and Contested Societies, 61–71.

STEVE MOKWENA

THE MAKING OF THE YOUNG LIONS: ANATOMY OF A MASS-BASED YOUTH MOVEMENT

Young people first emerged as political stakeholders in the resistance movement in the 1940s. Although established in 1912, it was not until the 1940s that young people played a serious role within the structures of the African National Congress (ANC). The emergence of youth leaders in the ANC Youth League, under the leadership of people like Nelson Mandela and Oliver Tambo, injected a new sense of urgency in the ANC. It was this radicalism that was largely responsible for the momentum behind political protest in the 1950s. This was also a period of hardening attitudes on the part of the Nationalist government, which was insistent on pursuing its apartheid ideology. Unwilling to entertain any notion of democracy, the white minority government responded with viciousness to all forms of protest. This was manifested most vividly in the Sharpville Massacre where the police shot into a crowd of 5,000 peaceful protesters, killing 69 and wounding 180. In this period resistance organizations reconsidered their non-violent methods, and this led to the formation of covert military structures such as Umkhontho we Sizwe (ANC) and Poqo (PAC). It was at this time that the government apprehended, prosecuted, and jailed many prominent leaders and forced many others into exile. With state violence, mass arrest, and the exodus of prominent leaders, the resistance movement was contained.

The 1960s became known as the quiet decade. It was not until the late 1960s, with the resurgence of student-led organizations such as South African Students Organization (SASO) under the leadership of Steve Biko (who was later killed in detention in 1977) that young people found new outlets for their political and social concerns. The black consciousness movement promoted the ideas of black power, black pride, and self reliance. It instilled a new assertiveness and opened new channels for antiapartheid resistance. Although black consciousness was enthusiastically embraced by a small group of university-based students, it remained limited in its ability to become a mass movement. It was not until the mid-1970s that a new form of resistance to apartheid exploded, owing largely to the changes in the political, demographic, and social make-up of urban black communities.

Rapid industrialization and urbanization led to a growth in the population of urban black communities. Consequently, the numbers of black children attending schools had grown in proportion. In trying to deal with these changes as well as the needs of an industrializing economy, the government had injected increased amounts of money into black education, expanding the numbers of black children in secondary education. Although black education remained inferior and punitive, increasing numbers of black school-leavers were entering clerical and low-level white-collar jobs raising, therefore, the expectation of social advancement at a time when white supremacist ideas were firmly entrenched in the social, political, and economic system.

On the other hand, in 1973 black workers had gone on strike in Durban after years of silence. At the same time, the people of neighboring Angola and

Mozambique had successfully defeated the Portuguese colonialists. These factors helped to nurture a critical consciousness among black youth. So, unlike their parents, young people were eager to challenge the power of the white government. The stage was set for the emergence of a politicized and radicalized generation that would write the last episode of the struggle against white supremacy in South Africa. As Hyslop (1988) noted, "By 1976 the political conjecture, the structural reorganization, and changes in the political culture of urban black youth combines to give rise to a critical situation." An explosive cocktail waited to be ignited.

Student protest was triggered by the government's insistence that black children should be forced to use Afrikaans as a medium of instruction, a language that neither the young people nor their teachers had mastered. This explicit symbol of racial domination provided the initial focal point and spark for the student protests. On June 16, 1976, 20,000 schoolchildren marched on the streets, refusing to learn Afrikaans and shouting "black power" slogans. The response of the government was heavy handed, as it resorted to deadly force to contain schoolchildren. The first victim of the police shooting was Hector Pieterson, a 13-year-old student from Soweto. This was the beginning of protracted running battles between students and the police. Between June and August of 1976 over 500 children died at the hands of the police. This reverberated throughout the country, leading to spontaneous rebellions in far-flung places with young people lashing out violently aginst anything that seemed to represent the white government. In hindsight, the student march in Soweto stands out as the definitive movement in the final push against apartheid. What started as a spontaneous, student initiated strike against education policies laid the basis for the evolution of a powerful youth political movement. It thrust young people onto the political centre stage at a scale hitherto unseen in South African politics.

Education remained a trigger for subsequent confrontations with the state throughout the 1980s. By the mid-1980s, the students had taken on a plethora of education related issues such as the use of corporal punishment, discriminatory examination policy, the low pass rates among black students, curricula, and so forth. It is only when students drew a clear connection between education issues and national politics that a strong youth-based political movement organized and launched from the schoolyard made young people leading the force in the national struggle for democracy.

FROM SPONTANEITY TO ORGANIZATION

Between 1976 and 1979, youth protest was essentially spontaneous and sporadic. The youth movement took some time before it cohered into a formidable political force with clear objectives and organizational expression. By 1979 two major youth-based organizations emerged: the Congress of South African Students (COSAS), which was dedicated to mobilizing middle and high school students, and the Azanian Student Congress (AZASO), which was started by university students in the black universities.

These two organizations provided a platform for the articulation of a coherent political movement with a clear ideological and political content necessary for the movement to grow from a series of localized youth struggles. These student organizations also sought to align themselves with organizations such as the United Democratic Front (which had become the primary antiapartheid coalition within the country) and by appropriating the symbols and rhetoric of the exiled ANC.

COSAS and AZASO (which had been inspired by the black consciousness philosophy of Steve Biko) saw themselves as the student arms of the banned ANC and openly espoused its philosophy as contained in the Freedom Charter. On the other hand Azanian Students Movement (AZASM)--the high school equivalent of the black consciousness inspired groups--aligned themselves with the black consciousness inclined groups and, later, the Pan Africanist Students Organization (PASO) aligned itself with the Pan Africanist Congress. By the mid-1980s youth activism and youth protest was firmly within a political mould that transcended student/youth issues.

Although education remained a critical political issue, young people began taking on community-wide struggles around issues such as rent, transportation, attacking puppet local government structures, and demanding the release of political prisoners, among other things. Young people also actively aligned themselves with trade unions and civic structures. The frequent skirmishes with the police and the army gave the protest movement an insurrectionary and violent character. It was during this time that young people became known as the "Young Lions" of the revolution – leading the onslaught against apartheid.

Efforts to organize young people outside of the schools and universities had proved to be difficult at the beginning. Although ANC aligned organizations proliferated in many townships and rural areas, it was not until 1987 (the International Year of Youth) that sufficient basis was laid for the emergence of the South African Youth Congress (SAYCO). SAYCO emerged with a decidedly militant stance as reflected in its trademark slogan, Freedom or Death, Victory is Certain. SAYBO vowed to and eventually succeeded to make South Africa ungovernable. By mid-1987, SAYCO was claiming over 1200 local structures with over half a million members and a support base of over two million (Seekings, 1993). This excludes many young people who participated in protest activities without being paid-up members of political organizations. It is fair to say that the overwhelming majority of black youth growing up in the 1980s participated in the struggle in one way or another. The term "comrade" came to be associated with black youth everywhere. Almost from its inception, SAYCO faced police harassment, and many of its young leaders spent extended periods of time behind bars and some were killed in the process. State repression notwithstanding, the deluge of popular protest had become unstoppable. Observing the mood in the 1980s, Straker concludes that, "From the perspective of the youth, this was a time of euphoria as well as terror. They had a new found sense of power and a vision of the future. They saw themselves as leading the older generation to freedom. Liberation was in sight and they were the authors of it."

The heightened climate of resistance created the basis for the emergence of youth leadership at all levels. Forced to analyze, critique, organize, and strategize, high school students and their counterparts outside schools gained increasing eloquence and intellectual sophistication. And many were driven by the sense of being a participant in a process of political change. There is also evidence of significant adult mentoring, particularly as people who had been involved in the struggle for long periods of time were tapped for their understanding. Ironically, the mass imprisonment of young people also put them into contact with veteran resistance politicians who helped hone their understanding and fuel their enthusiasm. Sadly, such leadership also came at a price as young people become the primary victims of state sponsored violence and killings. It is also important to note that, because of the different ideological strands, young people were often locked in bitter and sometimes deadly conflict for political control. The government did much to create suspicion and conflict as a way of dividing young people and their communities.

FROM STRUGGLE TO DEVELOPMENT: THE CHANGING NATURE OF YOUTH POLITICS

How does South Africa create adequate mechanisms that continue to engage young people in the political process? How does young people's energy and enthusiasm remain the defining feature of a fledging democracy in the absence of conflict and struggle?

It was not until the end of the 1980s that the Nationalist Party agreed to a negotiation process. The recognition of the ANC and other political organizations as well as the release of political prisoners and the return of exiled leadership was a major turning point in youth resistance politics. For the most part youth organizations were brought under the control of "adult" leadership. In a climate of negotiation and a move away from confrontational politics, the youth movement began a process of demobilization. Struggling to reconcile the politics of negotiation with the highly confrontational and volatile nature of youth politics, the ANC Youth League admitted that "they faced the task of balancing a tradition of militancy with support for the ANC's chosen strategy of negotiation. Simply put, the Young Lions were steeped in the politics of oppression that excluded debate with the enemy." With these changes came a gradual but steady decline in youth participation in politics. Today, the number of young people who are actively engaged is a small fraction of what it used to be in the 1980s.

A FOCUS ON INTEGRATING YOUTH INTO THE "MAINSTREAM"

Young people should become an active part of nation building, reconciliation, reconstruction, and development.

President Nelson Mandela

Dimensions of Exclusion

A study conducted under the auspices of the Joint Enrichment Project in 1991 found that 3.5 million young people were considered marginalized or facing difficult circumstances. It also found that 43% of young people were at risk, that is, showing increasing signs of alienation and having fewer resources and opportunities. Five percent were thought to be severely disengaged and showing very high signs of trauma, alienation, and possible participation in crime, violence, and other unhealthy behavior. As the decade of the 1980s drew to a close, young people were gradually losing their identity as an engine for change. Concerns were highlighted about the impact of inferior education, high unemployment, and exposure to violence on young people. Some started to think of a generation of young people who grew up in the turbulent decade of the 1980s as a "lost generation." Many feared that young people would derail the democratic process as the youth resistance movement dissipated into a criminally inclined sub-culture.

It was in response to this growing fatalism that the Joint Enrichment Project (JEP), a youth-based organisation started by the South African Council of Churches (SACC) and the Southern African Catholic Bishops Conference (SACBC) convened political youth organisations, social groups, and non-government organizations to discuss a strategy for addressing the concerns and challenges facing young people in the post-apartheid era. The gears had shifted and a new search for lasting solutions to re-integrate youth into the social mainstream had begun.

At the root of South Africa's search for solutions was the notion of organizing broad-based cross-political support for young people's issues under the rubric of youth development. Prior to the 1990s, attempts to bring different groupings together could not materialise owing largely to the adverse political environment. Youth organisations were often sharply split along ideological and political lines. Sometimes this translated into intense political tensions and bitter conflict. Attempts to come together often fell apart. It was not until the 1990s that attempts at seeking broad-based cooperation seemed to bear fruit.

The first successful attempt to establish common ground was with the establishment of the National Youth Development Coordinating Committee (NYDCC) and the National Youth Development Forum (NYDF) under the auspices of the Joint Enrichment Project (JEP). At this time, youth serving NGOs came together with youth-led and youth-run organisations to define a youth development vision for the country. The NYDF declared that its strategy was to create an enabling environment for youth development to prevent the marginalisation of youth and children and to create specific programmes to reverse the Apartheid legacy as it affected black youth. The NYDF was short lived; it ceased to operate within a year of being launched.

After extensive consultation and discussion, youth organisations lobbied for the establishment of a national structure to secure the representation of young people within the structure of the new government. After much debate about the establishment of a national ministry of youth, it was agreed that what was needed was a broad-based structure that cut across the different departments in order to ensure that issues of young people were not marginalised and placed in an inferior position. This was the logic behind the Youth Act of 1995 that led to the establishment of the National Youth Commission (NYC).

The National Youth Commission

The National Youth Act of 1995 laid the basis for the establishment of the National Youth Commission (NYC), a government structure made up of publicly nominated and appointed commissioners. The NYC was also located in the Office of the President. The Commission is made up of five full-time official commissioners, five part-time, and nine additional members representing the nine different provinces. All members of the Commission are supposed to be under the age of 35 to ensure that young people participate fully in addressing their concerns and working towards the solutions. The National Commission is to establish a comprehensive framework for the development of solutions. In 1997, the Commission developed a National Youth Policy after an elaborate process of research and consultation. After extensive consultation the NYC presented the National Youth Policy to President Mandela. Among other things, the policy states the following:

- To provide a framework for youth development nationally, to ensure that youth are given meaningful opportunities to reach their full potential;
- To address the major concerns and issues critical to youth and to give direction to youth programs and services provided by government and nongovernmental organizations; and
- To provide the basis and foundation for a National Youth Action Plan.

After three years in office, the NYC has not been able to get much traction in the area of programme delivery. Policy formulation is yet to translate into concrete opportunities for young people. However, the NYC has presented draft legislation on a National Youth Service Program. Such a programme is intended to provide young people with opportunities for training and skills while contributing to national reconstruction. According to the green paper on National Youth Service, the vision of National Youth Service is to:

> Provide long term and effective means of reconstructing South African society through physical rehabilitation and renovation of community resources as well as rebuilding the social fabric of communities. The NYC will enable young people to promote a spirit of Nation Building by inculcating a sense of service culture, a common nationhood and ensuring integrated youth development through service and learning activities.

It remains to be seen how the service programme will be implemented and whether it does provide viable and meaningful opportunities for youth development. The danger of youth service programmes around the world (even when they work well) is simply that they can be used as a way of placating and containing youth. There are ample examples of how under the name of service and nation building, young people become a form of cheap labour with no meaningful opportunities for individual development or roles in decision making and governance.

YOUTH PLATFORMS: CHALLENGES AND LIMITATIONS

In this period, there are two main achievements to be highlighted. First, the establishment of the NYC marks a clear political commitment to providing young people with the space and avenues for them to influence policies and to propose solutions. Second, the Commission has managed to bring together young people (leaders) from different organisations to work together. With this comes a new culture of nation-building and reconciliation. More significantly, it is a demonstration of a political commitment to make sure that young people take their rightful place as full partners and participants in the shaping of a more democratic and caring society.

However, this process is not without its challenges. Facilitating youth centrality on policy formulation and nation-building through coordinating structures or platforms (be they in government or in civil society) is sometimes fraught with contradictions. Thus it is not uncommon for them to be vilified and celebrated at the same time. Here are some contradictions that have emerged over the past four years.

Representation and Centrality in Policy Does not Equate with Delivery

Coordinating structures generally succeeded in articulating policy positions. However, they have yet to translate policies into concrete delivery. This is because the institutional framework required for promoting youth participation and centrality in decision-making and policy formulation is very different from the organizational framework required to design, implement, and manage programmes and services. In fact, it is clear from the legislation that these structures are not implementing bodies.

Such structures have a role in shaping such interventions, but they are not sufficient. The two are not mutually exclusive objectives, and the latter does not flow naturally out of the former. Representation does not equate delivery. There is evidence from other countries that suggests that such structures are used by government to contain youth dissent and thus do not have to bother to provide real opportunities. They serve to contain the main youth organisations and their leadership. Youth bodies of this nature also attract younger politicians for whom programme design and implementation was unchartered territory. However, the inability to inform delivery is often not of their making. The NYC and its provincial counterparts have come up against significant hurdles in the generally uncooperative ageist bureaucracy. They also lack the budgets required to attract and secure the technical resources for developing and implementing programmes.

The Perils of Consensus and Compromise

Over the past eight years, we have laboured under the assumption that the potential for delivery rests with developing consensus amongst the different stakeholders, especially political youth organisations. Inherent in the creation of coordinating structures is the inertia that comes with consensus. The bulk of our efforts and resources have gone into crafting and nurturing such structures. This method of organising was informed by the political culture of negotiation that led to the Government of National Unity (GNU). The NYC like the NYDF brings together divergent political groups and can only move on the basis of compromise.

Most times this leads to a tendency for agreement reached only on the lowest common denominator. Such bodies are perpetually on the path of least resistance and, by implication, the path of least innovation. Consensus building is an important part of the strategic objectives of a democratic government. Yet consensus is not an end in itself; it is useful only when it galvanises support for concrete action.

Centralisation

Over-arching structures tend to lead to a centralisation of resources and power. This plays itself out in the tensions between the coordinating bodies and NGOs. Funders and the government easily look towards these bodies as the first port of call when deciding who to fund and how to fund them. This then leads to a concentration of power and resources in the hands of structures that do not have an automatic and natural interest in supporting and representing the range of stakeholders on the ground, especially NGOs. In fact it is not uncommon for coordinating structures to compete in the same funding market as the non-government organisations that they purport to be supporting.

Centralisation, often done in the name of coordination and rationalising resources, can breed control as it frequently leads to disengagement with civil society organizations (especially community-based initiatives). This is because participation in processes and access to resources is dependent on a pyramidical political process. Organised bodies select representatives from national offices who often have little contact with the grassroots members. In addition, organisations rarely have adequate consultation mechanisms to keep their grassroots members informed and engaged.

This creates a rift between the elected few who preside over these structures and young people generally. Contrary to the rhetoric of empowerment, such structures are rather remote from the ground – a major handicap to innovation, enterprise, and genuine participation. They can speak and act on behalf of young people, yet unlike constituency-driven structures, they do not have mechanisms and structures to facilitate debate and engagement with young people. They answer primarily to the state, which after all is responsible for their financial sustenance.

Centralisation also leads to gate-keeping. Such structures determine who is in and who is out. Such processes are not always above board and lend themselves to undemocratic forms of decision making. This has an impact on who gets selected for appointment and employment within these bodies. It is particularly counterproductive when political criteria rather than the ability to deliver determine the process outcome.

Finally, these centralised bodies (government or civil society) tend to create an expectation that solutions to problems that affect young people will be brought from above. They have to present themselves as being able to engineer large-scale solutions from above in order to justify their existence. They also thrive on depicting young people as a "problem" that only they can solve. Despite the well-worn rhetoric of youth empowerment, such structures are less inclined to galvanise grassroots youth activism, certainly not of the kind that may challenge the government. For an example, with the second democratic election in May, 1999, the turnout of voters between the ages of 18 and 24 was appallingly low, marking a disconnection and perhaps disenchantment with the formalised nature of politics.

The Challenge of Accountability

Creating structures for coordination (and lobbying on behalf) of young people is an important part of ensuring that young people themselves represent young people's interests. The principle that young people must be centrally involved in the determination of social policy is not only important for youth development, it is a democratic imperative. Achieving this by fostering cooperation among bodies that have not collaborated in the past is also good in building a democratic and pluralistic society. Achieving these objectives (however laudable) does not necessarily translate into programmes and services for young people and should not be confused as such.

At best this creates the semblance of youth representation. The central challenges of youth structures the world over is their capacity to remain connected and accountable to youth constituencies. Again international experience shows that youth coordinating structures are notorious for turning into self-interested, inward looking entities with little or no connection to young people, ultimately defeating the very principles of youth participation.

Questions of accountability are not easy to answer. That said, coordinating vehicles created to promote and maintain the participation of young people in the political process should be tested against the following criteria:

1. If they are able to engage and mobilise grassroots support in a way that advances the ability of young people to be involved in their own development and the development of their communities.

2. If they are able to bolster the efforts of civil society (non-governmental organisations and community-based organisations) channelling resources from the state to citizens who can then take action to change their circumstances.

3. More importantly, if they are able to advance the youth development agenda inside the government without becoming marginal and assuming an

uncritical relationship with the state, thereby limiting the capacity of the political youth movement to lobby effectively for lasting social transformation.

CONCLUSION

> We must devoutly hope and work to make sure that young people, black and white, emerge as architects and builders of a new society. If renewal is the pulse of the African Renaissance, the young people are its heartbeat.
> – Ignatius Jacobs, former youth activist and MEC for Education

Evaluating the track record of the NYC purely on the three themes alluded to above, it is fair to say that much remains to be done. One must stress that we should not throw the baby out with the bathwater. Youth coordination structures or platforms can serve a purpose, but only if closely monitored by their constituency, that is, young people themselves. If not, they can defeat the very objective of promoting youth participation. It is up to young people and youth organisations to strive to make such structures more accountable and to use them in a way that promotes their wishes. We have to avoid the temptation of developing strategies and programmes that reduce young people to consumers of top-down initiatives with little or no room to become equal partners in the process of social change.

Steve Mokwena
Johannesburg, South Africa

REFERENCES

Hyslop, J. (1988). *Student school movement and state education policy.* Lawrenceville, NJ: Africa World Press.

Seekings, J. (1993). *Heroes or villains.* Johannesburg: Ravan Press.

Straker, G., Moosa, F., Becker, R., & Nikwala, N. (1992). *Faces of the revolution: The psychological effects of violence on township youth in South Africa.* Athens, OH: Ohio University Press.

SANJA SPANJA

THE PRONI CENTER FOR SOCIAL EDUCATION: EFFECTIVE YOUTHWORK PRACTICE IN CONTESTED SPACE

ABSTRACT

Youth in Croatia live in a shattered society, suffering from the civil war that brought youth a high rate of unemployment, lack of initiative and apathy, a desire to leave the country, and the normalization of violence between two nationalities. In partnership with the PRONI Institute of Social Education in Sweden, the PRONI Center of Osijek/Vukovar aims at increasing the participation of young people in creating a democratic and multi-ethnic Croatia. PRONI provides University level training in leadership and developmental youthwork, and it supports a network of youth organizations and youth clubs. The key principles of training in youthwork are based on social and informal education, including preparation for life by working from the *milieu* of the social inconsistencies and problems of daily life, learning from experience, participation in making decisions, and acceptance and understanding of others.

These days, young persons who remain in Eastern Croatia resemble Alice in Wonderland, standing in front of the mirror that will, the next moment, become the path to the world of unbelievable, newly experienced and unimaginable events. He or she feels, at the same time, fear of the unknown and a kind of pleasant tremor, a sense of wonder, brought by the new, unexplored world. But, when you find yourself in this "beautiful new world" on the other side of the mirror, two steps backward follow each step forward. Discovering oneself and others occasionally becomes an empty wish; each step backward takes a piece of the existential part from the young person who is threatened by the vacuum, which is hard and painful, and sometimes impossible to fill in the post-war environment of Croatia.

According to data provided by the State Institute for Statistics in Croatia, based upon the 2001 population census, 898,734 people between 15 and 29 years of age live in the Republic of Croatia and comprise about 25 percent of the total population. From 1953 to now, the percentage of young persons in the total population has declined, which means that the Croatian population on the average is becoming increasingly older. The most significant consequences of these negative demographic trends is a reduction of the ratio of the fertile population and actively employed population to an increasingly large and aging population who they must care for.

Doug Magnuson and Michael Baizerman (eds), Work with Youth in Divided and Contested Societies, 73–83.

Despite the decline in the percentage of young persons in the total population, we are confronted with a growth in the number of unemployed citizens under 29 years of age. Young people marry at an increasingly later age at the same time that the percentage of divorced persons younger than 29 years of age is increasing.

Existing data on young persons indicate a trend toward prolonging youthhood and socio-economic dependence. The causes of these, among other factors, is the prolongation of the education process, more difficulties in finding the first permanent job, a more complex condition for access to material goods (regular incomes, credit, ownership of real estate property, etc.), and the marginalization of youth in the decision-making processes.

Today in the Republic of Croatia there is no suitably developed governmental institution in charge of youth, as is the case in the majority of European countries where there is a public administration body with a suitable level of authorization and appropriate financial, organizational, and personal support for more active participation of youth in social and political life. Moreover, there are many examples indicating that political structures (one party and governmental bureacracies) attempted to prevent, weaken, or minimize initiatives appearing on the youth and student scene during the 1990s.

Research has shown that the majority of young persons are aware of their own political marginalization and that the reason for this is to be found in the lack of readiness among older persons to relinquish a share of the political arena to them but also in the incompetence of their own generation. They are provided with insufficient information about civil society, democracy, the process of political decision-making, and the manner of political activity.

Although the majority of young persons consider that their political involvement has a purpose through various forms of organization, a very small number of them decide to participate actively. Interest in politics and political events has dropped significantly. The majority of young persons are dissatisfied with the level of representation of their generation in public bodies and, therefore, think that in order to improve their participation in the decision-making processes, it would be necessary to apply so-called quotas for youth in the party election lists.

Still, simultaneously with poor participation in political institutions, there are greater participations of youth in NGOs and voluntary associations of citizens. Yet there is no cooperation between NGOs and political institutions. Since both sectors have the same field of activity, being the improvement of the quality of life and the social status of youth, such cooperation and exchange of information, ideas, and experiences--as well as financial support--would lead to better results.

Negative demographic trends in Croatia and the departure of qualified young persons from the country are a warning that it is necessary to improve the overall social status of youth and initiate actions that would have the goal of increasing their participation in the social processes and institutions.

In the post-war environment of Croatia, especially in Eastern Croatia--the Slavonija and Baranja region--the younger generation has been exposed to the influence of an environment which in all respects was shattered and all criteria of humanity, especially basic human values, was changed in a negative way. The general climate of poverty, destruction, violence, intolerance, and posttraumatic shock was unhealthy for everybody and especially for the young people. It is much easier to develop prejudice in the areas where conflict exists and conflict is easier to develop where there is prejudice. The prejudice is a result of fear and not reality.

In this conflicted space they live in a cruel reality, suffering consequences from the devastating civil war that brought a high rate of unemployment, lack of initiative, apathy, a wish to leave the country, and a reality that violence is normal way of communication between two nationalities.

THE CASE OF VUKOVAR

Vukovar is one of many towns in Croatia seriously affected by war in 1991. Vukovar is situated in the northeastern part of the Republic of Croatia, and it is the centre of the Vukovar-Sirmium county. It borders the Danube river and is across the river from Vojvodina in Serbia. The problems with the Vukovar economy are extremely complex, so they have to be viewed with respect to the war and post-war consequences. The difficult economic situation of the firms that used to sustain Vukovar development before the war represents the biggest problem. Most of these firms are currently either insolvent or undergoing privatisation and are, at the same time, burdened with debt, employee surplus, obsolete technology, massive damages to the plants, loss of market, and a lack of highly educated experts.

As human resources are the prime movers of any development, one should bear in mind that predominantly older generations have returned to Vukovar, and 70 percent of the students who study outside the county do not return. Considering such a significant drain of qualified personnel, it is extremely difficult to find a highly educated person with the required work experience.Vukovar is also burdened by an unemployment rate of 36 percent even among a much smaller population than before the war. According to the national census of 1991, Vukovar had 46,000 inhabitants, and in the 2001 national census, Vukovar registers 31,500 inhabitants.

CONTESTED SPACE

Youth in Vukovar have their own contested experience of living in a segregated city within invisible walls. In the segregated community they do not have a right to have "adolescent crises." For example, in a secondary school two groups of young boys--Serbs and Croats--had a fight because of a girl. This was the main story on the national evening news, explaining this incident as example of intolerance between two nationalities.

In this divided society the main thing for young people is who you are and whether you attend a Croatian or Serbian school. In only 1 of 7 primary schools in Vukovar do children of different nationalities attend classes in the same school building. Even in that school the classes in Serb and in the Croatian language are conducted in different shifts. In the remaining six schools, the classes are conducted exclusively in either the Serbian or Croatian language. Most of the young parents and parents-to-be are very much concerned with the current segregation of children as a direct outcome of the divided society. They are worried because they do not see any other perspective for their children other than this gloomy one.

Although political integration is a fact in East Croatia, the process of integration and reconciliation between the Serb and Croat/Hungarian communities is a difficult and painful process. The disastrous economic situation does not make this easier. For young people alternative perspectives are few, participation in vocational and higher education is low, and jobs are only available for a few. Further, the Croatian and Serbian communities in Vukovar are strong so that individuals are afraid that having any contact with the other side will isolate them from their own community.

We argue that youth in Vukovar are a forgotten social group that could lead to their disappearance as a meaningful social category and put youthwork in the corner of the society.

YOUTH POLICY

In 2001 the State Institute for the Protection of Motherhood, Family, and Youth appointed a working group for the Preparation of the National Programme of Action for Youth, consisting of the representatives of numerous ministries and public administration bodies, scientists, experts dealing with problems of youth, and representatives of youth themselves. In the beginning the working group consisted of 25 members, including six representatives of the youth NGOs. (PRONI representatives were in this working group.) Respecting the principles of active participation, The State Institute decided to include more young people during the preparation of the action plan itself.

All the participants in the preparation of the National Programme of Action for Youth agreed that Croatian youth live in an extended circumstance of social risk. They unanimously concluded that the relatively high expectations of the society towards youth have not been accompanied by appropriate actions and measures insuring the well-being of youth.

This National Youth Action Plan includes national policy toward youth, the strategy for implementation of national policy, and the action programme itself. It was intended that 111 objectives (activities) be realized in a five-year period. Such a large number of planned measures imply numerous problems and solutions that have not, until now, corresponded to the needs of youth and have been obstructing the development of their potential. At the beginning of September, 2002, the plan was adopted by the Croatian Government, and it was forwarded to the Croatian Parliament with the goal of discussion and adoption.

Acceptance of the National Youth Action plan by the Croatian parliament is, therefore, a clear and encouraging political statement that young people are looked upon with interest from the decision-makers. When aims and objectives are set in accordance to the needs of young people and described in the National Youth

Action plan, the upcoming challenge for the Croatian authorities will be the implementation of the designed activities.

From March, 2003, a representative from the PRONI Centre has been a member of the implementation group organized on the national level by the State Institute for the Protection of Motherhood, Family, and Youth for the development of youthwork education in Croatia. The aim of this implementation group is to establish all necessary preconditions for implementation of the 111 objectives of the National Program of Action for Youth in the Republic of Croatia.

PRONI CENTRE FOR SOCIAL EDUCATION

The PRONI Centre for Social Education is a non-governmental, non-profit membership organisation. It works for community development in divided societies and provides people with new learning opportunities in an informal creative process based on tolerance so they can bring about change suitable for their own lives.

In partnership with the PRONI Institute of Social Education in Sweden, the PRONI Center of Osijek/Vukovar aims at increasing the participation of young people in creating a democratic and multi-ethnic Croatia. Since 1997 PRONI implements activities for and with young people and organises trainings for young people and teachers throughout and beyond the war-torn area of Eastern Slavonia, Baranja, and Western Sirmium (East Croatia). In 2002 PRONI widened its activities in other post-conflict areas in Croatia, such as Knin-Benkovac.

Through its education and training programmes PRONI offers young people in Croatia an opportunity to develop their skills and to contribute to the development of their own society. The University training in Leadership and Developmental Youth Work is a tool to reach these aims. At the same time, PRONI supports a network of active youth and youth organisations, connecting them to the wider world through mutual visits, exchanges, and joint training programmes.

Youth Clubs

Young persons attending the youth clubs find a safe place, a micro-world in which alternative values operate. In the safe environment without drugs, alcohol, or negative behaviour, youth of both nationalities jointly learn, play, and create. Outside this safe micro-world, this Vukovar is not real. In the youth club, tolerance, mutual understanding, social education, prejudice redaction, creativity, and promotion of a healthy and active life is a way of working. On the other side, residents of Vukovar live their lives with intolerance, prejudice, and mistrust. Because of and apart from the conflict, drug use, alcohol consumption, and aggressiveness are accepted. Our youthworkers try to make each young person in youth clubs important and give each a chance to contribute something to the life of the group, with the leader no more and no less than the member.

Yet sometimes a tension exists between the expectations of club members and the reality of everyday life in segregated Vukovar. Very often they are confused and even angry that in the safe environment of the youth club they develop one model of behaviour and outside the club is a cruel world where they, with newly developed values, lose their protective shell and risk being hurt.

Because of that the policy of our youth clubs is to make connections with the wider community by organizing many different activities in different community locations. Included in these were organized gatherings between youth club members of different nationalities, sport competitions, creative workshops, and outdoor activities on the streets of Vukovar such as painting the bridge in the centre of the town and a costume parade through the streets. With those activities youth clubs try to draw attention of the community to their activities and show examples of cooperation and communication between young Serbs and Croats in public. Of course, it is hoped that offering positive models and creating action outside of the safe space of youth clubs decreases the perception of the impossibility of communication between two separated groups.

PRONI has ongoing activities in 18 youth clubs all over Croatia where our graduated students are working as youth leaders. There are officially 1330 youth club members under 30 involved in regular activities, but that number in much higher if we count temporary involved youth, visitors, and participants on special events. Our clubs are highly visited. Monthly there are 11,400 visits in the clubs, which mean more than 135,000 per year.

Youthworkers together with youth try to explore the needs of young people in different places based on regional specifics, mentality, and customs. Together with their members, youthworkers take an active part in the community, building the bridge between youths' contested spaces and society.

It is hard to measure the long-term impact of their actions in the community, but we are happy and feel it an enormous success if, after some activities organized by youth clubs, young people of different nationalities continue to gather together outside of the youth club.

Youthwork Education

PRONI offers young people a course in "Leadership and Developmental Youth Work," until recently unknown in Croatia. During the course students are introduced to the theories of social work and youthwork and Western models of community work with special emphasis on integration and participatory methods and approaches. Through teacher-trainings, PRONI enhances the possibilities of teachers in primary and secondary schools to be able to catalyse the process of integration and reconciliation in the schools, targeting pupils as well as their parents.

The PRONI Center also aims to develop the capacities and qualifications of its staff in order to meet the Croatian and European regulations by the end of the project period. The PRONI Center Croatia is at present facing a period of rather turbulent growth and development that challenges volunteers, tutors, support staff, and the organisation as a whole. Cooperation with local authorities is increasing as well as with the central government, specifically, the Ministry of Science and Technology and the Ministry of Education. Special attention is also given to relationships with the local, regional, and national authorities as (potential) strategic partners in the development of an open democratic society in which young people can play an active role.

We believe that youthwork is ongoing work that benefits not only young people but all citizens. We try to find recognition of young people in their own community and increase awareness of their significant role in society. Therefore we promote development of youthwork inside local communities and the involvement of state and local authority toward responding of the needs of young people. Our aims are:

– To encourage personal development through social education;
– To increase young people's participation in building civil society using social education as a tool;
– To support and participate in developing a permanent structure that provides ongoing work toward meeting the needs of young people by working in partnership with local communities, NGOs, and authorities on the local and national levels.

We offer two years of university studies from the University of Jonkoping, Sweden, for those who want to support and work with young people. The certificate is recognized by the European Union. The first year is A–level: Leadership and Developmental Youthwork. The second year is B–level: Training for Trainers. We also organize international study and student exchanges.

The Beginning: PRONI organized the first project in this area with 20 students in 1997. It was taught in six modules involving tutors from Northern Ireland and Sweden who traveled into the area for periods of two weeks at a time. The course followed six themes that are approved by the University of Jonkoping. On our university course we are using methods of informal education where ideas of young people are shared, skills developed, and values tested. The course reflects on some of these methods and includes:

– Individual and small group study to develop skills such as listening and questioning;
– Practical work methods such as documenting the process of practice;
– Written work;
– Self-assessment;
– Study blocks and residential.

The university course, following the social education model, prepares youthworkers to be active and to make a conscious attempt to change and intervene in such a difficult reality. In this sense "education" (*educare* or to nurture) stands for the planned or spontaneous activity of the community whose goal is to transfer social values, knowledge, and experience with and through young people. The process of education, which includes development of the mental, moral, and physical abilities represents one of the radical postulates of the human existence.

Social Educational Principles: Historically, social education represents a kind of preparation for life by accustoming people in the *milieu* of the social inconsistencies and problems that the existing social development imposes. With its organization, goals, assignments, and progressive functions, education in this sense embodies a crucial factor of social and human development. The act of knowledge is the synthesis of perception and concept, and only perception and concept together constitute a whole. With education (both formal and informal) one is preparing for life (*ad vitam paramus*), upgrading its personality and developing its moral, ethic, and progressive values.

An old Latin saying is that "experience is the best teacher, so we should learn from it" (*hoc est vivere bis vita posse priore frvi*). In social education, experience is one of the key foundations of youthwork. Together with theory, an experienced youthworker knows how to take a group through the path of personal development, one of the core principles of youthwork. In this phase or part of youthwork, young people are getting the chance to experience things that will develop their skills, values, knowledge, and attitudes. Through creative work and challenging activities, which occur in the safe and supportive environment, young people are encouraged to express themselves and talk without prejudices.

A second core principle of youthwork is participation in making decisions. In this phase they are learning about inequalities in the society and how to change, shape, and develop their experiences.

A third core principle of youthwork is acceptance and understanding of others. Youthworkers are role models to young people in their groups. They have to be conscious, persistent, ambitious, and without prejudices or negative attitude. Maria Montessori, in *The Montessori Method,* said "Learn from the child how to perfect yourself as an educator." Conversation between the youthworker and young people in the group is important because, without mutual correspondence, understanding, and trust (that they have built), that group cannot function in a desirable way.

Social Education Practice

There are no theories that can explain the problems of young people in a post-conflict community or a young person with a broken heart or the meaning of life to a young person who was betrayed by life. There are thousands of questions without answers, and the task of youthworkers is to try and give answers to some of them.

It is difficult to describe in advance how a youthworker would carry out a program of social education with a group of young people. Each group has a tendency to become harmonious or less harmonious--it depends on the group members, their mutual communication and understanding, and also on the youthworkers' ability to create environments for young people where they can feel free to speak their minds and cooperate with each other.

In UNESCO's essay, "Learning Societies," about modern society and education, the author writes,

> The current urge, fuelled by a desire to let reemerge a diversity of worldviews, meanings, and understandings around notions such as development, progress, knowledge, intelligence, wisdom, family/ community, cultural production, diversity, freedom, social justice, happiness, health, technology, ecology, dissent, etc., is to unfold a net of

plural learning paths composed of experiments and traditional practices related to deep and meaningful learning.

The main question that this university course provokes is how to promote cognitive-behavioural as well as emotional growth in order to achieve balance in transformation of theory into a practice that will effectively prepared future youthworkers for practical work with young people, especially in a difficult situation like we have in Vukovar.

Theory to Practice and Back Again

How do we connect theory that we are presenting with real life and needs in specific communities like Vukovar? How do we make it simple but keep it at a high academic level? In our work we try to follow the principle that *"Everything is connected."* All the parts of the puzzle called Social Education and Leadership and Developmental Youth work and all aspects of the program need to be connected on many levels during the course. We try to come back to the same points cowered on previous modules of teaching.

We are constantly aware that *"Attention must be paid."* As tutors on this university course we do need to draw conclusions about all matters concerning groups that we work with, the connection with social and political moments in our society, and to make our work relevant and part of everyday reality. The experience that tutors bring into this work is a huge *Ground of Experience.* Using examples from real youthwork situations, we try to cover the theoretical parts of the course.

Another challenge is to create space and atmosphere for learning using experiences, creativity, and knowledge within the group of our students rather than teaching them: to help them create, not consume. The program process has demonstrated that the methodology of our work is a model of educational intervention that provides young people with a vocabulary for discussing critical issues while widening perspectives, increasing empathy, creating an awareness of choices and opportunities, and preparing students for being responsible youthworkers. Based on the principle that students are adult learners who can continue to develop their knowledge, skills, and understanding of their roles as youthworkers over time, we also offered a model of successful professional development for students whose elements have broad interdisciplinary applications.

EXPANSION OF THE PROGRAM

The large-scale project began in 1998 and had two teachers from Northern Ireland who taught week-by-week. In 1999 the first local teacher was trained and employed. By this time a large body of materials was developed according to the local needs in this area of work with young people. From 2000 on almost all course materials and lecture were provided in the local language.

A large number of students have reported great satisfaction with the form of lectures and connection with practice nature of work. Others have expectations derived from previous experience with formal education where respect is owed to rote learning and formal content. Our own aims were changing attitudes and skills development, raising awareness about taking responsibility for decisions, and active participation through practical placement in the community. Success derives from combination of all features, and students are becoming more readily aware of our approach as times goes by. Many times students come back to tell us, "You changed us!"

From 1997 until now, more than 400 students have completed our education, and 47 percent of graduated students continue to work in the community as youthworkers or starting their own NGOs and taking active part in the society.

Within the University course every year students run approximately 35 small community projects with young people called Practical Placement. Through a number of activities we try to take active part in community development:

- Organizing community projects in cooperation with other local NGOs;
- Opening youth clubs/NGO centres trough Croatia;
- Organising training on different subjects relevant for youthwork and community development;
- Organising OUTHREACH projects (street youthwork, festivals, performances, exhibitions, and public debates.
- Actively participating within the working group of the State Institute for the Protection of Motherhood, Family, and Youth in last stage of designing National Programme of Action for Youth.

FROM PERSONAL DEVELOPMENT TO POLITICS

Issues like racism or powerlessness in our community are so big that it is difficult for young people to see what we can do about them. The very word "politics" is enough to strike horror into the hearts of youthworkers and bring boredom to the faces of young people. Youthworkers often say that their work is not political. That is not true at all, because ignoring politics in our day-to-day youthwork may be restricting people's ability to meet their developmental needs.

Personal and social problems and experiences can only be fully understood and acted upon when they are seen as both private "troubles" and public issues. This is the task for a critical social education and youthworkers. They need to create opportunity for action with young people. This is our challenge for the future, to help young people to be more connected to the political process, so that then young people could improve and change conditions in their community. Until then they will stay in the contested space of their youth clubs.

Saonje Spanje
University of Jonkoping/PRONI Center for Social Education
Vukovar, Croatia

REFERENCES

Council of Europe Youth Policy Advisory Mission: Final report of the visit of a group of experts to Zagreb, Croatia. (7 – 11 April, 2003). Youth programme Third Country cooperation, available from www. europa.eu.int

Hugo, M. (1999). Social reconstruction in Croatia. *Pedagogik D* (pp. 61- 80). Gothenburg University, Sweden.

Peko, A., Jindra, R., & Munjiza, E. (2003). *Perspective of coexistence: ethnic attitudes and fear of the other nation.* Osijek, Croatia: Philosophy Faculty.

Adinda Dulcic, A. (2003). *The State Institute for the Protection of Family, Maternity, and Youth: The National Programme of Action for Youth.* Zagreb, Croatia.

Smith, M.. (1982). *Creators not consumers* (2nd ed.). NAYC Publications (now Youth Clubs UK).

INTRODUCTION TO RESEARCH, THEORY, AND YOUTH IN CONTESTED SPACES

Like all practice, work with youth in contested spaces is informed by local and global values and beliefs about effectiveness, fitness, and worthiness. The volume of research and theory about this work is rapidly increasing and has a distinctly international hue, maybe more so than any other type of youthwork. Perhaps this is because violent conflict draws outsiders in, whether they have a direct stake in the conflict or not.

Local practitioners and international researchers are asking important questions about the extent to which these research tools and the theories on which they are based can be used in local settings. The Women's Commission for Refugee Women and Children conducted a brilliant participatory action research project in northern Uganda that pushes the boundary of our beliefs about the limits of research under these conditions. Siobhán McEvoy-Levy and Katy Radford show how conflict is reproduced and expressed in the lives of young people, with interesting descriptions of marginalization and unexpected takes on where the "divided" in "divided and contested" may lay. Grattan and Morgan, Harland, and Morgan and Veeran all reflect on the experience of conflict in Northern Ireland—historically and in comparison with other places, such as South Africa.

Research

- What research should be done in your context? In the context of the article you're reading?
- What about the phenomenon(a) of contested spaces asks to be studied?
- How must research on contested spaces be framed, conceptualized, planned, carried-out and reported?
- Is research a viable approach to contesting your contested spaces?

Youth and Practice in Contested Spaces

What do contested spaces teach us about...
- Being a young person there and elsewhere?
- Growing-up there and elsewhere?
- Direct youthwork with young people?

- What forms of youthwork are permitted and accepted and which are not by virtue of working in violently contested space?
- What auspice must *not* be used for youthwork in the article you are reading? In your context?
- Indirect youthwork on behalf of youth?
- Is there any indirect youthwork in your context?

Theory
- What theory counts—and why—in contested spaces?
- What kinds of theory are needed?
- Whose expertise is needed?
- What does theory contribute to effective work with youth?
- In what ways is theory local or global?
- How should we evaluate the legitimacy of a theory?
- Can the various theories about the work be organized coherently?

SIOBHÁN MCEVOY-LEVY

YOUTH NARRATIVES IN CONTESTED SPACES AND THEIR IMPLICATIONS FOR YOUTHWORK[62]

ABSTRACT

Young people's everyday activities – walking the streets, going to school, taking part in leisure pursuits, as well as their violent actions - are collectively narrated and are processes of peer education with important implications for youthwork in contested societies. This paper examines narrative data collected through focus groups in Northern Ireland in the years since the Belfast/Good Friday Peace Accord to explore the conflict reproduction roles of "experiential" learning on the streets and informal education among youth. The paper shows how narrative construction is organic to the everyday interactions of youth and helps create politics (or political meaning). The stories the young people construct, the frames and metaphors they use to describe their experiences of violence and attitudes to peace, and the dynamics of the focus groups themselves capture processes of collective meaning-making that shape how conflict evolves. The importance of these findings for youthwork is discussed in the conclusion.

Paramilitary ceasefires in Northern Ireland in 1994 began the public phase of a peace process culminating in the 1998 Belfast/Good Friday Agreement. This peace process followed almost 30 years of political violence during which approximately 3500 to 4000 people were killed and 35000 to 40,000 seriously injured (O'Leary & McGarry, 1993; NISRA, 1998) out of a population of approximately 1.7 million people (CAIN, 2001 figures). Parts of the cities of Belfast and Derry/Londonderry were landscapes of bomb damage, makeshift street barricades, and elaborate military fortifications. While most of that landscape has

[62]The author would sincerely like to thank the following people who provided insights or consented to formal interviews that have informed this research: Teresa Devlin of the office of the Northern Ireland Commissioner for Children and Young People (NICCY); Paul Donnelly of the Belfast Interface Project; Alan Delargy and Philip Hutton of Mount Gilbert Community College; Tony Gallagher, Queen's University Belfast; Hugh Green, St. Peter's High School, Derry/Londonderry; Eilis McDaniel, Children and Young People's Unit, OFMDFM; Laurence McKeown, Coiste na n-Iarchimíl; Jack MacLucas, Waterside Youth Center, Derry/Londonderry; Michelle Miller, Mount Vernon Community Center, and; especially, all of the young people who participated in the focus groups. However, none are responsible for the paper's interpretations or conclusions save the author. The research for this paper was supported by a Fellowship from the Joan B. Kroc Institute for International Peace Studies at the University of Notre Dame and by a Butler University Faculty Research Grant.

Doug Magnuson and Michael Baizerman (eds), Work with Youth in Divided and Contested Societies, 87–108.

largely been dismantled, memories live on, violence continues, and the street barricades returned in the post-agreement period.

On the one hand, a very visible marker of the post-ceasefire period has been the redevelopment of Belfast city center, including many new cafes, bars, hotels and a famously sleek, $58 million (USD), glass-fronted conference and concert facility. Quickly, Belfast was called one of the "hippest UK travel spot[s]" and "the friendliest and comfiest 'war zone' around" (Latimer, 1990; Pogatchnik, 1999). This last description (from a Canadian tourist publication) hints at the city's contradictions – and at how quickly Northern Ireland has been transformed in the global imagination.

Yet just a couple of miles from the revitalized downtown, residents of long-warring Protestant (Loyalist) and Catholic (Nationalist) neighborhoods continue to paint their curbstones in national colors, paint murals, hang rival flags, and throw stones and bottles at ethnic interfaces. Seasonally, because of contested Orange Order parades, and sometimes around sports events, tensions explode into violence. For young people[63] who are involved in these activities, often termed "recreational rioting" (Jarman & O'Halloran, 2001), going downtown is not hip, friendly, or comfortable. It is a place of interaction with youth from the other side: a place of antagonism. Adults in their communities, including youthworkers, point out that this is in part an imagined or exaggerated threat. In other words, it is a constructed world of youth who live on the margins. But out of this construction, a politics develops containing ideas about war and peace.

The first part of the paper explores the stories, frames, and metaphors that working-class urban youth use to describe their everyday activities and their involvement in riots and politics. Then the paper concludes with a discussion of the significance of these findings and narratives in general for youthwork practice. The field research on Northern Ireland was conducted through focus groups[64] with youth ages 12 to 25. Each focus group began with just three questions: What is violence? What is community? And what is peace?[65] The focus groups were followed with written questionnaires asking the same questions and inviting qualifications and additions. However, often the participants in the focus groups could not or did not want to stick to this agenda. Some groups focused on other issues that most interested them. At the time of the research these issues were inter-communal riots, street fighting, and the peace process. This was the case in the focus groups reported on below.

---

[63] Young people under age 24 compose 33% of the population in Northern Ireland according to the 2001 census. 54.6% of the population is under 35 years old. (CAIN)

[64] Useful literature on the importance of focus groups for research on contentious issues and for identifying cultural knowledge can be found in Hughes & Dumont (1993), Johnson (1996), Morgan (1996), Morgan & Krueger (1993), Nichols-Casebolt & Spakes (1995).

[65] See McEvoy-Levy (2000), and McEvoy-Levy (in press) for further discussion of this methodology.

YOUTH NARRATIVES IN CONTESTED SPACES

The interpretations and dramatizations of youth in Northern Ireland emerging in their accounts of their everyday interactions with friends and rivals are the subject of the next four sections of this paper. The first excerpts of the focus groups deal especially with religion, gender, and ethnicity, and the intersection of these with the experience of adolescence and economic deprivation – intersections that emerged naturally from the conversations themselves. The participants in this first extract were all female and between 13 and 18 years old. They were from the Mount Vernon estate in North Belfast.[66]

"[M]ost of Them's Just Bitchy:" Religion, Adolescence and Security

The topic of religion emerged in the girls' discussions of their future aspirations. Talk about where they would get married prompted one girl to wonder whether there would ever be a church built on their public housing estate. Another responded, "Mount Vernon is not the place for a church." The conversation continued as follows:

> Q. Why [is Mount Vernon not the place for a Church]?
> Lindsay: It's just not the place for a Church.
> Elizabeth: It's not a Christian place.
> Q. It's not a Christian place? What kind of place is it?
> Elizabeth: They do their own things. They don't have to do what people tell them. Like, did you ever see Christians? They talk to God. I don't believe [in] that, because every Christian has done somethin', they've either killed somebody or wrecked somebody's life, and they're only turnin' to God, so they are.
> Sarah: We've all done bad things in our life.
> Elizabeth: I don't believe in Christians.
> Ann: Believing in God is different from believing in Christians. I believe in God; I don't believe in Christians.
> Elizabeth: I don't – they're Bible bashers.
> Q. Do you mean they believe in the Bible literally and they're very religious?
> Sarah: [interrupts] Prods don't. It would be more the Catholics goin' like this [makes a sign of the cross] - Holy Mary and all that.
> Lindsay: There's Christians on both sides.
> Elizabeth: They're not really that different, like.

---

[66] The focus group was conducted at Mount Vernon Community Center, North Belfast, June, 2001. The names of the participants have been changed.

> Sarah: They're Catholics and we're Protestants – that's a quare [big] difference.
> Lindsay: They believe in Holy Mary and we believe in God, that's the only difference. [agreement]
> Elizabeth: But that's not really much of a difference.
> Sarah: It is. Because they believe God hasn't rose and we do.
> Q. Catholics do believe that Jesus rose from the dead.
> Sarah: Yeah, but why do they believe in Holy Mary?
> Q. Well...
> Lindsay: Because they're Fenians [derogatory term for Catholic].
> Sarah: They never grew up.

It is unclear if Elizabeth is referencing Loyalists (Protestants) who have become "born again" in prison or Catholics who kill, or both. But in defining "every" Christian as having "either killed someone or wrecked someone's life," she seems to situate herself outside the stereotyped confines of the conflict. It is a position that Elizabeth cannot completely sustain, for her peers interject. She does not back down. But her peers, who evoke the sectarian lens, have the last word and set the agenda.

This narrative shows how the identities "Protestant" or "Prod" and "Catholic" or "Fenian" spiral out from ill-conceived notions of religious difference. Yet for these youth, they are identities primarily constructed not in relation to a faith tradition but to their physical insecurity. They continue the conversation by introducing a theme of their confinement, a reworking of the "siege metaphor" that has been central to Protestant identity in Northern Ireland since the 12th century (See Buckley & Kenney, 1995). Protestant identity, colloquially being a "Prod," means not being be able to travel downtown because of youth from the other community:

> Q. What does it mean to be a Prod?
> Eizabeth: Support your country. You are who you are. Fight for your country.
> Sarah: This was our country.
> Elizabeth: This is still our country. Ulster.
> Lindsay: "For God and Ulster."
> Sarah: Means being mohawked by Taigs.

> Q. What does "mohawked" mean?
> Sarah: Killed. We can't even go into town. See if you go into town you end up getting beat. Me and my mate went to the cinema one night and they near killed her and there's this wee lass of 21 and they're near killed her.
> Q. How did they know she was Protestant?
> Sarah: I don['t] know.
> Q. Can you tell by looking at someone?
> Elizabeth: No.
> [Pause]

Sarah: Some people.
Lindsay: Catholics have wee mustaches and...
[In unison]: The way they wear their hair!
Sarah: And zits and all. Wee hellions.
Q. What's the hair like?
Sarah: It's way, way high.
Lindsay: Some of them have skinheads.
Q. The men?
Elizabeth: No, the kids.
Ann: See the men are just as bad, so they are, they coax the wee lads to join [paramilitary groups] and all that.

Most people agree that it is not possible to tell Catholic and Protestant people apart by any physical characteristic. But locally, people do practice identification based on accent, place of residence, school attended, and use of certain words or pronunciations. Clothes of specific "national" colors (orange or green) and the uniforms of soccer teams (like Celtic and Rangers) are more accurate markers. There is also a formal means by which youth in particular are categorized and identified whether they wish it or not. Most attend religiously-segregated schools, most of which have mandatory school uniforms, making it easy to identify Catholic and Protestant school children. In this way, the everyday is a conflict narrative with almost all youth in Northern Ireland constructed from an early age as conflict actors. They walk the streets to school in uniform and pass mirror images of themselves, dressed as "other," collectively (re)creating the conflict.

However, the young people in this focus group take the enemy-imaging a stage further. Notably, they begin by saying that it is not possible to tell a person's religious or political identity through visual cues. Then one says "some people." Finally, they announce a collective wisdom about how to identify Catholic girls: "The way they wear their hair!" Escalation occurs as part of the process of collective deliberation but it emerges from commonly held understandings. As a result, the familiar siege metaphor, expressed in an ethnic or racialized form in the localized slang of being "mohawked," is nuanced by an adolescence frame.

Most adults interviewed either were not aware of a hairstyle as a group identifier or had heard young people talk about it and believed it comical and inaccurate. But the perception was quite widespread among working-class Protestant youth in Belfast. Earlier, a similar conversation took place in a focus group among Protestants--male and female--in a school in the west of the city. Like the Mount Vernon group, this group from the Shankill, who participated in a focus group in 2000, described their leisure times as when they "just muck about" or "walk about" locally because, they said, their social lives were curtailed by risks of personal or small-group street assaults. They explained:

Tanya: Older ones would go downtown, but it's risky cause there's loads of Catholics.
Q.Why?
Tanya: Get in fights and stuff.

Q. I don't understand. How can you tell a Catholic or Protestant when you're downtown?
Tanya: Catholic girls wear hair [tied] up high.
Paul: Different colored clothes and such.
Claire: Boys wear caps back on their heads [and] have moustaches.
Tanya: They dress like tramps--scruffy looking. [They] don't look good in clothes--wear them either too big or too small.
Paul: When you walk in a Catholic area or downtown you can tell by looking at a person, tell by the way they get on [act].
Claire: Their hair is curly. They tie it in bobbles.
Tanya: Some of them are dead-on, but most of them's just bitchy.[67]

Hairstyle is the first group marker mentioned. It precedes even the obvious wearing of particular colors. On the surface, these two groups construct a politics of racialization. But the racial or ethnic frame is blurred with a frame of adolescence. Catholics are universally recognized by their "zits," "curly" tied up hair, and most are "bitchy." They are also at times infantilized as a collective: "They never grew up" and are "wee hellions."

"Self defense narratives," Lakoff (2001) argues, usually contain an asymmetry of good and evil. Here, the villain is not "amoral and vicious" (Lakoff) but unattractive and "bitchy." Lakoff argues that "metaphors are ways of reasoning" that "determine and constrain" our actions. In this case, the perspective that Catholics are unruly, threatening, immature, and ugly emerges not just from a sectarian reasoning but also from a teen reasoning. And one reinforces the other.

The sectarian conflict (the existence and threat of an "other") militarizes adolescence. This, in turn, recreates the racial/ethnic "other." The cycle serves to "determine and constrain" actions that might otherwise lead to peace. Youth are integral actors in creating their own politics of militarized adolescence. Indeed, the core of conflict reproduction in intercommunal conflicts may lie in the crucible of adolescence exploration and performance within and on the boundaries of their historically conflicting communities.

However, examined from another angle, the peacebuilding potential within this narrative can be uncovered. While a militarization of society creates confinement, so perhaps does the adolescent body. Maybe it should be no surprise, then, that these youth use a discourse of the body as a weapon in their everyday lives and as a symbolic barrier against empathy with "the other." Their life stage puts them regularly on the streets – to attend school and for leisure – at the time when they are also a self in physical transition. Surely, this enhances their sense of self-conscious vulnerability. In this, they may mirror teens worldwide, demonstrating their ordinariness.

Their narratives, then, may seek to take a little control of that terrain which often is, in fact, dangerous. Remarkably, while they seem to reproduce, even escalate, the conflict, the youth also critique the status quo. These young people conceptualize the conflict not just, or even primarily, in terms of national or

---

[67] The focus group was conducted at Mount Gilbert Community College, Belfast, 2000. The names of the participants have been changed.

political aspirations that are curtailed. In both cases, they begin with a story of teenage aspirations curtailed: "We can't even go into town." Telling this story of being socially excluded underscores that peace agreements need to provide (at least perceptions of) tangible benefits. Their criticism is not hidden in the narrative. It is an overt and political statement. When the girls emphasize that they cannot "*even*" go downtown, they suggest the tip of an iceberg of exclusion. They create politics (notions of who gets what, when, and how) together based on an understanding of their collective experience.

"Fifty Stitches – You're Rich!" Gender, Riot and Economic Exclusion

In the preceding narratives, rival girls are dramatized as teens with bad skin, but boys are described, perhaps in more threatening terms, with reference to skinheads and moustaches. However, the girls also sought to deconstruct this "hard" masculinity and reverse gender stereotypes. They suggested that the Catholic boys were "coaxed" by adults into participating in violence. But they insisted on their own agency in being involved in riots or "protests." Although this analysis reflects sectarian thinking, it also narrates a politics of gender:

Q. So will you be out tonight rioting?

Elizabeth: No. It doesn't start till Sunday.

Ann: It's not riotin'. Its protestin'.

Sarah: But it turns out to be riotin'.

Q. What's the difference between a protest and riot?

Ann: There's a peaceful protest and then the police come and that's when everybody gets really sick of it and pissed off and then they start getting the bottles and the bottles go everywhere.

Q. And what time do they go on to?

Ann: About 5 the next morning.

Q. Do you stay out all that time?

Elizabeth: No, we stay until about 1 or 2.

Lindsay: I stay until I see my uncle comin' and bolt.

Q. So what do your parents think of it?

Sarah: My mummy agrees with it, so she does.

Q. She's not worried about you?

Sarah: She is worried about me but she's always with me, so she is. But my mother agrees with it.

Ann: Because they know we are supporting the country. They know, see by the second night of protest, the police provoke us.

None of these participants mention fathers, although one uncle appears from the margins. The dominant image is of supportive mothers, contrasted with the provocative police. This sets up an interesting gender layer in which the girls take on ambiguous roles as "citizen warriors" (Lakoff, 2001). They are active participants in the violence but are outraged at how the police use their batons on "even pregnant women" and "women and children." In adopting these roles, they deconstruct a conservative moral order in which "stern fathers" supposedly dominate (see Lakoff, 2001), asserting a feminine alternative leadership. But, at the

93

same time, they reproduce that order with their story of women and children as victims.

The earlier sectarian infantilization of Catholics is qualified by the fact that these girls adopted parental positions generally. The Mount Vernon group described a Protestant being "mohawked" who was "a wee girl of 21" when they were several years younger than this themselves. In other parts of the discussion they dramatized themselves as the protectors of younger children and of the elderly in violent situations (McEvoy-Levy, 2006). So while their shifting, gendered positions entail contradictions, these girls narrate central and positive roles for themselves in intercommunal violence. However, their stories contrast with the mainstream narrative in which paramilitary men direct violence and girls are not present as in the following account of rioting that erupted in North Belfast in May, 2002.

In the wake of a soccer match between Glasgow Celtic and Rangers, one local newspaper described how "Police were confronted by gunmen, petrol bombers, stone-throwers, and thugs wielding makeshift weapons such as a hatchet, a meat cleaver, a golf club, and a pick axe." The news story reproduced the following edited transmissions from different police units in the area as the crowds left the football arena:

> 16.58: Crowd coming out from Brompton Park roundabout.
> 17.01: About 30 children on the "green" side and approx 12 now on the "orange" side. There is no stoning at present.
> 17.06 A group of approx 20/30 heading from Alliance Road towards the shop fronts.
> 17.06: Approx 60 heading from Brompton Park area, towards the shop fronts.
> 17.15: Both factions have come together at the roundabout - need more assistance.
> [...]
> 17.25: Large crowd of youths here with bottles - will need permission to fire baton guns here soon.
> 17.26: Need permission to fire - situation getting serious. Reply: Permission granted.
> 17.26: One PBR (plastic bullet round) fired - one hit - beige top and beige trousers.
> 17.29: Need more resources here - orange coming into green.
> [...]
> 17.41: One PBR fired at male with hatchet wearing a Rangers top and blue track bottoms.
> 17.42: Male has now taken hatchet to the vehicle.
> 17.44: Crowd is trying to overturn our vehicle over here.
> 17.50: Three baton rounds fired. Two hits.
> 17.50: 13 baton rounds fired.
> 17.50: Green side moving back into Brompton.
> 17.54: Approx 50 youths in Brompton Pk pushing bins [trash cans] into ground.

[...]

18.26: Fireworks being fired at police.

18.29: Five petrol bombs thrown.

18.31: Further petrol bombs being thrown. One struck military LandRover.

18.38: One member of our crew has been injured - need ambulance...

18.48: Call from a female - stated Catholics are coming up to Crumlin Road/Hesketh, coming to shop fronts.

18.49: Nine petrol bombs thrown. A large number of people now heading towards Hesketh. It looks like the loyalists are coming out to meet them.

18.55: Approx 300 people here at Hesketh rioting.

[...]

18.58: Hesketh Park - report of person in area with guns.

19.04: Call from Crumlin Road, report a male in the area, tall wearing white top... he has a meat cleaver.

19.08: One shot fired from the orange side (at police) at Hesketh Park.

19.10: We can confirm one strike to this vehicle.

19.12: Gunman in sight at Hesketh Park.

[...]

19.49: Report Jim ------- (prominent loyalist) agitating crowd to attack police. (Gordon 2002)

This account describes how children, youth, and adult paramilitaries are involved in stages as a riot unfolds and escalates. There is a ritualized quality to the event with children as the advance guard in a clash that the police describe in purely sectarian terms as "orange" versus "green." This is the same pattern described in the focus groups by girls themselves in relation to a different riot one year earlier:

Elizabeth: There's [little] kids but they don't stand in the road, they wait at the bonefire [bonfire] field, you know what I mean. Then there's the likes of us, 13 to about 18, 19. We're the ones that blocks the road and then when all the riotin' starts, the older ones arrive.[68]

Yet the only woman mentioned in the newspaper and police narrative is one who calls the police for help. The "children" in the news/police account do not have genders and the "youth" are male. In the focus groups, the girls seemed aware of their own invisibility in the public eye, for they note in other parts of the discussion that they are not listened to, even though they have knowledge of where and when street violence is taking place or is imminent (McEvoy-Levy, 2006). But they do not link invisibility to gender inequality. Nevertheless, their actions--and some of the narrations of their actions--critique and destabilize the mainstream narrative.

Another politics – this time a class politics – is expressed by young people, both Catholics and Protestants, in the focus groups. In a rare point of agreement youth from both traditions perceived that police provocation led to or exacerbated riot situations and was motivated by material gain. Catholic boys in one group agreed that the security forces were motivated by "danger money" because they are compensated for injuries obtained during the course of duty, as summed up in this

---

[68] This quotation is examined detailed context in McEvoy-Levy (2006).

quotation from Kieran: "They [the police] get a hundred pound a stitch. With fifty stitches - you're rich!" Similarly, in a Protestant girl's explanation, the police enjoyed public disorder because they could earn overtime money. Elizabeth: "If there's any riotin they get paid more. See if they're on seven pound an hour, they get triple that. In case any of them get hurt. That's why they love it, they get more money."[69] The perceived economic motivations of the police help to justify the involvement of these young people in street violence. Their strategic thinking is shaped by an economic opportunity structure in which the acquisition of 5000 pounds (50 stitches multiplied by 100 pounds) is perceived to equal wealth. This class frame – which crosscuts the sectarian division – provides another critique of the peace process for it underlines the young people's sense of economic exclusion.

A more unusual economic frame was also used to explain the *intra*communal violence that has been a feature of the post-agreement period in Northern Ireland. During the period of this research, violent internal feuding between rival Loyalist (Protestant) groups displaced 269 families in the upper Shankill (the site of one of the focus groups). A month later 109 had still not been re-housed. They were reported to have suffered financial hardship, disruption of school schedules, as well as psychological trauma. In the local press, one mother spoke of the upheaval in these terms: "Our children are the future. They are losing out on so many things in life – if their own community is doing this to them what chance do they have?" (Bonner, 1999).

This "children are our future" versions of events, which the media tends to highlight, is countered with a somewhat different narrative when young people from the area speak about the events in a focus group four months later. Since the violence was intracommunal, they sought an alternative to the siege frame. And instead of bemoaning "their own" doing this, they fastened on the Balkans, child soldiers and refugees, as a metaphor for their own condition.

> Claire: There's lots of Kosovars moving into Britain now. [I] Saw the house on the TV the other day. It was lovely.
>
> Tanya: In Bosnia there's kids of 8 shooting at army, kids been shot to death.[70]

The first girl expresses envy for a "lovely" house in Britain, which seems more a reward than a hardship for the Balkan refugees she references. In doing so, she identifies her own locality's economic deprivation (officially one of the most deprived parts of Europe) and her own attraction to domesticity. But her peer links this longing with the active participation of children in violence. She raises the possibility of kids shooting and being shot in their own locality. The specter, of course, (following the Balkans analogy) is of escalating ethnic violence. Together, these girls create a vision of mounting violence rooted in economic exclusion. But

---

[69] These focus groups were conducted in St. Peter's High School, Derry/Londonderry in 2000 and Mount Vernon Community Center, Belfast in 2001. This second quotation is examined in more detailed context in McEvoy-Levy (2006). The names of the participants have been changed.

[70] Focus group at Mount Gilbert Community College, Belfast, 2000. The names of the participants have been changed.

they also point to economic development as a peacebuilding mechanism and, once again, critique the peace process.

"Peace is Not a Real Goal:" Politics and Resilience

It was a distinctive feature of all the working class Protestant groups that escalation, even catastrophic war, was envisioned for the future. In contrast, working-class Catholics tended to envision a stagnant pseudo-peace typified by "ordinary" problems such as drugs and AIDS becoming more prevalent and a continuation of the sectarian rivalry at street level (McEvoy-Levy, 2006). But they too were skeptical about violence ever being consigned to the past. For Catholics the frame was typically more overtly and conventionally political and expressed an experience of being second-class citizens. One young Catholic likened Catholics being beaten up by the police to historical US slavery and more recent assaults on Rodney King:

> Kieran: There's always going to be violence. Like in America – blacks and whites. Way back the blacks were all slaves. Now they've got their freedom but they're still being treated like slaves. There's always goin to be fightin', its just the same over here.
> Malachy: They are still slaves in some parts, aren't they? It was on the news the other night. Rodney King.[71]
> Connor: When you are involved in violence you feel good because you feel your point is getting across, you know you're getting heard. [You do it] because you feel you're not being listened to. It gets on the news and is shown around the world.[72]

What is remarkable about these explanations is how conventionally violence is framed as a political instrument. The global connections in these narratives on the one hand seem to normalize political violence but, on the other, lend themselves to a quite rational skepticism about peace processes and inter-group reconciliation. They are at least realistic about the promises that accompany historical rapprochements. These boys constructed a peer group transcending time, space, nationality, and race to identify with other minorities. Their empathy with these "others" did not translate into empathy for their Protestant rivals at home. Yet they demonstrate their strong capacity for empathy in this regard. And in both sets of focus groups (Catholic and Protestant) some young people did express such empathy and maintained their arguments against the criticism of others in the group.

The critique offered by the Catholic boys in these focus groups, then, is two-fold: On the one hand, they present a conventional critique of the British state that has historically repressed the Catholic population. On the other hand, they confront, in a pessimistic but analytical way, the grand concepts of peace and peace

---

[71] For a fuller discussion of this focus group with 13-16 year-old Catholic boys at St. Peter's High School, in Derry/Londonderry in May ,1998, see McEvoy-Levy, 2000.
[72] The focus group was conducted at Waterside Youth Center, Derry/Londonderry, in 2000.The names of the participants have been changed.

processes. Sean tells the researcher that "it's hard to explain to someone who doesn't live here" that violence will always be a reality of life in Northern Ireland. He expresses and reinforces what is the common understanding of the group: Peace processes do not mean an end to violence or a new era of justice. No one contradicted him. But this prediction is not offered as a desirable outcome. The speaker intends to educate the researcher to this harsh reality.

Catholic youth who were activists in Sinn Fein, a political party associated with the paramilitary Irish Republican Army (IRA), created narratives within which the youth, gender, and class issues were also quite central. These activists (who were university students in their early twenties) explained why they worked for Sinn Fein rather than the more moderate nationalist party the Social Democratic and Labour Party (SDLP). [73]

> Sinead: A lot of people feel that the SDLP are out of touch with them. We've [Sinn Fein youth] been involved in protests against the landlords. The [student] housing is very bad and the rents are so high, you know. There's loads of people that have had to drop out [of university] because they can't afford to pay the fees and it used to be free. So we want to get somethin' done about that. They [SDLP] never pushed for any of these student issues or anythin'.
>
> Most people still feel that nationalism is a big concern whereas they [SDLP] feel they're post-nationalist, and obviously nationalism and unionism are still a large part of the problem. But the SDLP for some reason think that because there is a peace process that it's all over and done with. There's no one to represent young people, and there's hardly any women in the party either. The party leaders are mostly men. It's just very unrepresentative. The SDLP are all just sort out for themselves. Sinn Fein have been working to get [pedestrian] crossings – small things like that. They've redeveloped the whole town [...] There's goin' to be a youth center too and a recreation center.
>
> Joseph: They're on the ground. If you go through any small town or area where Sinn Fein is a prominent party, you can tell who is Sinn Fein because they mix through the people an[d] all. There was one SDLP councillor in the same estate as us, and she owned a big grand house and very rarely spoke to us. She was like a councillor at one time but she thought she was very grand because of it. Her (Sinead's) uncle was our mayor for a while and he worked in the summer in the concrete factory. He worked shoveling cement into a mixer, you know, and he was a mayor at the same time, you know. He was so down to earth, it was unbelievable. The Catholic people respect us because they can talk to us easily.
>
> Sinead: Usually, when people have problems with their houses, you know, they're on to the Sinn Fein councillors and its done right away.... Ordinary work.

---

[73] This focus group was conducted at Coiste na n-Iarchimí (Ex-Prisoners Committee), Belfast, in 2001. The names of the participants have been changed.

Joseph: The SDLP are not an invigorating party. They don't have a real goal. Peace is not a real goal. You need somethin'. You need a reason why peace is there. You have to bring down the barriers that created the war in the first place, which was partition. And the SDLP never really dealt with partition the way Sinn Fein has.

The argument that "peace is not a real goal" contains an analysis of peace as inevitably involving an end goal of a United Ireland. But beyond this is a multilayered explanation of the attraction of Sinn Fein as a political party that, in fact, transcends the partition question and (perhaps strategically) does not mention armed struggle at all. Most of the defense of Sinn Fein versus the SDLP references ordinary local politics. They cite initiatives to help the elderly, for economic development, and the working class credibility of Sinn Fein candidates. The Sinn Fein candidates not only get the "small things" done, but they are approachable, hard-working members of the community, rather than career politicians. The SDLP councillors are perceived as "grand" even when they live in the same housing estate, pointing up, perhaps, the importance of relatively small differences in economic status in an environment where economic expectations and opportunities generally are low. But the key theme is of authenticity and community loyalty. The image of the man of the people who "worked shoveling cement into a mixer" while also serving as mayor was quite sincerely offered and explores the same theme expressed by the younger participants in the focus groups (from both communities) when they said the police were motivated by "danger money."

Moreover, these focus group narratives also demonstrate how engagement in community-based activism can be psychologically rewarding on an individual basis. These older, politically active youth are clearly more confident and articulate not just because of age or education but also because of the strong sense of positive identity and belonging they have gained through their political involvement. "The Catholic people respect us," states Joseph, underlining the positive affirmation he receives from a perceived leadership role. As Straker (1992) has pointed out in her study of township youth involved in anti-apartheid activism in South Africa, mental resilience seemed to be enhanced for those who had leadership role in the youth movements.

Power and Silenced Voice

In contrast, the younger girls in Protestant/Loyalist groups did not perceive themselves to be respected: "People don't listen to us." In the Mount Vernon focus group, the girls ended the discussion in response to these questions:

Q: I sense that you're quite angry about a lot of things. Is that right?
Elizabeth: Yes.
[silence]
Q: Do you think this is a good place to be a young person?
Elizabeth: Yeh.... [unsure]
Sarah: This is where you learn about these things... about Catholics and all.

> Q: Do you find it useful to talk about these things?
> Elizabeth: Doesn't bother me.
> Ann: Helps you forget about it some times. Helps you forget if you're a Catholic or a Protestant.
> Q: How often do you think about these things?
> Elizabeth: When somethin like this [Drumcree] is happening we talk about it.
> Lindsay: Sarah's thinking about it all the time. She's going: "Oh, please be riotin, oh, please, please."
> Ann: How long will you be in Northern Ireland, miss?
> Q: Until the 9th of July.
> Sarah: [exclamation] The 9th of July! But how are you goin' to get home? There's a rumour goin' about that if there's any trouble or any riotin', North Belfast is getting shut down, supermarkets an[d] all. And Drumcree is what? The 9th of July?
> Elizabeth: No, the 7th, this Sunday.
> Ann: Can we have a break?

One of the participants reveals with the word "Miss" that she views the researcher as a teacher and that, whether rioter or protester, she is a schoolgirl, too. Some of the others sniggered at that – demonstrating the same. There is some weariness, sighs, and boredom at the end. There is sadness: "helps you forget." And then they brighten again for a moment at the further discussion of anticipated riots. Demonstrating that their worlds are small, they presume that the researcher is staying in their area and will be affected by any violence. But the final word is that the rioting will shut down *even* the "supermarkets" and it will curtail the author's and other adults' movements. In other words, riot entails power over the everyday, over domesticity, livelihood, over business, over interpretations, over the researcher, and over uses and abuses of their words and lives. And the prospect is exhausting. Still, while they claim some control in this way, they need permission to withdraw from the conversation. They cannot yet open, close, or control the narrative. Perhaps, this is because they perceive that no one is listening, or because they do not conceive of themselves as participants in the creation of politics. However, like the other youth who participated in the focus groups, these girls do indeed create politics with both their actions and their narrations of those actions.

Several common themes emerged from all the working-class, urban focus groups, Protestant and Catholic, male and female. A strongly expressed and idealist desire to serve and defend (their own) was one shared theme. A vaguer sense of economic (in)justice was another. An awareness of youth or teen identities as creating a distinct worldview slides in and out of the narratives but does not quite solidify. Even less awareness of the significance of gender politics is expressed, but the narratives demonstrate that gender inequality and tension are their lived experiences. While the Protestant participants adapted the very old siege metaphor in their narratives, the Catholic participants reproduced the traditional counter narrative containing nationalist ideas of freedom, dignity, and voice. In both cases, we can see the conflict reproducing in the familiar narrative being adapted (in greater and lesser degrees) to a new time. Yet even as they reproduce the conflict, these young people critique it.

These youth present themselves as angry, excluded, rejected by and rejecting religion, confused, curtailed, concerned, domesticated, independent, longing, tribal, teen, school girl/boy, protesters. They are simultaneously excited and bored with it all. Some are cynical, others engaged, radical men and women of the people. Globally aware, they reach out for identifications that might somehow better explain what it is like to live as they do. However, failing to note the agency of youth in creating politics, many adults are tempted to dismiss young people's talk as uneducated and illogical. But experience is an education, and Ross (2001) notes, "Although it is often easy to dismiss in-group explanations as incorrect or irrational and therefore irrelevant 'just-so' stories, to do so would be as foolish as for a psychoanalyst to tell a patient he or she has just recounted a stupid dream" (p. 159).

These young people do not only reveal subjective understandings that lie at the heart of the conflict reproduction process. They also intelligently (though not always overtly) prescribe constructive change. They warn of the dangers of escalation in war and stagnation in peace, and they point to concrete and specific social problems to be addressed.

IMPLICATIONS FOR YOUTHWORK PRACTICE

These dialogues help clarify that involvement in street or organized violence appeals to youth where there is a combination of unfulfilled needs, militarized experience, and compelling collective narratives, and together make a case for holistic and integrated youth policy responses. Youth are key connectors in society and have important roles in both making meaning in society and cultural (conflict) reproduction. A challenge for youthwork is how to engage with, indeed, rely upon the narrative construction and peer education process that is organic to young people's everyday activities. Further challenges involve how to expand and build on school-based programs and reach non-school youth. Creative, street-based (as well as center-based) programming that is oriented towards a balance of skills development and ideas and reflection (service learning models, for example), and unattached youthworkers who can work on the streets and in collaboration with youth service providers in youth centers and schools should be funding priorities in deeply divided and contested societies. The basic principle of youth design and consultation is also strongly indicated by this research.

As these dialogues show, violent behavior and prejudiced and divisive attitudes and speech emerge in the context of collective and personal trauma, negation of rights and lack of security, political and economic marginalization, and collective narratives of loss and threat. Sectarian or ethnically homogenous social groups, armed groups, and gangs (see Spergel, 1995) offer physical protection, group solidarity, cultural and/or religious identification, moral and political education, self-esteem, honor, economic hope, voice, engagement, and excitement. Summarized in Figure 1, these factors suggest that youth policies should monitor the rights and security of young people and address their recreational, community service, participation, economic development and training, and narrative-building needs.

As Figure 1 illustrates, *narratives* are part of *the context* of contested societies. Narratives also are *motivating factors*. They facilitate recruitment to armed groups and express and structure and create motive for belonging to such groups. Narratives should also be addressed *in practice/policy*. It appears that the impact of narrative construction is the least well acknowledged for youthwork and so this aspect is discussed further below.

A. In contested spaces there is a context of
    ▶ collective and personal trauma
    ▶ absence of rights/security
    ▶ political and economic marginalization
    ▶ collective narratives of loss/threat

B. Armed group and gangs recruit by fulfilling needs for
    ▶ physical protection
    ▶ social solidarity or surrogate family
    ▶ cultural and/or religious identification
    ▶ moral and political education
    ▶ self-esteem, honor and respect
    ▶ economic hope
    ▶ recreation and excitement
    ▶ voice and engagement

C. Youthwork implications/ youthwork should offer
    ▶ a service and participation component
    ▶ a recreational component
    ▶ an economic development and training component
    ▶ a monitoring of rights and security of children/youth
    ▶ a narrative-building component

Figure 1. Implications of Narratives for Youthwork in Contested Spaces

Narratives as Sources of Authentic Information

Consultations with youth, whether in focus groups as in this study, in surveys, or through youth councils or consultative forums, are essential for acquiring authentic and refined information about youth needs. The needs expressed through the dialogues collected in Northern Ireland make a case for holistic and integrated youth policy responses. They help clarify the need for educational access, job skills training, and employment programs that address the economic exclusion of youth. The complex and sometimes unusual frames that the participants in the focus groups used suggest direct connections between their economic exclusion and their attitudes both to intercommunal violence and to authority figures. The role of youth services in providing recreational activities and, additionally, in providing opportunities for community involvement and service are powerfully supported by the ways in which these youth identify themselves as socially excluded (unable to go into town, for example) while at the same time socially-anchored community actors.

Likewise, policies of citizenship education, conflict resolution, peace education, trauma counseling, and reconciliation initiatives are strongly supported by the findings of this research: Young people's militarized experience involves layers of trauma that work against empathy and revolve around retellings of poorly understood or inaccurate stories of the other's beliefs, motives, and presence in conflict. Context-specific gender differences must also be considered. As this study suggests, girls, for example, may be involved in or report being involved in riots and protests in a poorly understood subversion of gendered expectations. Education about gender may usefully precede dialogue about the overt conflict in this case (but not in others).

Monitoring and prioritizing children's and young people's rights and security and publicizing these findings are also important work for youth service providers for three reasons. First, personal (as well as group) insecurity is indicated as a central preoccupation of youth in contested spaces. Second, human rights monitoring can work towards undercutting cycles of conflict by providing early warning of conflict escalation and addressing the defensive and redemptive appeals of violence. Third, it may be desirable that youth are offered opportunities and skills to be human rights monitors in their own communities. However, distrust of adults and feelings of being ignored are pervasive themes of youth narratives in contested spaces. So, it is equally important that young people have, and perceive that they have, dedicated adult advocates.

Moreover, the narratives that youth create in their everyday interactions are not static, so ongoing attention is required. Emphasis on relationship-building between adults and youth and youth-to-youth mentorship is necessary but not sufficient to identify the trends and deep texture of youth marginalization, which also requires more systematically recording and analyzing the data – the narrative data--that emerges from close conversation, dialogue, confidence, trust, and friendship. Only in honestly engaging youth in this process as co-participants in gathering and recording their own knowledge, reflections, and prescriptions for change can such an approach produce the most authentic information and possibly be productive of better relationships, peace, or social justice.

Narratives as Sources of Politics and Culture

As well as providing more authentic information about youth needs and conflict dynamics, youth narratives are important in another way. They help create politics and culture. Youth create stories in their everyday interactions that sustain and create violence-legitimizing myths and memories. They also critique, deconstruct, and adapt established narratives to prescribe for positive change/peace. It is ironic that, although often socially, politically, and economically excluded, youth are key connectors in society. Youth participate in a variety of social institutions and spaces including school, home, the street, workforce, voluntary and leisure organizations and church, synagogue or mosque. Depending on the situation, these spaces of youth interaction may also include refugee camps, political movements, peace groups, interactive media such as internet discussion forums, and various forms of armed organization such as official militaries, rebel, terrorist, and spoiler groups, or criminal gangs (see McEvoy-Levy, 2006). Since youth are key connectors among these institutions, the narratives they create have wide distribution including to younger siblings.[74]

The cultures of divided societies or contested spaces are understood in many different ways depending on the standpoint of the actors involved. Such cultures may be defined as cultures of violence, death, or occupation, gun-cultures or drug-cultures, cultures of gender, racial or ethnic inequality or injustice, cultures of distrust or fear, cultures of solidarity or struggle, or some combination of these. Youthwork policy and practice is shaped by (and helps shape) these many politicized conceptualizations that often stereotype and scapegoat youth. However, it is important to recognize the active roles that youth themselves play in culture- (and conflict-) building, processes in which adult control is dominant but not absolute.

When young people in Northern Ireland write the graffiti "UTH" – meaning "up the hoods" – to rival the monograms of paramilitary groups, they are insisting on recognition as political entity (that is, a power-seeking group with negotiable interests and needs). They have politicized their marginal position and politicized what, as Darby (2001) reports, the police in Northern Ireland call "Ordinary Decent Crime."

In a different way, when young people generate conflict narratives, whether coherent political analyses or simply rumors of sectarian threat, these narratives can have concrete conflict outcomes such as triggering violence at community interfaces or recruiting other youth. Community workers in Northern Ireland have had some success with mobile phone networks used to contact youth and community workers "on the other side" and deflate fears of attacks that are

---

[74] Research in Northern Ireland shows that some 3-year-olds are able to recognize and express preference for "their" community's symbols (Connolly, Smith, & Kelly, 2002)

often generated by rumors. Crisis or conflict management of this kind is a vital activity that requires community and youthworkers who are willing to physically place themselves on the frontlines and work the irregular hours that political conflict and public disorder dictate. Longer-term initiatives such as education programs and encounter groups also address narratives by discussing enemy images and/or self-concepts. But these may not deeply impact students' everyday lives, and they may result in the "legitimation of difference" rather than the fostering of "shared space and identity" (Gallagher, 2004, p. 111).

Reaching Youth

A further set of challenges for youthwork emerges in how to reach youth who are beyond school age, do not attend school, or who are disaffected from reconciliation-oriented models. School-based citizenship education can hopefully address the latter and potentially reach a wide audience of young people. But it is also essential to go to the other places where youth are and this means funding youthworkers and educators to engage with young people on the streets, in bars, and at workplaces as well as in schools and established youth and community centers. Moreover, it will require that both teachers and youthworkers are adequately prepared and rewarded for developing effective partnerships through professional development, compensation, and promotions.

Yet it still remains to be seen if it is possible to engage youth in the process of constructing narratives in ways that both validate and challenge political understandings, encourage creativity, and promote shared identities and interests. Perhaps the integration of service-learning and narrative-based methodologies into youthwork programs can support such a goal. Story-telling or history-writing methodologies in inter-communal youth groups may reveal, humanize, and legitimize "the other's" story, precisely because they provide the same space for and acknowledgement of one's one history (see Adwan & Bar-On, 2006). Local history or memory projects that involve youth on the streets taking testimonies and collecting the stories of older people or their peers in a service-learning format involve the production of and reflection on a variety of narratives.

More formal truth-telling initiatives, such as Truth and Reconciliation Commissions, are increasingly popular and, while they may not be practical or productive in all contexts, open avenues for thinking about how youth may be engaged in national narrative-building. For example, even where such processes may be generally difficult, there may still be room for youth-only processes. National or local youth truth commissions may be more feasible if confined to a particular time-frame such as the period *since* a peace agreement (which is counter-intuitive to the established models). Such an approach would not deal with a whole contentious past but only that past that certain youth cohort has directly experienced. Inviting youth into a process of constructing their common story in such formats – whether local or national narratives – may be desirable because it would entail leadership roles for youth and require them to participate in community consultation and consensus-building.

Yet existing youth development programs often have difficulty meeting target participation levels, and there is resistance to cross-community work in favor of dealing with intracommunal tensions and development, as suggested by the North Belfast Community Action Unit (NBCAU) Evaluation Report (2004) of youth development programs:

> In many cases there was demonstrable opposition to working with the *"other side."* Views expressed during the consultation included, *"they won't talk to us"* and *"we have no interest in working with [that community] in the near future."* While a number of [Youth Development] Consortia had sought funding for "Single Identity" programmes, no evidence was available to show that the longer-term impact of these would be move groups towards cross community activity. (p. 24)

There are also dangers associated with public speech in contexts where informing has serious consequences or where traumatic memory may be activated. Sufficient support services and a community-wide agreement on its value would be necessary to validate and protect the participants. This is where the bigger challenge for youthwork emerges: how to create a culture in which the inclusion and recognition of youth as political actors can exist alongside the protection of children and youth as vulnerable human beings.

Children's rights advocates and statutory bodies for children's services have built-in prejudices in favor of the protection of children and children's welfare. Where a political agenda is extended it is focused on changing public values about children and childhood writ large promoting, for example, that children *have* rights or that corporal punishment is abuse. Less commonly, children's agencies respond to local political events or to specific and politicized forms of containment strategy such as paramilitary punishment beatings or Anti-Social Behavior Orders (ASBOs). The agenda of the office of the Northern Ireland Commissioner for Children and Young People (NICCY) demonstrates such an approach. The Children and Young People's Unit (CYPU) in the Office of the First Minister and Deputy First Minister (OFMDFM) similarly focuses on under 18s, employing a United Nations Convention on the Rights of the Child rubric. These are positive initiatives, essential to building sustainable peace. But it is not clear to what extent these institutions are conceptualized as contributing to the peace process in Northern Ireland or if the impact of the conflict on children *and* the impact of children on the conflict are to be central foci.

It seems that so far these children and young people's institutions have developed their agendas in response to consultations with youth. If it is the case that children and young people do not prioritize dealing with the conflict, the past, or political and sectarian street violence, they must be listened to. However, 34% of young Protestants surveyed by the North Belfast Community Research Project (2003) stated that youth should be involved in policy making. And there is a need for more intensive, extensive, and longitudinal consultation with youth in their different spaces of interaction. In societies in which armed conflicts have been intractable, young people, like adults, may be in denial about the extent to which societal militarization is a collective problem and responsibility. Moreover, as Smyth et al. (2004) found, it may be that the most frequently experienced conflict experiences of youth are the least visible: "[R]are experiences, such as being the victim of a punishment attack or joyriding, are highly publicised and visible to the wider society, whilst the more common experiences, such as being stopped and questioned by the police, or being attacked on the way home from school, are comparatively ignored" (p. 97).[75]

Another potential problem is that if key decision-makers come to rely on a children's rights context as the major or only space for deliberating on issues of youth violence, economic rights, or political agency, older young people (over 18s) may be further marginalized. Moreover, while building a culture of children's and human rights is essential work in "post-conflict" or contested spaces, it is at the same time important not to depoliticize children in their own local context. Each context is different in this regard. For example, in South Africa, children and youth were central actors in anti-apartheid activism and saw themselves in that light, but they were politically marginalized in the transition to democracy. In Northern Ireland, a key challenge resides in whether children and youth are recognized at all as political agents. The dialogues in this paper suggest that everyday narratives create politics--or political meaning--whether the participants see themselves as political actors or not (see also McEvoy-Levy, 2006). It remains to be seen whether adult observers and decision-makers will recognize this as politics and, in turn, how they will or can respond.

Siobhán McEvoy-Levy
Butler University

REFERENCES

Adwan, Sami & Dan Bar-On. (in press). Sharing history: Palestinian and Israeli teachers and pupils learning each other's narrative. In S. McEvoy-Levy (Ed.), *Troublemakers or peacemakers? Youth and post-accord peacebuilding.* University of Notre Dame Press.
Arlow, M. (2003). Conflict and curriculum change in Northern Ireland. In S. Tawil & A. Harley (Eds.), *Reframing social contracts. Curriculum policy reform in societies emerging from civil strife.* Geneva: UNESCO International Bureau of Education.
Bonner, A. (1999). Shankill families ask for "emergency" state. *Irish News,* October 25.
Buckley, A. D., & Kenney, M. C. (1995). *Negotiating identity. Rhetoric, metaphor and social drama in Northern Ireland.* Washington and London: Smithsonian Institution Press.

---

[75] These researchers found that the most common and least visible conflict related experiences were: "Frustration with politics; isolation from adult world; experience of house raids; feeling persecuted, feared, and blamed by adults; [being] stopped/questioned by police; feelings of stigmatisation due to community identity; underage use of alcohol; [inability to] talk about issues; negative experiences and attitudes towards police; experience of segregation; fears for safety of self and family; sectarian verbal abuse; avoidance of certain areas; lack of contact with or knowledge of 'other' community." (See Smyth et al. 2004, p. 98).

Darby, J. (2001). *The effects of violence on peace processes.* Washington, DC: United States Institute of Peace Press.

CAIN: Conflict Archive on the Internet. http://cain.ulst.ac.uk/ni/popul.htm. Accessed February 6, 2005.

Cairns, E. (1996). *Children and political violence.* Oxford: Blackwell.

Connolly, P., Smith, A., & Kelly, B. (2002). *Too young to notice? The cultural and political awareness of 3-6 year olds in Northern Ireland.* Belfast:Community Relations Council.

Education for pluralism, human rights and democracy. (2002). UNESCO Center. Coleraine: University of Ulster.

Gallagher, T. (2004). Interculturalism in a divided school system. In D. Powell & F. Sze (Eds.), *Interculturalism: Critical issues* (pp. 11-117). Oxford: Inter-Disciplinary Press.

Gordon, S. (2002). Shameful: Soccer thugs target Army personnel as post-match violence escalates in north Belfast last week. *Sunday Life,* 12 May.

Hughes, D., & DuMont, K. (1993). Using focus groups to facilitate culturally anchored research. *American Journal of Community Psychology (Special Issue: Culturally Anchored Methodology), 21*(6), 775-806.

Jarman, N., & O'Halloran, C. (2001). Recreational rioting: Young people, interface areas and violence. *Child Care in Practice, 7*(1), 2-16.

Johnson, A. (1996). "It's good to talk:" the focus group and the sociological imagination. *The Sociological Review, 44*(3), 517-539.

Lakoff, G. (2001). Metaphorical thought in foreign policy. Why strategic framing matters. *The Frameworks Institute.* Available online at:

http://www.frameworksinstitute.org/products/metaphoricalthought.pdf

Latimer, J. (1999). Belfast bounces back. This Northern Ireland city has transformed itself into a vibrant urban centre.http://www.canoe.ca/Travel/Europe/UK-Ireland/2003/09/08/179689.html Accessed October 6, 2005.

Lynagh, N., & Potter, M. (2005). *Joined-up. Developing good relations in the school community.* Belfast: Corrymeela Press.

McEvoy (-Levy), S. (2000). Communities and peace: Young Catholics in Northern Ireland. *Journal of Peace Research, 37*(1), 89-96.

McEvoy-Levy, S. (2006). *Troublemakers or peacemakers? Youth and post-accord peacebuilding.* University of Notre Dame Press.

Morgan, D. L. (1996). Focus groups. *Annual Review of Sociology, 22,* 129-152.

Morgan, D. L., & Krueger, R. D. (1993). (Eds.). *Successful focus groups: advancing the state of the art.* London: Sage.

Nichols-Casebolt, A., & Spakes, P. (1995). Policy research and the voices of women. *Social Work Research, 19,* 49-55.

NISRA/Northern Ireland Statistics and Research Agency. (1998). *Annual Abstract of Statistics,16.* Belfast: Author.

North Belfast Community Research Project: Local Initiatives for Needy Communities (LINC) and Institute for Conflict Research (ICR). (2003). *Young people and politics in North Belfast. An outline of a survey by the North Belfast Community Research Project.* Author.

North Belfast Community Action Unit. (2004). *Evaluation of the youth development programme 2003-2004 final report.* Belfast: Deloitte MCS Limited.

O'Leary, B., & McGarry, J. (1993). *The politics of antagonism. Understanding Northern Ireland.* London: Athlone Press.

Ross, M. H. (2001). Psychocultural interpretations and dramas: Identity dynamics in ethnic conflict. *Political Psychology 22*(1), 157-178.

Smyth, M., Fay, M. T., Brough, E., & Hamilton, J. (2004). *The impact of political conflict on children in Northern Ireland: A report on the community conflict impact on children study.* Belfast: Institute for Conflict Research.

Spergel, I. A. (1995). The youth gang problem: A community approach. New York: Oxford University Press.

Straker, G., Moosa, F., Becker, R., & Nkwale, M. (1992). *Faces in the revolution. The psychological effect of violence on township youth in South Africa.* Athens, OH: Ohio University Press.

WOMEN'S COMMISSION FOR REFUGEE WOMEN AND
CHILDREN[76]

AGAINST ALL ODDS:
SURVIVING THE WAR ON ADOLESCENTS
PROMOTING THE PROTECTION AND CAPACITY OF
UGANDAN AND SUDANESE ADOLESCENTS IN
NORTHERN UGANDA[77]

ABSTRACT

It is just over 200 kilometers from Uganda's bustling international capital of Kampala to the northern Districts of Gulu, Kitgum, and Pader where this study took place. Travel from south to north appears not much different from that in many countries in Africa. Crowded city streets with indoor shops turn into long stretches of deteriorating road punctuated by noisy and colorful roadside markets. Traffic jams give way to streams of bicycles laden with harvested grass and sorghum. The dirt road is a walkway where women and girls proceed step-by-step, erect in the blazing sun, supporting baskets of fruit on their heads and infants on their backs. The landscape is an abundance of brilliant greens and orange, of rich arable land, and of seeming tranquility. The only signs of conflict are a few military checkpoints along the way and a soldier here and there, resting under a tree, his rifle across his knees.

But the tranquility is only a mirage, and the road, flanked by tall grass and trees, is a blind burrow through treacherous forest. For 15 years, the region has been the scene of some of the worst violence committed against children and adolescents in the world. Roads, schools, villages, and families are falling apart. It is a society in the process of disintegration. If you are under 20 and living here, you have known nothing but armed conflict in which you are a prime target. You learn from adults the lessons of traditional social norms, but you have little chance to practice them. Unprotected and left to fend for yourself, you are instead a master at coping with the realities of this world you have inherited, a world with troubles you do not deserve.

Every day you peer into the tall surrounding brush knowing that the Lord's Resistance Army (LRA) is out there, somewhere, not too far away, and at

---

[76] The Women's Commission thanks the Andrew W. Mellon Foundation, the McKnight Foundation, the Moriah Fund, BNP Paribas and the Eleanor Bellows Pillsbury Fund for their support of our work in Uganda and their ongoing concern for adolescents affected by war and persecution.

[77] This paper is excerpted from a report by the same name, available from www.womenscommission.org/pdf/ug.pdf The editors thank the Women's Commission for Refugee Women and Children for permission to publish this report.

Doug Magnuson and Michael Baizerman (eds), Work with Youth in Divided and Contested Societies, 109–139.

any moment may suddenly appear to abduct, rape, torture, or murder you. Worse, you think of your friends who have already been taken. Regular news about the LRA's whereabouts and latest atrocities travels outward from its epicenter, and countless stories about being in the wrong place at the wrong time fill your head, making you wonder, "Am I next?" The Ugandan Army (the Ugandan People's Defense Forces [UPDF]) is supposed to make you safe, but the fighting continues, and you wonder sometimes what they are actually doing. "How could it be so hard to round up these small groups of rebels?" Other times you know exactly what they are doing because they are robbing or raping you.

Thousands of you live in extremely crowded, sprawling, and unsanitary displaced persons camps, "for your own safety," you are told. But there you regularly go hungry, contract diseases and are not actually very safe. The camps get attacked, too.

You see plenty of rich land before you, but if you choose to plow it and grow crops or swim in the streams, you may be attacked. You are told you have free, universal primary education, but you cannot go to school, because you might be abducted there, your teachers have been killed, there is not enough money for supplies, and the school is too far away. Secondary school is out of the question: the fees are too high, and you must feed your stomachs before your minds.

You would turn to your parents, but they might not be alive: Many parents have died of HIV/AIDS or been murdered by the LRA. Even if they are there, they cannot protect or take care of you. You must take care of your siblings, but you cannot get a job, a loan, or any training. You are pushed into marriage when you are barely 12 – how else will you eat? All most adults will say is: "You youth don't respect us anymore."

If you are a refugee from southern Sudan, you fled attacks by the Sudanese government forces, abduction by the Sudan People's Liberation Army (SPLA) and deprivation at home. You are supposed to be safe here. But now you must also fear the LRA and some of the Ugandan nationals, too, who hate you for also needing the land. You are not out of reach of the SPLA, which circles freely around you, attempting to reel you in. And you are hungry, always hungry.

Even your personalities are a contradiction. Shouldn't you be hardened to the world after all this? Don't you hate the ground you walk on? Instead, you dance traditional and new dances, you laugh with your friends, you care about your communities, and you look for solutions. You care for your brothers and sisters, pay for their schooling, and try to form livelihood cooperatives with your friends. You hold onto some of the lessons of kindness of generations past. You do not talk of revenge but of peace – when you can bring yourselves to hope. You worry for those among you who are living on the streets, turning to drugs or prostitution. There are so few to help you. You deserve much better.

The lives of young people like these are described here from a study using focus groups, surveys, and individual interviews designed and carried out by adolescents. The findings of this research are organized into sections, but the concerns are three-dimensional, overlapping, and interconnected in the minds and experiences of the adolescents who own this report. Massive insecurity – physical, psychological, economic, social, spiritual – is the force that binds them together in a rhythm of brutal contradiction for young people.

Both Ugandan and Sudanese adolescents feel – and are – betrayed by virtually everyone involved in this conflict including families, communities, governments, UPDF soldiers, the SPLA, and the international community. Young people realize that they are pawns in a much larger conflict and offer intelligent and constructive solutions for building a better world. At the same time, they do not often recognize their own capacity to bring change or how they can do it.

Young people in northern Uganda desperately need and have a right to support. They call for an end to the conflicts in their countries and a commitment to ending poverty through development and education, including support for the most vulnerable. They want to help, but no one is asking them. The findings of the focus groups and case studies conducted by adolescent researchers with over 2,000 adolescents and adults in their communities, combined with additional Women's Commission research, flesh out the details of the effects of armed conflict on adolescents – on their roles in society and virtually every aspect of their lives. Insecurity is at the root of all other concerns. Lessons learned about adolescent participation, information on international, national and local responses to adolescents' concerns, and prospects for peace are also considered, calling for increased attention to adolescents' concerns and support for their leadership.

ADOLESCENT RESEARCHERS IN CHARGE: METHODOLOGY AND LESSONS LEARNED ABOUT ADOLESCENT PARTICIPATION

Adolescent researchers asked their peers and adults to discuss the question: "Who are adolescents or youth,[79] and what is their role in Uganda today?" Strong responses reflected a keen awareness of young people undergoing changes at an accelerated rate and an awareness of a community in crisis where traditional values and culture are not sufficiently recognizing or responding to the dilemma of young people.

Central to the approach of this study is a belief in the need and right of adolescents to participate in the decisions that concern them. Adolescent participation in this study and adult support for this participation took several principal forms, which are reviewed here in the context of the approach to the research. Adolescents were lead researchers, advocates, and research participants who were interviewed by the research teams.

Adults were advisors to the adolescent researchers, research coordinators, advocates, supporters, and research participants who were interviewed by the research teams.

---

[79] International organizations such as the World Health Organization (WHO), UNICEF and UNFPA categorize adolescents as 10-19, youth as 15-24, and young people as 10-24. The Women's Commission report *Untapped Potential. Adolescents Affected by Armed Conflict*, 2000, p. 10, states that adolescence is defined chronologically, as pertaining to certain ages; functionally, as a process during which individuals make a critical transition from childhood to adulthood; and ultimately by its cultural and societal context, which vary widely. The Convention on the Rights of the Child considers children to be "every human being below the age of 18 years unless, under the law applicable to the child, majority is attained earlier."

The Research Teams

Fifty-four Ugandan and Sudanese adolescents living in the Gulu, Kitgum, and Pader Districts of northern Uganda participated as "adolescent researchers" in this study. They were the principal researchers, in collaboration with the Women's Commission. They designed and shaped their methodology, organized and conducted the research, and analyzed and reported their findings.

The young people worked on two separate teams, one in Gulu, known as the Gulu team, and one in Kitgum and Pader, known as the Kitgum/Pader team, with 26 and 28 adolescent researchers respectively. Eighteen adults serving as "research advisors" assisted them in their responsibilities, nine on each team. A local, Kitgum-based youth non-governmental organization (NGO), the Watwero Youth Group, served as a "youth coordination group" for the Kitgum/Pader team, and a group of four adult individuals acted as a "youth coordination group" for the Gulu team. Many of the adults involved also worked with NGOs in the region[80] and were respected members of the community, including parents and teachers.

The International Rescue Committee (IRC), Uganda's Psychosocial Program in Kitgum, and World Vision Uganda's Children and War Center in Gulu provided invaluable support to both of the teams, encouraging and facilitating their work from start to finish.

The objective of the teams' work was to identify and investigate key issues facing adolescents in their communities and to identify solutions for these concerns. The results of their work is used for advocacy purposes to bring international, national, and local attention to adolescent and youth concerns in northern Uganda and the surrounding region. Their recommendations inform decisions made about programs and policies implemented in northern Uganda, including strengthening current efforts and implementing new pilot projects for young people that *involve* young people. It is also hoped that the process will inspire young people and provide them with ideas about ways they can take action on their own behalf, with or without help from adults.

---

[80] Staff members from Canadian Physicians for Aid and Relief (CPAR), Rural Focus (RUFO), Red Cross Uganda (RCU), the Concerned Parents Association (CPA) and Gulu Support the Children Organization (GUSCO) were among the adult research advisors in Gulu. Local and international groups were stakeholders in the project in other ways as well, helping with project planning, team nominations, and project implementation. Associazione Volontari per il Servizio Internazionale (AVSI) nominated a young person to the Kitgum/Pader team and some transportation for their work. CPAR, RUFO, RCU, CPA and GUSCO also supported the work of the team in Gulu with nominations and in some cases arranged focus group sessions. All organizations expressed their enthusiasm for learning from the process and its outcomes. Team trainings and post-research analysis sessions were conducted in the Teacher Training Center in Gulu and at St. Joseph's Hospital in Kitgum.

Selecting the Adolescent Researchers

The Women's Commission laid out basic guidelines and developed criteria for selecting adolescent researchers, adult research advisors, and the youth coordination groups according to a terms of reference laid out for each. Diversity was a key criterion to ensure the representation of the range of experiences and perspectives of young people in the community and to ensure the maximum opportunity for the researchers to learn from one another.

As a result of consultations with adolescents and local and international NGOs in the districts, the research teams were chosen in a variety of ways from a process of democratic, community self-selection to interviews with the Women's Commission. Team participants were of both sexes, from 10 to 20 years old, and included returned abductees, internally displaced Ugandans, Sudanese refugees, adolescents living in and out of camps, those orphaned by war and by HIV/AIDS, students and out-of-school youth, working youth, adolescents with disabilities, youth activists (e.g., for peace), and adolescent heads of household. They also included adults with a commitment to and/or experience working with young people.

In Kitgum and Pader, adolescents also represented four distinct settings: Sudanese refugee settlements (Achol Pii, Pader); internally displaced (IDP) camps (Padibe, Kitgum); isolated and war-torn villages (Omiya Anyima, Kitgum) and a town center (Kitgum Town Council, Kitgum). The Gulu team had representatives from Gulu town, the Awer displaced persons camp, and rural villages outside Gulu town.

Designing, Organizing, and Implementing the Research

Each team participated in a three-day training in which Women's Commission researchers and local professionals guided them through a process of identifying their purpose as a team, learning about research, and developing and practicing their methodology. The Women's Commission provided a framework for the researchers, including the following general questions: "What are the main problems of adolescents/youth in northern Uganda, and what are some solutions?" and "Who are 'adolescents' and 'youth' in northern Uganda today?" A combination of focus groups, case studies of individual interviews, and a survey for ranking adolescents' top concerns were also suggested.[81] After the training, the research teams conducted their research for roughly three weeks, followed by a week of analysis and two weeks of drafting a team report.

---

[81] The focus groups provide an overall qualitative look at the range of issues of concern to adolescents and details about these concerns. The case studies provide a more detailed look at specific issues uncovered, and the surveys help identify the relative importance of the range of issues described.

Beyond this framework, which the adolescents approved, the adolescent researchers identified topics and sample questions to be covered in focus group discussions and individual case study interviews. They also designed their own surveys, containing a list of concerns, of which research participants were asked to rank their own top ten. Although each team worked separately, they developed very similar questions, and their survey categories were virtually identical. Consequently the same survey was used for each. The case studies conducted by the adolescents covered a range of issues and experiences they identified in their work, providing a more in-depth look at typical adolescent experiences.

In both teams security and logistical restrictions played a role. While the full Kitgum/Pader team was trained together and did their final analysis together, four subgroups of the team conducted their research in each of the four sites where researchers lived. Security constraints prevented each of these groups of young people from traveling outside of their area to conduct research. In Gulu, security problems restricted the team to the town limits and nearby villages and "protected camps," which are home to thousands of IDPs. All of the Gulu researchers had the opportunity to work together in all locations. Of the IDP camps included in the research, a total of seven were involved: Anaka, Awer, Lugore, Pabbo, Pagak and Parabongo in Gulu District, and Padibe in Kitgum District.

Focus groups and surveys were carried out by smaller groups of the larger research team, including two to four adolescent researchers, accompanied by one adult research advisor. The adolescent researchers in these small groups took the lead explaining the project to participants, posing questions, generating dialogue, taking notes, and administering the survey. Following the sessions, the adolescents also wrote up summaries of the overall findings of the sessions. Adults acted as guides, helped the young people to organize themselves, and endeavored to intervene only when needed. Adolescent researchers acted individually to invite research participants to be interviewed separately for case studies. These interviews at times lasted several hours, following which the adolescent researchers wrote written reports of their case studies.

Each focus group/survey session aimed to involve no more than eight to ten people to provide ample opportunities for individuals to speak.[82] Sessions were conducted in the language of choice of the participants, mainly Luo, also known as "Acholi," the native language of the Acholi people. Although the length of the sessions varied, in general the groups spent 90 minutes talking in the focus groups and then 30 minutes completing the surveys. Attendance at the sessions was voluntary for participants, and they were informed that their testimony might be used in printed reports but that their identities would be kept confidential for their protection. The taking and publication of photos were only permitted with the verbal agreement of the research participants.

Table 1 lists the target participants for the focus groups. The central role of youth coordinators in Kitgum and Pader, in contrast to the Gulu Team, demonstrated perhaps the most significant difference between the two Districts. In

---

[82] In practice, this limit was often exceeded due to community interest, logistical constraints and the researchers simply not wanting to turn people away. While the sizes of the groups were in the majority very manageable, some were very large and reflected a more typical forum for local community discussion, where a big group gathers outdoors to consider an issue.

Kitgum and Pader, for example, the Watwero Youth Group took responsibility for coordinating all of the team's training, research, analysis, and reporting activities, facilitating the young peoples' initiative in undertaking these activities. In Gulu, because no established youth entity could be identified, a group of four adult individuals acted as a coordination group and directed the organization of the research process in a more centralized way. Under the leadership of the Watwero Youth Group, with help from IRC, the team selection process in Kitgum and Pader was well organized with essay competitions and an election by peers. With the Gulu team, in the absence of a youth coordination group, the team selection took place before the formation of a coordinating body of adults. Young people were nominated by their community, with the help of World Vision and other NGOs in Gulu, and then interviewed and chosen by the Women's Commission. The survey design and results were nearly identical, and both teams did a thorough and exceptionally thoughtful job, but in many respects it was ultimately easier for the youth group to support the activities of the adolescent researchers than the group of adults.

Table 1. List of Interviewees

Adults	Youth
mothers/fathers/guardians	females
teachers	males
religious leaders	males and females together
widows	orphans
elders	the disabled
women vendors	refugees
refugees	internally displaced persons
internally displaced persons	primary and secondary students
the disabled	those out-of-school
	former child soldiers
	heads of household
	working young people
	prisoners

Note: The Women's Commission also interviewed NGO, government, military and United Nations (UN) representatives in the three districts and in Kampala.

Comparing the Youth Coordination Function in the Two Districts

The Watwero Youth Group, for example, found it much easier to coordinate and motivate the adolescent researchers than did the adult-led coordination body of the Gulu team. Notwithstanding their dedicated and hard work, it was still much harder for the Gulu coordinators as a group of adult individuals randomly brought together to depart from a relatively stratified approach to project implementation and to create a non-traditional atmosphere of youth-led teamwork. The budgeting and management functions of the study were also less in the hands of young people in Gulu, who at times felt stunted in their activities and argued that "adolescents should be coordinating this work." This may have led, in part, to fewer opportunities for the adolescent researchers on the Gulu team to hold focus group sessions. A total of over 1,400 respondents were interviewed in Kitgum/Pader compared to more than 500 in Gulu.

The Watwero Youth Group, in contrast, was used to regularly convening young people, garnering their opinions and energy, and knowing how to combine work and fun. They had an easier time encouraging and supporting the natural energies and inspirations of the adolescent researchers. At the same time, the youth group had other issues to contend with, struggling to reach consensus on the management of finances and on planning the future direction of the organization. In general, those who were more active and involved in the project were more interested in deepening the scope and expertise of the organization. Those less involved were more concerned about short-term gain and opportunities.

While it is perfectly possible and very important for adults and adolescents to work together to create successful participatory experiences for adolescents, where adolescents play strong leadership roles the adults involved must be able to create a balance between young people's need for autonomy and support. Individuals with youth organizing experience, including young activists, are likely to be particularly familiar with the dynamics of youth leadership and better equipped to support it.

Findings

Findings from the study are grouped into the categories of a) developmental issues of adolescence and youth, b) protection from abduction and sexual violence, c) ending insecurity, d) education, e) livelihoods and dependency, f) health, g) psychosocial reintegration, and h) coping and resilience.

ADOLESCENCE AND YOUTH: A COMMUNITY IN CRISIS

Adolescent researchers asked their peers and adults to discuss the question: "Who are adolescents or youth, and what is their role in Uganda today?" Strong responses reflected a keen awareness of young people undergoing changes at an accelerated rate and an awareness of a community in crisis, where traditional values and culture are not sufficiently recognizing or responding to the dilemma of young people.

An Age and a Stage of Life

The new National Youth Policy of Uganda defines youth as "all young persons, female and male, aged 12 to 30 years." The policy also states that youth should not be regarded as a homogenous group fitting into age brackets, but rather as a group involved in a process of change[83] (Ministry of Gender, Labor, and Social Development, 2001, p. 9). Uganda's Principal Youth Officer, Kyateka Mondo, told the Women's Commission that determining the age range for the policy was a "contentious issue" and that "people in the localities define youth with very different scenarios in mind."[84]

Both adolescent and adult responses conveyed the importance of defined roles that supercede chronological ages. They used, for example, a variety of words in their local languages to describe people at different stages of life according to clan traditions. Ugandan and Sudanese Acholi adolescents, for example, offered a series of words, *latin, bulu, ladongo, luditu* and *rwot,* to correspond with the English for child, adolescent/youth, adult, elder, and chief. Sudanese refugees from the Latuka and Didinga ethnic groups provided two other sets of corresponding words in their own languages. They explained that their definitions related to age, level of maturity, and an individual's standing within the community.

Some said that girls are adolescents from ages 13 to 17 but are women as soon as they marry, even at 12 or 13. Youth are considered to be from ages 15 to 30 and distinct from adolescents in that they are sexually active. This includes females from age 12 to menopause.

Sexual development can cause problems for girls if they seek to attend school and/or resist early marriage, adolescents said, adding that girls come under other pressures imposed by the physical maturity that marks them for womanhood. They also said that adolescents can be increasingly stubborn and at times overly sensitive.

A person becomes an adult upon marriage and only then commands full community respect. George Omono, former Director of Gulu Support the Children Organization (GUSCO), agreed: "Before you are married, no one really takes you seriously and you are not consulted on issues of concern to the community. Respect means that you can express your opinions in public and that people listen to them. I married late and only got respect after that. It's not about money or experience."[85] Other adolescents longed for the freedom they perceived to come with adulthood. "As a grown up, there must be freedom. I have no freedom. We cannot go outside the gate," said one adolescent girl whose father was killed by the LRA and who lives in an orphanage.

Elders are older people with authority; they carry sticks, as do teachers, and require respect from young people. Betty, 24, from Gulu, said that she feels like a young person when she is out in the world, but that when she gets home she is treated like an adult with adult responsibilities. Betty was orphaned when she

---

[83] The youth policy does not undermine or seek to change the definition and interpretation of a child as stipulated in Uganda's Children's Statute of 1996, which defines a child as "a person below the age of eighteen years." The policy also states that it seeks to be harmonious with the programmatic definitions of international agencies, including United Nations agencies that define youth as persons between 15 and 24 years old, and the Commonwealth Youth Program definition of 15 to 29 years. The National Youth Council (NYC) statute of 1993 enacted by the Ugandan Government had previously provided identified youth as 18- to 30-year-olds in naming them as eligible to become members of the NYC. The new policy thus creates a definition that bridges overlapping definitions of childhood, adolescence, and early adulthood by using 12 to 30.

[84] Women's Commission interview, Kampala, May 3, 2001.

[85] Women's Commission interview, Gulu, May 10, 2001.

was eight years old and took on the care of her sister's two children when her sister died of AIDS. One of the children also has AIDS.

Traditional Roles Under Siege

In the best of circumstances, adolescence is a difficult period in which physical and emotional changes, intergenerational conflicts, insecurity, and rebelliousness can reflect social norms and a healthy developmental process. Uganda's National Youth Policy recognizes adolescence as a "period of great emotional, physical and psychological changes that require societal support for a safe passage from adolescence to full adulthood" (Ministry of Gender, Labor, and Social Development, 2001). In northern Uganda and in the south of Sudan, there is no such safe passage. The lifespans of most adolescents have been dominated by more than a decade and a half of war marked by terror, displacement, isolation, and poverty. Social structures are unraveling with an accelerated force. Relationships between adults and adolescents are undergoing tremendous upheaval without any corresponding cultural adaptation recognizing the pressures young people are facing and without support for their capacities to cope.

Most adolescents and adults are subject to extreme pressures. They are crammed into refugee and internally displaced persons (IDPs) camps with few options for self-sufficiency and little physical or emotional space to develop their skills, capacities, and self-confidence. Adolescents are forced to take on adult responsibilities beyond expectations of earlier societal norms and are left to fend for themselves. An increasing number of orphaned adolescents, especially girls, are left to care for themselves and for their families.

The traditional age for marriage has dropped sharply. Girls from an IDP camp in Gulu said that the ideal time to get married would be 21 for girls and 25 for boys.[86] They reported, however, that girls in the camp were now getting married as young as 12, primarily for economic and security reasons. They are under constant threat of abduction or rape; their parents are unable to take care of them adequately, and girls are denied future opportunities to find gainful work. Boys, on the other hand, struggle under other constraints that have cut short their own adolescence. They are under great pressure to produce a livelihood in a poor economic setting that also undermines their sense of confidence. Should they wish to marry, they are still required to pay a traditional bride price, which few can afford.

Psychosocial pressures of war have also resulted in a decline of "morality" and of traditional respect for the authority of elders, according to both adult and adolescent respondents.[87] Many adults complained that adolescents no longer respect their parents or other adults and that they can no longer control

---

[86] Women's Commission interview, Awer IDP camp, Gulu, May 12, 2001.

[87] Adolescents consistently cited "immorality" as a concern, indicating it involves a general lack of values, where adolescents behave disrespectfully or selfishly and/or engage in acts that are considered by many to be improper, such as socializing at modern discos, watching videos, having sex or committing crimes.

young people. Some young people, they said, spend all their time watching videos in video stores, going to discos and traditional dances without permission, and engaging in casual sex. There is little social support for the dilemma of adolescents, and many feel abandoned by an adult society that is not responding to their insecurity or to the level of responsibility they are taking on.

Young people are feared as threats to stability, especially those who have fought with the LRA or SPLA forces, even if they were abducted. Deference to authority is still demanded and reinforced through such behaviors as very authoritative teaching methods. "The one with the stick is in charge, as the teacher," said one adolescent. The Resident District Commissioner for Gulu, Musa Ecewero, said, "We see these kids as a risk to the future of the country."[88]

Out of their own fears and pressures from this rapid change, many adults feel out of control and are clinging tightly to traditional values and structures in which adults are providers, commanding authority, while young people are required to follow a strict code of respect. These views and lingering traditional beliefs about roles and responsibilities can blind communities, including adolescents, from recognizing and bolstering the incredible strengths and coping skills of young people.

Many adults also understand and can articulate the deep social crisis and their inability to parent well as a result of unrelenting war, poverty, and disease. "Our children are being raised by babysitters,"[89] said one Sudanese mother, reflecting on the struggle of many parents who must leave their children with other people for long periods to go to work and make ends meet. "We are really in a dilemma," said George Omono, formerly of GUSCO. "Our family structure is disrupted and children grow up with little guidance. With the war, the 'fireplace values' passed on through storytelling are no longer there."[90]

Some Solutions

Overall, adults and young people articulated the strong need to improve intergenerational understanding and dialogue. This means meeting the challenge to better understand and accept how cultural tradition is being forced to recreate itself in new forms. It includes making conscious decisions about values—which to keep and which to change—in order to support the healthy development of adolescents. It means adults helping their children by communicating, supporting their capacities, and providing them with the opportunity to develop responsible and independent decision-making skills. Any successful outcome must involve the whole community in valuing the opinions of young people and their contributions.

---

[88] Women's Commission interview, Gulu, May 8, 2001.
[89] Kitgum/Pader research team and Women's Commission interview, Achol Pii refugee settlement, Pader, May 21, 2001.
[90] Women's Commission interview, Gulu, May 2001.

119

PROTECTION: ABDUCTION AND SEXUAL VIOLENCE PLAGUE ADOLESCENTS

In the eyes of children and adolescents, protection is mostly about growing up in a safe and secure environment.[91] In the northern Uganda Districts of Gulu, Kitgum, and Pader, young people are anything but safe or secure, and both Ugandan and Sudanese refugee adolescents have identified insecurity as the overarching preoccupation and devastating reality of their lives. On one level, the dire circumstances of war seem "normal" because they are all young people know. On another level, adolescents and youth are acutely aware that it is not normal to be abducted; forced to fight, kill and steal; forced to labor; sexually enslaved, exploited and abused; hungry; uneducated, without hope for a livelihood, and; without the care and love of parents who are no longer with them as a result of war. Young people in northern Uganda are calling for an end to the wars in the region, an end to their suffering as principal targets of war, and for immediate attention to be paid to the economic development of the north.

Both Uganda and Sudan have ratified the Convention on the Rights of the Child, affirming their commitment to upholding the rights of children and adolescents, including during armed conflict. They have also signed the 1951 Convention Relating to the Status of Refugees and its 1967 Protocol guaranteeing protection to refugees, including children and adolescents, within their borders.[92] Despite these commitments, the Ugandan and Sudanese governments have failed to adequately protect children and adolescents in northern Uganda and southern Sudan, and young people in these areas remain the targets of extreme brutality.

Abduction: Children and Adolescents Forcibly Recruited and Sexually Enslaved by Rebel Groups

Perhaps the most conspicuous and overtly damaging hallmark of the conflict in northern Uganda Districts of Gulu, Kitgum and Pader has been the abduction of thousands of adolescents. Abductions are most frequently carried out by the LRA,

---

[91] International protection involves efforts to ensure the range of human and humanitarian rights of individuals and communities as established under international law and reflected in national law. Among others, these include the right of children and adolescents to be safeguarded from armed conflict and of refugees not to be returned to the country from which they have fled persecution. Governments have the primary responsibility for ensuring the protection of their citizens, refugees, and others within their borders, and nongovernmental and intergovernmental organizations, communities and individuals, including young people, all have important roles to play. For more information on the protection of refugees refer to *Protecting Refugees, A Field Guide for NGOs*, produced jointly by United Nations High Commissioner for Refugees (UNHCR) and its NGO partners. See also *Guidelines for the Protection and Care of Refugee Children* from UNHCR, the Convention on the Rights of the Child and the Summary of International Treaties Pertaining to Children Affected by Armed Conflict, UNICEF Sub-NGO Working Group in Children in Armed Conflict.

[92] As described throughout the report, the LRA and SPLA are major violators of children's and adolescents' rights. While they are "non-state actors" and are not signatories to international treaties agreed to by governments, they should be pressured to adhere to the same principles of humanitarian and human rights law.

120

which has abducted more than 11,000 children and adolescents since 1986, but sometimes also by the southern Sudanese SPLA rebel force. Usually accompanied by forced fighting and killing, labor and sexual slavery, abductions have intensified the insecurity of young people, not only those who have directly suffered the consequences, but all those who fear it may happen to them. All the young people and adults interviewed stated that they live in constant terror of sudden attacks and abduction or reabduction by the LRA, which lurks unseen in the surrounding bush.

Long-term patterns of abduction by the LRA. Notwithstanding the very recent and potentially temporary shift in the pattern of abduction, many young people testified to the LRA's reign of terror and pattern of abduction that has existed over the past 15 years in northern Uganda. The rebels mainly abduct adolescents, according to some reports between the ages of 14 and 16, though they do abduct younger children and adults as well (Human Rights Watch, 1997; U.S. Department of State, 2000). Abduction and murder remain adolescents' principal fears.

Adolescents who have managed to escape their captors depicted compelling scenarios of their abduction – some lasting 6–10 years. These mostly involve raids by small LRA bands where children are rounded up in schools, at home, or elsewhere and forced to carry heavy loads between 50 and 100 miles to southern Sudan, receiving little food along the way. En route to Sudan, many are forced to commit acts of violence and thievery, including against other children. They are warned that refusal to obey will result in their own deaths. Once in Sudan, they are trained as fighters in LRA encampments and, after training and indoctrination, they are often forced to return to Uganda to commit atrocities against their own communities and the UPDF. Some young people are even forced to kill members of their own families and communities. As a result, many believe they can never return home because of the terrible acts they have committed.

Abducted girls reported being raped, sexually enslaved, and forced into domestic servitude while smaller numbers are forced into armed combat. While most victims are Ugandan, Sudanese refugee adolescents living in settlements in northern Uganda have not been spared LRA attack and abduction.

Sudanese refugee adolescents also abducted by the LRA. At least eight Sudanese refugee adolescents testified to having been abducted from the Achol Pii refugee settlement in Pader District during LRA attacks.[93] The most recent attacks on the settlement by the rebels occurred in February, 2001.[94] Having already fled conflict in southern Sudan, one young refugee described the double jeopardy of his situation. "We fled the Arabs in Sudan, and now we must flee the LRA here," he

---

[93] Sudanese refugee adolescents are known to have been abducted by the LRA in other areas in northern Uganda as well.

[94] The first attack, on February 14, resulted in the looting of property (including foodstuffs, household items, clothing, and money) and the abduction of six people (four nationals and two refugees, aged 18 and 11). The second, on February 23, resulted in the looting of 20 households, abduction of five nationals and three refugees (all three escaped within several hours), and the severe beating of one refugee (International Rescue Committee, 2001).

said.[95] Other accounts by Sudanese refugees convey the effects of abductions on their young lives.

Daniel, a refugee in Achol Pii, was abducted by the LRA in 1996 at the age of 16. "The 'Otang,' which is the Acholi name for the rebels, attacked the block, burnt all the huts, and killed nearly 200 people," he reported. "They looted and took our food and forced me and three girls away with them. We didn't know where we were going until we reached southern Sudan." Kept at a place called Natotopoto training camp, the adolescents were subjected to "relentless indoctrination" and rigid discipline. Basic training consisted of "running around the camps hour after hour, carrying stones on our shoulders. Anyone who spilled stones or collapsed was killed immediately," Daniel said. "Meanwhile, the three girls were forced to have sexual intercourse. After the training, we were forced to go and fight; our target was to kill. We were forced to kill our own people."[96]

Another Sudanese refugee, Peter, 19, also abducted from Achol Pii said: "Once abducted, you are forced to ferry very heavy luggage, move bare-footed, [suffer] insufficient feeding, and forced to have sexual intercourse [in] the case of ladies. If you refuse their commands or are completely tired and cannot move, you are murdered. The rebels are butchers of adolescents."[97]

Rape and sexual slavery of captive girls.   Thousands of girls have been among those abducted by the LRA over the past 15 years. Reports from escapees reveal that most of these young women are forced to become the sexual slaves, or "wives," and domestic servants of commanders or other fighters. They are repeatedly raped, and many bear children in the harsh conditions of the bush or in LRA encampments with barely enough food to survive and no health care. Some reports indicate that the LRA has also sold and traded some children, mostly girls, or provided them as "gifts" to arms dealers in Sudan (U.S. Department of State, 2000).

Mary, an adolescent girl from Kitgum, told a psychosocial worker about her brutal experience with the LRA.

On May 17, 1996, I was 14 years old, and around midday, I was sitting outside a hut in our compound with my cousins. A man came by and asked us to show him the way to the next village. My cousin didn't like the look of him, but I wasn't scared because our home is by the roadside and many different people pass by to fetch water or take a bath in the stream nearby. Less than five minutes later, five more men came in our compound with guns in their hands! I thought I was dreaming, but reality dawned on me as they ordered us to remain where we were and

---

[95] Kitgum/Pader Research team and Women's Commission interview, Achol Pii refugee settlement, Pader, May 2001.

[96] Kitgum/Pader Research team interview, Achol Pii refugee settlement, Pader, June 1, 2001.

[97] Kitgum/Pader Research team interview, Achol Pii refugee settlement, Pader, June 14, 2001.

122

each one of us was chained together with ropes like goats. I started crying for my grandmother. I couldn't imagine how she was going to react when she finds out I was abducted. I was hit very hard for crying and we were led to the next village where we found more captives tied up in the same manner. We were then given luggage to carry. We walked the rest of the day until evening, and older female captives cooked, we were given food and we slept, tied up together under heavy rain. On the third day, we reached Palutaka in Sudan, and there were many children there.

That evening all girls were separated from the boys, and we were divided up among different men. The man I was given to had two wives. That night, he called me to him. I went obediently, expecting him to ask me to do something for him like take some drinking water. Instead, he told me to sit next to him, and he started to feel my breast. I pushed his hand away in disgust. I was so embarrassed I wanted to insult him. He told me to lie down. I refused. He asked me if I had ever seen a dead body. I said "No, I hadn't." Then he said, "You will soon see your own corpse." He pushed me down and laid on top of me and raped me. I cried out and begged him to stop but, instead, he pushed his hand into my mouth and threatened to kill me if I didn't stop. He raped me three times that night. In the morning, I crawled out of his hut and went to one of his wives. I thought she would console me, but she scolded me and told me that she was not my mother to nurse me! I crawled around, boiled water, and nursed myself. My hip joint felt like it was coming out of its socket and my private parts were very painful. I could not urinate without crying out in pain. I could not believe it when two days later he called me again and raped me twice! My life went on like this for months.[98]

Short-term abductions and forced labor. While the numbers of abducted children and adolescents are estimated at over 11,000, actual numbers may be much higher, as many young people were abducted for shorter periods of a few weeks and made it home without further report. In a group interview with 21 randomly identified adolescent orphaned girls in the Padibe IDP camp in Kitgum, the Women's Commission asked for a show of hands of those who had been abducted. Every hand but one went up.

The principal characteristic of these short-term abductions is forced labor. The girls in Padibe, for example, told stories of being forced to carry loads and do other chores for the rebels before being let go. This labor, along with money and supplies looted by the LRA, help to sustain the LRA's survival and campaign of terror.[99]

---

[98] Case study prepared by Aneno Maria Palma, formerly IRC Psychosocial Program Assistant, Kitgum. Undated.

[99] While the vast majority of the Acholi and Sudanese people interviewed stated their abhorrence for the activities of the LRA, many acknowledged their belief that there are those among the Acholi people in northern Uganda and abroad who profit from (through receipt of stolen goods and protection) and/or support their insurrection.

Abductions by the SPLA, abetted by the Ugandan government. Many of the adolescents who fled Sudan escaped forced recruitment into the SPLA. But the risk did not end once in Uganda. Significant support to the SPLA by the Government of Uganda has made it relatively easy for the SPLA to come and go in and out of northern Uganda, where their presence is commonplace. Although less visible in recent months, perhaps due to a tightening of control of the Uganda-Sudan border by the UPDF, young people said that the SPLA are still very much present, and they are identified by their dress as well as their use of Arabic. Family members of some SPLA commanders and soldiers even reside in the Achol Pii settlement.

Gender-based Violence

Adolescent girls have been and are prime targets for rape, sexual assault, and sexual exploitation, including sexual slavery and prostitution.[100] In nearly every interview, adolescent girls described personal knowledge of "rape and defilement"[101] either against themselves or their peers. Adolescent girls and boys told researchers that girls are raped, or "defiled," in IDP camps, the Achol Pii refugee settlement, and in non-camp settings. The perpetrators and their tactics vary by location and include the LRA, UPDF soldiers, Ugandan nationals, IDP camp and refugee settlement residents, neighbors, and family members and adolescent males.

Girls surveyed in Gulu, including those living in six IDP protected villages, named "rape and defilement" as their third most important concern behind "insecurity, abduction, and murder" and "displacement," and both boys and girls in the village of Omiya Anyima ranked "rape and defilement" as among their top five concerns. This unrelenting violence causes girls to endure terrible psychological and physical harm, including increased teen pregnancy, sexually transmitted infections (STIs), and other health concerns. Girls who have not been raped suffer the constant fear that it will happen to them.

In the Achol Pii refugee settlement: rape by other refugees and Ugandan nationals. Sexual attacks in Achol Pii reportedly are committed mainly by other refugees, Ugandan nationals—who live near the settlement—and LRA soldiers. Refugee girls said their freedom of movement is severely restricted, as they fear sexual attack by

---

[100] Adolescent boys may also be the victims of sexual violence, but there is little evidence, perhaps due to cultural taboos surrounding the occurrence and discussion of such violence.

[101] Under Ugandan law, "defilement" includes any sexual contact outside of marriage involving girls younger than 18 years of age, regardless of consent or the age of the perpetrator. While defilement carries a maximum sentence of death, that punishment has never been given to a convicted rapist. Violence against women, including rape, remains common. Polygamy is legal under both customary and Islamic law, and a wife has no legal status to prevent her husband from marrying another woman. Men may also "inherit" the widows of their deceased brothers. From: *AFROL Gender Profiles: Uganda,* AFROL, undated, www.afrol.com/Categories/Women/profiles/uganda_women.htm. The words rape and defilement are used interchangeably in this report.

Ugandan males if they wander away from the main areas of the settlement to collect firewood or attempt to journey into town. Women report that rape is common, including within marriage, and is often accompanied by other forms of domestic violence, including physical and psychological abuse. Adolescent males are, by their own acknowledgement, frequent perpetrators of rape.

Robert, a teenager from Achol Pii refugee settlement, stated that "many of the defilement cases come as a result of girls refusing to have sex with a boy after she has committed to a relationship with him. They can go together, and he will do things for her with the expectation that at a certain point they will have sex. If she ultimately refuses, he gets angry and will force her."[102]

In the IDP camps: UPDF soldiers are the main perpetrators. Internally displaced Ugandan girls and young women living in protected villages and camps said that they, too, live in fear of rape, but in their case it is committed mostly by UPDF soldiers who are supposed to be responsible for providing security. Girls stated that sometimes the UPDF will lie in wait for them along roads at night, ambush them and rape them, or even go straight to their huts and rape them. They also explained that girls who refuse sex in exchange for gifts or other goods or services are often forced to comply.

Rose, 14, who lives in Awer IDP camp in Gulu, told researchers that: "The soldiers ask girls to spend time with them, and they give them gifts. They expect them to have sex with them, and if they don't, they just defile them anyway. Sometimes they don't even ask about anything, they just ambush you and attack you while you are in your hut or while you are walking in the bush."[103]

Sylvia, 15, from Padibe IDP camp in Kitgum, stated that girls are particularly afraid of being raped by UPDF soldiers at night as they are walking along roads. "They will just suddenly jump you and defile you. They are supposed to be protecting us and, instead, they are raping us."[104]

When asked what they wanted to do when they grow up, several girls said teachers and nurses but one girl said, "Be a policewoman." When asked why, she said simply, "for security."[105] She felt so unprotected that she was determined to join the police for her own safety and to improve the safety of the community.

In towns and villages. Researchers also heard testimony from adolescent girls living in towns and villages who described similar sexual and gender-based violence as that reported in the IDP camps and refugee settlements. The perpetrators varied from family members, neighbors, and teachers to UPDF soldiers and street criminals. Betty, who is 19 years old and lives in Gulu town, said that she sometimes sleeps at her workplace instead of walking home late at night for fear of being raped by the UPDF or street thugs. Another adolescent girl, Alice, who is

---

[102] Kitgum/Pader research team and Women's Commission interview, Achol Pii refugee settlement, Pader, May 2001.
[103] Gulu research team interview, Awer IDP camp, Gulu, June 2001.
[104] Ibid.
[105] Ibid.

still in primary school, said: "Big men rape children, especially girls. A big man raped his daughter. The mother of the girls was already dead. That is the biggest problem that we girls face."[106]

Some Solutions, Including International Efforts

Young people said that enforcing Ugandan law would go a long way toward helping to prevent sexual violence in their camps and communities. They all agreed that communities should also become more sensitized about sexual violence to promote prevention and that the practice should end. However, the reality is that sexual and other violence against girls and women is centuries old and exacerbated by the current environment of violence and instability. Thus, girls also believe the violence would diminish if the war ended, particularly if the IDPs could return to their home villages where there would be more space for privacy, and families and neighbors would not be living in such a cramped and pressured environment.

ENDING INSECURITY MUST GO BEYOND RESTORING PHYSICAL SECURITY

Young people recommended a wide range of insightful and cogent solutions to end the abductions and to bring peace. These include talks between the Governments of Uganda and Sudan and between the Government of Uganda and the LRA, as well as between the Government of Sudan and the SPLA. Such efforts, they said, should be accompanied by a cease-fire and followed by a rehabilitation program that addresses social and economic differences within society, emphasizing food, health, education, and security. Special attention must be given to orphans and unaccompanied minors, including internally displaced and refugee young people.

Adolescents also expressed the need to build a culture of tolerance and reconciliation among the Acholi people and all of the people of Uganda through civic education and community and government action to support the amnesty process. They said that Acholi leaders must continue to put aside any differences between them and unite for peace. Believing that LRA leader Joseph Kony will not negotiate with President Museveni and that Museveni's government has not yet acted in the full interests of protecting children and adolescents in the north, the young people also expressed concerns about a real possibility for peace while Museveni remains President. It is clear that Museveni has much work to do to win the confidence of young people in the north whose hopes for peace have been dashed repeatedly throughout their lives.

At the same time, despite complaints that the UPDF has not adequately protected young people and even that their increased presence has been destabilizing and often abusive, the adolescent respondents call for improved living conditions for the soldiers. In so doing, they believe the army will become more professional and better able and willing to protect the people in the north.

---

[106] Kitgm/Pader research team interview, Kitgum Primary School, Kitgum, June 2001.

Young people propose deployment of international monitors in the north to observe efforts to create peace as well as a UN peacekeeping force to help halt the abduction of youth. They feel that these efforts should be matched with monitoring of international assistance so that government corruption cannot deplete resources meant for the citizens. They also believe that the international community has a role in collecting guns from the rebels. In addition, young people specifically called on the UN Special Representative of the Secretary-General for Children and Armed Conflict, Mr. Olara Otunnu, to increasingly intervene wherever possible on their behalf.[107]

EDUCATION: A FUNDAMENTAL RIGHT DENIED

"We want to go to school! Please help us!"

Cries for education from the adolescent girls and boys in Acholiland are strong. Virtually every single adolescent interviewed said getting an education is very important to them, selecting it from the survey as one of their top five concerns. As young people in Gulu, Kitgum, and Pader struggle to cope with the insecurity and adversity in their lives, their dedication to education is remarkable. Despite countless barriers, especially for girls, they are desperate not to lose their opportunity to learn – they know it is central to maintaining a level of stability in their lives and their hope for the future.

The dream of education, however, has become nearly impossible for most adolescent boys and girls. For over a decade and a half, war in northern Uganda and southern Sudan has caused the destruction of schools and the abduction and killing of students, teachers, and school administrators. Thousands of adolescents, especially orphans, displaced persons, and refugees, face enormous barriers to getting an education and have no access to school. Those who do manage to attend school find massively overcrowded classes and poor facilities, ill-equipped for learning. Few young people see any clear paths to a steady job or income, and they feel their right to an education has become a luxury overshadowed by a constant preoccupation with meeting basic survival needs.

Without education, adolescents are losing hope and confidence in themselves and in the future. They blame a lack of education for what they see as an increase in "immorality" among young people and society as a whole, including an increase in early marriage, forced prostitution of girls, drug and alcohol abuse, and the number of street children. Ugandan young people are frustrated by the knowledge that when they become adults, their communities will lack the full range of skills needed to recover from war, create lasting peace, and get a foothold on development. Sudanese refugee adolescents similarly will lack many of the skills they need to build new lives in Sudan or to successfully integrate into Ugandan society.

---

[107] *Promoting the Protection and Capacities of Adolescents in Northern Uganda, Kitgum Region,* Kitgum/Pader research team report, 2001.

Universal Primary Education (UPE) Flounders in the North

In the districts covered by this research, a number of barriers have made sporadic attendance, late arrival, and dropouts in primary school seem the norm. Primary school levels run from P1 through P7, beginning usually at age five. Dropouts occur mostly in the later years of primary school when young people are entering adolescence. Adolescents and school officials report that many young children are starting P1 at seven, eight, or even nine years old, and others try to complete their primary studies when they are older and have missed some years. Huge numbers of young people are unable to attend school at all because of other responsibilities and barriers. These include child-care, long travel distances, security problems, and an inability to pay school fees. Many adolescents told the Women's Commission that they had completed a number of primary school years but simply could not continue. Gender discrimination is also a huge factor in the lower enrollment and higher dropout rate of girls.

Many young people show up late or do not make it to school at all. The distant location of schools and insecurity both in school and on the way to school puts them under the constant threat of attack and abduction. The LRA targets schools, abducting students and killing teachers. As one boy from Gulu recounted: "When the LRA took me, I was in school. They said, 'We are going to celebrate this day because we are destroying this school.'"[108] One adolescent in the village of Omiya Anyima said that the nearest primary school is 17 kilometers from his home and that the journey takes a long time and can be very dangerous. As a result, he is frequently late or misses school and has trouble keeping up. Adolescents who do attend frequently spend less than half a day in school because of insecurity and the need to travel back and forth. Distances to secondary school can be much greater.

Lack of money for school supplies, clothes, exams, and tuition not covered by the UPE also result in low attendance and high dropout rates. Although free UPE makes education more accessible financially, parents must still pay for supplies and some school costs, including examinations. Tuition for a term of primary school costs about 5,000 Ugandan shillings (US $3) per term, with three terms a year, a fee that many families simply cannot afford. Moreover, the UPE only covers four children per household, imposing greater prohibitive costs on households with more children. Many young people have only one set of clothes to wear and may be embarrassed to go to school. This is a particular problem for girls, who worry about having a set of clean clothes during their menstrual periods. In addition, orphans and many others cannot afford these expenses.

Food shortages leave young people distracted and weak. IDPs and refugees especially are often malnourished and weak. Coping with the physical effects of hunger is often a higher priority than school.

---

[108]Women's Commission interview, Gulu town, Gulu, May 14, 2001. One of the most famous cases of abduction occurred when 139 girls from the St. Mary's School, Aboke, were abducted by the LRA in October 1996.

Many adolescent boys in the Achol Pii refugee settlement, particularly those who are unaccompanied minors, are also late to school because of their responsibility for communal cooking. Each must take turns performing the task of preparing meals for others in the mornings, making them frequently late for school. Sometimes they have to leave school during the day to run home to cook meals.

In some of the strongest illustrations of young people's acceptance of taking responsibility for their predicaments, many are also making enormous sacrifices to help one another find ways to get through school. In some adolescent-headed households, siblings take turns working to pay for one another's tuition until they both manage to complete school. John, who is 15, from Kitgum Town Council, established a kiosk with help from IRC, where he sells candy and other goods to pay for his older brother's school fees and to care for his much younger brother. When his older brother finishes school, John plans to take his turn, finishing his own education while his older brother works.

Access to higher education is an even greater struggle. While dropout rates are high in the latter years of primary school, access to secondary school becomes even more limited. The huge fees and small number of schools make secondary education out of reach for most adolescents. At present, 509 sub-counties in Uganda have at least one secondary school. The remaining 347 sub-counties without a secondary school are located predominantly in rural areas like northern Uganda. Fees for secondary school range from 50,000-100,000 Ugandan shillings (about US $56) per term, with three terms per school year and four years of secondary school S1-S4.[109] Putting that against an average income of perhaps 70,000 Ugandan shillings (US $39) per month needed for all other expenses, paying for even one child to attend is nearly impossible for most.

The IDP camps in Gulu have no secondary schools. If IDP adolescents from Gulu, for example, can pay the fees or gain sponsorship, they must be boarded in or near Gulu town where several secondary schools are located, adding yet another cost. Dropouts increase in secondary school, because the financial burdens are astronomical by comparison to primary school. Girls face additional barriers to education. For example,

> ...after I passed my Primary Leaving Examination, I was admitted to S1. But when I asked for school fees, my step-mother said, "If you want to go to school, you will have to wait until my last born is up to university and I've bought myself a coffin. Then you can go."[110] Rachel, 16, from Kitgum Town Council

Solutions to the Problems of Education

Despite these overwhelming barriers, adolescents and other community members place enormous hope in the education system to solve many of the problems of the

---

[109] The secondary school system in Uganda is roughly based on that of the British system. Following seven years of primary school, young people go on to four years of secondary school, following which they take "O-level" (Ordinary Level) exams. If they choose to go on for additional secondary schooling, they study for two more years and then take "A-level" (Advanced Level) exams.

[110] Kitgum/Pader research team interview, KICWA Center, Kitgum Town Council, June 2001.

community. Without help from inside and outside of the community, the system will not even begin to deliver on some of these hopes.

Young people reiterate their deep conviction that an end to their insecurity and increased livelihood opportunities would result from improved opportunities for education. They call on the Ugandan government and international donors to work together to improve the education system and increase opportunities for children and young people to attend school. Boys and girls agree that girls' education must be prioritized and that all education efforts should be linked to livelihood opportunities.

To increase their financial support for school, young people propose some concrete steps. These include a combination of grants, loans, and education incentives. They ask the Ugandan government to adopt and implement an affirmative action education program for children and adolescents living in the conflict areas. Young people suggest that a special fund be established to pay for the secondary education of students in northern Uganda. They also call for the expansion of sponsorship programs by the government and NGOs, particularly for orphans, formerly abducted children, and children from the poorest families.

Young people believe there is widespread administrative corruption in which education funds are siphoned off for personal gain. They feel that the Ugandan government must take strong action to zealously investigate and eliminate corruption to ensure that the funds reach their designated targets – the schools and other education programs.

They ask that their curriculum be expanded to include reproductive health education, conflict resolution, hygiene, peace education, and civics. Girls and boys agree that reproductive health education should inform them about the dangers of early pregnancy, early marriage, and STIs, including HIV/AIDS, as well as family planning and birth control. They also call for more flexible scheduling and for practical training, with schools that are better equipped and more able to focus on vocational skills training. School schedules that accommodate their other responsibilities should also offer some adolescents better opportunities for completing their education. They say that teacher training colleges and better conditions for teachers are especially urgent in order to secure the necessary number of qualified and committed teachers.

In general, young people also believe that teaching styles should become less authoritarian and more participatory and that the education system should focus more on practical training and less on theory and rote academic learning. All of these improvements will require teacher training, improved facilities, and better equipment. They believe that an improved school system would attract higher attendance and win the full support of parents.

Young people also suggest that travel programs should be established to allow young people from northern Uganda to study education systems in other countries so that they can bring new ideas to their communities and suggest practical examples for making changes.

In addition to these suggestions, adolescents call for increased investment in regional development that will lead to employment opportunities for school-leavers and graduates. Without opportunities for young people to get through all levels of school and other training that they can put to use in their communities, they are convinced that the most skilled people will leave the region and, for the rest, it will be a continual struggle to survive.

LIVELIHOOD: OPTIONS ARE LIMITED AND DEPENDENCY DEEPENS

In the face of terrible war-induced poverty, adolescents are trying desperately to find basic sustenance for themselves and their families. But they are also left carrying the heaviest burdens. Inadequate protection and safety conditions prevent young people from cultivating arable land. They have precious few opportunities to learn, use viable skills, or find support for self-generated livelihood initiatives. Instead, they are learning to become dependent on outside humanitarian aid. Many young people are unable to attend school because of added responsibilities. They find survival in prostitution or are pushed into criminal activities. Other out-of-school adolescents struggle to make enough to pay the school fees of their brothers and sisters, sacrificing opportunities of their own for the well-being of their siblings.

Some adolescents are leaving their homes in IDP camps to find jobs in towns, but with little success. Adults believe that this migration is decreasing Acholi ties to ancestral lands, and they fear that without parental guidance, adolescents living on their own in towns are led to "bad behavior" that is undermining family structures and culture. Some rural and urban adolescents faced with no opportunities to earn a livelihood have turned to crime and prostitution, both of which have greatly increased in recent years, adolescents assert. Some of these adolescents end up as street children, a phenomenon that was previously unknown in Acholiland. Adults told researchers that criminals are looting at night and participating in ambushes and robbery, and that many of them are young people without jobs but with basic needs to meet.

Adolescent-led Livelihood Initiatives

The research identified many youth-led livelihood initiatives and revealed an urgent need for livelihood and income-generating opportunities, including skills training and micro-credit. As described above, many Sudanese young people are working together and cooperating with Ugandan nationals outside the camps to form cooperatives and associations in which a small group of young people jointly undertake projects. These include helping each other raise pigs or goats and then sharing profits. They have found some support for these activities from organizations like the IRC in Kitgum, but much more is needed.

Many young people expressed their strong desire for livelihood opportunities that will provide the opportunity to pay for school fees and allow them to attend school. Although a few such income-generating programs are linked to education, they are largely restricted to formerly abducted adolescents. The Ugandan government, international donors, and NGOs need to fund and work with local NGOs like the Concerned Parents Association (CPA) to develop more of these programs for the general adolescent population. Adolescents in all three districts called on the government to give grants and loans to the most vulnerable adolescents, especially school dropouts, orphans, and those living in IDP camps and to offer micro-finance schemes to youth and the wider community to improve livelihood and reduce poverty.

HEALTH: CHRONIC CAMP CONGESTION AND VIOLENCE UNDERMINE ADOLESCENT HEALTH

Among the myriad problems facing adolescents affected by the war in northern Uganda, adolescents and adults identified the difficulty of meeting basic needs such as food, water, health care services, and medicine as major concerns. Virtually all adolescents cited the spread of disease, lack of reproductive health services and education, sexual and gender-based violence against girls, and the HIV/AIDS epidemic as the leading problems created and compounded by conflict and insecurity. Adolescents maintain that a lasting peace and the dismantling of the camps would dramatically reduce most of northern Uganda's health problems. According to the Gulu research team report, adolescents believe that "If peace predominates and the soldiers return home, then the culture of dignity, love, respect, and hospitality would be revived through family communication at the 'fireplace.'"[111]

Food insecurity is rampant. Poor security, lack of protection, abduction, displacement, and the disability and death of able-bodied adolescents stops young people from cultivating the fields for food. As reported in the Gulu research team report: "Malnutrition was unheard of in Acholiland before the insurgency because the land would produce all the food needed for healthy growth and development. The insurgency led to a concentration of people in camps with restricted movement and the destruction of property, including entire households and agricultural products. This has completely prevented us from cultivating the land and has created malnutrition, starvation, and anemia."[112]

Adolescents living in crowded towns and, particularly, those in the over-congested internally displaced camps and Achol Pii refugee settlement say that their minimum needs for water and sanitation are not being met. "People are drinking dirty water from the rivers because there is no clean water, which makes them sick," said one Sudanese boy in Arum Primary School in Achol Pii. Many adolescents echoed this statement made by an internally displaced adolescent: "For us, the war means that there aren't enough places to go to the bathroom."

Adolescents said that living in camps without adequate latrines or safe water leads to the quick spread of diseases such as cholera, diarrhea, measles, malaria, and tuberculosis. It also leads to high morbidity and mortality rates. A survey conducted by the NGO African Medical and Research Foundation

---

[111] *Problems and Solutions Identified by Adolescent Researchers in Northern Uganda.* Gulu Research Team report, Gulu, Uganda, 2001.
[112] Ibid.

(AMREF) found that over 50 percent of Gulu households indicated chronic ill-health (United Nations Population Fund, 2001). In response to the health problems caused by poor conditions within the camps, adolescents called for the dismantling of the camps as a critical component of any improvement. In the meantime, they urged the construction of latrines in camps and towns, the protection of water springs, the improvement of the drainage system, and increased health education in all camps as well as in primary and secondary schools to prevent diseases.

Both Ugandan and Sudanese adolescents complained about inadequate medical supplies, poor medical facilities, high hospital fees, the poor performance and corruption of some health workers, and unevenly distributed hospitals. "The only existing health unit is 17 kilometers away from our home, and we lack trained personnel and have poor medical equipment," said a 16-year-old boy who lives in Omiya Anyima village in Kitgum.[113] The Achol Pii refugee settlement, which stretches approximately 21 kilometers, has two health facilities and one doctor, which must serve up to 26,000 refugees registered in the settlement and an additional 10,000 Ugandans living in the vicinity.

Adolescents called for the development of health infrastructure in all sub-counties to better dispense medical supplies and doctors within the community, including internally displaced camps and villages. They also called on the church, NGOs, and the government to help minimize corruption and maximize efficiency.

Reproductive Health and Sexual and Gender-Based Violence

Reproductive health services, rare enough due to cultural restraints, are even more limited by the conflict. Acholi cultural practices, norms, and attitudes prohibit open discussion about sex, leaving many adolescents, especially girls, uninformed about the consequences of sex and other reproductive health issues. In addition, the majority of operational health units are church-run and offer very limited reproductive health services and education for adolescents. Nevertheless, many adolescents are engaging in sex, including by force, from ages as young as 12 or 13. A large number of girls said they could not say "no" to unprotected sex, and some boys said that they didn't like condoms and would not wear them during sex. Others reported having no access to condoms, especially in the IDP camps. Girls also reported that they lack sanitary supplies during their periods.

The majority of adolescents viewed many of the reproductive health problems facing adolescents as resulting from "a decline in moral values" due to the conflict. This morality gap, they say, has led to early sexual activity between adolescents, prostitution, and an increase in domestic and community violence involving rape and sexual assault. In order to reduce the incidence of rape and resulting early pregnancy, adolescents suggested that soldiers' barracks be relocated farther away from the population and that communities be sensitized about the ill-effects of drinking alcohol, which they believe contributes to violence against girls and women. In addition, they urged that contraceptives and family

---

[113] Kitgum/Pader research team interview, Omiya Anyima, Kitgum, June 2001.

planning be encouraged at all levels of society in order to reduce the number of child mothers and unwanted children.

PSYCHOSOCIAL REINTEGRATION IN AN ENVIRONMENT OF DISINTEGRATION

> Coming back from the bush I thought of committing suicide because I was so embarrassed to live with people who knew me after doing these shameful practices...I thought I might have contracted STIs, including AIDS, so life was useless since I had a short life expectancy. People my age laughed at me and called me abusive names, and I could not stay with them. I have lost friends and company. I am lonely. (Betty, 19, from Achol Pii refugee settlement)

The psychosocial[114] consequences of war on the lives of adolescents last long beyond its end, and as long as war persists they involve an ongoing and simultaneous process of disintegration and reintegration. As young people bear and cope with physical and emotional upheaval, they are continually coping in an ongoing process of recovery.

As the principal targets of war in northern Uganda, adolescents are under constant attack, their spirits depleted and their healthy development short-circuited by violence and insecurity. Surviving adolescents face drastically altered social relationships that often include physical and emotional abuse from families and communities. Violence has spread from warring parties to families and neighbors, where domestic violence and sexual abuse are on the rise. Adolescents named child abuse as one of their top five concerns.

Feeling hopeless and alone, young people are desperate for support and protection. They also protect themselves against their own vulnerability with defensive, aggressive, or detached, often anti-social behaviors. Yet they are proactively surviving and continually strive to improve their lives in many creative and constructive ways.

Young people are both hindered and helped along their path to recovery by a community that views them with alternating and simultaneous suspicion and sympathy. The conflict has altered young people's lives and their roles in the

---

[114] As described in the Women's Commission report, *Untapped Potential, Adolescents Affected by Armed Conflict*, "psychosocial" can be defined as follows, as referenced from: *Cape Town Annotated Principles and Best Practice on the Prevention of Recruitment of Children into the Armed Forces and Demobilization and Social Reintegration of Child Soldiers in Africa* and UNICEF's *Interregional Programming Workshop on Psychosocial Care and Protection.* "The term 'psychosocial' underlines the close relationship between the psychological and social effects of armed conflict, each the one type of effect continually influencing the other. By 'psychosocial effects' is meant those experiences that affect emotions, behavior, thoughts, memory, and learning ability and how a situation may be perceived and understood. By 'social effects' is meant the ways in which the diverse experiences of war alter people's relationships to each other, in that such experiences change people but also the experience through death, separation, estrangement, and other losses. 'Social' may be extended to include an economic dimension, as many individuals and families become destitute through the material and economic devastation of war, thus losing their social status and place in their familiar social network." Dr. Mike Wessells, a professor at Randolph Macon University and expert on the psychosocial effects of armed conflict on children, further comments that the meaning of "psychosocial" varies according to cultural context.

community at an accelerated rate. They are seen increasingly as "immoral" and disrespectful, and their role as perpetrators as well as victims in the conflict has invoked confusion and fear in the hearts and minds of their families and communities.

A huge gulf is emerging between the generations as local traditions and war-related stresses discourage young people from open discussions with adults, including public officials and teachers, about their situation and changing roles. Some adults and several local organizations are, however, working to support the needs and strengths of adolescents, although most of them address the urgent and immediate needs of those returning from captivity. Support for the countless other adolescents living in dire circumstances is also urgent, but less forthcoming. Psychosocial and reintegration interventions should maximize young people's direct involvement in decision-making and implementation, and there should be continuous follow-up on their circumstances and progress.

Recovery and Reintegration of Former LRA Abductees

Former abductees carry to freedom the memories and emotions of agonizing experiences, symbolic reminders of the heavy burdens they were forced to carry during captivity. Many remain haunted by the acts of violence they have suffered and have been forced to commit. Some experience nightmares, emotional disconnections, acting out, even violence and other symptoms of what in Western medicine is called Post Traumatic Stress Disorder (PTSD). To many young people, these dreams and experiences reflect spiritual distress in which they are troubled by the spirits of those they have harmed, and they feel wracked with guilt.[115] Formerly abducted young people also know that they are among the most vulnerable to LRA attack. If re-abducted and recognized, they are likely to be killed immediately. Many escapees have been pursued by rebels and killed. Relatives and friends of those who escape may also pay a similar price.

Many formerly abducted young people stated that they are so afraid of re-abduction by the LRA that each night they sleep in the bush instead of in their huts, believing they are less likely to be found there should the LRA attack their homes and villages. Like dozens of others, one former abductee from Omiya Anyima told the Women's Commission: "We don't sleep at home. We are very vulnerable to re-abduction, and our huts are dangerous to stay in at night."[116]

Formerly abducted young people are haunted by many other worries: that they will not find or then not be accepted by their families and peers; that they will be stigmatized as killers and thieves or, in the case of sexually abused girls, especially those with children, tainted and shamed; that they are infected with HIV/AIDS and will not live long. Will they be able to catch up or even return to school? Will they find employment? In addition to these weighty emotional

---

[115] Traditional religion has its own version of PTSD in which the fears and demons are externalized. The healing lies in family or community actions and/or rituals rather than individualized therapy performed by a professional.

[116] Women's Commission interview, Kitgum Uganda, November 2000.

burdens, formerly abducted young people have lost much trust in a world that has failed to protect them and even betrayed them.

Adolescents said that these fears and anxieties are further reinforced by LRA indoctrination. The rebels warn them repeatedly that, despite promises of amnesty, the UPDF will punish, torture, and kill them rather than allow them to return home. The rape and sexual enslavement of girls, many of whom have borne children, has been used as a deliberate attempt to tarnish their virtue in the eyes of their community and make it more difficult for them to return. This in turn can undermine the value of formerly abducted girls to society and make them the potential objects of ridicule, humiliation, or further sexual violence. Sexual violence also serves to stigmatize girls returning to their communities as potentially diseased, including with HIV/AIDS.

Little data exists on increased violence committed by returned and other youth within their communities, but it is much discussed. Many adolescents stated that desperate poverty is driving orphans and other young people to steal and that some former abductees are turning to crime out of difficulty in readjusting to civilian life and finding jobs. Others blame the pervasive culture of violence within the LRA from which it is hard to break free. Unconfirmed reports from juvenile justice experts in recent months have included reports of violent acts of banditry committed by bands of youth, sometimes pretending to be LRA or UPDF soldiers. In IDP camp settings and in the Achol Pii refugee settlement adolescent boys are raping adolescent girls.

Often preoccupied with their own concerns and unsupported themselves, families and communities have limited energy or patience to give to the returning adolescents. Young people reported that many adults face the return of young abductees with a confusion and an ambivalence that range from anger to compassion, fear to protection. Moreover, families and communities often expect the returning adolescents to behave like adults while still having the authority to treat them like children.

Despite the numerous obstacles in the way of healing and reintegration, communities have worked hard to welcome and accept the young people. They struggle to face many difficult conflicts. For example, parents of abducted girls wonder what they might do if their daughters return home pregnant or with a child. While they would rejoice in seeing their daughter, they question how they would feel about a child whose father is a rebel and how that child would be treated by the community. In general, communities are also willing to offer forgiveness and support amnesty for the LRA. Adults said that they try to remember that the young people abducted by the LRA were not there by choice, but under the threat of death.

Community groups also recognize that reintegration is about far more than curing medical ills. They understand that healing is a long process for young people and their families that requires determined and ongoing follow-up, even in the face of frustration, discouragement, and other setbacks. Communities also understand that education and livelihood activities are particularly important to young people, giving them some hope for the future and helping to provide for the whole family. They know that the authority and responsibility their children may have had while in the LRA is hard to let go once they are back to civilian life, especially if there is nothing else to occupy or make them feel good about themselves. They believe that if young people know they can begin to lead productive lives post-abduction, they will be less likely to return to the LRA should they be overwhelmed or disappointed by life outside captivity.

A number of community groups have formed to help these young people and their families. Most notable is the CPA, which supports families of abducted children, helps to reintegrate the former abductees, and prepares them and the wider community for their return home. CPA helps parents and other community members confront fears about their children's transformation and develop the support they need to give to the young people upon their return.

Programs by KICWA, GUSCO and the World Vision Children of War Center in Gulu help adolescents find their families and reintegrate into their communities. They believe that music, drawing, and other creative and sports activities have a powerful healing impact. Young people in all the centers are engaged in chores that serve the whole group such as helping to prepare meals or cleaning up. These organizations also work with the young people afterwards to follow up on their integration and provide skills training and other educational opportunities that the former abductees overwhelmingly want and need. They also work to minimize the time young people spend in the custody of the UPDF following their escape[117] and ensure that while in custody they are treated with full care and protection. Each center also does its best to create a safe and secure environment for the young people and, to this end, each center is placed in the relatively safe town centers of Gulu and Kitgum.

There is debate among organizations over the best approach to reintegration. Some argue that the process should avoid institutionalization, which is believed to contribute to the further stigmatization of young people. They also believe that young people should return home as swiftly as possible, where the most critical part of the healing and recovery process takes place. These organizations provide shelter in traditional structures known as "ot lums," or grass houses, which are familiar to the former abductees and to which they will be returning. They build the capacity and skills of local community members, including parents, to work with the returnees, rather than leaving the challenge of reintegration to outsiders or those with formal education.

A different approach assumes that successful transition to community life requires more extended rehabilitation time in a center, including longer periods of exposure to Western-oriented individual counseling. This approach also involves a more dormitory-like atmosphere for the young people. Despite these differences, the majority of former abductees interviewed reported having had good, helpful experiences under each set of circumstances.

However, none of the rehabilitation programs make sufficient use of the capabilities of young people who have already been successfully reintegrated and who should be made an integral part of helping new arrivals. With further training and by involving them in decision-making, these young people could work with and inspire confidence in the new arrivals and would likely create ways to further

---

[117] Many former abductees end up in UPDF custody as they make their journey home. The UPDF holds them for a period of time, interrogating them about their experience and then releases them.

improve the process of return and reintegration. It would also offer all formerly abducted young people opportunities to continue to build networks of solidarity and support and expand the reach of the organizations to conduct follow-up.

Religion and Ritual

Many young people find solace in traditional rituals and by attending the Christian churches that flourish in the north. Churches provide spaces for prayer and an offer of forgiveness from God and the community. Many young people rely on churches and their belief in God for strength and to create a bridge to full community acceptance. In the case of KICWA, support is also provided to families who choose to perform traditional Acholi rituals to cleanse and renew the young person who has returned. Often until such a ritual is performed, neither the community nor the young person will be at rest. In such a poor region, however, the necessary materials to perform these rituals are often out of reach without assistance. In most cases, such activities provide enormous relief to all involved and help the healing and community acceptance process of the young person.

Adolescent Coping and Resilience

Adolescents in northern Uganda and southern Sudan have shown enormous strength in coping with situations of crisis. Some of the skills they developed have helped them survive armed combat, extreme poverty, and deprivation. They are incredibly resilient and have attempted to weather each new crisis as it has arisen. They demonstrate skills such as staying alive in the bush, foraging for food, lighting fires and building shelters while attempting to simultaneously find work, stay in school, and care for siblings. These adolescents are resilient and dedicated, not just to their own survival but also to a better future. Their ideas, strengths, and abilities will form the basis for continued community recovery.

While young people in northern Uganda may have few opportunities to influence community decision-making, many are actively asking for help from the adults around them despite frequently being turned away or disappointed. In perhaps one of the most stirring examples of desperation and tenacity facing adolescents in asking for help, a 15-year-old boy saw Women's Commission researchers on the street in Gulu and randomly said hello. Not even knowing their names, he later traveled over 80 kilometers along a dangerous road to Kitgum to find them again and ask for help. Like countless others, he was an orphan with many brothers and sisters to care for, with no one to help pay for his schooling or other needs.

Young people's commitment to education in school and elsewhere is overwhelming. They cling to the possibility of an education with great hope and do whatever they can to be able to finish their schooling. If they cannot go to school, adolescents still desire to and do participate in non-formal education and learning activities.

Some former abductees, including boys in the village of Omiya Animya and Awer IDP camp, have formed their own support groups. They said that sometimes a group of former abductees will get together to plan a project or they will just sit together, talk, and pass the time. These meetings help them to feel supported and give them confidence. While former abductees do very much interact with other young people, they tend to look to one another for solace and support. As fewer girls have escaped than boys, it is not clear that they have opportunities for mutual support to a similar extent.

Young people's strengths and coping must increasingly be transformed into leadership. Young people must find ways to recognize how their survival skills can be built upon to increase youth-led organizing and activism that constructively and democratically addresses key adolescent and community issues. Support for young people's capacities and involvement in decision-making is urgent, and it must be balanced with protection and humanitarian and development assistance that addresses their immediate needs for security, food, education, and health care.

Women's Commission for Refugee Women and Children
New York

REFERENCES

Friedman, S. (2001). *Participatory approaches to UNICEF programming, Section II*. New York: UNICEF.

Human Rights Watch. (1997, September). *The scars of death: Children abducted by the Lord's Resistance Army in Uganda*. New York.

International Rescue Committee (IRC). (2001, June). *Assistance to Sudanese refugees in Pader District Achol Pii Refugee Settlement*. Sub-project Monitoring Report, pp. 3.

IRIN. (2001, August 21). *Uganda: IDP treatment "Runs counter to humanitarian principles."* Gulu, Uganda.

IRIN. (2001, August 23). *Uganda: Acholi leaders urge government to dismantle IDP camps*. East Africa News Brief.

Ministry of Gender, Labor and Social Development. (2001). *National youth policy: A vision for youth in the twenty-first century*. The Republic of Uganda.

Ojwee, D. (2001, May 12). UPDF kill four civilians. *The New Vision*.

United Nations High Commissioner for Refugees (UNHCR). (1999). *Protecting refugees: A field guide for NGOs*. Author. Available at:
http://www.unhcr.org/cgi-bin/texis/vtx/partners/opendoc.pdf?tbl=PARTNERS&id=3bb33b192

United Nations High Commissioner for Refugees (UNHCR). *Guidelines for the protection and care of refugee children*. Author. Available at:
http://www.unhcr.org/cgi-bin/texis/vtx/protect/opendoc.pdf?tbl=PROTECTION&id=3b84c6c67

United Nations Population Fund (UNFPA). (2001). *Components in the 2001 inter-agency consolidated appeal for Uganda*. New York: United Nations. Available at:
www.unfpa.org/tpd/emergencies/caphtml/uganda.htm

U.S. Department of State. (2000, February). *Country reports on human rights practices: Uganda*. Washington, DC: The Bureau of Democracy, Human Rights and Labor.

U.S. Department of State. (2001, February). *Country reports on human rights practices: Uganda*. Washington, DC: The Bureau of Democracy, Human Rights and Labor.

KATY RADFORD

"IT'S NOT JUST BAGELS AND *BHAJIS:*" REFLECTIONS ON A RESEARCH REVOLT, YOUTH PARTICIPATION, AND MINORITY ETHNICITY IN NORTHERN IRELAND[118]

ABSTRACT

This chapter records the methods used to conduct participatory research with young people from minority ethnic communities in Northern Ireland. Some from minority ethnic and faith-based communities in Northern Ireland see it as a place of a diminished sense of belonging, of value, and restricted opportunities. These views are considered in the context of a region emerging from violent conflict.

Northern Ireland is "in recovery." At the time of writing many committed practitioners working with young people are trying to be effective within communities in Northern Ireland that have been described as "no longer at war," "sustaining peace," "emerging into a post-conflict situation" and my particular, somewhat nebulous favorite, "being in a transitional phase."

Youthworkers, social workers and educationalists are expected to have a predisposition to developing good practice when working with young people in heterogeneous societies. Yet for many years, this aspect of their work has been tempered and restricted by bridge building or fire-fighting between the needs and expectations of two majority cultural traditions within Northern Ireland, distinguished if in name only, as coming from within the Christian traditions. This chapter is offered as a backdrop to a debate that has recently begun in both policy and practice terms across a number of sectors about mainstreaming issues of minority ethnicity and faith within this social and political context.

The chapter looks at the process of conducting a research project about cultural diversity. A resulting publication, *Count Me In,* from the research is now used as a tool in strategy and policy development by a range of organisations in Northern Ireland. The training manual, *Think of Me, Think of You,* which also came from the research, was written and developed by the research participants. This award-winning resource is being used across the statutory and voluntary youth sector and by the teacher training establishments.

---

[118] Empirical evidence in this article is drawn from research commissioned by the Department of Education, Northern Ireland, conducted in collaboration with the Youth Council for Northern Ireland, the Northern Ireland Council for Ethnic Minorities, and the children's rights charity, Save the Children.

Doug Magnuson and Michael Baizerman (eds), Work with Youth in Divided and Contested Societies, 141–151.

The process of co-ordinating the project is revisited from the perspective of someone whose work is informed by an anthropological training. Since Scholte (1972) proposed the practice of reflexivity, it is not merely fashionable but now a well-versed discourse within anthropological theory and ethnography to consider the researcher's impact on information elicited in the field. It is so rehearsed that Cohen (1992) refers to it as a "weary old truism" (p. 225). For many years, thoughtful ethnographies have problematised the relationship between the researcher and their host communities (Hendry, 1992; Rabinow, 1977) and others have carefully interpreted this material within a format situated at the interface between autobiography, biography, and theory, (Clifford & Marcus, 1986; Matsunaga, 2000; Okely & Callaway, 1992). There is also a growing body of work that focuses on the effects on all participants of the research process and of the particular inequalities and challenges faced when working with young people, vulnerable participants, and family members. However, critics of the reflexive practice view such reflections as gratuitous, a somewhat egotistical exercise, taking it as read that the permutations of gender, race, familiarity with the subjects, and the personal expectations of the researcher are among any number of factors that influence the choices made in the information solicited, proffered, and written up.

When I began working on this chapter, I presented the editors with a training manual, some scattered thoughts, and a few bullet points. They asked me to consider framing it by drawing on a process of reflexivity and write from within this established genre. Focusing on the first person with such an approach, it was suggested, would provide an opportunity to complement the novelty of the experience and what uniqueness was to be found in the research. It was argued by the editors that to harness and translate my idealism and experiences as a "whole" person might appropriately highlight human and humane motivations shared with others from different disciplines who also work with, advocate, and campaign for young people who are perceived to be vulnerable.

To that end it is worth acknowledging that any symbiosis between myself as facilitator and the young people who took part in the research was influenced to some extent by a variety of factors including my:
- experiences as a child growing up in Northern Ireland during the height of the conflict in the 1970s,
- being a member of a minority community,
- family history: as the mother of one of the participants in the research, as the daughter of a refugee and as part of a family where genocide, related to ethnicity, has imprinted an inter-generational legacy.

To subject all the events and encounters of the research process to my interpretation and reinterpretation would, I believe, constrain the material and the effervescence of its formation. To focus with any depth on the authorial voice in this instance will undermine rather than complement the young people's achievements. Distorting the participants' voices with the power of the adult narrative, as Van Manen (1999) suggests, would be to permit the sub-plot to subvert the main plot.

While my observations and facilitation undoubtedly provided safety nets, rubber boundaries, and both intentional and unintentional stimulus, the success of the project was its process and that remained firmly rooted in both the interactions of the participants and their confidence to redefine the parameters of the work and their engagement with it. Any growth and power that emanated from this process signalled an organic young people-centered form of community development. The most valuable information gleaned from this project did not emerge from my interviews with or exerted influence on them but, rather, as a result of the anthropologically-defining methodology of participant observation that we all undertook.

This chapter outlines a research "revolt" and the merits of the participants' influence on the process as well as the outcomes of their agency in the area of citizenship.

METHODOLOGY – A REVOLTING EXPERIENCE!

One of the unpredicted outcomes of the research was that a core group of 12 refined the direction of the project over a six-month period in what I refer to as a research "revolt." Of these participants who took part in the development of the training resource, all had experience of family living in diaspora and, for some, this was reflected in their status as asylum seekers and refugees fleeing persecution. All had some experience of traumatic loss with six having either a family member or a friend with a family member who had been shot dead as a political act. The group comprised one Jew, two Muslims, two Sikhs, five Hindus, one Christian, and one Buddhist. Their countries of origin included Palestine, Ireland, Sri Lanka, India, Mainland China, and Hong Kong.

All the quotations here were taken from these children and young people, (aged between 10 and 18) who met originally when they were part of a larger sample of young people who took part in the qualitative research project funded by the Department of Education in Northern Ireland (Radford, 2004a). Initial aims were drawn up by adult representatives of these bodies without consulting any young people. The research was conducted with 100 young people from a number of different ethnic, faith, and national backgrounds.

The initial research sample was determined by access which was facilitated by one of the partner-sponsors, Norther Ireland Council for Ethnic Minorities (NICEM), a membership organisation representing ethnic community groups that, in turn, selected participants on the basis that their identity would remain confidential and any quotations would be unattributed. The 100 participants self-identified as coming from a variety of nationalities and faith-based communities. All were able-bodied and lived with one or more birth parent. None had experience of living in the care of social services. All were financially dependent on their families, with none of the young people in paid employment. Some lived in families totally financially dependant on public/statutory benefits, with experiences of living in hostel and temporary accommodation. The views of both first- and second-generation migrants to Northern Ireland were represented and all considered themselves to have shared allegiances to Northern Ireland and to another place or "imagined community" (Anderson, 1983). "It's not that we forget about 'back home,' but our parents are not in Albania now. We're growing up here and so now this is where we are from."

The study at this stage was standard and uninspiring, comprising formal and semi-structured interviews with young people. However, as the participants' confidence and engagement with the process increased, some articulated concerns that their input and narratives were being "used" for information by others and that they would have no control over this. They were unhappy with the anonymity clauses decided by the sponsors on their behalf: They felt that others' bargaining for the terms and conditions of their involvement in the usage (albeit with the best of intentions), effectively rendered them peripheral to the process and this was a clear example of adult disempowerment of youth.

Up to this point, the participants had little say in the direction of this (and other) research nominally being conducted on their behalf with minimal ownership of the research findings. Independently, a number said they were concerned that they were being "over researched," in particular due to the legislative duty placed on statutory agencies to consult with young people and those from minority ethnic communities as outlined in Section 75 of the Northern Ireland (1998) Act. At first sight, this duty is a welcome application of the United Nations Convention on the Rights of the Children where youth participation is a cornerstone. Yet the participants recognised that consultations they had previously been involved with were flawed. This, they suggested was principally due to:

- the limited accountability of researchers to consultees, and
- the lack of any obligation to implement their recommendations or comments.

Within the context of a small black and minority ethnic sector, the participants' comments raise questions about how youth consultation is conducted and the political rhetoric being embodied in the box-tick consultation. "People want to know all the time what we think about – but why should we do this for their benefit? Or they want us to turn up with food and in our saris to dance. What purpose is it for us if people just write about us. We can do this for ourselves." For the participants, then, it appeared that the value placed on their participation was a simple binary between being expected to either validate goal-directed outcomes by researchers or to be token and decorative, providing what Mohanty (1994, p. 146) describes as "a harmonious, empty pluralism." This latter practice of affirming essentialised notions of community was later termed the "Bhaji and Bagel approach" by one of the participants. In their discussions, the young people used the expression to represent the way those from the majority communities gathered evidence from or worked with them.

Given that relatively few young people in Northern Ireland are in positions to comment on issues of minority ethnicity, it is perhaps unsurprising that participants to the research felt tokenised. They spontaneously debated the increasing pressure being placed on them to respond to requests to take part in discussions on a range of matters that they are frequently neither pre-disposed to consider nor have knowledge about, for example, changes to policing arrangements or, in this case, youth service provision within a post-conflict situation.

To address their growing disquiet, the research revolt was initiated by the twelve when they came together in a neutral space to discuss and resolve the issue collectively. They negotiated and agreed to continue in the research only if they were enabled to participate in creating a training resource. They spent the following three months working on the development of the design and content of this material negotiating the terms of their contribution with the organisations funding the research.

> I don't like the pictures with us holding out our hands; it looks like we are begging for something.

> Make sure there's pictures of us together--not on our own--so people know we're a team.

It's a Sunday afternoon in Belfast. Raj, Grace, and Rabia are waiting for the rest of the group to arrive so they can sign-off on the artwork for the training manual they have been working on.

> The problem page should definitely go at the back. That way we can end it by putting in some of the embarrassing questions we asked before we really got to know each other.

> You mean the ones you asked. I was *sussed* from the beginning.

The work they entitled *Think of Me, Think of You* is a publication in which they decided to be identified as co-authors and in which they chose to have photographs of themselves. The title reflects their pluralistic approach and their intention to focus on areas of commonality within their diversity of experience. Agreement to develop this aspect of the project was reached in consultation with the original community organisations, and a methodology more meaningful to the participants was developed that included a series of workshop activities including photography, role play, drawing, life-story telling, and problem-solving exercises in an extended process that focussed on aspects of individual and group identity. Workshop design was informed by a variety of practices and methodologies grounded in the principle of youth participation (Fajerman, et al 2000; Treseder, 1997; Sheehan, 2004).

RECLAIMING OWNERSHIP

The participants began the process ill-informed of one another's experiences, of any conflicts within their families or their communities of origin, and with a lack of familiarity with the micro-dynamics of Northern Ireland's emergence from conflict. "I don't really know who is on what side here, so I just don't talk about anything political in case I say the wrong thing to someone."

Some forthright questions were asked of one another and responses were given with equal frankness and candour. "What do you mean you're an asylum seeker? I thought they were all men. How did you get here, in a trailer or what?"

145

"Yes, we travelled for four days in a sealed container." *The participants desired that the information from these workshops would be incorporated into the design of the anti-discriminatory material which, in turn, they hoped would be used as a tool* to build more positive community relations. Based on the information that they shared, they decided to develop material that used reflective action and talking points to address some of their experiences of stereotyping, ostracism, and of different forms of social exclusion. "What do you think people see when they look at your style of dress? What is your favourite item of clothing and why? Think of someone else's style that you like, would it suit you? Why not? If you had to accompany your sister to the police station each week to sign in as an asylum seeker, how do you think you would feel?"

SAFE SPACES

Participants in the study chose to work with the project in places they defined as "their" spaces. Initially this was at their homes, residences, or in community centres they used on a regular basis. Defining notions of home and community can be a paradox for individuals and communities where migration, transience, displacement, and spiritual and physical estrangement directly affects a sense of belonging or alienation (Rapport & Dawson, 1998). Both community and home are concepts that warrant specific attention when applied to young migrants and, in particular, to asylum seekers seeking a sense of place after fleeing persecution. For the participants in this project, their ambiguous and fluid notions of belonging, home, and community were re-defined together into the need to work within "safe" spaces. Safe, in this instance, was characterised as being "with people that are like you," "with kids who are the same age and have the same sort of beliefs even if you are from a different religion," "where there is no alcohol and no one is going to talk about sex or drugs or that sort of thing," "with people who will understand what we can and cannot do."

Kousalyaa explained that the message each of these statements conveyed to them was that a safe environment is created "when there's no need to explain." Yet in workshops where diversity was explored, the participants' demonstrated on a number of occasions a willingness if not a need to explain difficult experiences to each other. This was particularly evident when past images of brutality, loss, and conflict emerged as powerful and deeply embedded memories that resonated with their current experiences in Northern Ireland.

"One time I was coming home from school with my mates. Some boys fired a pellet gun at me and shouted racist names. I didn't get hurt, but it really, really upset me. Even now it upsets me to think about it." He pauses, and one speaks. The group neither looks to me nor to one another for guidance. Some look down. All wait. He draws breath and looks at the ceiling. Slowly he begins to speak again.

> You see, it reminds me that the reason we first came here was because we had to leave our home when my oldest brother was shot dead. He was doing nothing, just delivering fish with my dad, but he was caught in a crossfire with soldiers. Later on that day, when we told my grandfather,

he had a heart attack and died. So that's why I couldn't tell my parents what happened on that day those Irish boys fired at me. It would have broken them even more to think that where we thought we were going to find safety, we were not safe at all.

After a period of working together the group spontaneously began to share intimacies that could be expected to leave them vulnerable and exposed. Revealing and poignant statements were punctuated with supportive silences. Participants appeared to instinctively allow for safe spaces to emerge and here they enabled and allowed for one another's emotional openness to blossom rather than wither.

As an extension of their concerns about the notions of safety and of belonging, the concepts were further explored in discussions within the context of a growth in violent crime within Northern Ireland and how their exposure to this occurred within both a sectarian and racist context. "One time when we were coming back from the temple, we were waiting for a taxi. Some cars kept circling and circling round us and round us and the people inside were calling us racist names. It was so frightening. We decided not to go again. We just don't know who people are or who they represent so we don't talk to anyone about it."

As stories began to flow more freely, layers of concerns were revealed when they began to think about nationalism and religious ideology as they related both to their lives in Northern Ireland and in their countries of origin. As a partial response to such external pressures and forces, they discussed cultural and gender specific traditions that emphasized family centeredness. It was clear that inter-generational support was crucial to their perceptions of safety. From within their distinctive traditions, they collectively recognised that the extended family and respect for traditions provided forms of social capital that they expected and wanted to call on to provide buffers to deflect wider community challenges.

It was particularly noticeable that within this context their views mirrored the findings of other research projects with minority faith and ethnic communities (see, for example, Desai & Subramanian, 2003) where high levels of gender conservatism were articulated and women were expected to be responsible for the maintenance and dissemination of cultural values, traditions, and both child and elder care. However due to the size and marginalised status of their communities, a "taking care of your own" expectation did not always appear to provide sufficiently supportive structures to withstand the taunts of others in Northern Ireland, in particular those from communities emerging from conflict.

NEGOTIATING COMMUNITIES - NEGOTIATING IDENTITY

In Northern Ireland, young people's exposure to physical and armed violence is *de rigueur* (Brett & Specht, 2004; Byrne et al, 2005). It is solidified in their psyche through its appearance on walls in murals (McIntosh & Jarman, 2005), in popular culture and music (Radford, 2004b), as a norm in the culture of engagement with the police and criminal justice systems for some youth (Hamilton et al, 2004; Radford et al, 2005) and in the form of paramilitary punishment beatings and shootings for others (Byrne, 2005; Feenan, 2004; Kennedy, 2002). Segregation, created through access to public education and housing, is well documented

(Murtagh, 2002), with sectarianism and racism both realities that young people and their families experience on a regular basis (Jarman & Monaghan, 2004).

Rabia is 17. She lives in an exclusively Protestant residential area on the edge of a Loyalist estate with her mother, younger siblings, and her uncle who insists she attend a single gender school. Until recently she attended a state school close to her home. Rabia wants to become a doctor, but that school did not provide her with the science classes that she needed to take at A level in order to fulfill the ambition. The nearest single-gender school that provides her with the classes is almost three miles away in an exclusively Catholic area. To travel there, she has to pass through a number of invisible interfaces between Protestant and Catholic residential areas in a uniform that marks her out as attending a Catholic school. Church-led assemblies, the school chapel, and the celebration of mass as a school are a focal point of the school day. Rabia was discouraged from attending this school by Protestant neighbours and has been taunted and on the receiving end of a number of racist comments since she began her walk to and from the bus stops at either end of her journey by both Catholics and Protestants. Her uniform has been customised so that her head, arms, and legs are fully covered and when not at school she is particularly assertive in defending her wishes to wear full hijab when challenged by others

> People see my clothes as a cloud that hangs over women to oppress us. What they don't see is that it is a smokescreen for me. I feel correct and proper when I am dressed as I am now. I don't believe it's got anything to do with men controlling women; it's a woman's choice to dress modestly and to observe *hijab*; it's a sign that shows self-respect and that women should not be judged on their appearance.

Goaded in the street, discouraged by neighbours for attending a non-local school, Rabia, with her thick Belfast accent, suggests that she walks a thin line between feeling a part of her school community and being apart from her neighbours and recognises that others' allegiances to her are contingent on whether she is, as the old joke goes, "a Protestant Muslim or a Catholic Muslim."

Rabia's experiences elicited similar stories from other members of the group: "We're the only non-white family in our neighbourhood. People are nice to us, like, but I've never been into anyone's house and, even though I walk home with people from school, no one would ever come into mine." The responses resonate with those of young people from minority ethnic backgrounds living in rural Wales (Scourfield, 2005). Participants in both studies at no stage choose to describe themselves as Black nor do they articulate any cultural affinity or association with the area in which they live. In this research, participants were unwilling to describe themselves as exclusively Irish, Northern Irish or, in the case of the Scourfield report, as Welsh. "I know I'm a mix of my Chinese and my Irish family and that both bits are important to me, but people look at me and make assumptions."

At one level the participants welcomed the fact that a fusion of their British/Irish/minority ethnic and faith identities could be sufficiently hybrid to defy pigeonholing but recognized that this also created a dislocation from their wider environment. As statistical minorities, there was a recognition that they remain at a disadvantage.   Their experiences are those of a cohort that one participant described as being "inside-out."[119]

For the participants in this study, having and making opportunities to articulate experiences that clearly impact on their worldviews appeared to be useful. It informed their ability to meaningfully connect with one another as well as their willingness to transform hurts and vulnerabilities into catalysts for reconciliation and moving forward.   Through the process of sharing, a sense of solidarity occurred where intense feelings of social togetherness and belonging arose in keeping with Turner's ritual notion of *communitas,* and an active attempt was made to address essentialist notions and reductionist views of their identities. What the participants created throughout the course of the project was an environment where psychological and social constructs drawn from shared interests, preoccupations, and intimate understandings of one another provided a collective focus and group identity.

What appears to have developed from this deepening participation in the project should not be perceived as the creation of a homogenous community of youth "otherness" in contrast to the majority communities.   Rather, it was the creation of "safety spaces" where peer group friendships were able to develop irrespective of territorial and ethnic allegiances, age, gender, and faith.   There they were able to create a project where they could address and challenge others' responses to their multiple individual and group identities.   This in turn provided an opportunity for their voices at their most robust to articulate the discrimination and prejudice they experienced by those from the majority communities that allowed them to create a model of good practice and the anti-discrimination training resource through which they could address these issues with their peers.

CONCLUSION

This chapter began by rejecting the appropriateness of writing predominantly from within a reflexive idiom because neither my insight and histories nor those of the other participants were the principal issue here.   The moral and ethical basis for this chapter was to expose a process of working, privileged and preferred by the participants, that enabled them to build on shared concerns in a safe environment.   This in turn allowed for the conception, planning, and implementation of a training resource and this material is now being used to improve good relations more extensively in Northern Ireland.   What emerged from the procedure confirms fundamental principles of community development.   It was evident that given adequate tools, young people, irrespective of their age, ethnicity, faith, social status, baggage, and cultural expectations can, through their dynamism and potential, bond and bridge gaps between themselves that adults have not yet been able to address.

---

[119] Director Gurinder Chada explores this issue of the insider-outsider status, along with the ethnicity and culture of young Asians in Britain in a number of her films and documentaries including *I'm British But.., Bhajis on the Beach,* and *Bend it like Beckham.*

In this instance, their results were not used for individual cathartic purposes as had initially been desired but, rather, were developed into a good practice resource for the wider benefit of Northern Ireland society. The youth who participated in the research inherently understood that their revolt was not just possible but necessary to ensure that policy is not built on narrow conceptions of a "Bhaji and Bagels" approach to inter-culturalism. The consultation process that they rejected had come to artificially represent the totality of their expected contribution to policy development. What they replaced that with was the creation of a resource that represented an opportunity for them to create change and influence decision-making that impacts on the quality of their lives. In doing so they were also able to explore and strengthen social networks both within and without the communities that they come from and that they live alongside.

Because of the complexity of their multiple identities, some of the participants' friendships, just like the spaces in which they live, come from, and seek out remain contested in particular circumstances. But most still see one another, some regularly and others less so. But what they are all now able to do is to draw on a shorthand of a shared social capital that provides a collective buffer and boundary when they negotiate and renegotiate their relationships.

POST SCRIPT

It is September, 2005, and eighteen months on. I receive an invitation by phone from Raj to an event that he's organizing in the Indian Community Centre, a leadership course for young people from throughout Northern Ireland. He intends to use the *Think of Me* resource as a training tool. "Raj, I didn't think you wanted to continue with youthwork." "I don't, but this isn't work – it's just what we do to *make* things work."

Katy Radford
The Irish School of Ecumenics, Trinity College Dublin

REFERENCES

Anderson, B. (1983). Imagined communities: Reflections on the origin and spread of nationalism. London: Verso.

Brett, R., & Specht, I. (2004). *Young soldiers: Why they choose to fight.* London: Lynne Rienner Publishers.

Byrne, J., Conway, M., & Ostermeyer, M. (2005). Young people's attitudes and experiences of policing, violence, and community safety in North Belfast. Belfast: Institute for Conflict Research.

Clifford, J., & Marcus, G. E. (1986). *Writing culture: The poetics and politics of ethnography.* Berkeley and Los Angeles CA: University of California Press.

Cohen. A. P. (1992). Self-conscious anthropology. In J. Okely, & H. Callaway (Eds.), *Anthropology and autobiography* (pp. 221-241). London: Routledge.

Desai, S., & Subramanian, S. (2003). Color, culture, and dual consciousness: Issues identified by South Asian immigrant youth in the Greater Toronto area. In P. Anisef, & K. M. Kilbride (Eds.), *Managing two worlds: Immigrant youth in Ontario.* Toronto: Canadian Scholar's Press.

Fajerman, L., Jarrett, M., & Sutton F. (n.d.) *Children as partners in planning: A training resource to support consultation with children*. London: Save the Children.

Feenan, D. (2002). Community justice in conflict: Paramilitary punishment in Northern Ireland. In D. Feenan (Ed.), *Informal Criminal Justice*. Ashgate: Aldershot.

Hamilton, J., Radford, K., & Jarman N. (2004). Learning to listen: Young people and the police in Northern Ireland. *Youth and Policy. 84*, 5-21.

Hendry, J. (1992). The paradox of friendship in the field: Analysis of a long-term Anglo-Japanese relationship. In J. Okely, & H. Callaway (Eds.), *Anthropology and autobiography* (pp. 163-167). London: Routledge.

Matsunaga, L. (2000). Recollections of life crisis: Distancing the personal. In P. Dresch, W. James, & D. Parkin (Eds.), *Anthropologists in a wider world: Essays on field research* (pp. 167-185). Oxford: Berghan Books.

McCormick J., & Jarman, N. (2005). Death of a mural. *Journal of Material Culture, 10*(1), 49-71.

Mohanty Chandra, T. (1994). On race and voice: Challenges for liberal education in the 1990s. In H.A. Giroux, & P. McLauren (Eds.), *Between borders: Pedagogy and the politics of cultural studies* (pp. 145-166). New York: Routledge.

Murtagh, B. (2003) *The politics of territory: Policy and segregation in Northern Ireland*. Basingstoke: Palgrave.

Okely, J., & Callaway H. (1992). *Anthropology and autobiography*. London: Routledge.

Okely, J. (1994). Thinking through fieldwork. In R. Burgess, & A. Bryman (Eds.), *Analysing Qualitative Data* (pp. 18-34). London: Routledge.

Rabinow, P. (1977). *Reflections on fieldwork in Morocco*. Berkeley and Los Angeles: University of California Press.

Radford, K. (2004a). *Count me in*. Belfast: Save the Children.

Radford, K. (2004b). Red, white, blue and orange. An exploration of historically bound allegiances through loyalist song. *World of Music, 46*(1), 71-89.

Radford, K., Hamilton J., & Jarman, N. (2005). It's their word against mine: Young people's attitudes to the police complaints procedure in Northern Ireland. *Children and Society, 19*(5), 360-370.

Rappaport, N., & Dawson, A. (1998) *Migrants of identity: Perceptions of home in a world of movement*. Oxford: Berghan Press.

Scholte, B. (1972). Toward a reflexive and critical anthropology. In D. Hymes (Ed.), *Reinventing anthropology* (pp. 430-457). New York: Randon House.

Scourfield, J., Evans, J., Shah, W., & Beynon, H., (2005). The negotiation of minority ethnic identities in virtually all-white communities: Research with children and their families in the south Wales valleys. *Children and Society, 19*, 211-224.

Shephard, C., & Treseder P. (2002). *Participation Spice it Up!* London: Save the Children.

Smyth, M., & Robinson, G. (2001). *Researching violently divided societies*. London: Pluto.

Treseder, P. (1997). *Empowering children and young people*. London: Save the Children.

Van Manen, M. (1999) *The practice of practice*. In M. Lange, J. Olson, H. Hansen, & W. Bÿnder (Eds.), *Changing schools/Changing practices: Perspectives on educational reform and teacher professionalism*. Louvain, Belgium: Garant. Retrieved September, 2005

http://www.phenomenologyonline.com/ max/articles/practice.html

TONY MORGAN AND VASINTHA VEERAN

WINNING THE WAR:
RHETORIC OR REALITY FOR YOUTH IN NORTHERN
IRELAND AND SOUTH AFRICA?

ABSTRACT

The foci of this paper are the similarities and differences of youthwork between
South Africa and Northern Ireland, within the framework of understanding social
capital in a post-conflict sense. Youthwork, in order to make a profound impact on
the youth, needs to understand influences at a macro-, mezzo-, and micro-level.
This includes the legacy of violence that has been structurally perpetuated and
often casts a veil over youthwork practice. Youthwork policy in a post-conflict
situation is influenced by the pre-conflict and conflict stages. This results in policy
and practice that reinforces the norms of inequality which are often the
precipitating factors for the violence in the first place. Youthwork policy and
practice fails to recognize the nature of inequalities in a post-modern society. The
divided societies of N.I. and S.A. appear to be further apart in terms of integration
and the distribution of resources.

Northern Ireland and South Africa remain battlegrounds of intense internal
political strife. Although the design of the conflict within these countries is
conceptually different, the social, physical, and psychological impact on its
recipients seldom differs. The historical background of apartheid and the troubles
of Northern Ireland are not only central to the development of youth programmes
but directly and indirectly influence how policy is shaped. Northern Ireland, like
South Africa, is in the process of moving from a conflict situation to a post-conflict
situation. Although the troubles of the North are not as institutionalised as those
experienced by black South Africans during the apartheid regime, the scourges that
face both societies are very real and, indeed, rooted in a long-standing relationship
with politics and propagandist ideology (Veeran, 2002). Any work undertaken with
youth within these contexts needs to be aware of these "imbedded" issues in order
to understand the barriers to progress.

The conflict perspective espouses that violence and its sequalae are central to
our understanding of societal structures, influencing and shaping our thinking and
social conscience. Macionis and Plummer (2002) "envisage society as an arena of
inequality that generates conflict and change" (p. 24).   The ongoing conflict
between dominant and disadvantaged groups revolve around factors such as

*Doug Magnuson and Michael Baizerman (eds), Work with Youth in Divided and Contested
Societies*, 153–163.

gender, race, class, and ethnicity. Young people, especially young men, are--through their masculine culture and upbringing--prone to violence as a means of moving through the rites of passage. Many young males in deprived areas see it as desirable and as a means of survival. Regrettably, in the face of extreme manifestations of violent behaviour, violence has been sanctioned as an acceptable means of socialization, discipline, and social control (Henderson, cited in Barbarin & Richter, 2001).

THE IDEOLOGY OF YOUTHWORK

The practice of youthwork is a complex process that is influenced by various factors. Of significance is the context within which it is practiced. As agents of social change, youthworkers have to be aware of the ecological context (macro), which includes the legacy of violence, the needs of the youth (micro), and the objectives and philosophy of the agency (mezzo). This complex set of interacting variables makes youthwork a difficult proposition in normal society, let alone contested spaces. With this in mind, youthwork can be interpreted by drawing on the ideology of social capital.

Social Capital and Youthwork in Conflict Societies

Not only is there a need to rid the community of the prevailing conflict and its sources, it is also imperative that any lasting and sustained change must also be accompanied by changes in frames of minds. It is from this perspective that the significance of social capital in youthwork practice is being viewed. Not only has conflict left many young people emotionally traumatized and psychologically alienated, but it has also disconnected and isolated them from social networks within the community often exacerbating deprivation. In acknowledging the role that young people play as the interface between the past and the future, Veeran (2003) stresses the need to heed the call for greater investment in social capital. Bourdieu (cited in Field, 2003) stated that social capital "...is the sum of resources, actual or virtual, that accrue to an individual or a group by virtue of possessing a durable network of more or less institutionalized relationships of mutual acquaintances and recognition" (p. 15).

Veeran (2003) says that investing in social capital among young people reinforces their interconnectedness. The level and extent of interconnectedness is variously experienced in the N.I. and S.A. contexts. For example, in South Africa this distinction is made based on the unique characteristic of *Ubuntu,* which means "a person is a person through other people" (Veeran, 2002, p. 102). *Ubuntu* exemplifies community as the locus of human relations and in doing so reflects a differing view from the dominant Western (in this case N.I.) emphasis on community and relationship. The West views an individual as a discrete entity and the predominant African view stresses context and relationship to others with emphasis on the community (Musa & Fraser, cited in Veeran, 2002). The nature of youthwork may, therefore, be influenced by either an approach that espouses the development of the individual as the primary focus of the work with the community having a less significant role to play or the collective needs of the community with the individual being an integral part of a wider social grouping.

Field (2003) states that "relationships" are central to the understanding of social capital. If we accept Field's version of social capital, then it seems logical to assume that youthworkers can contribute to building social capital, as relationships are the basis of their work. Building networks and shared values are at the heart of power or influence in the social setting that people find themselves. However, what Field leaves open to speculation are the essential ingredients for relationships. In addition, he adds that there is a dark side to social capital. By this Field means that some relationships can lead to members of society being part of a clique or prescriptive set of values without even knowing they are part of these pre-designed phenomena. But the dark side of social capital offers a most interesting insight and will be discussed later. (It was in N. I. that Field conducted his research).

Bourdieu (cited in Field, 2003) also believed that in order for social capital to maintain its values, individuals had to work at it. However, Bourdieu saw social capital in terms of a hierarchical structure with the capital coming from the possibility of creating social inequality and, hence, equality as a vehicle for those in power to decide what equality meant. Bourdieu's insight into social capital revealed "… different individuals obtain a very unequal return on a more or less equivalent capital (economic or cultural)" (p. 16).

For Bourdieu social capital simply was about using it to reduce inequality among people. He further concluded that capital is gained through solidarity within networks and is only possible because membership gives rise to profits, both materially and symbolically. In applying this theory to youthwork, the cultural deficit may be evident in the lack of creative and resourceful ways of confronting and addressing conflict. Youth are generally the vehicle through which cultural perceptions and practices are transmitted. So, in essence, practitioners are tasked to build on the social capital reserves of young people in a way that they will be able to heal fractured relationships. This is easier said than done. The problem arises when the divided society compounds the problems associated with moving outside their comfort zone, as shown by the example from Belfast where young people wanted a job in their own area and felt unsafe looking for employment outside the area. The practice of youthwork in these contexts has to deal with competing variables that are detrimental and compromise the development of useful social capital of youth in disadvantaged situations.

While the preceding discussion highlighted that macro-level factors are critical in the development or non-development of social capital, we see also that it can be influenced by micro-level factors. At this level peers are deemed to be an important source of social capital. Coleman (1961) suggested that peer influences (including disapproval) were more likely to shape teenagers' views than those of responsible adults such as parents or social workers (cited in Field, 2003, p. 22). This moves social capital into the realms of negative equity, especially where negative influences and experiences dominate. Indeed, Coleman and Hoffer (1987) state that communities were a source of social capital that could offset some of the impact of social and economic disadvantage within the family. Social capital, while being caught up in the collective conscience of a community, nevertheless has to deal with the more individualistic modern society, especially in youthwork.

Social capital can be influential on what is assumed to be traditional youthwork, and it challenges sectarian behaviour. For example, some youthworkers in N.I. are themselves from the same background as the youth and are sometimes accused of not challenging sectarian behaviours and, more seriously, of colluding with this type of behaviour due to their political and religious background and beliefs (Jeffs & Smith, 1990).

Putman (2003) explains that by deconstructing social capital into bridging (inclusive) or bonding (exclusive), one can identify its deficits or influence. He suggests that the former is about building linkages between citizens and external assets for greater reciprocity and collectiveness. Bonding is about reinforcing exclusive identities and the maintenance of homogeneity that widens the gap between citizens (deemed to be at the bottom of the social scale in terms of power and influence) and the wider social structure. This relates to the challenge between the collective interest at local level and the more individualistic approach of agents of change in society, such as school and the pursuit of individual credentials.

Fehnel, Sisulu, Kodwa, Mohamed, and Perold (2000) emphasized the importance of *bridging networks* as a key element in the process of building social capital in South Africa's highly fragmented society. Bonding networks were much more prevalent among the disadvantaged groups in South Africa, where common themes of suffering, deprivation, and conflict kept communities focused and united in order to counter these adverse social conditions. The value of bonding is well articulated by Kawachi & Berkam (1997): "Strong networks can provide a context where young people acquire a sense of status and self-esteem that promotes their integration into the wider community, with a particularly marked impact in reducing the prospect of conflict" (p. 121).

The focus of youthwork can, therefore, offer youth the opportunity to determine what type of social capital they need but, more importantly, how they can achieve it. This means that they can use youthwork to complement aspects of social, cultural, economic, and intellectual development that will enhance their chance of material well-being in personal terms. However, it may also mean that youthwork enhances the very social capital that gave rise to violence in the first place, for example, poverty, lack of housing, and low educational achievement. Social capital may draw from some of the less desirable aspects of society such as inequality and disadvantage that were present before, during, and after the violence.

It is to the dark side of social capital that we turn. Is the work, even if rhetorically correct, nevertheless having little or no impact on the lives of young people in areas of conflict? Field and Schuller (2000) say that social capital helps reinforce inequality and anti-social behaviour. They state that cooperative actions that benefit the participants may produce undesirable effects for the wider society or negative externalities for participants. They are referring to the role of paramilitaries and freedom fighters, in the context of N.I. and S.A., and suggest that social capital, like any other form of capital, can be used towards malevolent purposes. This has resonance for N.I. and S.A. where group solidarity in human communities for survival and safety is often purchased at the price of hostility towards out-group members. Field (2003) believes that "...hate groups...benefit from access to reserves of social capital just as much as anyone" (p. 73). An example of this is that access to different networks is unequally distributed. Field cites the example of education as a way of perpetuating inequality. In N.I., this is achieved by the middle classes holding onto power through the use of examinations within the school system, while in S.A. the power to withhold education from most blacks perpetuated inequality. Education is used to keep young people out of a very important social capital vehicle.

Bourdieu's (1997) account of the abuse of social capital shows how social capital remains the property of privileged groups alone through what he called "mutual back-scratching and self-advancement." Youthworkers, according to Field (2003), who are often indigenous to disadvantaged communities "also tend to have networks which are made up of people in a similar situation to themselves, who are therefore of only limited use in accessing new resources" (p. 78).

Therefore, while inequality is an aspect of social capital, especially where violence is consequential to the development of a certain type of capital, youthworkers may have little or no influence in creating additional social capital that is both useful for young people and free from social inequalities. In some communities in N.I. and S.A. the paramilitaries and gangs employ young people to sell drugs, steal, and hijack cars, thus creating employment and indeed a form of perverse social capital which can, at a later date, be cashed in for violent behaviour deemed necessary for the so called protection of the community.

Social Capital and Single Identity Work

Using the N.I. experience, Field (2003) draws attention to inequality in areas of both deprivation and conflict.

> ...much community development work has historically been concerned with building social capital through single identity work, designed to build community confidence to a level where people are prepared to engage in the risky and painful process of attempting reconciliation across the two communities. Yet... this rests on a "spurious and uncertain connection" between two quite different processes, and the end result – intended or not – may be to build exclusive bonding forms of social capital... (p. 131)

On the one hand, youthworkers have to develop the individual within a community while at the same time deal with the inequalities of the social structure they find themselves working within. Harland, Muldoon, and Morgan (2005) showed that one of the main functions of youthwork for young people is to give them coping skills to deal with their marginalized status through interpersonal development, but the link with social and human capital for employment was tentative.

The contexts of youthwork occur in a multi-system network, namely, the youth's daily life (micro), the web of interacting relationships between the family and community (mezzo and exo) and the culture and policies of society (macro). Given that youthwork does not occur in a vacuum, the influence of these systems cannot be ignored as highlighted by Vygotsky (1978) and Piaget (1964), who showed that collaborative learning was characteristic of teachers, parents, and peers who provide support and scaffolding for learning and development.

Through the network of relationships within the family, peers, school, and other social outlets, educational opportunities, life skills, jobs, and social support are envisioned outcomes. The case for community youth programmes have been strongly advocated in addressing conflict and violence as a symptom of structural discrepancy at the macro-level. In line with the dominant African culture in which the spirit of *ubuntu* is strongly entrenched, community youthwork in the South African context has a place, because it is based on developing social capital that is about the collective needs of society and the need for citizens to feel part of the "new" post-conflict society. The norms, through the collective *ubuntu* ideology, permeate youthwork principles in both word and deed. South African youthworkers are advocates on behalf of, and with, the youth of the country. This has led to a rejection of many practices from Western European culture, which some South Africans see as barriers to the development of a collective approach to youthwork.

One example cited by visiting youthworkers from S.A. to N.I. was the use of youth clubs to carry out youthwork. The comments were simple but insightful in that they wanted to know why young people attended the youth club nearly every night and why their parents and families were not part of the young persons' youthwork experience. In N.I., the reverse may be applicable. For example, in N.I. youthwork is synonymous with a strong youth service (statutory) and a healthy voluntary youth culture. Young people are well serviced in this part of the world, but one of the consequences is the lack of control they have over this youthwork. Indeed the continued bureaucratization and litigation through rule and regulations has made youthwork nearly impossible in this part of the world. This is an indication of the playing out of Western culture on the shape and impact of risk taking in youthwork.

CHALLENGING CURRENT MODELS OF PRACTICE

Understanding youthwork practice in N.I. starts from the strategic plan of the Youth Service of Northern Ireland (Youth Council for Northern Ireland, 2003). This states that youthwork should contain a central theme of personal and social development, a commitment to preparing young people for participation, testing values and beliefs, and promotion of acceptance and understanding. The strategy also indicates that young people should take responsibility for their own actions and, in order to achieve these central goals, the model suggests that youthworkers are required to "...pay careful attention to all the elements of the Model, have a knowledge of social structures and policy, have high levels of youthwork skill and a deep understanding of educational/youthwork theory and methodology" (p. 17).

No reference is made to the issue of inequality inherent in society. The document is largely reflective of the Western world's obsession with administration and accountability in terms of protecting the agency against litigation. Youthworkers decry the problems they face with mountains of paperwork and accountability around issues that are normally unrelated to their practice. Another example explains the disconnect. The mission statement of the Youth Council for Northern Ireland's *Strategy Document* states, "To ensure opportunities for children and young people and young adults to gain for themselves knowledge, skills, and experience to reach their full potential as valued individuals" (2003, p. 1).

A critique of this statement would be difficult, as would a more concrete measurement of the outcomes or outputs that the strategy espouses. The issue is that the rhetoric may not reflect the needs of the youth on the ground and, to be more cynical, the dominant language makes life more difficult for those on the ground to work out exactly what it is that is on offer from a youth service. What exactly does reaching their full potential mean to many youth who are still living with the trauma of a post-conflict and divided society? This area of work requires much more empirical research.

Suffice to say that in N.I. there are policy documents for nearly everything and procedures for doing nearly every aspect of youthwork. However, the question is whether this is helpful to the development of young people and whether this model can be replicated in South Africa in terms of what is expected from those involved in youthwork.

One could argue that the importance of this language is that it reflects a movement in N.I. accentuated by the European Union towards accountability. Without these outcomes that are more about accountability, targets, and outputs rather than personal growth and integration, funding will not take place and financing for further development will be curtailed even though most workers see European funding as additional bureaucratic paperwork which is soul destroying. Accountability has a way of assuming a certain middle-class nature, which uses the dominant language and is often an anathema to the practice of youthwork. This is because many of them see it as impingement on the time they have to work directly with young people. Often they will say that if they wanted to work in an office they would not have become youthworkers. The challenge for youthworkers is to define a new language that underwrites the "real" values and contributions of youthwork in a post-industrial world but which will be cognizant of youthwork in S.A. and N.I. as they are at different stages in post-modern development industrially, economically, and socially. Similarities exist in youthwork in N.I. and S.A. especially in the relationship between the rhetoric and the reality of youthwork. South Africa and Northern Ireland are two distinct cultures with varying post-conflict contexts that are underpinned by different economic stages of development, varying interpretations of a post-conflict situation, developing capitalistic material well-being and, therefore, *de facto* different needs in terms of youthwork.

In contrast to the South African context, youthwork in Northern Ireland is highly structured and organized and is regulated by youthwork policy, legislation, and practice that are supported by human and financial resources. However, bureaucracy has suffocated the basic fundamental principles of youthwork in N.I. The further bureaucratisation of this basic work through administration and deconstruction has resulted in a fragmented service. While all the parts of the jigsaw are present in the *Model of Effective Practice* (2003), the big picture is missing.

South Africa, on the other hand, can point to fundamental needs of youthwork, which has a resonance with the N.I. experience at the turn of the century and what made the work meaningful, for example, nurturing, educating, and protecting youth. In much the same way as N.I., the rhetoric of having well articulated policies also pervades youthwork in South Africa. Yet, it remains aloof from grassroots youthwork. Great strides have, however, been made in youthwork within the new South Africa, but its impact is yet to be felt. For example, there is a National Youth Policy (1997) that youth helped create. The most recent developments relate to the recognition of Child and Youth Care Workers as a profession (South African Council of Social Services).

Notwithstanding the structural discrepancies, these developments illustrate that the intent and purpose of youthwork is becoming more evident as well as carving a niche for itself. However, in contrast to N.I, most youthwork in South Africa is provided under extreme constraints, not least of which is the lack of appropriately trained youthworkers. The backlog created by the omission of services to young people for decades by the apartheid regime makes this an enormously difficult task for the development of youthwork. Thus, both regions are still drawing on structural understandings that were present before the violent struggles. This has led to a reduction in the impact of youthwork. The ending of violence or the struggle(s) within both communities has led to the assumption that things are better for marginalized youth and that youthworkers can "now" move onto more important work with young people. Yet the reality is that life for many marginalized youth is still unacceptable and, although the violence has been reduced, they have not seen any direct benefit.

IMPLICATIONS FOR YOUTHWORK

What does this mean for youthwork in conflict situations in both countries? It may mean that youthwork needs to take more notice of the economic well-being of young people as a pathway out of poverty and deprivation. But although many of the ills of society are perceived as the menu from which youthworkers can choose, this has, according to research by Harland, Morgan, and Muldoon (2005), led to confusion about what exactly youthworkers do or think they do.

There are two common constants in both countries that are worth noting in terms of dealing with conflict in divided societies. One is that some young people need additional support from adults at certain stages in their development. This depends on their social, economic, emotional, physical, and material situation and is dealt with by a variety of groups, including youthwork. Secondly, the context in which they live is additionally made difficult by either political conflict or the legacy of conflict. This leads to compounded problems for youth at times when they are both going through personal change in a context of social change. Added to this problem is the difficulty of shaking off the dark side of social capital or the legacy of violence associated with some areas. Workers in these areas need to be developed to use the full range of resources that impact on social, economic, and intellectual development rather than drawing only on their contextual and often limited understanding of social change. They should additionally be aware of how the legacy of violence has hindered their understanding of the macro-economic influence on youthwork and their role in this change.

The only thing that does not change is that there are young people having to deal with these societal changes, which are so complex most adults never fully understand them, never mind deal with them in any meaningful way. One example of a strategy for dealing with conflict is from S.A., where some of the principles espoused in the Truth and Reconstruction Process (post-apartheid programme to address the conflict and its sequalae) are also evident in the juvenile justice programmes.

Youth involved in violence and conflict participate in a Youth Empowerment Strategy (YES), which focuses on helping them to acknowledge their role in perpetuating conflict and violence. In doing so, the youth engages in a cathartic process that precedes the ability for acknowledgement and acceptance. It is expected that this will prepare youth for atonement, repentance, reparation, and compensation (Veeran, 2002). Examples of the success of this programme have been documented from pilot projects undertaken by the Inter-Ministerial Committee on the Transformation of Child and Youthwork (1996). The authors believe that the answer, therefore, lies with the young person being given the skills to navigate a world that is changing irrespective of what that change looks like. It could be change to their family life, personal sexuality issues, social problems, bullying, or emotional and physical issues etc. Young people need to be offered training to become self-aware, to understand the context in which they live, and what this means truthfully for their development.

Regrettably, some youth in both contexts have perceived violence to be the only way of dealing with conflict. However, the belief in non-violent social change can transform one's conflict management strategies and techniques. The case, therefore, for conflict resolution skills to be part of the educational programmes is a compelling and common approach for youth from N.I. and S.A. Some subjects in school should be jettisoned in favour of informal educational approaches to learning. Learning should be central to educational institutions, not subjects, and there should be a role for informal education organisations to deal with issues, including conflict resolution and truth. Dealing with conflict as if it was outside the normal issues for young people is doing both the young people and their needs a disservice.

CONCLUSION

Youthwork and youthworkers are at a very interesting phase of development in the post-conflict societies of N.I. and S.A. Youthwork is at the interface of deficits (as a result of the conflict) and potential for change (post-conflict). Notwithstanding the socio-economic differences between the two countries, they face the same challenges of transcending micro, mezzo, and macro barriers to the development of social capital. On the micro-level, youthworkers need to broaden their horizons and embrace ideologies external to their worlds and recognize diversities in beliefs and values of society as a whole. Youthworkers will give young people coping skills to deal with difficult compounded situations that will give them the inner strength to move forward (whatever that means for them) in a constructive and self-preserving manner, such as returning to education to achieve qualification or dealing with life in a violent situation.

On a mezzo-level, for some youthworkers autonomy and self-belief comes from local involvement in response to violence and conflict. The local arena offers a sense of local democracy for those left behind and for those who do not want to or cannot move on. On a macro-level, organizations that are charged to deal with these difficult situations may, as Hamilton (2002) suggests, have the rhetoric through the dominant literacy but lack the tools to create an impact on the ground because of the confused and confusing message they are trying to get across to individuals who are working from a different frame of reference about the perceived and real needs of marginalized youth.

Tony Morgan
University of Ulster
Vasintha Veeran
National University of Ireland, Galway

REFERENCES

Barbarin, O. A., & Richter, L. M. (2001). *Mandela's children: Growing up in a post-apartheid South Africa.* New York: Routledge.

Beck, U. (1999). *World risk society.* Cambridge: Policy Press.

Beinart, W., & Dubow, S. (1998). *Segregation and apartheid in twentieth century South Africa.* New York: Routledge.

Bourdieu, P. (1984). *Distinction: A social critique of the judgement of taste.* London: Routledge.

Bourdieu, P., & Wacquant, L. (1992). *An invitation to reflexive sociology.* Chicago: University of Chicago Press.

Coleman, J. S. (1961). *Adolescent society: The social life of the teenager and its impact on education.* New York: Free Press.

Coleman, J. S., & Hoffer, T. (1987) *Public and private schools: The impact of communities.* New York: Basic Books

Connolly, P., & Maginn, P. (1999). *Sectarianism, children and community relations in Northern Ireland.* University of Ulster (N. I.): Centre for Conflict Studies.

Fehnel, R., Sisulu, S., Kodwa, G., Mohamed, N., & Perold, H. (2000). South Africa. In H. Perold (Eds.), *Worldwide workshop on youth involvement as a strategy for social, economic and democratic development.* Johannesburg: Knoxville Press.

Field, J. (2003). *Social capital.* London: Routledge.

Field, J., & Schuller, T. (2000*)*. Networks, norms and trust: explaining patterns of lifelong learning in Scotland and Northern Ireland. In F. Coffield (Ed.), *Differing Visions of the Learning Society: Research Findings.* Bristol: Polity Press.

Hamilton, M. (2002). Sustainable literacies and the ecology of learning. In R. Harrison, F. Reeve, A. Hanson, & J. Clarke (Eds.). *Supporting Lifelong Learning* (vol 1). London: Open University Press and Routledge.

Harland, K., Muldoon, O., & Morgan, T. (2005). *The nature of youthwork in Northern Ireland: purpose, contribution and challenges.* Department of Education (N.I.).

Jeffs, T., & Smith, M. (1990). *Young people, inequality and youthwork.* London: Macmillan.

Jeffs, T., & Smith, M. (1998).The problem of "youth" for youthwork. *Youth and Policy Journal, 62,* 45-66.

Jeffs, T., & Smith, M. (2002). Individualisation and youthwork. *Youth and Polciy Journal, 76,* 39-65.

Kawachi, I., & Berkman, L. (Eds.). (1997). *Social epidemiology.* New York: Oxford University Press.

Marcionis, J. J., & Plummer, K. (2002). *Sociology: A global introduction.* Harlow, England: Prentice Hall.

Morgan, T., O'Hare, B., & Campbell, H. (2001). *The excluded adolescent. An exploration of marginalised young people in Northern Ireland.* Belfast, N.I: YouthNet.

Mtshali, M. O. (1988). *Give us a break: diaries of a group of Soweto children.* Johannesburg: Skotaville Publishers.

Musa, F. (1997). *Cantilever, 4,* 4-9.

Nasson, B. (1986). Perspectives on education in South Africa: In S. Burman, & P. Reynolds (Eds.), *Growing up in a divided society.* Evanston, Illinois: Northwestern University Press.

Northern Ireland Government Statistics: WWW.NISRA@GOV.UK

Piaget, J. (1964). Cognitive development in children. *Journal of Research in Science, 2,* 176-186.

Veeran, V. (2002). Youthwork in contested spaces: A South African perspective of past legacies, present challenges and future prospects. *Scottish Youth Issues Journal, 5,* 93-106.

Vygotsky, L. S. (1978). *Interaction between learning and development.* Cambridge, MA: Harvard.

Youth Council Northern Ireland. (2003). *Model for Effective Practice.* Belfast, NI: Author.

ALAN GRATTAN AND SUSAN MORGAN

YOUTHWORK IN CONFLICT SOCIETIES: FROM DIVERGENCE TO CONVERGENCE

ABSTRACT

Based upon initial research in Northern Ireland and South Africa, this paper examines the role of youthwork and youthworkers in conflict and post-conflict situations. Using Antonio Gramsci's concept of the "organic intellectual," we argue that the youthworker as an organic intellectual is in a unique position to empower young people in the democratic political process. It is particularly critical in situations when communities are in the process of both divergence, moving towards conflict, and convergence, in the process of reconciliation and reconstruction. Youthworkers of and from the indigenous community can be the catalyst for understanding and expressing the common sense philosophy and worldview of the respective communities. As such, they can be key mediators in the divergent and convergent processes.

> *For all of our languages we can't communicate*
> *For all of our native tongues we're all natives here*
> *The scars of the past are slow to disappear*
> *The cries of the dead are always in our ear*
> *Only the very safe can talk about wrong and right*
> *Of those who are forced to choose, some will choose to fight.*
>
> *Natives,* by Paul Doran

> *It is the realisation that the most potent weapon in the hands of the oppressor is the mind of the oppressed.*
>
> Steve Biko

In the ten years following the initial ceasefire in Northern Ireland, many advances in socio-economic, political, and psychological terms have been made. As a result of the "end" of violence, a number of significant changes took place, including development of the local economy with inward investment aimed at regeneration and peace-building. Additionally, the development of new political structures not only increased dialogue between antagonistic political groupings but also created a new sense of political optimism. During the same period in South Africa similar significant developments took place. With the end of the oppressive

Doug Magnuson and Michael Baizerman (eds), Work with Youth in Divided and Contested Societies, 165–175.

apartheid regime, a sense of widespread optimism was underpinned with the development of new political arrangements that, for the first time, allowed political participation for the majority of the population. As an integral part of the nation building process, new programmes, including the regeneration of housing, education, and health, were initiated.

Despite this context of renewed optimism, Northern Ireland and South Africa remain contested spaces, which brings opportunities and challenges. In relation to Northern Ireland, the issue of contested spaces tends to be manifested through ongoing inter- and intra-communal conflict. This conflict involves paramilitary power struggles for control over territory but also control of economic opportunities. Within South Africa, contested space takes the form, again, of an economic and political struggle within the townships and informal settlements. It is also expressed in tensions and outbursts of sectarian violence between the various ethnic groups and communities.

Furthermore, the level and extent of external investment feeds a growing impatience (among indigenous communities) with the speed of reform and nation-building. Still, both societies are taking tentative first steps towards a new set of social arrangements. With the increased levels of inward investment, this will provide new opportunities in relation to education, skills development, employment, and increased potential for individual and communal prosperity.

The challenge, however, is to sustain such development, which will necessitate the embracing of cultural and religious diversity and an integration, respect, and understanding of the various established communal "certainties" and "truths." This will mean that animosity and fear must be replaced by trust and, in the short to medium term, an element of uncertainty and insecurity will remain. Given the generations who have experienced the conflict and violence in both societies, this will be a slow and developmental process.

Using the concepts of Gramsci and building upon Lederach's (2002) "Actors and Approaches to Peacebuilding Model," this paper will help clarify the unique contribution of youthwork in contested spaces to engage positively in developing the potential and capacity of young people in their immediate environment.

YOUTHWORKERS AS ORGANIC INTELLECTUALS

People [youthworkers] who work in these kinds of settings, with these kinds of issues are grounded in some kind of "programme theory, that is, they have some kind of idea of what they are setting out to do, and the ways in which they work are determined by a view of the world and a concept they want to change/make happen" (Youth Work in Contested Spaces, 2004).

In using the "Youth Work in Contested Spaces" (2004) terms of reference statement, we are suggesting that those indigenous people involved in youthwork have a view of the world embedded in the common-sense philosophy of their community borne of conflict emanating from their sense of oppression, injustice, and inequality. They recognise and understand the need to make positive change through a process of initiating the involvement of young people within their community. In this context the youthworker therefore takes on the role of the organic intellectual.

Gramsci's Concept of the "Intellectuals" and "Common Sense Philosophy"

> History and politics cannot be made without passion, without this
> emotional bond between intellectuals and the people-nation.
> Antonio Gramsci (Hoare & Nowell-Smith, 1971)

Gramsci was one of the most influential political activists and theorists of the 20th century and was imprisoned for his ideas by Mussolini. When sentenced to imprisonment in 1928, the prosecuting attorney is alleged to have said, "For twenty years we must stop this brain from working." Gramsci died in prison in April, 1937 (Hoare & Nowell-Smith, 1971).

Gramsci came from a poor and disadvantaged background and, as a physically disabled person, was subject to oppression and discrimination. As a young person he began to articulate his challenge to the existing social order. Gramsci's theory can be encapsulated in his most widely articulated phrase, "pessimism of the intellect, optimism of the will" (Forgacs, 1999). What Gramsci was referring to was the capacity and ability of the marginalised and subaltern groups in any society to achieve elements of power and control over their own destiny in the face of what appears to be insurmountable odds.

One way of understanding this process of change, according to Gramsci, is the central role of the organic intellectuals in developing an alternative or counter-hegemonic view of the world. Gramsci extends the definition of intellectuals to all those who have the function of organisers in all spheres of society including economics, politics, culture, and community. Each social grouping in society will have its intellectuals. Part of the role of these intellectuals is to articulate and disseminate the philosophy of that social grouping irrespective of their position within civil society. In this respect Gramsci also makes a distinction between organic and traditional intellectuals. Traditional intellectuals tend to be those who are seen as having a monopoly on what is deemed to be acceptable and legitimate knowledge. The traditional intellectual articulates the dominant ideology and in doing so helps perpetuate the position of the powerful and ruling groupings in state and society (Simon, 1986).

In contrast, Gramsci refers to the organic intellectual of the subordinate groups in society. These organic intellectuals arise from within and are of the subaltern peoples in any society. The organic intellectual makes sense of the world through a common-sense philosophy. In this context common sense philosophy is "The conception of the world that is uncritically absorbed by the various social and cultural environments in which the moral individuality of the average man [sic] is developed" (Forgacs, 1999).

Common sense philosophy must be seen as both a relative and dynamic concept due to the fact that it takes countless different forms in conformity with the immediate social and cultural context. In essence the organic intellectual must be able to analyse, understand, and intellectualise what may be seen as a "chaotic aggregate of disparate" commonsense views of the world that are "ingrained" within his or her own social grouping (Forgacs, 1999).

Therefore, part of the function of the organic intellectual is to articulate and disseminate this common sense worldview. They are essential in the development of the political consciousness of everyday life with the view to changing the position of their social grouping within civil society. It is from their indigenous position that they attain the passion and understanding of the people (Cavalcanti & Piccone, 1975). The contemporary history of both Northern Ireland and South Africa bears testimony to the idea that, despite long-term pessimism, dramatic change can take place when the will and optimism of the people prevails.

Much of the work with young people within the communities in Northern Ireland and South Africa is both significant and pivotal in relation to the reality of conflicted space. The majority of those organic intellectuals involved in youthwork operate, for the most part, according to a common-sense philosophy. Such a common sense philosophy is borne of their sense of belonging to a community that espouses a particular religio-political or ethno-political worldview and has shared experience of conflict. Furthermore, this sense of belonging brings with it an understanding of the psychological and sociological realities associated with this particular community. Such an understanding, in turn, brings with it a legitimacy, acceptance, and level of trust denied to those perceived as outsiders.

One of the difficulties of a common sense philosophy and the differing forms that it may take is spontaneous and *ad hoc* action based upon perceived localised and immediate needs. This may often be of a contradictory and counter productive nature, in that it may deal with a here and now individual or community issue, which runs counter to the core values, principles, and longer term aims of youthwork.

This is partly due to the existence of different interpretations of the community experience and the consequential actions, i.e. a violent response thereby exacerbating paramilitary activity or, alternatively, dialogues towards convergence and finding a solution. The inevitable co-existence of different interpretations of the common sense philosophy often leads to a contradictory consciousness pulling young people in different directions. Dealing with these contradictions is the reality and challenge for the organic intellectual/youthworker.

In conflict and, indeed, post-conflict situations, young people are often placed in a position where they must choose to defend their community or to resist involvement in direct action. Their choice depends upon individual worldview but also upon the intensity of the common sense philosophy of their community and peers. For the young person, involvement in direct action will bring peer group and community acceptance whilst resistance to such pressure may provoke both psychological and physical intimidation. Equally, the youthworker/organic intellectual will be placed in a similar position of maintaining the trust and respect of the community and young people according to the stance they take. To encourage or condone direct action runs contrary to the principles and practice of youthwork.

However, a positive aspect of the common sense philosophy is that the organic intellectuals are close to the issues that impact on the community and, by and large, they maintain the trust and credibility of those people, including the young people and those actively engaged in violent conflict. The youthworker as an organic intellectual is in a unique position to provide active, empowering, and sustained leadership.

> The mode of being of a new intellectual can no longer consist in the eloquence, which is an exterior and momentary mover of feelings and passions, but in active participation in practical life as constructor, organiser, permanent persuader, and not just a simple orator.
>
> Antonio Gramsci (cited in Hoare & Nowell-Smith, 1971)

The motivation of the youthworker as an organic intellectual is that through active participation with young people, they will improve the opportunities and the quality of life within their own communities, thereby building a more optimistic future. Additionally, this also has the potential for evolving into a form of participative and collective action, aimed towards achieving both social justice and social change. This in many respects is a common element that shapes youthwork in contested societies throughout the world.

YOUTHWORK: DIVERGENCE TO CONVERGENCE

Lederach (2002) identified the role played by local leaders at the grassroots level. He acknowledges their intimate and practical understanding of the people: "These people [grassroots leadership] understand intimately the fear and suffering with which much of the population must live" (p. 42). Those who Lederach refers to as the grassroots leadership (see Figure 1) we interpret as Gramsci's organic intellectual.

Lederach places the grassroots workers at Level 3 of his model. We, however, would take this further and suggest that the organic intellectual/ indigenous youthworker plays a more central role in divided societies. Whereas Lederach's model firmly locates the grassroots leaders within the peacebuilding agenda, further development of this model will help us to understand the place and role of the organic intellectual/indigenous youthworker in conflict and post-conflict societies.

We would suggest that the organic intellectual/youthworker is a significant actor at all levels and stages in both the divergence and convergence processes of societies experiencing the consequences of conflict. In this context, when a society or community is involved in the process of divergence, all attempts at avoiding conflict through mediation and dialogue appear to have been exhausted or rejected. In such a situation, society is moving towards confrontation or a military--as opposed to a political--solution.

In contrast, the process of convergence represents the end of conflict, or post-conflict phase. During this phase, individuals and communities move towards attempts at reconciliation and arriving at a political solution. While many issues still remain unresolved and tensions still exist between the parties to the conflict, nevertheless non-violent solutions are sought.

In both scenarios, the youthworker/organic intellectual can be, and often is, a key person and a catalyst of this process within the community (see Figure 2). In any society the monopoly of power and influence over civil society lies with the state. This is often maintained through a hegemonic process involving the combination of the establishment leadership, specifically, the military, professional

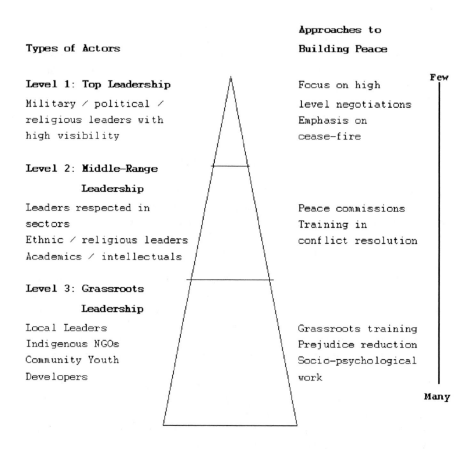

Figure 1 Actors and Approaches to Peacebuilding

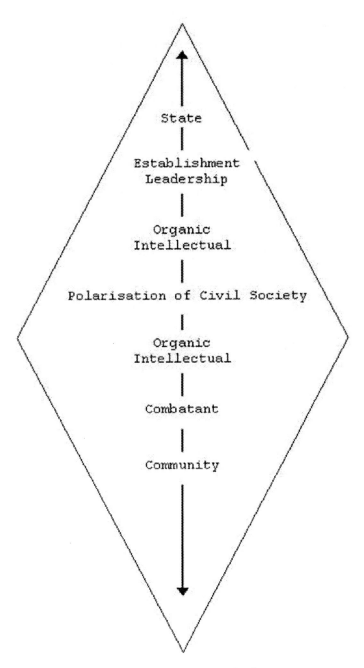

Figure 2. Model of Society in Conflict

politicians, judiciary, and so on, working in conjunction with the traditional intellectuals, specfically, lawyers, academics, and clergy. Together these groups maintain hegemonic consent for the dominant ideas of that society or administer the coercive means for its maintenance when it is deemed to be under challenge.

In a society where any community or social group perceives an injustice, often their course of action is to withdraw consent from the state. Some members of this community may be prepared to enter into violent struggle and conflict. The state response often results in coercive measures against that social group or community. Whilst generally violence emanating from a community is totally against the state and its representatives, it can also escalate into intra- and inter-communal conflict involving those who give active consent to the establishment and align themselves with the mechanisms of the state.

In this situation and when conflict is at its most intense, the communities from which the combatants arise will and do give varying degrees of active and passive support to those who take up arms. In short the combatants are of and from the community and as such are an integral part of that community. Without such indigenous community support the combatants cannot survive. Likewise, but in comparison to the combatant, the organic intellectual must also maintain an element of community support in order to be able to practice in an influential and effective manner.

It is in this extreme and competitive environment that the organic intellectuals such as youthworkers and community developers must operate. What the organic intellectual and the combatant have in common is the knowledge, experience, and understanding of the common-sense philosophy and worldview of their community. They also share the trust and credibility of the community. Where the organic intellectual/youthworker and the combatant diverge is in the application of their shared common-sense philosophy, with one taking direct violent action to effect social change while the other professes a more developmental route to change.

In the middle of any conflict scenario are the young people, some of whom are more directly affected than others. Of those young people who live with direct political violence in their community, some are often faced with the dilemma of how to respond to pressures imposed by their peers and significant adults to become involved with violence. This can also bring the youthworker into an ideological struggle with the combatant for the hearts and minds of the young, especially male, adult. The lure of the status and prestige afforded to young people who involve themselves in the violent conflict should not be underestimated. It is in this situation and against such pressures that the youthworker with a different view and approach to that of the combatant must operate.

The organic intellectual can be regarded, at times, as the voice of reason in the midst of what the rest of civil society and, indeed, the state see as a violent and untrustworthy community. The organic intellectual is in a pivotal position between their indigenous community and the rest of civil society and the state. As in Figure 2, the youthworker as an organic intellectual can be the conduit through which an exchange of ideas between the various levels of a society in conflict can pass through. In the case of both Northern Ireland and South Africa, youthworkers were often the mediators between paramilitary organisations, combatants, and the wider community authorities and politicians, between both the grass roots and the establishment but also between the various communities.

Because of this position and their ongoing work with young people, the organic intellectual/youthworker is engaging in a battle of ideas as to how to effect social change for the young person, their community, and society as a whole. In this context the youthworker may also be regarded as the catalyst to instigate a convergence of ideas and action in the peace building process. However, due to the experience of conflict for many young people any change must be seen as real and meaningful.

Given the nature and complexity of a conflict society, youthwork must be more sophisticated and adaptable to the various interchangeable and dynamic dimensions of the needs and realities of young people. Figure 3 is an attempt to provide an understanding of the different youthwork interventions by the organic intellectual at different stages from violent conflict and divergence through to the de-intensification of conflict and convergence.

During the phase of divergence, the common-sense philosophies and worldviews that influence direct action begin to become entrenched and find a degree of legitimacy and affirmation within the respective communities. In this phase dialogue is at a minimum, and those who advocate a violent and direct action approach to the resolution of difference challenge the role and influence of the organic intellectuals/youthworkers. This phase also sees the intensification of violent conflict and further polarisation of those directly affected by the conflict. The role of the youthworker in communities directly embroiled in the violence tends to be one of containment, of keeping young people away from direct confrontation and involvement while at the same time promoting reconciliation and understanding whenever possible.

In contrast the phase of convergence sees a de-intensification of violent conflict thereby providing opportunities for increased dialogue and communication. This is the phase when the organic intellectual/youthworker can build upon and develop the on-going work from the divergence phase. This phase brings more prominence to the work and the nature and focus is increasingly multifaceted. In this context the youthwork interventions must include political education directed at social change, nation building, and power sharing with the once perceived "other."

While elements of the same work are on-going in both the divergence and convergence phases, the level of violent conflict, the upheaval, and consequences in the immediate community environment tends to determine the emphasis and priority of the youthwork.

CONCLUSION

Given the longevity of the conflict and struggles in Northern Ireland and South Africa, the organic youthworker has grown up and developed a view of the world within the context of societal instability. Often this is the primary motivation to

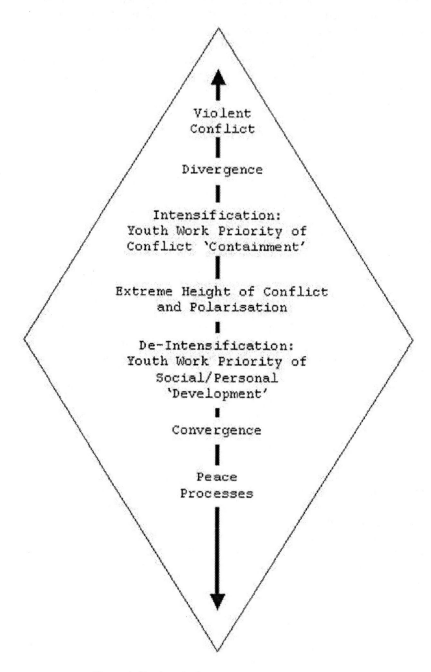

Figure 3. Youthwork: Divergence to Convergence

seek to improve the situation for young people within their immediate communities. Overtly underpinning much of the work within the communities is a commitment to bring about change for the better of young people. Central to this process is the work of the organic intellectual in empowering young people to bring about change for themselves. Whilst there are vast contextual differences between Northern Ireland and South Africa, one common element in many examples of youthwork is the central role of the indigenous community leader or organic intellectual.

Youthworkers in contested spaces are in the position to make a unique contribution to young people's capacity and potential to influence their immediate environment. This has been evident in the development of youthwork in both Northern Ireland and South Africa. Alongside the general issues and concerns experienced by young people that youthwork has responded to traditionally lies the added dimension of dealing with politically motivated violent conflict and its legacy.

In a fragmented political society it is even more crucial that youthwork has a political dimension. If young people are to become a part of a process that is sustainable, they need first to understand the political situation and also have a sense of their own power/ability to engage in their society to make a change for the better of themselves and others. Young people in Northern Ireland and South Africa have a political ideology deeply embedded in the worldview of their own communities. It is the right of young people to be afforded opportunities to explore, express, and develop ways to engage real political participation.

The youthworker is crucial to the development and process of the political empowerment of young people, with a unique potential to make the necessary links between the common sense philosophy and worldview of the young people from the subaltern groups and the wider socio-economic and political structures of society, thereby bringing young people into meaningful political participation.

Alan Grattan
University of Southampton, UK
Susan Morgan
University of Ulster, Northern Ireland

REFERENCES

Cavalcanti, P., & Piccone, P. (Eds.). (1975). *History, philosophy & culture in the young.* St. Louis: Telos Press.
Forgacs, D. (Ed.). (1999). *The Antonio Gramsci reader: Selected writings 1916-1935.* London: Lawrence and Wishart.
Hoare, Q., & Nowell-Smith, G. (Eds.). (1971). *Selections from prison notebooks of Antonio Gramsci.* London: Lawrence & Wishart.
Lederach, J. P. (2002). *Building peaceful societies.* Washington: Institute of Peace Press.
Simon, R. (1982). *Gramsci's political thought: An introduction.* London: Lawrence & Wishart.
Youth Work in Contested Spaces (2004). *Terms of reference document.* Belfast: YWICS.

KEN HARLAND

THE LEGACY OF CONFLICT IN NORTHERN IRELAND: PARAMILITARISM, VIOLENCE, AND YOUTHWORK IN CONTESTED SPACES

ABSTRACT

Since the early 1970s, the Youth Service in Northern Ireland has attempted to respond to the needs of young people within a context of extremely difficult and contested socio-economic and political circumstances. As our society emerges from a period of prolonged violence, old fears and traditions are still prevalent. Violence and paramilitarism has left its legacy, and there remain real threats and dangers. The delivery of youthwork in Northern Ireland faces both new challenges and exciting opportunities. This paper provides a brief context for the conflict in Northern Ireland and demonstrates the potential value and challenges of youthwork in contested spaces.

Reflection on any aspect of life in Northern Ireland must be considered in the context of a deeply divided and contested society emerging from over 35 years of conflict. Since 1969, Northern Ireland has witnessed widespread social, economic, and political upheaval through what is commonly known as "the troubles." Throughout this period, cultural and political identity has been fiercely disputed. Young people develop their sense of ethnic identity "in the midst of political crisis and sectarian confrontation" (Bell, 1990, p. 1).

Sectarianism and the effects of the troubles have had a significant influence upon young people growing up in Northern Ireland (Bell, 1990; Smyth, 1998). Connolly and Maginn (1999) found that sectarianism amongst children in Northern Ireland was rooted in their day-to-day experiences and, by the age of three, children had not only developed an understanding of the categories of "Protestant and Catholic" but were able to apply negative characteristics each to the other. Harland's (2000) inner-city Belfast study revealed that young males aged 14-16 grew up in polarized communities that made it difficult for them to build friendships and trust with young people from other traditions. They were wary of other males who were not part of their own peer group and extremely fearful of young men from other traditions. For these young men violence and the threat of violence was part of their everyday lives. They perceived social spaces such as schools as hostile environments where they increasingly felt marginalized, vulnerable, and anxious. They only socialized with their own mates and feared being alone. The fear that these young men feel is understandable when you

Doug Magnuson and Michael Baizerman (eds), Work with Youth in Divided and Contested Societies, 177–190.

consider that 9 of 10 of those killed during the Northern Ireland troubles have been male, with half between the ages of 15 and 29 (Smyth, 1998).

The fact that mainstream paramilitary organizations claimed to have ceased from violence in 1994 was irrelevant to the lives of these young men. Paramilitary activity such as punishment beatings, mutilations, and manifest forms of intimidation remained a constant threat that resulted in these young men feeling fearful and confused, particularly in regard to issues surrounding law and order. This is not surprising when you consider that from 1973 to 2004 there have been almost 3000 victims of shootings by paramilitaries (primarily on young males) and more than 2200 recorded victims of vigilante-style beatings (Kennedy, 2004). Complicating this further is the fact that in many communities throughout Northern Ireland the police are not formally recognized as a legitimate authority, and paramilitaries have become the informal police enforcing their own brutal forms of justice (Feenan, 2002).

"One of them pulled out an iron bar from inside a jacket and hit him across the face." This was the opening blow in an account of a paramilitary style beating on a 15-year-old boy who was taken to a bedroom by five masked men and was beaten with iron bars for twenty minutes (Irish Times, 12 March, 2001). This is a poignant reminder of the harsh realities of young peoples' lives in a society moving from conflict towards peace. The legacy of prolonged conflict has left many young people feeling trapped between the supposedly old rituals of violence and paramilitary control and the drive towards new and more democratic and inclusive processes. While the peace process has undoubtedly ushered a reduction in the number of paramilitary killings, there remains a strong paramilitary presence in the everyday life of working-class communities throughout Northern Ireland. For example, in 2002 there were 358 paramilitary style shootings, the highest level since the ceasefires in 1994, and 318 bombing incidents (Gordon, 2003).

There are also substantial financial gains for paramilitary groups through illegal racketeering. For example, a headline in the Belfast Telegraph, 7 October, 2004, stated that senior police linked a £1.2m. robbery of cigarettes in Belfast to a paramilitary group. Monopolizing the flow of drugs, alcohol, and cigarettes has become an important source of income for paramilitaries. Crucially, however, it has also generated bitter feuds between paramilitary groupings that have resulted in a spate of internal paramilitary shootings and deaths.

Whilst it could be argued that the majority of young people in Northern Ireland display resilience and have very successful outcomes (e.g. Muldoon, et al, 2000), a Cost of the Troubles study (Fay, Morrissey, & Smyth, 2003) revealed that the victims of the troubles have been overwhelmingly male with 3279 males being killed compared to 322 females. The study also revealed that the highest death rate for any age was for 20 to 24 year olds accounting for 20.2% of all deaths and Republican and Loyalist paramilitary organizations causing 80% of all deaths (Fay, Morrissey, & Smyth, 1999; Smyth & Hamilton, 2003).

Young people in inner city areas remain astutely aware of paramilitary presence and the very real threat it presents. This hidden reality is a complex political space in the psyche of young people throughout Northern Ireland. The legacy of the troubles has created an ambivalent consciousness of fear, injustice, anger, and apathy, particularly in relation to paramilitary activity. A poignant reality, however, is the fact that for some young people, particularly young males, joining a paramilitary organization can be a viable and even attractive option. The paramilitary call for solidarity and the potential financial benefits and status associated to paramilitaries have become a lure for recruitment. For those young people who choose not to join there is the danger of being singled out, which strikes fear into the heart of many young men.

These struggles undoubtedly cause acute stress and tension at an individual, family, and community level. Ferguson and Cairns (1996), in a study evaluating the effects of political violence on the moral development of young people in Northern Ireland, found that children from areas experiencing high levels of violence displayed lower levels of moral development than their counterparts from less troubled areas. They hypothesized that living in a relatively violent area may be a factor that adversely affects moral maturity. They also suggested that the segregation, sectarian attitudes, and negative stereotyping, more common in areas of greater conflict, may be hampering young people's progression to the highest stages of moral development. Ferguson and Cairns (2002) further suggest that "adolescents from areas characterized by high levels of political violence are more likely to cling to partisan ethno-political identities and provide greater support for the culture of violence" (p. 449).

THE BLUR BETWEEN PERPETRATORS AND VICTIMS OF VIOLENCE

A stable society is one understood to be characterized by people sharing a common sense of identity. In contrast, a contested society is one where there is no common sense of identity and where support for the institutions of the state are variable depending on the traditions and loyalties people belong to (Wilson & Morrow, 1998). In Northern Ireland the wider social context is characterized by a number of features that help construct and mediate the experience of political violence (Smyth & Scott, 2000). While throughout the Northern Ireland conflict it was predominantly young men who were both the victims and perpetrators of violence (Smyth, 1998), the distinction between victim and perpetrator can become blurred.

A recent study by YouthAction Northern Ireland (2002) explored the relationship between young men as victims and perpetrators of violence. For these 135 young men aged 14 to 25, violence and the fear of violence from paramilitaries and other young men within their community occurred in contested spaces such as school, geographical flashpoints such as interface areas, a contested space where two communities from different traditions are linked together, and city centers. Many of the young men also had experience of public violence (e.g. rioting, marches, sectarian and racial incidents, and alcohol related "weekend violence"), and several mentioned domestic violence. They spoke of a constant fear of being beaten and the threat of punishment and sectarian attacks. Bullying, both verbal and physical, was an ongoing hassle.

While the majority of young men perceived themselves as victims of violence, they were more reluctant to see themselves as perpetrators of violence.

They believed it was their duty to defend their family and community if under threat. In this capacity they believed violence was an acceptable response. They did acknowledge, however, that some forms of violence were unacceptable such as "attacking pensioners, child abuse, and paramilitary bullying." Importantly, however, they condoned the use of violence as a legitimate way of dealing with some of their problems. Additional to this was the buzz and excitement that many young men felt as a result of being involved in violence. Several young men perceived a society without violence as boring, suggesting that engaging in violence and other forms of risk- taking behaviour for some young males can be a rewarding activity.

Young people living in Northern Ireland have learned from the troubles that the use of violence can be a legitimate and effective way of resolving conflict. This is an important observation for those working with young people in spaces that are violently divided and contested. Firstly it challenges the assumption that all young people are opposed to violence as a means of conflict resolution. Secondly it demonstrates that some young people may be prepared to use violence to forward the cause they believe in. Thirdly it suggests that young people may struggle to identify any realistic alternatives to violence as a means of resolving conflict. These are powerful motivational issues that those working with young people in contested spaces need to consider.

Importantly however, this focus does not take into consideration the effect of violence upon the victim. There have been successful accounts in restorative justice programmes throughout the world that have encouraged perpetrators of violence to reflect upon the impact of their behaviour upon victims. Restorative justice seeks to meet the needs of victims, make offenders accountable for their actions, and offer a pathway into the community (McEvoy, 1998). Whilst to date this is not a formal aspect of youthwork in Northern Ireland, it has potential to help clarify the blur that exists between perpetrators and victims of violence. Particular challenges lie in discovering creative ways of engaging those who have been involved in violence to contribute to peace building programmes.

YOUNG PEOPLE IN CONTESTED SPACES

The young men in the YouthAction study reported that they did not talk to their parents or other significant adults about violence-related issues and did not think it was appropriate to talk to schoolteachers. They believed there were no real long-term solutions or alternatives to violence in Northern Ireland and felt powerless to bring about change. They were also confused and disillusioned in regard to political developments and struggled to see any immediate benefits to their communities of living in a post-conflict society. This raises concerns in regard to how young people in contested spaces seek emotional support. It also necessitates the need for more creative ways of engaging young people and exploring how they can play a more inclusive and influential role in building a post-conflict society.

This type of internalization also highlights a complex set of contradictions that may exist for young people within violently contested spaces. For instance, while young people may not wish to be violent, they may be fearful of the consequences of not being violent in certain circumstances. This necessitates that a young person must decide (often in a split second) which form of action they will take at a particular time. These subtle but profound decisions are negotiated by young people in many contexts, i.e. in school playgrounds, on the streets, in city centers, at football matches, on public transport, and they have important consequences. In these contested spaces young people can acquire status from their peers through their ability to fight or appear fearless. Conversely, young people, in particular young males, fear being shamed amongst their peers through their inability to defend themselves or their communities as this is contradictory to their masculine expectations.

At a recent conference in Northern Ireland, individuals told stories about how they became involved in violence as children and young people. For example one man from South Africa spoke of how defending your community was initially learned as a boy through using rolled-up newspaper as a sword. As this form of play developed the newspaper became short pieces of cardboard before being replaced eventually by a real knife.

While there are important lessons from these stories, they also present practical and ethical challenges to youthwork in contested spaces. Morally it could be questioned whether or not a former perpetrator of violence should have access to vulnerable young people as an educator. Conversely, a youthworker with this type of background is in a powerful position to empathize with young people in violently contested spaces and speak of the dangers whilst appreciating the potential benefits and acquired status that are often associated with violent behaviour. It must also be noted that many ex-members of paramilitary organizations have played a crucial role in the political search for peace in Northern Ireland. Similarly, the involvement of perpetrators of violence in youthwork has the potential to be an extremely effective dimension of conflict resolution. Paradoxically, in its attempts to attract young people away from violence to more democratic processes, the Youth Service in Northern Ireland could be perceived as in direct competition with paramilitary organizations.

YOUTHWORK IN CONFLICT SOCIETIES

Since the early 1970s, the Youth Service in Northern Ireland has attempted to respond to the needs of young people within a context of extremely difficult and contested socio-economic and political circumstances. As violence escalated in the early 1970s, youthwork attempted to keep young people out of trouble and off the streets (Smyth, 2001). As the Youth Service in Northern Ireland evolved, more specific initiatives were developed in response to the troubles around the themes of cross-community work and community relations. In 1992 Community Relations Guidelines produced by the Youth Council for Northern Ireland developed a five-level model of community relations. Crucially however, much of this work was based on a contact hypothesis (see for example, Amir, 1969; Pettigrew, 1986, 1997; Neins, Cairns & Hewstone, 2003) and avoided the more challenging and controversial issues associated with political education and civic responsibility (Smyth, 2001).

Wilson and Tyrrell (1995) described how the first contact projects in Northern Ireland were primarily concerned with bringing Catholic and Protestant children together whilst avoiding efforts at reconciliation between both communities. Smyth (2001) further claims that there has been a tendency amongst those who facilitate community relations programmes to attempt a position of neutrality or objectivity that has been underpinned by a fear of having one's core beliefs exposed. Connolly (1998) argues that much of this work may have actually been counter-productive and only served to reinforce existing stereotypes, while Bloomer and Weinreich (2003) found that community relations projects in Northern Ireland only partially achieved their intended outcome.

During the past number of years there have been significant trends in Northern Ireland society for a more consultative ethos through which young people were encouraged to become more involved in decisions affecting their lives (Youth Council for Northern Ireland, 1993). Terms such as participation, empowerment, education for citizenship, and rights and responsibilities reflect recent attempts to better appreciate youth potential and embrace diversity of culture. Understanding of the concept of citizenship is adapted from the late T. H. Marshall (1950) who suggested that citizenship was concerned with three main elements: the civil, the political, and the social.

The first comprises rights between individuals within civil society, the second defines individual rights *vis-à-vis* the state, and the third refers to entitlements to state-provided social programmes (Kelly, 2003). The Citizenship Advisory group (1998) stated that citizenship for education included learning about rights and responsibilities, community involvement, and political literacy. Citizenship education was a response by the New Labour government in the U.K. to apathy, ignorance, and cynicism about public life, lack of involvement in and community affairs, societal alienation from public values, and a low voting turnout by 18 to 25 year olds.

Despite this emphasis, many youthworkers in Northern Ireland have struggled to comprehend citizenship and question why citizenship education has become such a priority (Harland, Morgan, & Muldoon, 2005). Promoting an agenda for citizenship education and civic and democratic responsibilities with young people in communities who have experienced the brunt of sectarian violence is no easy task. It is understandable why certain young people may be suspicious of attempts to involve them in contributing to peace building processes. In such contexts, it is perhaps ambitious to expect youthworkers to be able to persuade particular young people of their future role in civic society.

Yet this is surely what lies at the heart of youthwork in a post-conflict society. Smith (1996) talks about supporting young people to have "civic courage:" the freedom to make choices and act upon them in relation to issues that affect their well-being and that of others in the face of contrary opinion or opposition. Whilst this aspiration is laudable, at present there are few structures in place to encourage those young people directly involved in violence or young people on the margins of society to engage in civic education.

It is important to note that not all young people participate on youth programmes, and significant numbers of young people who do participate on youth programmes disengage at an early age and struggle to identify any significant benefit from their involvement (Youth Council, 1998; NIVT, 1999). As noted by Geraghty, Breakey, and Keane (1997), "It would appear that neither the practice nor the ethos of Youth Service provision are either meaningful or relevant to them." This is not to undermine the dedication and commitment of youthworkers in Northern Ireland who have been at forefront of supporting young people at the sharp edge of community and political conflict. Nor should it deflect from the committed and sustained efforts made by practitioners and policy makers to establish clear principles for the delivery of youthwork in Northern Ireland.

The core principles laid down by the Department of Education (2003) are a commitment to preparing young people for participation, the promotion of acceptance and understanding of others, and testing values and beliefs. These three core principles underpin the personal and social development of young people and should be reflected in all youthwork. One constraint, however, is that the core principles can appear vague and do not specify how they can support or prepare young people for living in a society emerging from a period of prolonged conflict.

Recently, there have been two major Youth Service responses to further develop community relations work in Northern Ireland. Firstly, the Joint in Equity, Diversity and Interdependence initiative (JEDI) aims to:

- Develop a coherent strategy for community relations youthwork and education for citizenship.
- To embed the inter-principles of equity, diversity and interdependence into the ethos, policies, and programmes of organizations that make up the youth sector.[120]

Secondly, the Youthwork in Contested Spaces initiative was established in partnership between Public Achievement, The University of Ulster, and The Youth Council for Northern Ireland. This project aims to build the capacity of the youthwork community in Northern Ireland and to contribute to international best practice, particularly in preparing young people for life in a divided and contested society. Both these initiatives attempted to influence youthwork practice and policy in Northern Ireland by engaging young people in new and more creative ways. Morrow, Fyben, and Wilson (2003) argue that until recently "equity, diversity and interdependence have developed separately without any coherent strategy linking the strands" (p. 178). It has been a bold move by the Youth Service in Northern Ireland to attempt to implement equity, diversity, and interdependence as core principles of how youthwork should be implemented in the contested spaces of Northern Ireland.

The Youthwork in Contested Spaces initiative has enabled young people and youthworkers from other contested societies (i.e. South Africa, Serbia, Israel, Palestine, and Northern Ireland) to come together to share experiences, tell their stories, and provide insights into how they have survived their conflict.

---

[120] For more information on JEDI principles see Morrow, Eyben, & Wilson (2003).

Importantly, youthworkers from these countries have also had opportunities to share lessons from their youthwork practice with young people in their own contested spaces. Despite these exciting developments, huge challenges remain. Church and Shouldice (2003) suggest that sharing stories, experiences, attitudes, and feelings offer a spectrum of possibilities in conflict resolution beyond the direct programme participants. They add, however, that evaluation and measurement of such initiatives can be difficult and confusing, and whilst there is an assumption that any change transferred is positive, this is not always the case.

Youthwork in Northern Ireland is only beginning to understand and address the legacy of conflict and the potential role of education for citizenship. Although there are exceptions (e.g., Public Achievement and some youthwork programmes in schools) most youthwork in Northern Ireland occurs independently from formal education. In addition, the Youth Service in Northern Ireland receives only one percent of the overall budget for education, which seriously restricts the type of resources available to youth organizations. The influx of European Peace and Reconciliation monies as a result of the troubles has made a substantial contribution to youth programmes working with young people throughout Northern Ireland. It must be noted however, that this funding has been typically short-term and difficult to sustain (Harland, Morgan, & Muldoon, 2005).

PERSONAL EXPERIENCE OF YOUTHWORK IN CONTESTED SPACES

I have been directly involved in youthwork for twenty years. During this time I have worked with young people throughout Northern Ireland in both the voluntary and statutory youth sectors. In particular, I have worked with marginalized young people in inner-city areas who have witnessed the brunt of community and political violence. I have delivered youthwork throughout policy changes from cross community work to community relations work to implementing the principles of equity, diversity, and interdependence (EDI) and am currently involved in the Youthwork in Contested Spaces initiative.

For four years during the 1990s I worked on a project with the Belfast Education and Library Board called F.R.A.N. Each initial represented the first letter of four youth centers in Belfast, namely, Finaghy, Rosario, St. Agnes, and Nubia. The project operated during some of the worst periods of the Northern Ireland conflict. Two of the centers were Catholic and two were Protestant. Each year ten young people aged 14-18 years old from each centre participated on a 10-month programme that culminated in a seven-day visit to Formby, Liverpool. The project adapted the motto, "It is better to light a candle than complain of the darkness," reflecting the hope and optimism of the founders of the programme. The group met every Monday night and whilst the initial focus was contact it progressed to addressing more controversial issues such as identity and violence and difference.

I worked in a staunchly Loyalist area with a strong paramilitary presence, which made recruitment into programmes extremely difficult. Many young people were frightened to join as they feared the consequences of being associated with people from 'the other side'. Part of my role was to speak to parents and explain that community relations work was an important part of the youthwork curriculum. Whilst many parents accepted this, there were others who did not. Some withdrew their children from the youth center because they would be in contact with Catholics. Despite these difficulties, each year young people did fully commit to the programmes. Primarily this was due to the very positive feedback from members who had participated in previous years.

The main points I want to raise are related to personal safety, policy, and resilience. On several occasions when the bus arrived on a Monday evening to take us to the chosen venue, certain individuals (typically young men aged 15 to 17) from the local community would stand outside the center and direct verbal abuse at everyone involved. This was very intimidating and frightening. On one occasion I was struck on the head with an object. There were other occasions when the group could not meet because of troubles that had occurred that particular week such as shooting or a bombing in one of the areas. Despite such setbacks and personal fears, these young people were prepared to take huge risks, take a stand against personal threat, and build friendships with young people from another tradition who were perceived by many in their own community as the enemy.

I often questioned why, year after year, these young people continued to get involved in a youth programme that was potentially threatening and offensive to certain members of their community. For the young people I believed it was their desire for a better future without violence, hatred, and death. For other young people the programme was hope that life could be different. Whilst there were ongoing tensions during the ten month programme, the seven-day visit to Formby in England was always the highlight. Young people were able to relax and have fun in a safe and neutral environment. The masks they wore dropped and they could be themselves with young people regardless of what background or tradition they came from. Prejudices and stereotypes were challenged, and issues of identity became secondary to the overall experience.

One fundamental difficulty was the fact that when young people returned to their own contested spaces after the visit, they felt that the relationships they had established could not be sustained. Community pressures and old beliefs and attitudes quickly replaced the optimism that was generated during the programme. Many lessons have been learned through the myriad of community relations programmes in Northern Ireland. For the majority of youthworkers, however, the question of how to sustain community relations programmes in a divided society has not been resolved. Youthworkers still face the perennial problem that when young people go back into their own communities it is extremely difficult for them to maintain relationships with young people from other communities.

DRAWING PRACTICAL LESSONS FROM YOUTHWORK IN CONTESTED SPACES

This practical learning comes from studies and research in Northern Ireland with young people around the theme of violence and peace building. They are in no way meant to be prescriptive. Rather they are pointers to how youthwork practice around peace building has evolved.

Implementing the Principles of Equity, Diversity and Interdependence

At the core of the JEDI initiative was placing the values of Equity, Diversity, and Interdependence at the core of policy and operations. JEDI (2003) defines equity as a commitment to fairness, including the redressing of any identified undesirable or inequitable balance. Diversity encourages respect for and expression of the range of identities represented by young people in Northern Ireland and those who work with them in the youth sector. It is a source of celebration and interest as opposed to fear and suspicion. Interdependence recognizes and explores the ways in which our individual paths are intertwined. It is about building new relationships between the various people and groups in a pluralist society. These three principles are the building blocks of a society that functions in a sustainable and positive way. As such they are the also the building blocks of behaviour at the individual, institutional, political, and cultural level (p. 10).

The Creation of Safe Learning Environments

Harland, Morgan, and Muldoon (2005) found that youthworkers in Northern Ireland perceived building meaningful relationships with young people as the primary purpose of youthwork. The nature of this relationship is underpinned by the principle of voluntary participation and the fact that a young person can, at any time, withdraw from a programme, making youthwork distinct from most other professions working with young people. Morrow and Wilson (1998) argue that it is necessary to understand the importance of this relationship and to offer spaces where trust and difference is valued and alternatives can be imagined. Barriers that restrict young people from talking openly are related to personal safety, cultural identity, fear of being shamed, and lack of trust (Harland, 2001).

Improving Knowledge of Alternatives

Young people in the YouthAction study reported that they did not enjoy or relish many of the violent incidents in which they were involved, either as victims or perpetrators of violence. In many instances they were simply doing what they thought was expected of them or what they perceived as the only acceptable or safe option in the circumstances. They also perceived that the attitudes, values, behaviour, and lifestyles they were accustomed to were natural and normal.

Groupwork exercises such as role playing encouraged these young people to question norms and values and identify potential alternatives to violence in a context of personal safety. Individuals who were no longer involved in violence (such as ex-paramilitaries who were currently involved in containing violence) were brought into sessions to share their experience and tell stories about their role in violence. The young men quickly engaged with these older men who had, previously, been immersed in a world of violence. This type of intervention had a profound impact upon participants and enabled them to recognize that people who have been violent can change.

Skills Development

An important factor contributing to young men's involvement in violence was that they did not know how to evade violence or minimize the potential for conflict in certain situations. This can be attributed to a lack of skills in avoiding violence or an inability to choose potential alternatives. In order to improve knowledge of alternatives, a number of skills-development programmes were identified as relevant in supporting young men to make more informed choices in relation to violence and peace building. The themes for skills development included conflict avoidance, mediation, negotiation, self-defense, anger control, storytelling, identifying "red flags" (these were triggers that incited violence), recognition of feelings, and appreciation of masculinity.

The delivery methods encouraged young males to express themselves and reflect on their lives and experiences of violence. The programmes also demonstrated that these young men found discussion-based youthwork methods that engage, stimulate, and enthuse to be supportive, useful, and practical.

Combining Energy and Reflection

The approach and delivery methods used in the programmes were crucial in regard to the impact they had upon the young men's attitudes and behaviour. Young men said they found it useful to have a balance of interactive type exercises that harnessed their energy and creativity particularly when combined with sessions that facilitated reflective discussion and thinking.

Youthworkers as Educators

Youthworkers are in a powerful and unique position to positively influence young people. Their skills and knowledge enable them to build purposeful relationships with young people and offer them the possibility of change. Young people frequently cite the non-judgmental attitude and supportive approach of the youthworker as being central to their openness and comfort in expressing their views on violence and peace building (YouthAction, 2002). Their ability to engage young people effectively opens up the possibility of youthworkers reaching those who are on the very margins of society. This includes attempting to reach those young people who have been most affected by conflict. It also means engaging with those who have been both the victims and perpetrators of violence and attempting to engage them in dialogue as part of the quest towards a more peaceful and stable society. This may be perceived by many as a controversial and perhaps fanciful aspiration. However, in a society emerging from conflict to peace, part of any resolution must surely be to reach and engage those who have been most actively involved in the conflict.

CONCLUDING COMMENTS

Youthworkers, many of whom work at the coalface of community conflict, are in a unique and powerful position to engage with young people on programmes that facilitate personal growth and development. Crucially, through this relationship youthworkers have the opportunity to create safe spaces, as opposed to contested spaces, where young people can share their stories of violence and explore new possibilities.

Youthwork raises ethical questions about the motivational factors of youthworkers and the extent to which their political beliefs influence their relationships with young people. Further challenges exist in determining how best to engage and involve those who in the past have been the perpetrators of violence and are now willing to play an active role in resolving conflict.

At present there is ambiguity as to the role and contribution of youthwork in contested spaces or in societies emerging from a period of prolonged conflict. Clarity is needed in regard to how youthwork defines political and civic education and the extent to which this should be part of a youthworker's role. The youthwork curriculum in Northern Ireland addresses core issues of personal and social development: acceptance and tolerance of others and testing values and beliefs. Whilst this curriculum may be perceived as flexible and all embracing, it is perhaps too vague to support youthworkers in the delivery of youthwork in contested spaces. In addition, the outcomes of youthwork are often nebulous and difficult to measure. Although there is a danger of being too specific about measurable outcomes, there are growing demands from funders and policy makers in Northern Ireland for youthwork to produce more tangible forms of measurement and accountability.

Engaging and facilitating youthwork with young people in contested spaces is a challenging task. Addressing and facilitating potentially controversial issues with young people assumes that a youthworker possess certain skills, knowledge and attitudes. In recent years in Northern Ireland there has been a move away from generic youthwork practice that was typically carried out in youth centers to a more specialist form of youthwork that occurs in a wide range of settings. The craft of delivering youthwork in divided and contested spaces is an aspect of youthwork that should be reflected in the training of youthworkers.

Historically, the monitoring and evaluation of youthwork practice in Northern Ireland has been sporadic and not well documented. It will be of extreme value if the process of youthwork in contested spaces throughout the world is recorded and the learning shared with others. This in itself will demonstrate the value and potential of youthwork as an effective educational approach to engaging and supporting young people in contested spaces.

Ken Harland
University of Ulster, Northern Ireland

REFERENCES

Amir, Y. (1969). Contact hypothesis in ethnic relations. *Psychological Bulletin 71*, 319-42.

Bloomer, F., & Weinreich, P. (2003). Cross community relations projects and interdependence identities. In O. Hargie, & D. Dickson, D. (Eds.), *Researching the troubles: Social science perspectives on the Northern Ireland Conflict* (pp. 141-162). London: Mainstream Publishing.

Church, C., & Shouldice, J. (2003). *The evaluation of conflict resolution (part 11): Emerging practice and theory*. Derry/Londonderry: Incore Publications.

Connolly, P. (1998). Early years, anti-sectarian television – guidelines for a series of television programmes directed at anti-sectarian work with children in their early years. Belfast: Community Relations Council.

Department of Education, Northern Ireland. (2003). *Youth work: A model for effective practice*. Update 2003. Northern Ireland: Department of Education.

Fay, M., Morrissey, M., & Smyth, M. (1999). *Northern Ireland's troubles: The human costs*. London: Pluto Press.

Feenan, D. (2002). Community justice in conflict: Paramilitary punishment in Northern Ireland. In D. Feenan (Ed.), *Informal criminal justice*. Aldershot: Ashgate.

Ferguson, N., & Cairns, E. (1996). Political violence and moral maturity in Northern Ireland. *Political Psychology, 17*, 713-725.

Geraghty, T., Breakey, C., & Keane, T. (1998). *A sense of belonging: Young people in rural areas of Northern Ireland speak about their needs, hopes, and aspirations*. Youth Action Northern Ireland: Youth Action Publishers.

Gordon, D. (2003). *Police service Northern Ireland. First constables annual report*. Police Service for Northern Ireland Publications.

Harland, K. (2000). *Men and masculinity: The construction of masculine identities in inner-city Belfast*. Unpublished dissertation, University of Ulster, Northern Ireland.

Harland, K. (2001). The challenges and potential of developing a more effective youth work curriculum with young men. *Journal of Child Care Practice, 7*(4), 288-300.

Harland, K., Morgan, T., & Muldoon, O. (2005). *The nature of youth work in Northern Ireland: Purpose, contribution and challenges*. Research Report Commissioned by the Department of Education in partnership between the University of Ulster and Queen's University, Belfast.

Jarman, N., & O'Halloran, C. (2001). Recreational rioting: Young people, interface areas and violence. *Child Care in Practice, 7*(1), 2-16.

Joint in Equity, Diversity, and Interdependence (JEDI). (2002). *A framework for reflection in practice: Guidelines for embedding EDI principles in youth work practice*. Northern Ireland: JEDI Publications.

Joint in Equity, Diversity, and Interdependence (JEDI). (2003). *Placing the values of equity, diversity, and interdependence at the core of policy and operations* (Document One). Northern Ireland: JEDI Publications.

Kelly, D. (2003) *A study of the development of personal and social education and citizenship in a college setting*. Undergraduate thesis submitted to University of Ulster, Northern Ireland.

Kennedy, L. (2004). *Broken bodies, silenced voices: The paramilitary abuse of children in Northern Ireland*. Save the Children/Queens University: Belfast Publications.

McEvoy, K. (1998). Crime and punishment. Cited in *Andersontown News*, July. Belfast.

Morrow, D., Eyben, K., &Wilson, D. (2003). From the margin to the middle: Taking equity, diversity, and interdependence seriously. In O. Hargie, & D. Dickson (Eds.), *Researching the troubles: Social science perspectives on the Northern Ireland conflict* (pp. 163-182). London: Mainstream Publishing.

Neins, U., Cairns, E., & Hewstone, M. (2003). Contact and conflict in Northern Ireland. In O. Hargie & D. Dickson (Eds.), *Researching the troubles: Social science perspectives on the Northern Ireland conflict* (pp. 123-140). London: Mainstream Publishing.

Northern Ireland Voluntary Trust. (June, 1999). *Empowering young adults: Lessons from the unattached youth programme*. Northern Ireland Voluntary Trust Briefing Paper.

Pettigrew, T. F. (1986). The intergroup contact hypothesis reconsidered. In M. Hewstone, & R. Brown (Eds.), *Contact and conflict in intergroup encounters* (pp. 169-196). Oxford: Blackwell.

Pettigrew, T. F. (1997). Generalized intergroup contact effects on prejudice. *Personality and Social Psychology Bulletin, 23*, 173-85.

Smyth, M., Hamilton, J., & Thomson, K. (2001). *Age and generational politics in Northern Ireland's troubles and their consequences for justice and peace*. Paper to the British and Irish Social Policy Association's Annual Conference, July, 2001, Belfast.

Smith, A. (1996, June). *Education for democratic citizenship*. Consultation Meeting, Strasbourg, 1996.

Smyth, M., & Hamilton, J. (2003). The human costs of the troubles. In O. Hargie, & D. Dickson (Eds.), *Researching the troubles: Social science perspectives on the Northern Ireland conflict* (pp. 15-36). London: Mainstream Publishing.

Smyth, M., & Scott, M. (2000). The Youthquest 2000 survey. Derry/Londonderry: Incore Publications.

Smyth, P. (2001). Working with children and young people in violently divided societies: Papers from South Africa and Northern Ireland. In M. Smyth, & K. Thompson (Eds.), *Community conflict impact on children* (pp. 215-230). Belfast: Incore.

Wilson, D. & Morrow, D. (1988). *Supporting community youth workers in a contested society*. Northern Ireland: The Understanding Conflict Trust.

Wilson, D. & Tyrrell, J. (1995). Institutions for conciliation and mediation. In S. Dunn (Ed.), *Facets of the conflict in Northern Ireland* (pp. 230-250). London: St. Martin.

Young People Now. (2004, January). Modern folk devils. *National Youth Agency Publications* (pp. 14-15). Leicester, UK.

Youth Council for Northern Ireland. (1993). *Participation: Youth work curriculum guidelines* (pp. 9-10). Belfast: Youth Council for Northern Ireland Publishers.

Youth Council for Northern Ireland. (1998). *Benefits of the youth service: A study of the experiences of 14-18 year old members of registered youth groups in Northern Ireland*. Belfast: Author.

INTRODUCTION TO PROGRAMS AND ORGANIZATIONS

In these spaces much direct work with youth is composed of organizing and sustaining groups and organizations made up of young people and/or dedicated to helping them. Much indirect work for youth--work on their behalf--is also organization-bound, in that most of us work for, with, or against groups and organizations, and we envision, plan, and implement our purpose and activities through programs and organizations.

The programs and organizations included in this section are indigenous and international, charismatic and institutionalized, *ad hoc* and formal, political and apolitical. One characteristic that unites all of them is a developmental, political, and moral commitment to youth leadership of the organization.

Three sets of authors provided extended treatments of their organization: Rebecca Manski writes about Baladna, an organization of and for Arab youth inside Israel; Vesna Ognjenovic, Bojana Skorc, and Svetlana Ivackovic write about *Zdravo da ste*, including description of how social education and developmental principles can be applied to this kind of work, and Hammad and AlBakri write about the American Friends Service Committee's program that is built on the Public Achievement model.

Organization

- What do these descriptions tell us about why in their particular contested space the work was given and sustained in this type of organization?
- What do descriptions of programs in contested spaces over/under emphasize and distort about the program's purpose, goals, infrastructure, practices, or resources?
- How do program descriptions show the ways contested spaces work?
- What do these descriptions tell us explicitly/implicitly about which are "political" and why?
- What program descriptions are missing?

Contested Space

- What does each type of organization teach about the nature of contested space?
- What types of organizations committed to young people might be more/less reasonable, practical, permitted, and effective in your context?
- What types of organizations in your context are seen as "political," and what are the consequences of this perception/reality on young people, on youth programs, on the community, and on the contested space itself?
- What types of organizations in your context serve to enhance/diminish civic space?
- What are the youth-led youth organizations/groups/programs/projects/services in your context?
- What is the future likely to be for this type of organization if the violence subsides?
- Is a new cohort of youth leaders being trained to run organizations by these young people or by others?

Young People

- What does each type of organization teach about what is like and what it means to be a young person in a contested space? In your contested space?

Youthwork

- What does each type of organization teach about the nature and practice of direct youthwork with young people in contested spaces? And in your specific space?
- What does each teach about the possibilities of such work?
- What does each teach about the most/least effective host of direct practice work with young people?
- What do these suggest about "best practices," "worst practices," and what is acceptable and not as "youthwork?"
- What do these descriptions suggest about the professional practice of direct work, including initial and ongoing training, supervision, and the general conditions of practice in a contested society?

VESNA OGNJENOVIC, BOJANA SKORC AND
SVETLANA IVACKOVIC

DEVELOPMENTAL YOUTH GROUPS WITH WAR-AFFECTED CHILDREN AND YOUTH: THE YOUTH GROUP AS CO-CREATOR OF DEVELOPMENT

ABSTRACT

Zdravo da ste/Hi Neighbour began as a method to work with war-affected children and whose aims then evolved into developmental and political work with youth. Social education with war-affected children and youth begins with the actual daily lives of young people, works within the context of a group and dialogues, and works with culture as a means of development.

Vera Obradovic (2005), director and choreographer of the performance *Moving Equilibrium,* commented on her experience with the youth group:

> Work with young people from *Zdravo da ste/Hi Neighbour* has led to discoveries of new possibilities both in practical and theoretical senses....Nobody expected the performance that has been created. The joint creation exceeded all of us who participated in the process of creating. These young people are not dance or drama amateurs; they did not even practice dance or drama for recreational reasons, but they created the dance performance. In doing so they were supported by two professional dancers, an actress, and the choreographer. During the preceding years they participated in different program activities organized by *Zdravo da ste* and have achieved the openness that is necessary for acquiring creative contents as well as the ways how to perform creatively. (p. 4)

What emerged was not performance in one dimension but multi-leveled creation. The youth group continued building new meanings, and the symbolic function of language remained in a hidden form because of the newly discovered creativity of body language. The process of creating *Moving Equilibrium* could be described as a conversation performed by youth.

> In the beginning we discovered that we have a treasure: the treasure that is inside us, that we carry inside us, that we carry with ourselves. Together with treasure we have journeys. Journeys to the treasure, to ourselves, and to others, because... The perfect equilibrium is when we balance one another.

Doug Magnuson and Michael Baizerman (eds), Work with Youth in Divided and Contested Societies, 193–200.

VESNA OGNJENOVIC, BOJANA SKORC AND SVETLANA IVACKOVIC

INTRODUCTION AND BACKGROUND

The vantage point of this paper is an insert from a comment made by Krippner and McIntyre (2003), the editors of "Psychological Impact of War Trauma on Civilians," in reference to the programme activities of *Hi Neighbour* (*Zdravo da ste*): "The programmes are aimed at children as the repositories of hope for a more peaceful future" (p. 109). Founded in 1992, *Zdravo da ste* is an non-governmental organization headquartered in Belgrade (Serbia) whose activities have been aimed at protecting and promoting development and community building during the war and post-war crisis in former Yugoslavia. Although the organization serves people of all ages, the work with children and youth is the priority. The majority of young people participating in *Zdravo da ste* programmes were originally settled at collective centers for refugees and displaced people, some of them from 1992, some from 1994, and some from 1999 after the NATO bombing and Kosovo crisis. Some of them are still in collective centers. In 1996, David Tolfree, the external international expert for social work wrote,

> *Hi Neighbour's* work is a highly original approach developed in response to local circumstances. The model also reflects the drive and commitment of a group of psychologists who felt the need to develop an appropriate response, coupled with their particular theoretical orientation that emphasized strengths rather than weaknesses, the capacity for growth and development rather than propensity for despair, dependence, and depression. The resulting methodology provides a context for a special form of social interaction and set of "tools" which enable refugees to set their own agendas and work purposefully on many obstacles to their own growth and development, drawing primarily on the resources and strengths contained within refugee community. In particular, the HN approach builds on the great capacity of children for creativity and imaginative play, through which difficult issues can be explored, feelings can be expressed, and a sense of hope can be found despite the extreme difficulties facing them. (p. 122-123)

After the intrusion of the war in former Yugoslavia, a few hundred thousand refugees arrived in Serbia. The people who came first were followed by many others, coming in waves during a seven-year period, reaching a total of 700,000. The meaning of our lives was shattered.

Programme Orientation

The ideas that inspired us were from Russian psychologist Lev Vygotsky. His general genetic law states that "all higher psychological functions are internalized relationships of the social kind and constitute the social structure of personality" (Valsiner, 1987). The composition of higher psychological functions, including their genetic structure and ways of functioning, is social. Even when these functions become psychological processes, their underlying nature remains social.

The Field of Life

The field of life is seen as common, and the main source of further development was built through relations between people. Consequently, human development is an endless process and the human being is in a continual, lifelong process of change. The field of life is seen as an open space, and we tried to develop social relations by engaging collectively in building a common response to the social situation from an asymmetric position; by that we mean responding not only to what exists but also to what is becoming.

THE BEGINNING

In October of 1991, a pilot study was carried out in Belgrade with 110 preschool children attending public institutions for preschool education. The observation of children's free creative activities--drawing and play--indicated some changes, which we see as related to the intrusion of war upon the children's minds. The children's spontaneous activities of drawing and playing lacked playfulness and imagination. Observations and qualitative analysis of findings formed the base for the general programme guidelines.

Observation of Drawings

The content of children's free drawing included military equipment, weapons with many details, bullets, rockets, soldiers shooting at each other, burned flags, shelled houses: War scenes dominated the drawings. The drawings seemed as if they had been done under a magnifying glass. The brutality and violence seen on TV or heard about from others were easily recognizable in the drawings of some young boys. The visibility of war through drawings was higher in boys' than in girls' drawings. The details of war and military equipment appeared in drawings of girls, interrupting the content; military airplanes, rifles, red crosses, and soldiers intruded into landscape with flowers, butterflies, and children.

Compared with pre-war creative production, the use of colours in children's drawings was drastically reduced, with generally somber tones pervading many drawings. Black colour occupied more space and occurred in unexpected places and objects: sky, sun, flowers, leaves, faces, and houses. For example, a young girl asked to draw her self-portrait as a princess with a black crown on her head, black spots on her face, a black flower on her clothes and, in the middle of the room, a small black tank was shooting at her. The title of the drawing was *My Room.*

The children's play changed in many aspects. Role-playing with war content was more frequent than before the war, and it tended to interfere with or even dominate other play activities, transforming them into war play. Role-playing reflected details of war that had not been seen before in previous children's activities. The totality of the war context was visible through role-play activities: battlefield, hospitals, kitchens, shelters with warriors, doctors, nurses, cooks, refugees, victims. Girls took an active part by acting as nurses, cooks, and wounded or dead people.

It indicated that the reality of war occupied the children's play and its enormous diversity was reduced to activities related to war circumstances. Within the imaginative world of play, reality sequences appeared as intruders. The play is an inseparable part of participating in social life, and in play children consistently tried to cope with the interruption caused by war – to overcome discontinuity in everyday life.

First observations of refugee children showed that they, who directly experienced the brutality of war, did not play at all. Our first but strong impression of refugee children living in the collective centers for refugees completed previous findings: They lacked initiative for and within play, and some of them asked directly for help. It seemed that the play was frozen. During the NATO strikes in Serbia in March, 1999, our observations of children's play were confirmed. We again saw children's drawings and play activities losing playfulness. Many parents said that their children stopped playing, and toys were untouched for days. We saw refugee children in two collective centers making real shelters for protecting themselves rather than houses for common playing.

The Vygotskian concept of play emphasizes its crucial significance for future development: "In play the child is always above his average age, above his everyday behaviour; in play he is as if head-high above himself. Play contains in a condensed way (as in the focus of a magnifying glass) all tendencies of development; as if in play the child would try to rise above the level of his usual behaviour" (cited in Valsiner, 1987, p. 64). Faced with the fact that war had intruded upon play activities, in January, 1992, we initiated efforts to restore playfulness. The programme aimed at protecting and promoting development was structured. Since its initial implementation in 1992 up until now, the programmes of *Zdravo da ste* have been extended, expanded, and transformed.

PROGRAMME GUIDELINES AND STRUCTURE OF ACTIVITIES

In January of 1992 the main postulates of programme activities were constructed:
> *Life is value per se and there is always energy to go on.*
> *Life needs others who see, who hear, who feel.*
> *It is worth proclaiming that life is present even when it seems that everything else is lost.*

In considering possible strategies of how to protect and promote human development, *Zdravo da ste* gives crucial relevance to social interaction. The group is open for all participants, the size of the group is not strictly defined in advance, and the workshop leader does not have his/her group to work with. In order to revitalize human capacity for expression and creation, a special model of relational activities has been developed. Interactive play-like patterns of activities were structured in order to evoke and integrate individual and group creativity.

The programme of specially designed workshops tends to turn children/youth from the role of war victims to active creators of their own lives. It is oriented on the process (not on outcome), on the group (not on individual or the subgroup of chosen individuals), on experience of everyday life (not on special or unique experiences separated from life).

It Is Process Oriented (Not Outcome Oriented)

Most workshops in use today are structured according to the goals given in advance and oriented toward an expected outcome. In contrast, from our point of view, any group interactive process is potentially developmental, and the workshop gives a frame for group activities that could (but sometimes do not) occur within the frame. The openness to unpredicted and unexpected events is built within this frame. In short, the workshop is an open, divergent activity in which the facilitator is not a leader or manipulator but a partner in common activity.

It Emphasizes Group (Not Individual or Dyadic) Exchange And Mutuality

The relation between the group and the individual is one of the most important issues of psychology today. From the methodological point of view the workshop is a form of activity in which every participant is inseparable from the group activities and is actively working/learning through that experience (see Ognjenovic, 1996). The main activity is exchange within the circle – every participant is contributing to the group process. This gives an opportunity to each participant to create a social event using various expressive modes. It also prevents a situation of focused communication in which some members are favored while others are passive. Exchange in a circle emphasizes equality of participants. Many teachers/workshop leaders using this workshop programme reported that the structure of relations in the group changed: They were pleasantly surprised with newly-discovered capacities of children they had been treating as "retiring," "limited," "asocial," "shy," "closed." The group is seen as a creative unit that is much more than the sum of individuals. It is in continual and dynamic exchange with the social field.

It Is Strongly Connected with Actual Life (Not with Special or Unique Experience Separated From Life)

Borders between the workshop situation and everyday activities are not strict. The workshop is incorporated into everyday life. There is no particular end point for workshop processes, since they are going to be continued after the workshop is over. The workshop is running in reality in schools, common rooms, collective centres, public institutions, or somewhere else. These are places where everyday life is going on. Workshop activities were developed as complex and open interactions involving elements of play and creativity. During workshop activities participants express themselves through various modes: movements, gestures, voices, words, songs, drawing, painting, performances.

In order to evoke and promote symbolic divergent activity, a divergent action with "objects" is structured. This divergent activity was defined through special sequences of activities intending to make participants aware of symbolic means for expression moving from expected toward unexpected/unpredictable manipulation and to raise awareness of tools and take the step away from ordinary communication. The activities were built on expressive sources through flexible and guided use of voices, words, gestures, movements, colours, lines, shapes, and drawings. The participants were expected to express the meaning of the words by nonverbal means, to find the voice for something that is ordinarily voiceless, to find the colour for the voice, to express feelings by the movement, to find the colour for the gesture/movement and vice versa, to touch and sense the untouchable. Our assumption was that unusual and unexpected activities with the means of expression would provide an opportunity for internal symbolic activity to occur, develop, and integrate. We believe that this activity model keeps and promotes the totality of the process and prevents it from splitting up into internal and external activities.

PROGRAMME FOR YOUTH

Social activity is a producer of becoming.
Lois Holzman, Belgrade Youth Center, 7 December, 2004

Central to our approach is the belief that the developmental potential of intercultural and intracultural differences goes far beyond the mutual knowledge of traditional patterns of behaviours. Differences can be the source of development in an exchange that all the sides involved can mutually achieve common benefit. "The more multiple the relationships, the richer and more profound the individual and cultural experience" (Zur, cited in Holzman, 2000).

Activities with young people are performed as common activities of youth and adults. Working together is developmental for all participants. We believe that separating generations and doing things focused on stages (the stage of adolescence or adulthood) supports the generation gap and splits the social world according to traditional criteria of ages and stages. The possibility for common and mutual building by youth, adults, children, and elderly should be nurtured and kept because the socio/cultural exchange among generations is the source for divergent and creative activities.

Over the years the programme was further developed and transformed into activities such as the training workshops in traditional and artistic skills, ecological activities, ethno-art, open workshops/performances, and activities of building creative relations with culture (literature, painting, music, dancing). These workshops grow over the particular skills; they are open, creative, multi-leveled activities, wherein the products are not goals by themselves but a part of the process of building new meanings for future activities. *On each end there are many new beginnings*, said one of young participants.

Within the context, culture is the strongest social generator of development. It is not only the medium wherein the development is unfolding but, much more than that, it bears the seeds of development in the essence and gives opportunity to each participant to create events built on the totality of her or his expressive potential. Culture belongs to all the people and is being built by all.

During long periods of programme implementation and transformation, the process of production was observed and the final products were analyzed as an integrated part of the process itself. The responsiveness of all participants to the programme was positive. It was astonishing how quickly and easily an eruption of creativity had been evoked in spite of recent destruction, loss, and suffering.

CULTURE AS A PROMOTER OF DEVELOPMENT

We will begin with the questions we had been asked by our colleagues:

What afterwards? After a beautiful rise, is the return to reality harder or not?

To what extent is art larger than life and able to outshine it? Because art is the light.

Can creation cover everything and to what extent can problems be alleviated?

These questions are interrelated and there is a common answer. There is a call in them for a split in our minds, for a gap between the sublime and the low, between a rise and fall, as if the workshop is something different from life and art is something different than reality and the artist is someone different from the ordinary people.

But we will not accept this invitation. Art and life are one and the same thing. There is no fall after creation. Creation is not a rise; creation is part of us. It is active energy; it broaden us out. There is no fall after it. Art is not Paradise, and reality does not mean being expelled from Paradise. The dichotomies are in our heads; they are not necessarily real. A problem is where we see it is. A problem is not where we want it to be.

So let us go into art, into creation, and we are in our lives, in ourselves, and then there is no fall. It is life, and if it is, it is not a problem but part of our lives. It is activity (see Ognjenovic & Skorc, 2003).

At this point, we wish to pay attention to the history of this creation and to look upon it from a developmental point of view. Our practice built within social spaces strongly contested by war and conflicts taught us about life as we live it or, to say it more precisely, it taught us about the social sources of life. Through common activities, wherein the obstacles put by traditional social roles and labels vanish, the human exchange occurs in a genuine way and enormous capacity for learning for development become transparent. The majority of these young people have participated in the *Zdravo da ste* programme since their childhood and their creative participation does not represent their life experience - it is their life experience.

Vesna Ognjenovic, Bojana Skorc, & Svetlana Ivackovic
Hi Neighbor/Zdravo da Ste
Belgrade

REFERENCES

Holzman, L. (1997). *Schools for growth, radical alternatives to current educational models.* Mahwah, NJ: Erlbaum.

Holzman, L. (2004). *What is social in social development?* Lecture at the Youth Center, Belgrade.

Holzman, L. (2004). *Do boundaries inhibit the growth of new psychology?* Presentation at the 112th Annual Convention of American Psychological Association, Honolulu.

Newman, F. & Holzman, L. (1993). *Lev Vygotsky: Revolutionary scientist.* London: Routledge.

Newman, F. (1994). *Let's develop.* New York: Community Literacy Research Project, Inc.

Obradovic, V. (2005). *Search for perfect equilibrium through play and dance.* Presentation at the 7th Regional Congress: Dialogue between civilizations – CID/UNESCO, Ohrid.

Ognjenovic, V., Andjelkovic, D., & Skorc, B. (1996). *Self-expression of refugee children involved in the programme of psychological workshops. The influence of recent socio-political events on fine arts and on patient's* art (pp. 181-202). New York: The American Society of Psychopathology of Expression.

Ognjenovic, V., Skorc, B. (2003). *Evaluation of Hi Neighbour programmes.* Belgrade: Zdravo da ste.

Ognjenovic, V., Skorc, B., & Savic, J. (2003). Social sources of life. Rehabilitation in the former Yugoslavia. In S. Krippner & T. M. McIntyre (Eds.), *The psychological impact of war trauma on civilians: An international perspective* (pp. 171-177). Westport, CT: Praeger.

Ognjenovic, V., Skorc, B., & Ivackovic, S. (2005): Creating culture across generations. Presentation at Childhoods, Oslo.

Tolfree, D. (1996). *Restoring playfulness: Different approaches to assisting children who are psychologically affected by war or displacement.* Falun, Sweden: Radda Barnen Forlag.

Valsiner, J. (1987). *Culture and the development of children's action.* New York: Wiley.

Valsiner, J. (1989). *Human development and culture.* Toronto: Lexington Books.

Vygotsky, L. (1971). *Play and its importance in child's psychological development.* [Serbian: *Predskolsko dete, Beograd: SPDJ:, 48-61*].

Vygotsky, L. (1996). *Educational psychology.* [Russian: Moskva: Pedagogika – Press.]

SUZANNE HAMMAD AND TAREQ ALBAKRI

THE STORY OF "POPULAR ACHIEVEMENT": A MODEL OF YOUTH CIVIC ENGAGEMENT IN PALESTINE

ABSTRACT

This article focuses on youth civic engagement as one viable strategy for positive engagement of young people in Palestine, a strategy whose long term aim we believe could significantly contribute to strengthening constituencies for peace among Palestinian civil society and support the emergence of a true democratic Palestinian society and state. We present the story of the Popular Achievement program by tracing how it has been implemented in the West Bank and Gaza and analyzing its main implications and impacts on young people and the Palestinian community as a whole, the factors that we believe have deterred some young people from being civically engaged, and the range of services for youth, and interventions.

The Middle East is in the world news almost daily, and thus many believe they have a good grasp of the issues there, especially those between the Palestinians and the Israelis. Yet this perceived familiarity too often keeps these issues from being understood in their complexity and potency. This is true especially for youth, where usual images of individual and collective violence on both sides serve to distract attention from the everyday matters associated with being a young person in that context.

Young people in the West Bank and Gaza go about their everyday lives within and across a variety of contested spaces: geographic, faith-based, gendered, ethnic, social class, and family status. None of this is unique except in the particulars of the history and current violence of the Palestine/Israel conflict and in the larger strategies used to engage, marginalize, threaten, prevent or enhance certain forms of individual and collective ways of being and doing "youth."

In this paper we locate our primary strategy of youthwork, youth civic engagement, within short discussions of geography, history, and politics of Palestine that provide a context for understanding young people, their everyday lives, their daily challenges, and the organized ways adult society responds to them in terms of services, institutions, and opportunities. Our approach has been to engage young people as citizens now who can and do make viable contributions to their community and society while enhancing their skills and sense of personal, individual, and collective efficacy. This is the story of Popular Achievement, a project of the Quaker Service- American Friends Service Committee Middle East program.

Doug Magnuson and Michael Baizerman (eds), Work with Youth in Divided and Contested Societies, 217–234.

SUZANNE HAMMAD AND TAREQ ALBAKRI

IN CONTEXT: THE CONFLICT AND ITS IMPACT ON YOUNG PEOPLE

The population of young people in the Middle East is the largest compared to other age groups. In Palestine more than 47% of the population is below 15 years old and more than 60% are below the age of 24 (Palestinian Central Bureau of Statistics, 1999). This makes them vital to the social, economic, and political well-being of Palestinian society. This entire generation was born and lived through various stages of the Palestinian/Israeli conflict.

It has now been 55 years since half the Palestinians became refugees and the entire nation stateless. A population of around two million then, it is now approaching eight million. Of those, three million live in the area of Palestine occupied by Israel in 1967, specifically, the West Bank (including East Jerusalem) and the Gaza Strip. Another million live in Israel as citizens of that state. Nearly four million Palestinians have been refugees as a result of the 1948 exodus and reside in Jordan, Syria, Lebanon, other Arab countries, the United States, Europe and elsewhere.

Since the second *intifada* of September, 2000, and the breakdown of the Oslo peace accord, the overall socio-economic and political situation in the West Bank and Gaza has taken a dramatic shift with reoccupation of Palestinian cities, towns, camps, and villages and consequent tight closures, prolonged curfews, the erecting of the so-called "separation" wall, ongoing house demolitions, and sporadic checkpoints bottlenecking peoples' livelihoods under the pretext of security for Israel.

Such hard-line policies of the Israeli government have not enabled a viable, independent Palestinian state to emerge and have led to the escalation of the hardships and frustrations among Palestinians. Increased suicide bombings from radicalized Palestinian groups have sustained a cycle of violence between both parties. Moreover, a weakened Palestinian Authority has not been able to gain public confidence in its political vision, exacerbating the situation with this vacuum in local governance amidst the chaos of occupation. As a consequence of all the above, efforts for a just and lasting peace have not materialized to date and the on-the-ground situation continues to deteriorate.

Throughout, youth have paid the heaviest price: No Palestinian youth today has experienced school without forced closures, curfews, and severe restrictions on his or her movements. In the realities of their daily lives, young people and their families continue to be exposed to various kinds of violence (structural and physical) such as house demolitions, bulldozing of agricultural land, confiscations, killings, casualties, bombings, imprisonment, and tight closures within and between their own villages and towns. It is a burden to go through what should be a normal day when living in the West Bank and Gaza. Nothing is easy.

We found in a 2001 assessment of youths' needs that this continuous pressure and the difficult conditions that are a direct result of the ongoing occupation have created a sense of isolation, helplessness, and hopelessness among Palestinian youth (AlBakri & Hammad, 2001). Moreover, with limited economic resources and fewer political or social opportunities, young people feel they have no individual ability to change their basic living conditions or the social or political environment. Amer Daraghmeh, a youthworker from Bethlehem, said, "Life under occupation is like a big stop sign, a never changing light…life is in a freeze mode." While for some the growing sense of injustice and powerlessness has been demoralizing as expressed by Daraghmeh, it has also had the effect of pushing some to the edge. Some young people, even those who abhor violence, have come to accept that one of the few options to resisting occupation and reaching political aspirations of a future free Palestine is their own death as martyrs or suicide bombers. For many suicide bombers life under occupation is equal to death as there is "no value to life under these conditions." [121]

On the other hand, many young people still hold hope that a better future is possible; for them it cannot get any worse. Some have found that by participating in civil society organizations and voluntary work (e.g. with the Palestinian Red Crescent Society), they can feel that they are doing something that is directly beneficial in their struggle for peace and independence. With few appealing alternatives available to youth who do not want to join political groups or factions, a large proportion of Palestinian youth want to get engaged in constructive work to better their life and live with dignity and freedom but do not know how to do it. This is precisely our target group.

The impact of the conflict and ongoing occupation has been manifested in young people in a variety of ways. Some of these and their implications are:

- Accumulated frustrations and hopelessness due to ongoing military occupation, dispossession, and failure of political processes.
- Eroding economic resources/opportunities that directly impact livelihoods and prospects for improvement.
- Polarization in the means of expressing one's national identity, together with an inability to fulfill their right to self-determination.
- A sense of resentment at the world's (especially Arab world) impotence in intervening to end the conflict.
- In the two waves of *intifada* young people took a lead role in organizing on the ground anti-occupation activities but were not included in consequent political processes. These made them take rebellious and sometimes extremist positions or otherwise resulted in total apathy, while some chose to challenge social and political structures within Palestinian society itself.
- Growth of a highly politicized university student movement that was strongly affiliated with political factions left little space for young people to be active outside circles of political affiliation.
- Supremacy of political aspirations over any other social issues. It was seen that in order to address community aspirations priority should be given to fulfilling the right to self-determination, and once Palestinians have an independent Palestinian state then all

---

[121] This is a quote from an interview with a youth activist in Bethlehem whose brother was a suicide bomber. The interview was conducted in 2004 within the framework of an EU-funded project called Youth Work in Contested Spaces. What is most striking is the two contrasting paths the two brothers took as a form of resistance to the occupation: one chose death while the other chose life and is now a vibrant youth activist in his community.

will be easier to address. In this sense many of the social problems were blamed on occupation and political conflict.

–   Young men and women tended to be recruited by Palestinian activists as well Israeli intelligence agencies as informers on youth political activists as well as traffickers of explosives and sometimes drugs.

–   An overwhelming sense of community solidarity and caring within Palestinian society regardless of geographic, religious, or political affiliations due to the common experience of daily life. The opportunity for collective action and community solidarity outside of political factions is a relatively new phenomena.

WHAT HAS ADULT SOCIETY MADE AVAILABLE FOR YOUNG PEOPLE IN PALESTINE?

How young people are perceived by Palestinian society and authority figures has been evolving along with the socio-economic and political situation, and their roles in society are by no means consensual across political, religious, and generational lines. However, young people's presence in the West Bank and Gaza demands that something be done. How do adults (and young people) in the West Bank and Gaza respond to what it is to be a "youth" and to what and how young people participate in organizations in these two contested spaces? What institutions, services, and facilities have been made available to young people?

One approach to answering this question is to catalogue and then categorize what civic and social communities and government are doing to, for, and with youth. Such an analysis found twelve approaches to "working with youth/young people."

1. Formal education (public and private schools, including faith-based schools). Public schooling is mandatory until 15 years old or 10th grade. Youth are in the social role of student.

2. Sports and recreation. Organizations, entrepreneurs, and groups that define and service young people by addressing their individual needs and pathologies. It is assumed that young people (especially men) have plenty of leisure time and physical energy that should be channeled towards sports activities. This is seen to prevent possibilities of deviant or delinquent behaviors. Examples include football, basketball tournaments, and bodybuilding gyms. Many of the sports clubs were shut down before the 1993 peace process and young sportsmen were detained if any political activities were suspected to take place in the clubs. Youth here are in the social role of the client.

3. Vocational training--organizations that focus on enhancing vocational skills of young people to help them find jobs. The programs were designed to focus on one profession (e.g., carpentry, computer technician) or some general skills enhancement. The programs are designed in a way that tailors particular vocational programs to men and others to women. These programs are delivered by private or public training centers, colleges, and training institutes.

4. Political mobilization (factions and political parties). Established adult political parties and organizations recruit, train, and involve young people.

Examples include youth organizations affiliated with political parties such as the Fatah youth movement, Democratic Union of Palestinian Youth, Palestine Student Council, and People's Party youth. Here youth are in the social role of "mender."

5. Ongoing youth groups and organizations. A range of adult-run organizations and groups provide young people with opportunities in recreation, informal/non-formal education, safe spaces for social events, and/or voluntary programming. Young people participate in trainings, awareness-raising activities on health, education, human rights, and environment issues that are seen by others as of priority or relevance to young people's lives. Examples are the YMCA, Scouts, educational community-based centers, some public libraries, and some universities that had mandatory volunteering requirements. Youth here are members or simply "young people."

6. Religious involvement. Faith-based groups and organizations offer young people informal religious education, safe spaces for social events, and programming centered around faith, spiritual, and/or religious involvement. Examples are youth groups formed in churches and mosques or faith-based associations and youth centers. Young people here are in the social role of identity guardian.

7. Paramilitary involvement. Organized and recognized paramilitary groups and organizations involve young people in their socio-political, religio-political, and religio-social work. Examples are Hamas and the Al-Aqsa Brigades. Youth are in the social role of member, freedom fighter and, possibly, hero.

8. Relief and crisis work. Local, national, and international relief and crisis organizations recruit, train, and involve young people as relief volunteers in crisis situations. Examples are the Red Crescent and the Union of Medical Relief Committees. The social role here is relief work volunteers.

9. Employment. This is a mostly governmental strategy of finding employment for young people so they can earn a salary, pay bills, and support the survival of their nuclear families. Many families depend on income generated by young people in the family who work as day laborers in the Israeli labor market. Burdened by the social expectation to start their nuclear families, young people need resources to do so and are pushed into labor market in their early 20s. Some drop out of school to work in the informal economy. Young people are in the social role of worker, trainee, breadwinner, "adult," husband/wife/parent, son, and daughter.

10. Emigration. Some young people choose to leave. Well-off families send their sons and daughters to neighboring Arab countries or other places in the world for better education. Some of them choose not to go back to the West Bank and Gaza due to limited job opportunities. Mid-career young people choose to emigrate for economic or political reasons.

11. Policy of containment. By this is meant the policy decision to monitor and contain youth using policy development as the tools. The Ministry of Youth in Palestine works on organizing summer activities, youth leadership trainings, and organizing the structures of youth and sports clubs in West Bank and Gaza. It is quite dysfunctional due to shortcomings in its financial and organizational capacities, and it is based on the government's perception of youth as a threat to the regime or a particular person. On occasion force is used against university

student demonstrations. Young people are in the role of "trouble maker" and "radical."

12. Youth civic engagement, work to invite young people to become involved voluntarily in citizen work for the creation and sustaining of everyday civil society. Youth "become involved" in the social roles of citizen and participant.

Given the sociopolitical and economic tensions in Palestine, given the violence and the impotence of a viable civic society, and given the lack of non-political space to prepare young people to take on citizen roles now and in their future, it was clear that we could make a positive contribution to the range and types of available responses to the wants/needs of youth and of the society by facilitating the emergence of youth civic engagement initiatives. Such work is greatly influenced by individuals (and groups) deep desire, motivation, and commitment for making change towards democratic, inclusive, just, and equitable society. This puts people involved at risk of being hurt, because they call for change in social constructions or power dynamics. Thus it is not simply "doing the work" with young people but the persistent courage to do (and continue doing) the work on controversial issues in conflict torn society while aware of risks entailed.

It may be easier in our region to become crystallized by the anger and violence of others than to engage over the long-term the dissipation of hope. Youth civic engagement embodies both hope and courage as modes of being citizen, not simply as feelings. This implies a work in progress. In our context "engagement" means having young people decide on the prerequisites, conditions, scope, and momentum of their active participation in their communities to address what they define as existing challenges to the well-being of their collective space. In other words, it is the continuous process of inviting young people to express their life experiences of oppression, alienation, exclusion, and disempowerment through collective non-violent citizen action that challenges sources of existing "power" and root causes of such life experiences.

THE CONTEXT FOR CIVIC PARTICIPATION IN PALESTINE

In the context of conflict-torn communities, the notion of identity (national, personal, communal, ethnic) and, consequently, citizenship are continuously being negotiated and re-defined and influenced by a range of factors, internal and external, imposed and indigenous, and is worthy of further study beyond the scope of this article. The complexity of the political situation presents dilemmas related to the status of different "types" of Palestinians (refugees, displaced, East Jerusalemites, Gazans, Jordanian Palestinians, Israeli Palestinians) all of which impact perceptions and meanings one gives to oneself as belonging to a collective group or nation. Although fragmented throughout different parts of historic Palestine, the region, and the world, Palestinians share a bond of their "Palestinian-hood" and sense of affiliation to what they yearn for: a democratic Palestinian state that is free from occupation and that they are able to reside in if they so choose. In this sense citizenship is not defined in terms of one's membership in a nation state to which its citizens can be accountable and vice versa.

While this is important to flag, for the purposes of this article when we refer to citizenship we see it as the individual and collective effort that people freely make to better their community. Some contextual challenges to this kind of work include:

1. The conception of adulthood starts from the point of marriage and/or beyond the late 20s. Until then, young people are seen as inexperienced and tend not to be taken seriously when they attempt to get involved in public life. Credibility is attained after much hard work and sometimes involves fighting against the tide to assert themselves and be "heard" by adults and authority figures.

2. Few employment opportunities *vis-à-vis* the influx of new graduates and a weak private sector (actually a whole economy that is dependent on Israel) pushes young people to focus on the daily challenge of maintaining living standards. There is just no time for civic participation activities that do not "feed bread" (an Arabic saying). In many other instances, emigration for economic purposes is sought as the cure-all option.

3. In Palestine, programs have promoted empowerment through short-term skill enhancement and awareness raising training courses. Few opportunities were given to young people to use the skills they learned. Trainings tended to be planned, designed, and implemented by adults on behalf of youth who were considered subjects in these programs rather than creators, partners, and integral constituents. It was claimed that power was given to youth but in reality remained in the hands of adults and the highly professionalized NGOs giving lip service to real youth participation.

4. There is fear of youth from authoritarian dogmatic power structures, many of which are not ready to accept voices bringing controversial issues to public dialogue. These rigid power structures include the political, cultural norms, and religious, and they fear loss of control of the status quo and the perceived chaos, while others have a negative perception of change as an external threat imposed from the "west" to alter existing norms and traditions.

5. Supremacy of the national struggle against military occupation and the political upheavals, frustrations, and realities has real implications for how young Palestinians go about with their daily lives. The uncertainty and unpredictability of life in the Occupied Territories and strict control measures affect free mobility, put ones' life or well-being at risk and, consequently, deepens young people's sense of powerlessness that is often translated into indifference or lack of motivation. Yet for others, it may be the very fuel that challenges them to get involved to try to improve their reality.

6. Power and authority over decision-making in a patriarchal society like Palestine is usually held by the breadwinning older male of the household. In some situations the influence of the older males goes beyond the nuclear family to include cousins, nieces, and nephews. Thus a network of elderly relatives tend to intervene in many of the existential decisions that a young person takes such as continuing school, choosing and marrying a life partner, and choosing a career, and so there is little chance to feel in control over their lives since it is legitimized by society that "the adult knows best." This is reinforced for an authoritarian educational system and practices within the institution of the school.

7. A predominantly conservative society gives little space for young people (especially for young girls) to participate in public spaces. This confines young people to indoor private spaces with little opportunities for interaction with the

outer world. Generally speaking, there are limited public spaces for interaction and action for young people other than sports and recreation centers. Those gatherings that do exist such as unions, political parties, and student movements tend to be very closely monitored by government and perceived as a threat that needs to be contained.

STRENGTHENING CAPACITIES FOR YOUTH CIVIC ENGAGEMENT IN PALESTINE

The youth civic engagement program that we have been involved with in Palestine and Jordan, Popular Achievement, refers to the intentional work to invite young people to become involved voluntarily in effective "citizen work" that contributes to the creation and sustenance of everyday civil society.

Popular Achievement first developed as model of civic education in the name of "Public Achievement" (PA) at the Center for Democracy and Citizenship at the Humphrey Institute of Public Affairs, University of Minnesota, in the United States. It has since then taken an international dimension, particularly in contexts ridden by conflict with inadequate opportunities for young people; PA is established in countries such as Northern Ireland, South Africa, Turkey, Bosnia, and in Palestine. In each of these regions PA has taken a twist that accommodates the realities and cultural contexts of young people there.

The Quaker Palestine Youth Program of the American Friends Service Committee (AFSC) has followed a strategy of challenging young people from a stereotype (sometimes reality) of being apathetic, marginalized, or unengaged because of the lack of options for exploring new ways in which they can contribute positively to the advancement of their societies. In Popular Achievement, young people are engaged as citizens who have talents, capacities, and creative skills to address issues in their near environment (see Figure 1). The logo for the program is "We are citizens of today and not just the potential for the future," implying an immediate role and responsibility in the present.

Young university students are invited to become facilitators of youth groups/teams in their communities. A training program is then organized for new coaches that brings coaches from previous cycles as well as young participants to train and talk about their past experiences in PA. In these booster sessions, facilitators are trained in basic facilitation skills for team building and for maintaining group dynamics. Training of coaches also includes concepts of participation, community development, citizenship, and informal education.

Coaches are then asked to start teams of younger people from their own communities with the help of community organizations, schools, or youth clubs. Each team has 10-15 young members who are usually 14-17 years old. Over eight months team members engage in a weekly 2 to 3 hour session of critical dialogue, research, and conversations with community members to identify, act upon, and address what they collectively identified as prioritized community concerns.

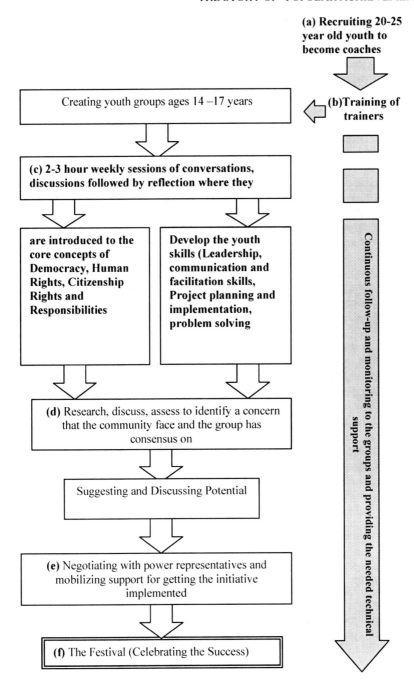

Figure 1. The Public Achievement Process

Young people learn to listen and respect each other, valuing and appreciating the diverse opinions expressed regardless of how naïve or radical they may sound. An essential element of the PA process is continuous reflection on what young people dialogue, see, feel, and think about in their community, while instilling confidence and freedom of critical thought within themselves and between each other. In the dialogue and reflection young people reach a common and deeper understanding of their realities without being intimidated by political, social, or economic power. Through this process young people draw lessons from lived experiences that they may not have been previously aware of and start to give meanings to their new self-created roles.

The next step is for young people to identify an issue of public interest that they will consider as a priority. Here young people conduct desk research, interviews, and surveys to validate and make sure that the issue they selected is of concern to the community. Throughout the exercise young people get to understand different perspectives related to real life situations and opinions that they have not been exposed to before. This adds another layer of critical thinking from analyzing findings of the research and then deciding on one issue to address as well as possible strategies to bring the desired change.

Young people then map the power centres in the society that positively or negatively affect the discourse about the problem they are facing and the change they are about to bring. Young people identify who could be allies or adversaries. This is a preparatory step to approaching those representatives of political, economic, or social power and negotiating support for the initiative. Participants simulate their meetings and negotiations with those in power. They learn how to make contacts, how to approach them, and how to meet them and present their case. Young people learn how to articulate themselves well and hold themselves and others accountable to their promises and responsibilities.

Throughout the eight-month cycle there are two major celebrations for all participants. The first is after young people identify the issues they want to work on. The second festival is organized by the coaches and young people at the conclusion of the program. Teams organize music, dance, and film performances in the one day festival.

As part of their reflection on the PA process young people are encouraged to write in any form, including short stories, poetry, cartoons, articles, or interview. These writings are published in a newsletter and on the website.

RESULTS, ACHIEVEMENTS, AND LESSONS LEARNED: YOUTH UNDER OCCUPATION REDISCOVER THEIR POTENTIAL AND POWER

Over the past four years, the Quaker Palestine Youth Program has conducted three eight-month cycles of Popular Achievement in the West Bank and two cycles in Gaza. A total of 130 teams have been active in this transformative action-oriented process throughout various refugee camps, villages, and towns of the West Bank and Gaza, mostly targeted because they are remote and/or underserved by major NGOs and service providers. With at least 10 participants on each team, approximately 1700 young Palestinian women and men have participated. One hundred and sixty university students have participated as coaches or peer educators. The initiatives chosen by youth have ranged from small school-based projects to large community-based activities that can contribute positively toward a tangible change that is of public interest. We encourage youth to think small and realistic, as the process is the real achievement rather than only the accomplishment of the goal.

At the school level: establishing science labs and computer centers where there were none or few, building additional class rooms where student density per class is high, developing youth-oriented websites by youth, addressing school violence.

At the community level: starting libraries accessible to the whole community, book collection campaigns, campaigns against early marriage, folklore exhibits and dances, lobbying for street lights in refugee camps, lobbying for internet connections to remote villages, community gardening, family planning campaigns, neighborhood clean-ups, cultural heritage education, and lobbying for a water pump.

Activities targeting less advantaged groups within the community: addressing poverty, organizing fun activities for children at residential orphanages, homes for the elderly, and institutions for the physically challenged.

Many of the projects required that youth pay visits to institutions within and outside the community, to present themselves, negotiate their project, convince authority figures or adults of the importance of the goal sought by this project, and seek their partnership to work together to serve the community through their initiative. Naturally, each project necessitates different kinds of interventions and activities depending on the nature of the project and the range of stakeholders to be involved.

Qualitative, Transformative Effects

One of the outcomes of PA is its transformative effect on youth, communities and, ultimately, the status quo that is shaped and reshaped by young peoples' initiatives and collective action. A participatory evaluation conducted by the American Friends Service Committee's Youth Program Assistant, Ureib Abdel Samad, found that participating in PA impacted youth in the following ways:

–Transformed their characters
–Enabled them to question and challenge what made no sense to them
–Helped them make new friends
–Gave them a chance to use unutilized talents
–Gained them recognition and a sense that they are productive members of their society
–Became less violent when they deal with their siblings

–Enhanced their skills in communication, conflict resolution, teamwork, and problem solving

–Learned and practiced using authority, power, democracy, and accountability

–Learned how to be persistent and resilient

–Rekindled a sense of community and caring

–Helped some get a job and internship placements

–Gave university students academic credit and practical field experience

Examples of Success Stories

These stories illustrate how youth civic engagement initiatives in Palestine have helped young people take control of and cope with their reality through continuous negotiation, defining new roles for themselves, and challenging stereotypes of young people by engaging in community action of positive benefit to the whole community.

Girls' perseverance in carrying out their project gains them community support: A group of fourteen girls, 14-15 years old, came together from the two communities of Birzeit and the Jalazon refugee camp to start a Popular Achievement team. Families of the young people became immersed in this youth-led project and it demonstrated the courage and commitment of young people in that community to accomplish what they defined as important to them in spite of some challenges. At the outset, the school principal did not approve of providing a space for the team to have their weekly meeting; he insisted on first getting endorsement for the project from the Ministry of Education. Though this endorsement is in place today, at that time waiting for such a letter from a government bureaucracy would have substantially delayed the project.

Yet the girls were not discouraged. Some of them convinced their peers to meet in the public playground in the village. In a society that is over-protective of young women, meeting in a public space outside the school represented a statement to the community that they are not ready to give up on their aspirations if it is blocked by existing authority figures. In another instance, a sporadic roadblock imposed by Israeli soldiers blocked the path of seven girls from the group who lived eight kilometres beyond the roadblock. However, this did not deter them from finding alternative means of getting to their weekly PA meeting: the girls took the risk of bypassing the checkpoint and walked the entire distance.

After several meetings the team decided to address the growing poverty in the community. They decided to launch a campaign to redistribute used clothing to families in need. They got in touch with charities, mobilized teams for collection, and over six weeks were able to collect 1000 pieces of clothing for about 35 families.

Girls' group advocates for issues to be placed on the community agenda: Another group of young girls in the village of Seelt il Daher near Jenin, a town in the north of the West Bank, identified 15 issues that they felt were important to discuss, including domestic violence, women's rights, early-age marriages, poverty, and unemployment. The girls identified a gap between their rights as girls in Islam and the societal practices they witness in their day-to-day life. The girls then decided to hold a meeting with the imam of the local mosque, asking him if he could address these issues from an informed Islamic perspective. This was an invitation to the imam to address the issues in the weekly Friday prayer that is attended by the majority of community members, especially men.

The imam listened to the girls and took their views seriously. In the following weeks he started tackling these issues one-by-one as requested by the girls, followed by an open discussion between young people and adult community members. The young girls successfully approached a representative of the religious institution who is quite influential in the rural context, and negotiated with him to use the weekly address to pay attention to concrete rights issues of concern to them.

"The Knights of Gaza" mediate community disputes and work to make Gaza greener: A group of young women and men from economically disadvantaged backgrounds came together and chose to call themselves the Knights of Gaza. Many of them worked summer breaks to supplement family income yet had the energy and motivation to do some community work in their spare time. In Gazan society, there are few opportunities for young people to express themselves, to learn about each other and get together while having fun at the same time. The group reached a consensus that their first project would be to create more green areas in Gaza City, a densely populated space. They identified 10 *dunoms*[122] in a housing project in the city that was a disputed area between the landlord and local authorities. The young people approached the landlord and the local authorities, gained the trust of both parties, and managed to plant it with habitat friendly bushes, flowers, and trees. The project gave the young people a sense of pride of accomplishment: not only were they able respond to a community need and help make a conflict-ridden congested space more beautiful, but they also were able to mediate effectively between adults and social institutions.

Young people challenge a predominantly adult-run board to reactivate the village youth club: The village of Ein Areek is located in the outskirts of Ramallah. In this village, the PA group met at the local church, bringing together young women and men, Muslims and Christians. They decided to work together on reactivating the village youth club that was governed by an all-adult board with no youth representation. It is quite unusual to challenge adult authority in small villages such as these in Palestine; the group faced resistance and their requests were not taken seriously. However, the issue of the youth club became a community issue and questions were raised as to why an existing public space for young people of the village was being underutilized. Members of the board came under the scrutiny of parents and community members and were asked to act upon their responsibilities.

---

[122]One dunom is 1000 square metres.

Moreover, despite the fact that youth failed in achieving their specific agenda and were demoralized for a while, they came to the realization that sometimes things can change if they are taken step-by-step and that they should stay persistent. Now the church and other community-based organizations organize periodic summer and recreational activities for young people such as football tournaments and summer camps.

Problems and Challenges

It is a continual challenge to maintain motivation and a sense of true empowerment in the disempowering context of an ongoing military occupation, daily challenges of living, disparities in power, and high levels of unpredictability and instability.

The difficulty of moving from one place to another has been a major crippling factor to the program. For staff this means more time spent on the road to reach teams in different areas. Staff members have detained by Israeli soldiers at military checkpoints for hours before they were allowed to continue their trip.

It continues to be a challenge to ask coaches to be as neutral as possible when facilitating discussions within PA teams. We seek to neutralize their role and the power they represent to the group (because of their age and status as university students) and conversely encourage participants to challenge the coach's influence in making decisions on behalf of the team.

Doing this kind of work and raising youths' awareness to challenge existing power structures (including some norms and attitudes) that restrain working for public interest has at times been perceived as a threat.

Lessons Learned for Practice

The motivation of young people is crucial. Most youth programs in Palestine are designed by adults on behalf of young people under the assumption that adults know what is best for young people. There have not been good examples of practice that truly encourage young people to be in the driver's seat, deciding what kind of program they would like, and what issues to address. Generally, in conflict situations adults and young people have very limited choices. In PA young people realize that they have a broader scope of choices: to participate, decide, design, and take action are all choices and decisions they need to make individually and as a team.

We have learned that for effective participation we need to explore and build on young people's motivation, specifically, giving them the free public space through which they (as individuals and groups) recognize and put their resources, talents, skills and creativity, wisdom, and experience into action. When encouraged and recognized for their growing capacities, young people develop a stronger sense of ownership of the initiative.

Stakeholders and program managers must be aware and committed to being process-oriented. We have learned that youth participation is a process and not an end. Practitioners are encouraged to be attentive and responsive to the openness of the participation process and be truly confident in young people's capacities to make a difference in their communities. This requires that youthworkers be willing to negotiate their own sources of power, influence, and authority to strengthen mutual trust and live the ethos of the program. Program staff (especially those in senior positions) compromise and negotiate their power positions with young people when they seek true, flourishing participation that will bring resources, energy, and talents to the table.

This implies a holistic understanding of youth participation that is not bound to a particular phase in the life cycle of the program but, rather, intentional in all aspects of organizational being such as collective planning, sharing, reflection, and action. In that sense practice should be responsive to where the group desires to go but with a clear, determined focus on the long-term goal.

Inclusiveness and diversity are necessary for youth participation to be meaningful. Engaging people across lines of economic, social, cultural, political, or age differences is key to the success of participation. The program should be inviting to as many stakeholders as possible. Within a framework that develops positive understanding and respect among all without judging or stereotyping, any voice can be a powerful tool for mobilizing young people and those around them. Engaging stakeholders (including parents and teachers) together with youth in the visioning, design, and evaluation of the program is key to strengthening a sense of community ownership of the program and to sustaining a vibrant movement.

Youthwork practice must be flexible and culturally situational in order to be meaningful. The practice should stem from a deep understanding of the local culture, conditions, and varying local realities of young people and should avoid being misperceived as a threat or intrusion. It should also be flexible and aware that societies are not stagnant but dynamic entities and aware that families can live in the same proximity but hold very different values and approaches.

This problem was encountered in some more conservative villages in the West Bank that did not approve of mixing males and females: Addressing this problem disrupted the process and led to an internal feud within the community. Youthworkers need to be skilled in respecting diversity of opinion and observing and acting appropriately within those situations. We should be flexible and ready to improvise, recognizing that in working towards social change there is no one recipe for all. Hence even after three years, the PA manual, while setting basic guidelines for implementation of the PA process, is still a work in progress and constantly adapting to feedback from practice and the reality on the ground.

DISCUSSION

According to Freire (1968), "Hopelessness is a 'concrete entity'" (p. 8) created by economic, historical, and social forces of oppression and is intensified in the absence of a "critical knowledge of reality" (p. 30). He counsels that the oppressed need to avoid seeing their predicament as irresolvable but to recast it as a "limiting situation that they can transform." We believe that within the Palestinian context, the PA model that we have used has been on target in the way it channels the prevalent hopelessness among young people, transforms the feeling that they are impotent in the face of the oppressive nature of the occupation, and shapes them into critical thinkers and actors who challenge these power structures. They have contributed to building a grass-roots, community-based democratic practice that liberates them from the fear of failure and unleashes their skills and talents. PA seeks to facilitate the creation and maintenance of a free space where young people are able to define their own roles.

As we enter the third year of Popular Achievement in Palestine and start to expand into other countries in the region, we raise the question of to what extent our work with young people is truly laying the foundation for viable authentic, meaningful, and effective youth participation that is able to challenge power structures (political, social, or economic) through non-violent means as intended. To what extent is this particular model of youth civic engagement effective within the context of a space that has experienced or continues to experience violence? How can we demonstrate that youth civic engagement is a stepping stone for building foundations of positive citizenship and peace?

With few prospects for a peaceful resolution of the conflict on the short run, an unstable new government, and a persistent military occupation of the West Bank and Gaza, it is worth noting that in Palestine, by necessity and by choice, youth civic engagement is in every sense "work in progress." The challenges described here are more than likely to continue to stand as obstacles in the face of proactive change that is stimulated from the grass roots, yet it is vital in maintaining hope for community-shaped, youth-led change.

Suzanne Hammad
Tareq AlBakri
Queen's University, Northern Ireland

REFERENCES

AlBakri, T., & Hammad, S. (2001). *American Friends Service Committee assessment of the needs of Palestinian youth in the West Bank and Gaza: Main findings.* Amman, Jordan: American Friends Service Committee.
Freire, P. (1968). *Pedagogy of the oppressed.* New York: Seabury.
Palestinian Central Bureau of Statistics. (1999). *Palestinian youth, facts, and figures.* Ramallah: Palestinian Central Bureau of Statistics.

REBECCA MANSKI

AN INVISIBLE CONFLICT: THE CLASH OF CIVIC, CULTURAL, AND NATIONAL IDENTITIES WITHIN PALESTINIAN YOUTH GROWING UP INSIDE ISRAEL

WHEN EXTERNAL CONFLICTS BECOME INTERNAL: AN OVERVIEW OF CHALLENGES FACED BY PALESTINIAN YOUTH IN ISRAEL

Palestinian youth – comprising over half of the Palestinians living inside Israel[123]-- are born in the midst of a complex spectrum of external and internal conflicts over their rights as citizens and human beings, over the transition from conservativism to modernity, and over their identities as Palestinians with Israeli citizenship.

The civic and political conflicts young Palestinians confront as citizens of Israel include the under-funding of public Arab schools compared with public Jewish schools,[124] the promotion of exclusively Zionist curricula and concurrent omission of Palestinian views of history, the repression of Arab student solidarity with Palestinians in the West Bank and Gaza, the treatment of Arab citizens as potential enemies, the perception of Arab births as a "demographic threat," and the maintenance of the Jewish majority and accompanying threats of transfer.

Always unique, sometimes stigmatized, and oft-forgotten, Palestinians in Israel live isolated from the Jewish majority, Palestinians in the Occupied Territories, the Arab World, and the rest of the globe. Even as their identity as Palestinians is repressed within Israeli society, the Arab world and their fellow Palestinians regard them exclusively as Israelis. Unable to travel to Arab countries that deny entry to Israeli citizens, they live isolated from millions of neighboring Arabs while surrounded by Jews. And, at the same time, most of the world is not even aware that they exist, much less that they are the original inhabitants of the land now known as Israel. All this compounds the personal and communal identity conflicts that arise as they sort through confusion over the civic, national, and cultural aspects of being an Israeli citizen and part of the Palestinian people and the Arab world.

---

[123]Palestinians in Israel are the population remaining after the 1948 conflict between Zionists and surrounding Arab nations. Almost all Palestinians in Israel, despite remaining within the bounds of what is now Israel, are internally displaced refugees.

[124] The Israeli public school system is divided into separate, segregated tiers for Jews and Arabs.

Doug Magnuson and Michael Baizerman (eds), Work with Youth in Divided and Contested Societies, 217–234.

© 2007 *Sense Publishers. All rights reserved.*

Unending Internal Displacement and Government Neglect

Almost all Palestinians in Israel are refugees or the offspring of refugees, internally displaced people who were forced to flee their villages or cities for shelter in neighboring areas. Sadly, this history of displacement is not over. The experience of continual displacement leading to overcrowding is compounded by profound government neglect. For instance, elementary students in the village of *Ein Mahel*, (adjacent to Nazareth) are forced to spill over to tiny impromptu classrooms in homes across the street because the government will not zone more land for their school to accommodate its growing student body. Meanwhile, a few kilometres away in the Jewish city of Nazaret-Elit, the local school boasts an Olympic-sized swimming pool and immense playing field.

The government plans threaten to demolish 45 "unrecognised"[126] Bedouin villages, remove their 70,000 inhabitants, and concentrate them in seven towns yet to be constructed (*Ha'aretz,* 2002). Then, the government claims, the Bedouin of the unrecognized villages will receive social services long denied them as residents of locales unrecognized by the Israeli government.[127]

Commonly, the so-called "modernization process" (and its accompanying practices of land confiscation, population displacement, and overcrowding) has rapidly transformed Palestinian agrarian-village culture while failing to build the infrastructure necessary to support industrial-urban society. Urban planner Harvey Lithwick (2000), of the Negev Center for Regional Development, compares the seven government towns built for the Bedouin in the 1970s with nearby Jewish settlements built by the government, capturing the paradoxes of Arab citizenship in Israel: "...down the road from all the other Bedouin towns are all-Jewish towns and luxurious residential suburbs. They feature private houses with green lawns and gardens, public swimming pools, expansive public parks, bustling shopping plazas, spotless streets and sidewalks, and modern new schools and community and youth centers" (p. 3).

Obstacles to Economic and Educational Advancement

As the modernization process has rendered traditional forms of Palestinian self-subsistence obsolete, economic alternatives have often failed to develop, leaving young workers without any hope of advancement. Somewhat ironically, the Bedouin – the Arab population promised the most by the Israeli government – also suffer the most extreme discrimination and the worst economic situation.[128]

---

[126] Villages not zoned or recognized by the Israeli government as legal entities.

[127] These tens of thousands of Bedouin are under threat of removal because the Israeli government refuses to accept their right to live in the villages in which they were born and negates their right to engage in subsistence agriculture on the lands they have roamed for over 500 years.

[128] One in six Bedouin first-graders are malnourished, 50% of children in "unrecognised" Bedouin villages are hospitalized in the first year of their life, and the Bedouin suffer the highest infant mortality rate in Israel. (www.rcuv.org)

As a result, tensions between Bedouin villages and the lush Jewish suburbs around them have grown. According to Israeli government statistics, in 2000 the Bedouin town of Tel Sheva was rated economically as the third most impoverished Israeli town out of a total of 204. Just down the road, the neighbouring Jewish town of Omer – which should be the most liveable town in Israel according to the same survey – has the highest rate of car theft in the country (Lithwick, 2000, p. 46). In the absence of basic educational opportunity and jobs, crime has become one of the only career paths available to the youth of Tel Sheva and many other Bedouin towns. [134]

The Negation of the Distinct Identity of Palestinians in Israel

Programming nurturing Arab students' cultural identity is conspicuously absent from state-mandated curricula. While Arab students in public schools study a wide range of aspects of Jewish history from an exclusively Zionist perspective, including the history of the Diaspora, the Holocaust, and the creation of the State in 1948, they graduate high school having learned next to nothing about the connection between their society and hundreds of years of Islamic civilization, their experience during the Ottoman Empire, or movements for an independent Palestinian state during colonial British rule. Nadem Nashef says that,

> The Arab education system is separate from the Jewish system and is run by the Ministry of Education, which has mostly Jewish staff. And it does not give money to independently-run Arab educational ventures. The Ministry as a whole has a proven agenda of deleting and canceling Palestinian identity. There is a tight control system on teachers and headmasters in terms of what they are allowed and not allowed to say. And there is also a kind of fear in the education system, because if you are a teacher, you know that if you talk openly about Palestinian issues, you could pay some kind of price. You could find yourself skipped for promotions, and in the 1970s and 1980s, many people were expelled from the system. Even today if you want to become a teacher, the first step is to go through a security check.
>
> The result is that teachers will not deal with these issues, and the kids do not have the opportunity to deal with them. And thus there's a lot of ignorance among Arabs about the most basic events in their own history. And when the kids learn, for example, about 1948 (the year over a

---

[129] The potential to develop as a society is fundamentally stilted by a lack of educational opportunity, and crime has supplanted other forms of economic activity: 25% of teachers serving the Bedouin community are unqualified to teach, 60% of Bedouin students drop out and, of those remaining, 6% pass their high school matriculation exams. According to the governmental unemployment index, which rates the 23 most jobless locales in the nation, the seven government towns are consistently rated the most underemployed of all communities in Israel. Not surprisingly, crime is rampant: From 1998 to 1999 alone, crime in the Bedouin community increased by 37%. See: http://www.rcuv.org, the website of the Council of Unrecognised Villages.

a million Palestinians became refugees on the eve of the declaration of the State of Israel) it's through a Zionist discourse. And you learn that, basically, the Arabs–who you are–were the enemy.

And at the same time you learn about the Jewish people, Jewish culture, the Jewish religion – all of this is compulsory. It is good to learn about these things. The problem starts when you don't also learn about where you came from, who you are, your identity, and then you can't know what it is you want to do with yourself, your society, in the future. From there start many problems.

So those of us who were facilitating conflict-resolution groups between Jews and Palestinians in Israel saw a big gap between Jewish kids and the Palestinian kids in terms of their level of social and political and self-awareness. You could see, very clearly, the difference in the quality of the education received and the results, the outcome of it, the gap in identity. The Jewish kids knew a lot about themselves as Jews, and the Arabs knew a lot about Jewish history too. But the Jewish kids didn't know anything about Arab history and, in many cases, neither did the Arabs. In these Jewish-Arab meetings, no special space was given to rectify this imbalance between Arabs and Jewish knowledge of the "other" or of themselves.

Arab Youth as Inherently Suspect: October 2000

The frustration of young Arab citizens concerning the impacts of budgetary inequity, a dearth of Arab political representation, and a general lack of voice in the wider Israeli public sphere was expressed during the cataclysmic events of October, 2000, in which tens of thousands of Arab youth took to the streets.

It was a kind of turning point to understand that one day, you may be a citizen and think that the state has some commitments to you…the normal relation between a citizen and the state…..and in a few days, or even in a matter of hours, you can become basically nothing, and your life worth can be worth nothing. (Nadem Nashef, personal communication)

In the months following the collapse of the Camp David Accords, tensions within Israel and the Occupied Territories escalated rapidly. Inside Israel, politically aware young Arabs noted no sign of implementation of education and budgetary reforms promised by former Prime Minister Ehud Barak; at the same time, young Palestinian workers found their economic situation declining.

At the height of tension, flanked by 3000 armed men, then Knesset Member Ariel Sharon pushed his way onto the grounds of the principal mosque in Jerusalem (Al-Aqsa). Worshipers at Al-Aqsa felt violated by Sharon's flagrant parade of military might and interpreted the presence of armed men as a sign of Israeli efforts to exert dominion over their holy site. Arab citizens, most of them youth, took to the streets. In the protests that ensued, police and racist Jewish mobs clashed with demonstrators, and the Israeli government's security forces killed 13 Arab citizens. Two of these youth had been chased into an olive grove, beaten severely, and shot at point blank range. One of these youth was a student in a co-existence program.

In an interview on Israeli Radio Reshet Bet one morning after several young Arab men had been killed by live-fire, Barak commended the police for their "restraint" as much as he lamented the general unrest: "....the police commanders....deserve great compliments for their self-restraint yesterday during the demonstrations, but I gave them the green light for any action necessary to bring about the rule of law...." (Dalal, 2003, p. 20). Nearly all Arab citizens of Israel, whether integrated or not, "Good Arabs" or "Bad Arabs," felt that they were perceived as enemies of the State.

Arab Children as "Demographic Threat:" Alienation & Fears of Transfer

As each year passes, and as the Arab population grows, every Arab child has come to be seen as a threat. A *Chicago Tribune* article (2002) noted the growing anxiety of Israelis concerning the growth of the Arab population in Israel: "Some say that ticking below the surface of the violent confrontation between Arab and Jews is a silent bomb, a demographic bomb." The once controversial "Koenig Report on Handling the Arabs in Israel" (1976) recommended: "Expand and deepen Jewish settlement in areas where the continuity of the Arab population is prominent....examine the possibility of diluting existing Arab populations." However taboo its assertions at the time, the Koenig Report's recommendations have become a core part of Israeli government policy and imbue the subconscious of many mainstream Israelis (Asher, 2002). Such thinking has dire impacts for future generations of Palestinians with Israeli citizenship and for decades has influenced Arab youth's feelings of alienation in their homeland.

As recently as February 5, 2003, a headline in the Israeli daily *Ma'ariv* read, "Special Report: Polygamy is a Security Threat," and detailed a report published by Herzl Gadge, the Director of the Population Administration Department, a department of the "Demographic Council" concerned with maintaining a "superior" number of Jews to Arabs.[130] Meanwhile, the open discussion of transfer in Israeli politics of late has lent legitimacy to the transfer concept and generally increased the public's receptivity to the idea of expulsion as a solution to either "the Arab question" or "the Bedouin problem" (Blecher, 2002; Haas, 2003). The reference of Beni Alon (former Minister of Tourism, founder of Ehud Leumi) to transfer rings in the ears of young Arab citizens determining their life paths and of parents striving to build a future for their children: "We will make their lives hard until they *ask* to leave" (*Ne'eman*, 2002). Ehud Leumi, among other far-right parties in favour of transfer, was invited into Prime Minister Ariel Sharon's coalition government, and their ideas have since become far less fringe (Arian, 2002).

---

[130] For instance, midway through the project, attempting to prepare them in some sense for the possible scenario in which Arabs are transferred by force or Jews are outnumbered by Arabs.

221

LIVING SIDE BY SIDE? LIVING SEPARATELY?
OR LIVING *TOGETHER*?

Unfortunately, although Jews and Arabs in Israeli society interact on a daily basis, surprisingly little dialogue occurs in these interactions, and "co-existence" efforts to address this reality have generally produced superficial results. Despite extensive investment in encouraging dialogue between Palestinians and Jews, and the proliferation of numerous co-existence projects, Arabs involved in meetings between Arabs and Jews often tend to feel tokenized. Thus the bulk of "co-existence" efforts thus far have tended not only to be insufficient for the resolution of conflict but in many cases to actually exacerbate inequalities. In the Palestinian context in Israel, the word "co-existence" has come to connote a spurious and contrived show of mingling mostly aimed at soliciting funding. Furthermore, for many the word itself suggests an ideal of "living side-by-side" rather than "living together." As a result many Palestinian youthworkers who at one time were interested in Arab-Jewish exchange have come to feel that the fundamental problems the next generation will face cannot be addressed through mere meetings or discussions with Jewish Israelis.

The Option of Exploring Narratives

Baladna's work has always unflinchingly referred to the historical roots of current perceptions. Baladna has initiated strategic planning for a project that will enable Palestinian youth to thoroughly and personally engage their own history and to share it with others in an enlightening way. In contrast with "co-existence" projects, which generally advise participants against "dwelling" on the past-- discouraging participants from engaging in a healthy inquiry about their origins and the origins of the "other"--this project will give youth an unprecedented opportunity to examine their pasts sufficiently that they may knowledgeably plan for their future.

The aim of the project is to instruct groups of Palestinian youth living in Israel and selected groups of Jewish youth as well in gathering stories from their grandparents about their dreams when they were young. We think it will be very interesting to see the similarity between the dreams of Palestinian and Jewish grandparents and the contrast between their levels of realization.

We believe that guiding youth through facing past realities will enable them to predict and explore how they want to react to any emerging negative or potentially positive realities.[131] Most importantly, we aim to help them to consider

---

[131] For instance, some Arab youth might wish for the Jewish people to simply go back to where they came from, and some Jewish youth might want the Palestinian people to simply accept living within the bounds of Israel as a "Jewish State" and accept that this means their refugee relatives will not be allowed to return.

what they realistically want for their futures. [132] By the end of the project, we hope that we can bring the youth involved to examine what having these wishes fulfilled would mean for the evolution of their own people and the well-being of the "other."

History has shown, time and again, that people who appear to "co-exist," who live side-by-side as neighbors throughout a lifetime, who eat together at work, and who sit next to one another at the movie theater, are nevertheless capable of slaughtering one another. Furthermore, while in everyday life all may appear calm, history shows that the strict roles upon which social constructs and political systems depend do not disclose themselves fully until the crucial moment – such as at the start and the end of an *intifada* or a regional war. Only genuine connections based on a deep understanding of friends and neighbors can withstand the ups and downs of the historical moment.

THE DEMOCRATIC POTENTIALOF THE MIDDLE EAST:THE FUTURE PALESTINIAN LEADERSHIP

The Oslo period and the subsequent cataclysmic events of October, 2000, showed, as many civil rights movements have realized before, that "Power concedes nothing without a demand" (Douglass, 1857). Adding to the important body of advocacy work being done by our fellow NGOs, Baladna seeks to rectify the sense of powerlessness felt among the previous two generations – shrouded in an atmosphere of fear of surveillance by Israeli secret service agents – and to lift a half-century hush in the Arab community in Israel about its status as the indigenous population of Palestinians who remained in the western part of historic Palestine when Israel was created.

It is Baladna's view that only when Palestinian youth have opportunities to know who their people are in all their diversity, what their history is, and what their rights are can they become true leaders of their community. In this way Baladna promotes the resolution of the internal identity conflicts that arise in Palestinian youth in Israel as a pre-requisite for any lasting and *genuine* resolution of the Israel-Palestine conflict. It has often been speculated that – should the Palestinian people see the fulfillment of their right to a state – the Palestinian people could have a unique role to play in the organic democratization of the Middle East from within. In turn, Arab citizens of Israel, with comparatively more experience with the democratic process than most in the region, could play a key role in democratization efforts in the West Bank and Gaza as well. Thus it is imperative that genuine and diligent efforts be devoted to establishing avenues for Arab youth to develop genuine access to the democratic system and to play a central role in any diplomatic process between Israelis and Palestinians. Furthermore, as 19% of

---

[132] The Israeli government has categorized the Palestinian people residing within its bounds since 1948 according to ethnic and religious classifications, drafting the Druze minority, recruiting the Bedouin, and accepting a margin of Christians into the Israeli army. Muslims who are not Bedouin have been deemed too "uncooperative" for army service, and placed in a separate legal category.

the total population of Israel, 13% of its voters, and 19% of the Palestinian people, Arab citizens of Israel could have unique influence over any future resolution to the regional conflict. As Israeli citizens and members of the Palestinian people, Arabs in Israel have come to know both sides of the conflict intimately and are well-equipped to grasp potential solutions.

Unfortunately, in 2002 89% of Israelis polled by the Jaffee Center for Strategic Studies at Tel Aviv University were opposed to inclusion of Arab citizens in "crucial national decisions, such as determining the future borders of the country" (Arian, 2002). Moreover, through all their years of intervention in the diplomatic process, the United States government, European Union, and the Arab world have barely acknowledged the rare perspective of Palestinians inside Israel. And, sadly, it must be acknowledged that the Arab community suffers internal disunity, exacerbated to the extreme via the classic colonialist strategy of "Divide to Rule." The extremity of the assault on the rights of the Bedouin, the unique history and status of the Druze, the many different experiences of Palestinians in the north versus the south of Israel, and enduring military occupation versus suffering rampant discrimination, have made it more difficult for Palestinians to relate to one another on the political level or to unite in fighting for a common cause.

We don't have a leader who thinks about what is good for the whole population, for the whole generation, for our future--a leader who plans for our future and is aware of our situation here inside Israel. Because of this I think it's very important to work on identity because the identity issue is very complicated here, for Arabs inside Israel.... I told you the youth sometimes feel it's okay if the Jews are above them... To be a leader they must know that: " I'm a Palestinian – I'm an Arab citizen inside Israel which claims to be a democratic state – so I have the right to be equal to the Jewish person and then this right I should use and not sit down and wait for the Jewish people to give it to me." They must know nobody gives you your rights. The circle of identity is connected to the circle of empowerment and the circle of rights.

-Rose Amer, Leadership Center Coordinator

As Palestinians throughout Israel, the West Bank, Gaza, refugee camps, and the global Diaspora face their particular predicament each in their own way, they share in common the tragedy of the division, displacement, and isolation of their people. For Palestinians in Israel – for whom the Israeli government's strategy of divide and rule has been a central challenge – remaining connected with their history, their people, and their culture constitutes a significant form of resistance.

THE RESOLUTION OF INTERNAL IDENTITY CONFLICTS
AS A PREREQUISITE FOR RECONCILIATION

Baladna programs and workers take Palestinian youth in Israel through overlapping phases of identity exploration and development necessary for the emergence of effective leadership qualities and community action: Individual and collective identity development, critical questioning, individual and collective action and experimenting with social action, and leadership through sharing energy and experience with others. All of these stages of *development, questioning,* and *action* lead to the emergence of young leaders able to extend the fruits of their experience in order to assist other youth in their own identity formation process. Baladna's approach, in which no one tells youth what to think or do or speaks for them, aims at the creation of a space in which youth can discover their interests, strengths, and weaknesses; develop their skills, and; take whatever path towards action such as art, teaching, protest, or media advocacy that makes them feel a sense of satisfaction and belonging.

Phase I: Individual and Collective Identity Development

At the heart of the identity development process lies the fundamental Baladna commitment to the principle of never claiming to bestow any magical solutions, never pushing slogans or forcing ideology, and working to offer an alternative to the official styles and contents of the formal education system. Our youth groups are centered on providing a healthy platform where youth may independently come to their own conclusions.

While engaging in autonomous inquiry as well as throughout the process of creating a safe space in which to collectively explore identity, it is crucial that Palestinian youth in Israel do not unintentionally isolate themselves from potential allies or from unpleasant realities. Opportunities for exchange with "outsiders" offer welcome respite and healthy perspective on the complex environment in which Arabs in Israel live. Part of this process involves connecting Arab youth with events organized by and with local Palestinian and Jewish organizations that respect Palestinian identity and are working for a common vision of a fully democratic country. Baladna also assures that Palestinian youth in Israel have access to a wide range of views and perspectives by linking Arab youth with the international community through youth exchanges, field trips, work-camps, and talks. Although in some ways the simplest aspect of Baladna's work, cross-cultural encounters are nevertheless in many regards one of the most fundamentally identity-shaping experiences Palestinian youth in Israel can have.

Furthermore, Baladna youth group discussions are always supplemented by the perspective of international human rights standards. Thus all Baladna youth learn about the United Nations Human Development Report, the Covenant on

Minority Rights, and the difference between general human rights and minority rights, citizen and human rights. All youth engage in activities about the connection between democracy and freedom, the tensions between rights of the minority and majority, and contradictions between different human rights. The international human rights dimension of Baladna curricula both allow youth to see that there are laws higher than that of the individual nation-state in which they live and also provide the basis for their understanding that the violation of human rights is an international phenomenon as well. Above all, awareness of international protocols can lead youth to be more assertive in breaking away from the segregated mentality and world in which they are born and making connections with like-minded individuals anywhere in the world, including throughout different regions of Palestine/Israel. Youth see that developing an internationalist, humanistic perspective can be an antidote to feelings of isolation.

Interestingly enough, when Baladna youth discuss feelings of isolation caused by racism and segregation, rather than engaging the question of racism between Arabs and Jews, questions about separation within the Palestinian community more commonly arise. Following an encounter with Black Bedouin in the south, northern youth expressed surprise that they did not know there were both Black and White Palestinians, an indication of the degree of isolation between Palestinians inside Israel.

To address youth's lack of awareness of the diversity within the Palestinian people, one youth group leader asked her youth to watch news from different sources and to observe the different lives that Palestinians lead: in refugee camps, under occupation, in unrecognized villages, in cities, and in villages. As the youth sorted through the many different conditions of life Palestinians experience, they were also able to note the commonalities within the Palestinian experience and way of life. In addition to giving the youth a greater sense of wholeness and connectedness with their people, they also came to see themselves as part of a larger body of people in the region, specifically, and not necessarily a downtrodden minority. Furthermore, youth saw that in comparison to other Palestinians, whether under military siege or in refugee camps, they live in a better economic situation and have far more access to the Israeli legal and political system. In individual cases, this realization can lead youth to feel a sense of power they may not usually feel and also to sense their responsibility to use what rights they have to make change.

During weekly meetings of a youth group living adjacent to the Green Line and right next to the West Bank town of Salfit, Baladna youth commented regularly on the irrationality of not being permitted to speak with or know Arabic-speaking Palestinians in the adjacent village, minutes away, while they are free to know Hebrew-speaking Israelis further away. They expressed concern about how their fellow Palestinians view them as well as how they had come to view themselves.

After considering common Hebrew words that delegitimize them as Palestinians and as citizens with full rights to their homeland, the youth considered the way the sudden classification of Palestinians who remained in Israel as

"Israelis" created a superficial semantic barrier that directly cut them off from the rest of the Arab World. The youth group members spoke of the feeling of watching Arab television shows and relating to them and then remembering that they cannot be part of the world they see. They asked Amer: "We speak the same language and we have the same culture, so why are we seen as enemies? Why can a foreigner go there but we, who feel so close to this culture and are part of it and have a real connection, cannot?" Thus, a simple piece of paper (an Israeli passport), which should signify their rights as citizens actually limits their freedom of movement to regions to which they are most culturally connected. This is a conflict that no youth group leader can resolve in his or her group, any more than she or he can solve it in life. Nevertheless, an exercise such as this can lead youth to make connections they might not otherwise make until much later in the lives, ushering in a humanistic clarity of values and assured sense of self that can to some extent liberate youth from their feelings of placelessness.

Phase II: Critical Questioning

For Palestinian youth born into an extremely complex situation, walking over the ruins of many conquerors, surrounded by the remains of their grandparents' villages, and living in the midst of new Israeli construction, the opportunity to discuss the past and present openly is vital to understanding why they live in a situation of conflict today. For instance, youth might notice recent Jewish immigrants from Ethiopia or Russia and wonder how they came here while some of their relatives who live abroad as refugees cannot move back. This kind of everyday observation may confuse or undermine their sense of belonging in the land in which they were born.

For instance, one youth group leader asked her members whether they would want to live in Palestine if in the future a Palestinian state were to be created. Half of the group answered that they would move to the Palestinian State (in most cases the more politically-minded among them) and the other half answered that they would not. The youth then asked each other, "Where is Palestine?" and explained to the leader that when she said the word "Palestine" they didn't know exactly what she meant: "Here" or "There." At this stage the leader explained that the right to stay on the land on which you born is a human right.

Because many Palestinian youth, like youth in other parts of the world, receive an abridged and often censored version of historical events than actually transpired, they often lack a basic sense of the connection between their rights to a home and the history of their home. While the generally boring, dry version they learn serves to discourage any interest in history, when they have the opportunity to make connections between historical events and the reality they see around them, history suddenly becomes a very lively subject.

For instance, when one group leader referred to at least 500 years of Palestinian presence in the region before 1948 and the impacts of the creation of the State of Israel on the Palestinian people, her youth group asked her, "If this is true and not made up, why aren't there history books about this?"

In response, the next week the leader brought her group a variety of different history books, oral histories, maps, and fact-sheets and asked them about the ruins of Palestinian homes they might have seen on the roadsides or as they walk in national parks. After discussing the books before them, they looked at mainstream Israeli textbooks, commenting that they were much more boring and furthermore concluded that their history is not represented there. Rather than offering an explanation, the leader asked them why they thought that was. The youth independently came to the conclusion that most history is the history of the strong, that it is told by those in control, as they document their victories. This same conclusion may well have ignited the beginning of the careers of many activists worldwide, snapping them out of youthful withdrawal and confusion.

Over the course of a year of youth group meetings, Baladna youth gradually come to see that unequal access to the wider discussion or representation in the official narrative occurs within their society as well, particularly with regard to gender dynamics. For many Palestinian girls, it is especially clear that if they wish to struggle for the rights of their people, they must first engage in personal struggles within their families to attend school, leave their home, travel abroad, and so forth. Thus recognizing their rights as women is, in pure practical terms, a precondition for full participation in wider struggles.

Unsurprisingly, at the adolescent stage of development, political questions tend to be overshadowed by gender questions and questions about family roles; out of all the discussions Baladna youth group leaders lead, the discussion of gender roles can be the most delicate to resolve. Furthermore, male or female, the first experience many youth have with making change often starts within the family. It is important that this process be a positive one, and while Baladna cannot help youth to directly contend with their private struggles, we do help them to sort through related questions so that they may focus on the larger picture and experience their full potential.

Perhaps my first big struggle was an internal conflict in the family, the village. I used to study Tae Kwon Do, and some men in the village were talking about me: "Why is a religious girl learning to be a black belt?" My father was a good, good man, but he tried to protect me from this gossip by preventing me from continuing. I put my foot down, and I wouldn't let him stop me because there was nothing else to do in the village and martial arts gave me so much power and energy! This was my first experience as a youth striving to find my way, and I always remember the potential of such experiences to develop into platforms for leadership when I work with young people today. I might have applied the techniques of debate if I had them then.

-Rose Amer, Leadership Center Coordinator

In a discussion of the rebellion of children against their parents' way of life, most boys in Baladna youth groups say that they do not like the norms their parents force upon them, while many girls felt that their parents' expectations are meant to make them feel secure, cared for, and protected. Interestingly enough, at other points in the discussion these same girls said that they fought constantly with their parents. In these situations, group leaders are faced with the challenge of pointing out the contradictions in the perspectives of the girls, without leading to more fights at home.

All Baladna youth are guided through discussions about relations inside the Palestinian family, engaging in role-playing activities, exploring gender stereotypes, and talking about limitations on freedom and the tension between individual rights and social strictures and assumptions. Youth come to understand the choice between safety and adventure and the ways that social norms can offer positive life-path guidelines as well as how the socialization process can make people less creative and free.

When one youth group leader asked her youth why conflicts between parents and children occur, the group quickly understood that conflicts between parents and children about gender are related to differences in appropriate reactions to different points in history. They also concluded that the family imposes gender definitions in undeclared ways through hidden messages and models of conduct based on the time period in which their parents navigated the maturation process and not always adapted to the present reality.

While some youth in the groups commented that they feel that things are changing for the better, observing that in Nazareth, at least, girls go to study, travel abroad, work, and sometimes meet boys, other students--mostly girls--said that this was a negative development exploited by both boys and by girls because it is often not accompanied by a full sense of self-awareness. In response, the Nazareth youth group leader asked the girls with more conservative perspectives to reflect on their own fashion tendencies, which at once follow the norm and yet are somewhat radical: "Are your low-cut jeans negative liberation or positive liberation?" she asked, which led some in the group to comment on the tendency of societies to reject those who fail to follow social norms, whether radical or conservative.

In the end of such discussions, youth often come to the conclusion that today, with such a mix of radical and conservative norms, it is no longer possible to always follow all of the traditional rules and current norms/fashions of society at once. Considering this question, Baladna youth groups often conclude that each person must make these decisions for themselves and avoid judging others for coming to opposite conclusions as they sort through similar confusion. This independent process is a more powerful, meaningful, and lasting lesson in understanding than the common "brainwashing for tolerance" in many schools. It also encourages youth to do more than "tolerate" difference: It shows them that they should actively *accept* it and encourages them to support one another's efforts to make more room for innovation in Arab society.

Phase III: Experimenting with Social Action

One of the greatest challenges youthworkers contend with is the task of dispelling the coercive associations many young people have with the idea of social action. While social change requires expertise and strategy and all youth require significant guidance in order to implement such a strategy, in essence the best way to teach youth to lead is to give them the space to explore their own interests and develop their abilities accordingly. In this way we strive to help youth see that there is no one path to change, no one definition of progress, and no single leader to follow. Even in our rather novice experience with the Public Achievement model thus far, we have quickly seen that, as youth watch their peers make decisions for themselves and implement their own visions, community action can be fun and contagious for young people.

In brainstorming a Public Achievement project of their own, one of Baladna's youth groups in the "recognized" government town of Rahat in the Naqab Desert first considered working on a variety of issues beyond the range of their community. Quickly they reflected that they were failing to see the problems right before their eyes: government neglect in terms of a lack of general services such as water, electricity, or education in their own town. Realizing their lack of awareness of their own experience with discrimination, they decided they would first educate themselves about their surroundings and then engage the situation of the unrecognised villages nearby. Afterwards, they would spread the awareness gained with their immediate peers and neighbours. Thus, just in the process of brainstorming, they came to critique their own approach and learned something about themselves.

Following extensive research into the current reality of unrecognised villages in this country, the reasons for their emergence, and the wider political context in which they continue to exist, they arranged visits to some neighbouring villages and presented their findings to local youth. Rather than being bored with apparently dull lectures about something far from their reality, the youth were instead thrilled to see the interest shown in their situation. One of the key results of the experience was that the youth in the audience expressed that they themselves should be doing more to address these concerns in their own community.

Perhaps if this had been an adult-led project, the youth would have felt that they had fulfilled their duties and the process would have ended there. Instead, the project, although complete according to the framework established by Public Achievement (just two months to brainstorm, research, and execute a project) was actually far from finished. From these initial talks emerged a further effort to lobby public officials at Rahat's Local Council to clean up a park that should have been a central gathering place for neighbourhood youth picnicking or playing football but instead housed a slew of drug dealers increasingly engaged in violent crimes. Out of this highly unusual meeting between the town officials at the Local Council and local Rahat teenagers came a promise to invest in greening the park and making it a safe place to play.

Only at this stage did an adult, Baladna's youth group leader, Omar Nasrara, step in to advise the youth. He explained that the chances of implementation of the promise were low but emphasized that the youth should remain proud of themselves for having the courage and sense of their rights to approach an adult in a position of power. The staff at Baladna were led happily to wonder: If all of Baladna's 400 youth did something similar, what could happen? Indeed, if thousands of youth felt empowered enough to hold decision-makers accountable to promises such as these, they could potentially be more effective than the individual, highly-skilled advocacy professionals who currently engage in lobbying to hold officials accountable.

ASAR: Before we were shy and couldn't talk to the society and say our opinion and now we talk and we are more involved. We have an active role in the society and our personality is stronger now.

AMIR: A lot of people want to do what we do now in the society but there is nobody to help them and to push them and support them.

ASAR: What we've learned, we want to give it to the next generation.

AMIR: We want them to learn and to pass on the process....Maybe to have a youth group with those who are younger than us. Maybe I could help and work in the society and maybe I will be a youth group facilitator one year.

ASAR: There is a fear about the future; we are not sure about it... One day is for you and ten days are against you. But there is a bit of hope and we still believe we can do something...

AMIR: We want to be involved because we look around and we see a lot of bad things happening and we want to change. Especially the cultural behavior that we think has a bad effect on the society and should be changed.

ASAR: For example our Public Achievement project was about youth and drugs and we wanted to do something to change this.

AMIR: And also early marriage. It's a phenomenon in our society that we would like to change. We meet once a week and we talk about all these things. We do activities for the younger children at the school... And we are members of the student's council at our school. And every year we are involved in the memorial day of the massacre of Qufr Qasem; we do activities on that day. Everything related to our society, we try to do something for the other generations...

AMIR: After discussing these issues and discussing them deeply, we decided to continue working on them. And we know a lot of things that we didn't know before. It has changed our personality.

- Members of Baladna's youth group in Qufr Qasem

Phase IV: Sharing Energy and Experience with Others:
Becoming Leaders in the Youth Movement

"Creating leaders," according to the common definition, that is, those who become renowned within the political system or media, is not Baladna's only aim. Neither is creating leaders according to the activist definition: a great speech-maker who leads mass protest movements. Of course, where our youth have the talent and interest to approach leadership roles in these ways, we are here to give them training, guidance, support, and inspiration. However, when the youth we deal with (i.e. the majority) do not have the personality types that one might classically associate with a leader, we strive to nurture whatever leadership qualities they do have and to link them with localized opportunities to lead, regardless of their potential on a wider scale. Above all, we work to prepare them to make challenging life choices in a fully conscious manner and to share their convictions with their immediate community, within their careers, and as citizens.

It has long been clear to Baladna that traditional advocacy for youth by adults can be just as disempowering to youth as any other kind of advocacy in which the community in need does not take part. Thus, most recently, Baladna has developed a grassroots approach to advocacy, a self-advocacy mentorship system in which a select group of motivated youth each year will learn the tools for advocacy themselves and *speak for themselves* as they engage in advocacy for all youth.

Clearly, one of the most basic aspects of youthwork involves mentoring, and youth find young mentors easier to relate to. Thus as an organization, our staff are also quite young. Although our National Coordinator is currently only 25 years old, she has an extremely wide academic, artistic, and NGO background for her years, herself a role model for those under her care. Our board is comprised of young and inspired community members who believe in the necessity of creating a youth movement and who themselves participate actively and regularly in Baladna's study tours, seminars, and exchanges. Baladna's established network of youth groups is fundamentally youth-led and youth-run. Every year, Baladna's newest community of youth group leaders emerge naturally from our annual leadership course in which former youth group leaders play a major role as trainers and presenters. In the next year, Baladna will encourage promising high school youth group members to become leaders once they graduate, offering young members leadership training following an adapted version of the curriculum our college-level leadership course trainees experience. In this way we will start to train older youth group members to recruit younger high-school youth, form a youth group, and thereby become leaders of youth groups of their own.

The prior experience of young adults at a later point on the historical spectrum – who have gone through the process of leaving home and coming to terms with some of those things they most rebelled against – can play a powerful mediating role between the generations, between the village and the city, and between the evolution of womanhood and manhood.[133] In particular, the opportunity to witness the way those only a few years older have dealt with the transition from Arab towns to predominantly Jewish universities can prepare youth for the adjustment from living in an environment in which you are surrounded by Arabs and the moment one suddenly becomes a minority and is treated as such.

It is not a simple task to guide Palestinian youth in Israel through the spectrum of social-change approaches available to them. Every Palestinian youth in

---

[133] For instance, the question of leaving home for college continues to be an issue in the Palestinian community in Israel particularly in the center and south of the country. Najwan Berekdar's youth group had many questions about her experiences as a university student. They liked the idea of meeting Jews and were curious about leaving the majority-Arab environment of Nazareth. Berekdar encouraged her youth group to organize a tour to a nearby university so that they might observe some of the contrasts between college and high-school and Arab life and Jewish life (i.e. more freedom and less control by teachers). During the tour, Berekdar led them to see how they might take advantage of the flexibility and opportunities of college life to try to change their reality, or to become active in the community.

Israel might at some point feel that they have to choose between working for their personal educational and career advancement as an Arab citizen, working internally for social change within the Arab community, struggling for the rights of all Arab citizens within the Israeli system, recognizing their capacity to work in solidarity for the rights of all Palestinians, or fighting for universal human rights everywhere. Baladna helps youth to navigate the burden and potential of these choices and work to show that it is possible and, perhaps, necessary to work at various levels in combination. Baladna believes deeply in promoting a holistic approach to the human rights of all rather than narrowly focusing upon individual rights or civic rights. The end goal of all this work is to strip away all barriers to solidarity between groups committed to true equality. And the means of this process involves distilling the simple value of cooperation between aligned individuals of all classes and religions.

We believe that even if the Arab community in Israel is not fortunate enough to see the emergence of a great leader and Baladna does not singularly produce a Martin Luther King or Nelson Mandela or Malcolm X, we are in a unique position to nurture the crucial perspective and vital conviction necessary for youth to recognize such a leader if she or he were to appear on the scene.

Like most grassroots organizations that believe in the necessity of creating people-led movements, we also work to show them that all movements that have managed to topple racist regimes have done so not merely through following a single leader but, rather, a multitude of freedom-fighters with a range of personalities, acting with a singular clarity of principle, were willing to take personal risks at major turning points in history.

Rebecca Manski
Baladna Association for Arab Youth
Haifa, Israel

REFERENCES

Arian, A. (2002). *A further turn to the tight: Israeli public opinion on national security* (vol 5, no. 1). Tel Aviv University: Jaffee Center for Strategic Studies. Tel Aviv University.

Blecher, R. (2002, Winter). Living on the edge: The threat of "transfer" in Israel and Palestine. *MERIP*, 225.

Channel Two [Israeli Public Television]. (2003). *Second view*, July 22.

Chicago Tribune. (2002). Birthrates alarm Israel. April 21.

Dalal. (2003). *Law and Politics before the Commission of Inquiry*. Adalah Legal Center, July.

Douglass, F. (1857/1985). The significance of emancipation in the West Indies [Speech August 3, 1857]. Canandaigua, New York.

Ha'aretz. (2002). The Bedouin have had enough of roaming. March 3. Jerusalem: Author.

Koenig, I. (1976). The Koenig Report on Handling the Arabs of Israel. Section 1: The Demographic Problem. *Swasia, III*(4), 1-8.

Lithwick, H. (2000). *An urban development strategy for the Negev's Bedouin community*. Negev Center for Regional Development and The Center for Bedouin Studies and Development.

Ne'eman, Y. (2002, February). Israeli Early Elections? Available from: http://www.meontarget.com/archarticles/arch020102/020202isrearlyelections.htm

SNEŽANA KRESOJA

HELSINKI COMMITTEE FOR HUMAN RIGHTS IN SERBIA

ABSTRACT

The Helsinki Committee (HC) Youth Group is established under the auspices of the Novi Sad branch office. Young people, some 25 of them, plan and realize the projects of their own design. Examples of the projects realized in the course of 2005 are *Toys for Peace, The Print Media & Perception of The Hague Tribunal, Children's Rights, Spitting Language, EXIT: Do Something for Your Conscience NOW (Not Only Words),* and *Children's Rights for Teens: Peer Education.*

The *EXIT: Do Something for Your Conscience NOW* project was conducted during the EXIT music festival in July, 2005, in Novi Sad. The Exit Noise Summer Fest is the biggest music festival in southeastern Europe and, in 2005, there were 150,000 people attending, of whom 15,000 were foreigners. The HC Youth Group Novi Sad office launched this project because it was the 10th anniversary of the Srebrenica massacre. This was the only EXIT event dedicated to the memory of the victims of the Srebrenica genocide.

The 10th anniversary of the Srebrenica massacre was the occasion for the world to once again speak up about this heinous crime and also about the Serbian genocidal policy in Bosnia-Herzegovina. Belgrade tried to "reform the crime" either by negating or "counterpoising" it with Serbian victims. Srebrenica was the biggest crime against civilians committed in Europe since WW II, the most heinous crime committed during the Yugoslav wars from 1991 to 1999, and the worst suffering by Bosniaks throughout their history. The crime in Srebrenica is incomparable with all other crimes committed during ex-Yugoslav wars. Srebrenica fully fits in with etiology and genesis of genocide.

From July 7 to 10, 2005, young activists of the HC Youth Group distributed *Srebrenica* informational leaflets to visitors at the EXIT festival. Along with distributing *Srebrenica* leaflets, over several evenings HC young activists asked the festival's visitors to express their opinion about topics such as "*What's your weapon?*", "*Which of your rights is being violated?*", and "*Srebrenica?*" They could write down their position for each of these topics on a large, empty placard. While the actions titled "*What is your weapon?*" and "*Which of your rights is being violated?*" proceeded smoothly, demonstrating visitors' considerable creativity and responsivness, the last evening was a different story.

On that Sunday (the eve of the Srebrenica anniversary of July 11), the process of gathering opinions about Srebrenica was marked by constant tension. Even the police warned HC activists that doing this was a risk they would have to

Doug Magnuson and Michael Baizerman (eds), Work with Youth in Divided and Contested Societies, 235–238.

take on their own and that the police would not protect them. Thanks to the festival's security guards, the action ended without any incident, except for verbal assaults and dirty words to which activists were exposed.

According to the Helsinki Committee's young activists Jelena, Dejan, Tamara, and Danica, visitors' views about Srebrenica were divided, ranging from heinous inscriptions to shame to claiming not to be aware. As one activist said,

I felt awful when I read one boy's inscription saying *"I wish it happened hundred times."* Some people just stood there listening to me telling them the Srebrenica story and said, "I know what happened and do not need you to tell me about it." However, they refused to write anything down. A girl approached me and said, "I know nothing about it." After my explanation, she scribbled "Awful." When I asked her what "awful" means to her given that she has been fully unaware, she replied, *"Well, if it's true that eight thousand people were killed, that's awful."*

Another activist said,

> In my view, the people who would not acknowledge what happened in Srebrenica take much stronger stands, they are more aggressive, and I feel terrible about it. Others just stand by and watch what is written down but cannot respond in any way as they face people filled with hatred and malice. A boy shouted in my face, *"What's that?"* He begun to tear down placards, crying *"I'll kill you all, you Ustashi!"*

Another boy wrote down, *"Knife, wire, Srebrenica,"* added four "s's" and said, *"If I had a bomb, I would throw it at you."* Someone else wrote, *"The worst of all is that people are much too frightened."* We were not afraid, in spite of the threats, said Srdjan: "You must keep the war crimes story alive, for once people understand what you are talking about, they are ready to devote thought to it. By the end of July, 2005, HC Youth Group launched an exhibition in Novi Sad called, *The Writing of EXIT*, composed of the written impressions.

This is one example of youth group activities conducted by the Helsinki Committee for Human Rights in Serbia, which is committed to the protection and promotion of human and minority rights and, for that matter, safeguarding Vojvodina's multiethnic character and curbing conflicts across ethnic lines. Vojvodina is the most developed and ethnically most heterogeneous part of Serbia. Over thirty religious communities pursue their activities in Vojvodina, and Germans, Hungarians, Slovaks, Serbs, Greeks, Vallachians, Romanians, Ruthenians, Ukrainians, Jews, Bulgarians, and Croats—at least 26 different ethnicities have settled in Vojvodina over many centuries. Novi Sad is the capital of Vojvodina province.

HC aims to systematically register and bring to public attention the human and minority rights violations by analysing the situation in the legislative and judicial systems, minority communities, Serbian prisons, and the educational system. Further, the Committee combats the overall social atmosphere that is still loaded with nationalism, xenophobia, and intolerance, and it supports the much-needed process of soul-searching *vis-à-vis* war crimes.

HC supports young people's proactive approach to decision-making processes at all levels of governance, particularly in the matters affecting human and civil rights, inter-ethnic relations, and the overall social climate, and it helps imbue young people with the set of values acceptable in the modern world and to raise their awareness about the disastrous effects of the policies grounded on hegemonism, ethnic bias, and conservative notions.

By opting for the activities that can be divided into "educational" and "fact-facing," the Committee intends to capacitate young people in Vojvodina for their actual and future roles in a complex community burdened by the negative experiences of the past and presently exposed to adverse influences. Therefore, HC wants to boost the group's sense of self-confidence by providing it with new knowledge and skills, assist those young people to become active participants and competent actors in social developments, as well as to improve their prospects of growing into policymakers able to squarely face the past and the future alike.

Namely, no one expected that the 10th anniversary of the Srebrenica massacre would draw such worldwide attention and stir up the moral dimension of the crime. Serbian nationalists overlooked the fact that Europe was standing up for its values in Srebrenica and that the time had made her acknowledge her own mistakes and failures in Bosnia. Srebrenica had questioned Europe's moral, political and military credibility, and that was the point Serbia completely missed.

Today's Serbia still refuses to acknowledge this crime as genocide. Various arguments are passed around. *"Others committed crimes as well,"* most people say. "The 'devil's circle' is closed – no one owes anything to anyone and everyone should receive his due, women were not killed…"

Three ongoing complementary processes in today's Serbia testify that the umbilical cord with the brutal and criminal policy has not been cut off so far. This is about the processes of relativization, normalization and depoliticization. As for relativization every mention of Sebian crimes results in the examples of crimes against Serbs. Normalization – crimes accompany all wars and all parties involved commit them. This not only blurs the difference between a criminal and a victim, but also boils down the crime of ethnic cleansing to a normal economic activity. It is not by chance only that the freedom of speech is used to justify the crime and that graffiti "Knife, barbed wire, Srebrenica" calling for a bloody rerun appear on the billboards reminding of the 10th anniversary of the massacre.

The backdrop as such mostly affects younger generations, regardless of their ethnic origin. The same as in other parts of Serbia, Vojvodina's youth have been raised on the Milosevic regime's warring propaganda brimming with ethnic stereotypes and intolerance, let alone the notion that any "otherness" is a threat in itself. Additionally crippled by the educational system that to this very day imbues them with conservative notions and misconceptions rather than capacitates them to use their brain, the great majority of young people are not only parroting all sorts of distorted arguments that have been presented to them by their teachers or families but also seem to be rather perplexed about an acceptable set of social values. It goes without saying that these are just some of the stumbling blocks in the way of young people's growing into tomorrow's modern policymakers.

This is the more so since in Vojvodina, the same as in all of Serbia, young people's awareness of the recent past and related stereotypes is mostly based on history textbooks presenting "one truth" alone. "Absolute truths" – i.e. national dogmata – and young people's vulnerability when it comes to the prevalent public discourse, are hardly encouraging to critical thinking. Thus, the majority of young people take that Yugoslavia disintegrated because of Slovenia and Croatia's separatism, Islamic fundamentalism of Bosniaks, and Kosovo Albanians' irredentism, let alone superpowers' interests (colonialism in the Balkans). Children knew almost nothing about human rights, as well as that the school system has not capacitated them to present their views individually and with sound argumentation. On the other hand, they readily spoke their mind while in group – actually, in chorus, they usually parroted the well-known stereotypes hued with nationalism.

Representatives of the Helsinki Committee instructed fourth- and seventh-graders from twelve elementary schools in Vojvodina during April, 2005, in notions such as human, children's and minority rights, rights of sexual minorities, racism, discrimination, stereotypes and bias. Just as an illustration: *"Serbs are the most courageous people of all."* Children welcomed this statement vigorously. They raised three fingers and chanted, "Serbia, Serbia!" Here are some of their comments: "Of course we are the most courageous people of all. We have won all the wars, rebellions, and bombardments. Our leaders have always marched in front of their armies. Emperor Lazar led the Serbian army in the Battle of Kosovo, while Murat lagged behind the Turkish army. Other people's influence on the Serbian people should be banned, since we have been anyway occupied by Turks for five centuries." Consequently, Milosevic is to blame for having "lost Serbian territories," while all warring parties have committed crimes and, therefore, either all should be called to account or "let bygones be bygones."

As long as young generations are not encouraged to think critically and question the prevalent discourse or governmental policies, as long as they are not capacitated to articulate their demands and proactively communicate with authorities at all levels of governance, and as long as they are not fully aware of today's world trends and set of values (that, among other things, excludes impunity for war crimes), Serbia's transition towards a market-oriented economy and integration into European institutions is doomed to meander through a rough and thorny way.

Snežana Kresoja
Helsinki Committee for Human Rights in Serbia
Assistant Coordinator, Novi Sad Branch Office

PUBLIC ACHIEVEMENT NORTHERN IRELAND

Belfast

Public Achievement began work in Northern Ireland in 1999, following a visit the previous year by a group of civic educators from Northern Ireland to the Hubert Humphrey Center at the University of Minnesota. The group, impressed with the young people at the school and the work that was happening, decided to pilot and adapt the programme in Northern Ireland. At its core Public Achievement believes that young people have an enormous amount to contribute toward the building of a more just, peaceful, and democratic society. The work supports small groups of young people addressing issues important to them at sites in communities, schools, museums and most recently, on the internet throughout Northern Ireland and museums in the Republic of Ireland. A "site" serves as a meeting place for one or more groups of young people working on an issue and are located in a community halls, youth clubs, schools, museums or on the WIMPS? (Where Is My Public Servant?) website. Once a group of young people chooses a public issue significant to them, they design, carry out, and evaluate their own projects; in the process the young people's perspectives are often challenged as they see the complexity and depth of the issues they are tackling. In the process young people learn skills and knowledge while developing an essential practice of active citizenship and democracy; young people make a meaningful contribution to the life of their community and the wider world.

Youth are supported in the process by adult volunteer "coaches" who challenge and encourage the groups' ideas. Coaches receive regular training by Public Achievement staff to sustain their work and the work of the groups. Coaches volunteer for the project through their work as teachers, youthworkers, museum staff, college students, and interested community members. Other innovations initiated within Public Achievement include the WIMPS? project, a developing coach training programme (in association with the George Williams College, London) and a project entitled Training Educators for Change, supported by the US Institute for Peace, the Department of Education (Community Relations Branch) and the Community Relations Council (Peace II). Public Achievement also works internationally with partners around the world, particularly in conflict regions such as the Balkans, the Middle East and Southern Africa.

Correspondence should be addressed to: Public Achievement, 87 Wellington Park, Belfast, BT9 6DP, Northern Ireland, URL: http://www.publicachievement.com/

Doug Magnuson and Michael Baizerman (eds), Work with Youth in Divided and Contested Societies, 239.
© 2006 *Sense Publishers. All rights reserved.*

ST. COLUMB'S PARK HOUSE

Derry/Londonderry, N.I.

St. Columb's Park House provides both a program and residential centre for the community. The centre began in 1994 as a reconciliation organization; a neutral venue for valuable work during the peace process. Today it continues its contribution to peace-building and social inclusion through a range of programs, largely for young people, that promote civic participation, human rights, and democratic pluralism. The training, educational, and research work engages the private and public sectors and provides outreach services when requested. Most of the programs work with those in contact with the organization.

Current projects St. Columb's manages include:

- *Education For Citizenship* supports schools and youth groups in developing skills of young people as active citizens in Northern Ireland.
- *Political Youth Wings* works with young political party members in the north and south of Ireland and the UK who regularly meet for weekend conferences to debate policy. The youth pick one policy issue per conference and engage in dialogue crossing all party lines. Issues in the past have included racism, war on terror, fair trade, and poverty.
- *Foyle YouthBank* is administered and supported by St. Columb's Park House. YouthBank is a grant making initiative run by young people for young people. A board of local young people provide small grants to youth with ideas of bettering their community.
- *Impetus Human Rights Award Scheme* awards good human rights practice throughout Northern Ireland in schools and youth centres. Awards are granted once a year.
- *Interact* focuses on active citizenship work in interface areas of conflict though youth-led initiatives. Training and support are also provided for youthworkers to further the work of the young people. The long term goal of the project is based on getting communities working together on issues of common concern.

St. Columb's Park House serves as a starting place for young people to build their capacities and confidence in doing this work that requires greater responsibility and leadership than they are typically given in their community. It acts as a gateway for many to more advanced opportunities after a few years of involvement. What stays with the young people after they move on, is the experience that someone asked and valued their opinion.

The St. Columb's Park House is based on the Waterside of Derry/ Londonderry, Northern Ireland.

Doug Magnuson and Michael Baizerman (eds), Work with Youth in Divided and Contested Societies, 241.

TANJA E. BOSCH

RESOURCE ACTION GROUP (RAG)

Cape Town South Africa

The Resource Action Group (RAG) is a community-based, youth development organization run entirely by youth and based in the township communities of the Cape Flats. The Cape Flats is a large sandy area, miles from the city centre, to which black South Africans were forcibly moved during the Group Areas Act in 1950 as part of South Africa's policy of apartheid or enforced segregation.

RAG is a youth development non-governmental organization (NGO) that aims to put South Africa's marginalized youth on the map by assisting individual youth and youth-based NGOs with material, organizational, and life skills in order to build their capacity and to become agents for social change in society. This is achieved through training, networking, support, and advocacy.

RAG was founded in 1993 by a group of unemployed youth who dealt primarily with the discussion of social and political issues at camps. This then developed into an organization that provided computer literacy training as a result of demand from the surrounding communities. Director Rodney Zeeberg explains that other activities became secondary, with computer literacy and skills training becoming RAG's main activities. Today RAG runs these activities in the Western Cape but also takes its training to rural areas further afield. A total of 14 computer training centres have been initiated by individuals in rural and urban areas after receiving training through RAG's "train the trainer" programme. Rodney describes RAG's vision as

> To have a supportive environment that recognizes the different and similar needs of young men and young women. An environment that allows them to develop their potential. So that in broad would be how we view young people and the context that we would like to see there for young people. And our mission, the way we set about doing this, would be through training, networking, making opportunities available to them through referrals that we make, and then skills training.

RAG works with youth from five Cape Flats communities, often referred to as previously disadvantaged: Bishop Lavis, Nooitgedacht, Valhalla Park, Langa, and Khayelitsha. Rodney explains that these communities still experience the legacy of apartheid despite a new democratic dispensation in South Africa.

Doug Magnuson and Michael Baizerman (eds), Work with Youth in Divided and Contested Societies, 243–245.

Now what we find in these communities is a situation where people are economically excluded from participating in the broader processes of society. We're looking at people that do not necessarily have access to higher education, we're looking at people who have been the victims of an escalating unemployment rate, you're looking at a community where health issues such as HIV/AIDS have become something that's quite worrying. I would say that gender-based violence, the abuse of young women specifically by their male counterparts − that would be one of the areas that's very serious and that's been very rife in the communities where we work. Unemployment, which you can link to most of these social ills which I've just mentioned, are some of the things that we've had to contend with.

With "each one teach one" as its motto, RAG offers youth in the Western, Southern, and Northern Cape training in computer literacy, media, leadership skills, personal development, strategic planning, and fundraising. It also runs educational camps. Much of its work is done in rural areas where such training is particularly needed. All of the training is done by RAG youth, for other youth, with the intent of ploughing their skills back into their communities.

One of the organization's main projects is the Civic Activism Project. "First of all the project was started as a result of a particular concern with regard to young people," said Rodney. "It was felt that young people do not engage in civic matters the way that they did in the past--it has sort of subsided or the form that it's taking is different from the way activists knew it previously, you know, mobilizing around apartheid, mobilizing around workers' rights, and stuff like that. And the question then came up, what were young people actually doing nowadays? And how could we re-engage them to become interested in their communities again? And that is where this Civic Activism project was born."

This project took place in the Northern Province, Gauteng, and on the Cape Flats. Groups of young people in these areas were formed and asked to identify areas around which they could mobilize. They came up with the two areas of gender-based violence and HIV/AIDS. The first stage was for the youth to carry out research on these issues in their communities and then to come up with strategies to address them. As Rodney explains,

The intervention strategy then entailed awareness days, pamphleteering, it entailed engaging people at strategic places like at a local shopping complex where our young people had a stall and they engaged young people, they distributed condoms. But also the project entailed raising awareness through physical interaction with actual victims of say HIV/AIDS. They, for instance, went to a house in Khayelitsha that specifically focuses on people who are dying of HIV/AIDS. There they interacted with the patients, they interacted with the medical staff, they've even gone so far as to clean the place, they've done a lot of things. And that has been more powerful than these awareness campaigns, because that actually rocked people, it moved them out of their comfort zones so they could actually come face to face with the real face of HIV/AIDS.

Another project that RAG is particularly proud of is the Response-Able Youth Project, funded by the Nelson Mandela Children's Fund.

And the project basically centered on career-oriented skills training and we've had quite a few successes in terms of this. I'm talking here especially about people that have been placed in various settings, either in an NGO setting or in a formal environment. These people have now found a niche for themselves because they can apply the skills that we have transferred to them in these settings. The project entailed…life skills training, then there's the administration skills training, and then there's the community awareness training. And all three areas have as their aim the holistic development of the person so that a person is not just trained in how to answer a telephone but is actually trained in certain social skills as well.

Sixteen-year-old Susan says, "I used to be a very shy person. Everybody seemed to have a problem with me. One day my mother told me about RAG. Soon I became a regular face at RAG meetings. The media project interested me a lot. Soon I got to grips with writing articles and eventually I went to rural areas and shared my knowledge about writing with marginalized rural youth. Now I am studying towards my National Diploma in Journalism and doing my in-service training for a year at an Afrikaans daily in Cape Town. I'd say RAG played a tremendous role in shaping me."

Despite the good work that RAG is doing, the organization faces closure as a result of lack of funds. Rodney has the last word on this. "As a training institution what is happening now is that we're starting to compete with government that has been establishing their further education and training colleges (FETs) or dealing with fairly established institutions already to run their FETs for them, and what is happening is that if you can't sort of adhere to the requirements, especially requirements that are quite costly, then the chances of you being funded is virtually zilch. This is exacerbated by the fact that most foreign donors tell you that we now have a democratic government, and you have to access funds through it. However, government has got their own training institutions, and obviously they're going to channel their funds through these institutions."

TANJA E. BOSCH

CHILDREN'S RADIO EDUCATION WORKSHOP (CREW)

Cape Town, South Africa

Bush Radio, a community radio station, is nestled at the foot of Table Mountain in Cape Town. This station provides a number of services to, for, and with children. For example, when a child goes missing, broadcasts are immediately interrupted with urgent calls to the public until the child is found. On Mondays *Positive Living* takes radio into the high schools with its outside broadcast unit, facilitating frank discussions about sex and HIV.

Bush Radio is the only radio station in the country that trains children in all aspects of broadcasting, with a six-hour on-air product, as part of their Children's Radio Education Workshop (CREW). According to programme integrator Adrian Louw, "Nobody wants children in the studios because they're going to break the studios. Yet we've had fewer breakages of headphones with the kids than with the adults, for example. We don't want to turn them into DJs or even adio broadcasters. We simply want them to understand media. And whether it is through radio or eventually through TV or the internet, we'll give them the understanding of media and how media operates; that's the aim of CREW essentially, not to make them broadcasters.

About sixty children show up at Bush Radio on Saturday mornings to learn about how to make radio. On an average Saturday, one sees children between age 6 and 18 writing scripts, editing their recorded materials in the production studio, discussing topics for the programme upstairs in the meeting room and, in the on-air studio, running all aspects of the live on-air broadcasts. The children and youth represent almost every group in South Africa: Black and White, Muslim and Christian, refugees, and middle and working class.

The Bush Tots consists of a group of fourteen children between 8 and 12, and the children are encouraged to discuss topics that interest them. One of the acilitators, Nashira, explains that "Basically what they do on air most of the time is taken up with discussion, and it's whatever they want to talk about. Whether it's where babies come from to what happens to your food when you swallow it, whatever they want to talk about. And sometimes they'll have a recipe in-between, or talk about something that happened at school."

Doug Magnuson and Michael Baizerman (eds), Work with Youth in Divided and Contested Societies, 247–248.

The Bush Teenz are 14-17 year olds and follow a similar format except that packaged pieces such as mini-features and vox-pops are mandatory. Their programme is more structured, with features such as a career slot, interviews, and calls from listeners. The teens often address topics such as HIV and AIDS, but they also deal with topics such as fashion and trends.

The next group, Street Philosophy, are aged 16 to 20. Nazli is another CREW facilitator and a Bush Radio volunteer who explained how this group works.

> They put packaged programmes together. So they spent a month off-air and produced fifteen-minute documentaries, which were personal accounts of family life and issues of race at school. They edited, they put together the sound, everything. As one of them explains, "We've just produced a series on generation gaps but each of us took a different angle. Thando spoke to his grandmother about sex and just asked her questions very openly and she would answer. Wendy spoke to her parents about the drug scene, the clubbing scene, what it was like then, and what it's like now. And then we also worked on this piece on racial differences among today's youth, Gabrielle being white and Leonie being black and them living together and being brother and sister." This group's radio programmes thus play a crucial role in their identity formation as they grapple with issues of history while growing up in a new era.

STEPHANIE GRIFFIN

PLAY FOR PEACE

An hour of play is worth a lifetime of conversation – Plato

Play for Peace is an opportunity for children, youth, and communities to see beyond conflict through play. Children are lifted out of their day-to-day realities of conflict and tension through play, laughter, and cooperative experiences. The children of these cultures inherit a legacy of mistrust, violence, and poverty. Unlearning these biases takes skillful strategies. Play for Peace developed a community-building model dedicated to fostering crucial social change for people from cultures in conflict. Play for Peace currently operates programs in Guatemala, Northern Ireland, South Africa, India, Israel/Palestine, and the USA (Chicago).

Michael Terrien, Executive Director of Play for Peace, describes it as a process of community building. Rather than being an event or program, it is the creation of ongoing learning partnerships that free each child to build positive connections with others. Especially among people with a history of inter-cultural tension, cooperative play is one of few bridges that promote cross-cultural relationships.

The goals are:

- To promote positive relationships among children from cultures in conflict.
- To create a non-threatening environment, free from fear, where children can experience the joy of play.
- To influence the behavior of adults through the positive example of children at play.
- To develop youth leadership skills and empower youth to act as catalysts of change in their communities.
- To draw positive global attention to areas in the world which experience negative media exposure.

Play for Peace develops local leaders who have a vested interest in positive change and who can most effectively advocate for those changes within their communities. Local youth, with the guidance and involvement of adults, can more easily win the respect of those children we need to reach and help. Cooperative games are at the heart of Play for Peace. Through cooperative play, children, youth, and adults learn to trust and respect others and to break down generations of cultural barriers. Play

Doug Magnuson and Michael Baizerman (eds), Work with Youth in Divided and Contested Societies, 249–250.

and highly-charged, energetic positive interactions form the foundation for a new mindset toward others. Playing together allows people to laugh together and begin to feel safe. Following this play process, participants reflect on their experience and discuss strategies used and how they work. This is often the first time they have come together and planned a common action.

The Youth Facilitators and the work done with and by them have become a signature characteristic of Play for Peace. The youth develop self-confidence and a deep appreciation for their own culture and the cultures of others. They learn facilitation skills and gain the ability to lead large groups of children though play sessions. The youth from each region connect with each other and share their stories. They see that there is a global culture of peace and that they are a part of it. This allows them to see beyond their immediate neighbourhood and expand their knowledge and friendships to include youth in many countries. To date there have been youth exchanges between South Africa and Northern Ireland, Chicago and Guatemala, and India and the Middle East. These exchanges and ongoing relationships allow the youth to develop connections and return to their home communities with a wider perspective of global issues and the realities of how other youth are living in contested areas and which creative abilities they are using to decrease tension and increase cooperation among neighbours.

INTRODUCTION TO STORIES FROM WORKERS

In these stories, most of which have been collected by Marko Gashi, from Serbia, Tanja Bosch, in South Africa, and Christine Velure-Roholt, who lives in Belfast and traveled to the Middle East, are moments of insight, conversion and transcendence, commitment, and terror. Each person confronts him or herself as reflected in the mirror of a divided society. Many have had the option to leave for more peaceful and pleasant surroundings but chose to stay. Some describe prophetic visions of possibility. All confront injustice, either as a citizen of the oppressor or as a citizen of the oppressed. Many are heroic, and most take great risks—physical safety, security, financial, interpersonal, spiritual, emotional, and psychological.

Few of these are true biographies. One is by Matt Milliken, whose compelling story weaves together his personal and occupational biographies. The others are stories that illuminate rather than tell about. We believe these stories illuminate the reader as well, in reflection.

Who are these youthworkers? How did they come to take on this vocational calling and do this work? How were they prepared for the work, if at all? What do they do? Why do they say they do what they do with young people (and not do something else)? What gives their work its shape and meaning?

What do these stories teach about…

   −my own biography? About me?
   −my calling to do this work?
   −everyday life in a contested space?
   −how such spaces work to shape everyday lives?
   −the power of such spaces to shape occupations, their communities, and their practices?
   −what it is like to be a young person?
   −what it means to be a youth in a contested space?
   −what it is like and what it means to be a "young person" who a youthworker "works with?"
   −the nature and forms of "youthwork?"
   −direct work with young people?
   −this work in a contested space?
   −your work?

ALAN
Israel

Interviewed by Christine Velure-Roholt

I am a Jewish Israeli. My interaction with Palestinians started when I was 16 in a youth exchange with youth from all over the world. It was the beginning of the *intifada*, the second *intifada*. We knew it was going to be hard, because the Palestinians were having a really, really hard time over there with tanks all over, and the Israel army all over. And we prayed then, because it was really, well, suicide bombers were like, everywhere, man. Let's say one suicide bomber in a month--it's quite a lot and they were killing an average of 15 persons each. And everyone was just afraid to go out into the streets, to shop, to go to nightclubs-- even the most basic things ... to go on a bus was one of the most terrifying things to do in Israel. So we knew it was going to be hard, because both sides suffered.

For instance, one of the leaders who came to our conference had just lost his father who had been murdered by the Palestinians a month before we were in conference. It was hard. For me it was the first time I met the Palestinians, because I saw them only on TV. We thought it was going to be hard, but we didn't realize it was going to be that hard. And once we got there we had the most terrible time of my life: being accused of murdering. And being accused of many other things that I just couldn't deal with. In one situation, someone went by us with a Palestinian group and he said, "Don't talk with the Jewish." He said it in Arabic, not realizing that I knew Arabic. They wanted to talk with us, but he was the leader and he told them, like, in a really awful voice, "Look, don't talk to the Jewish." It was like someone just came and took a knife and stabbed you. It was really terrible. We were in the same building but we didn't even talk to each other, not one word, because he refused to talk to us.

And I didn't realize how much they suffer: suffering just by trying to go on the bus to the other side of the city, or just trying to go to school or the shopping mall. And I didn't realize how much they suffered. And once we got there it was really...I didn't realize how ignorant we are about each other.

Because the Palestinians thought as much about us as we did about them, like, we are in our life and we go to the shopping mall. For me, I saw we had to do something about it. It's a situation we just can't ignore. Because I see young kids who can't go on with their life. They can't go to school. They can't do basic things like go onto the streets after 6 o'clock and they can't get out. Not to mention the group that came to the conference. They had to travel, like, three days just to get into the UK from Palestine, spending hours and days in the checkpoints. I realized it is not human to live in such a way. That is why I get involved in many

252

organizations, many actions for peace. Like, what I am working on today is through an organization called Youth Action. We know the kids in Palestine have loads of free time. They do nothing. So what we are trying to do is to bring Israeli students to teach them Hebrew or theater classes or do many other things. And to do the same on the other side, to bring Palestinian students to come over to Israel to teach them Arabic because Arabic is a compulsory language for them. And that's it.

OFIR GERMANIC
Jews, Arabs, and Ethiopians

I was the director of a youth organization in Israel, and most of the youth were teenagers from Ethiopia who came to Israel. Some of them were born in Israel, and some were born in Ethiopia. The Ethiopians in Israel are somewhere in the lower economic classes. And most of those Ethiopians are living in the same racially mixed cities where you have Jews and Arabs. And some of the Ethiopians live in neighborhoods with Arabs, and they do not get along well. And it's even worse than that as they always have something against each other.

We have this seminar--a youth council seminar. We took all the youth leaders, and before they start working with youth, we have a seminar. And we had some Arab groups, Palestinians who are living in Israel, and they came to the seminars as well. Because everyone is a social worker, and they are coming to make a change. But they never thought about the idea that they have to make a change. I mean, everyone wanted to make the change in their own communities, but they never came with the idea that changing their communities is not complete without changing the reality of their next-door community.

Once they were at a seminar, the Ethiopian and Arab leaders realized that they were really, really similar, that the Ethiopian culture is in many ways closer to the Arab culture than the Israeli culture. Even the word "hello" is the same word in Arabic and in Amharic, which is the Ethiopian language. We say *Shalom*, the Arabs say *Salem*, the Ethiopians say *Salaam*. But they never thought about it. I remember one of the Ethiopian leaders said, "You know, now that I think about it, my neighbors who are Arabs, they celebrate a wedding for seven days like we do. Yeah, you are Jewish, but your parents came from Europe."

So there are so many similarities between the Ethiopians and Arabs in Israel, but they couldn't see them. Because the Arabs treat the Ethiopians as Jews, who came recently to take their place. The Ethiopians wanted to be the best Israelis, and they wanted to prove to everyone that they are religious so they have to be against the Arabs. And the Arabs are the ultimate enemy. So they had so many clashes. Not far from Tel Aviv is a mixed neighborhood, and they are not working together. So we came up with a new project for youth called, "The Future Is in My Hand." And we tried to teach.

We said, "Hey look, this is all in your hands. If you want to change your reality first of all it's up to you. But if you want to do it, and you want to do something real, something that will last for long, you have do it with your neighbor." So we formed two groups: an Ethiopian group and an Arab group. And they worked separately, because to start with they couldn't cope with work together, it wouldn't work. Because the Arab would have to say something about the Ethiopian and the Ethiopian would have to say something against the Arabs, and so we decided to work separately. Later we can start taking them to meet the other group.

So we were working for a few months with two groups in that neighborhood. We had two projects and it was very successful. Each group learned about themselves, about their culture, because both cultures are being oppressed by the Israeli majority. They are being oppressed by the majority of the Israeli society who want to be really European. Even though we are living in the Middle East, we regard ourselves as European and we kind of neglect the neighbors we have, the music, the food. For example, to this conference we nearly brought the same food that the Palestinians brought, the hummus and everything. We share so many things.

We had a one-day tour to the north. So we drove all the way to the Sea of Galilee on separate buses and everything was fine. And there we had an activity so we got together. And I remember that I was sitting next to the Ethiopian group. A few kids were sitting and having lunch and at the next table there was an Arab group. And I remember the Ethiopians trying to listen to the Arabs to see if they could understand, because they started learning Hebrew at school.

Suddenly it was interesting. Normally they wouldn't listen or hear what was being said. But suddenly it was interesting. Then we had some more activities and they came to talk to each other and walk side-by-side. On the way back we decided to go in the same buses. And that was actually a disaster. Just taking them on the bus back to the city was a huge disaster. They had a huge fight about who was going to sit where. And then they started yelling at each other, "You stinky Arab," "You stinky black guy." We couldn't believe it. Just the two leaders sitting in the middle of the bus.

Still, I was happy actually and I'll tell you why. Before they used to just ignore each other. Now, maybe they had some fights, but they kind of had something to do with each other; they now cared. They wanted to do something; they cared about something. Or they had some kind of conversation. And we decided that the youth leader from the Ethiopian group would go and have a session with the Arab leaders, and the Arab leader to the Ethiopian group. And they see that they can work together.

It was very important to us, that children will see that. And then we had a meeting together about food. Every child would have to bring something, and suddenly again everyone saw that some of the food is similar and some of the music is similar and some of the customs are really similar and they began to chat with each other. And from that point everything went smoothly. This is their story of youthwork.

OFIR GERMANIC
Israel

About three-and-a-half years ago was the beginning of the second *intifada*. Then we had a kind of peace treaty with the Palestinians that everyone thought was going to be really helpful, blah blah blah. The beginning of the second *intifada*, just before Sharon went up to the Temple Mount, there was a big uprising of Palestinians in the occupied territories. But this time--unlike the other times--the Palestinians who were living inside Israel had something to say as well. They were raging against the Israeli policy. For the first time there were some clashes. It was the first time that there were big clashes between Palestinians who were living in Israel and considered by Israel as citizens. And because of those clashes thirteen of the Palestinians who were living in Israel were killed by Israeli police. And we're talking about citizens in Israel. I always thought or believed that Israel should treat all the Israelis as equal—it doesn't matter if you are Jewish or Arab or whatever. For the first time I took the time to realize that my government, my people, is shooting other citizens to death. It wouldn't happen anywhere, anytime, if they were Jews. Never. Not even if there would be a threat to the life of policemen or the army or soldiers.

I didn't think that the police force would shoot other Jews. But they are Arabs, so they kill them. So it's okay to shoot them. That was my feeling. It was the first time that I understood that something is really wrong here. I mean we are talking about equal rights for everyone. And I grew up in a city where there are loads of Arab villages around. One of my teachers was Arab-everything was fine. But they are crying and... Most of the people in Israel thought, look, I mean, even the people who live amongst ourselves are clashing with us. So we can't trust them any more.

So most of the people in Israel moved to the extreme right wing, against the peace process. I mean, the whole political structure actually moved to the extreme. And that caused me to react in the other direction. I became more left-wing in a way.

I remember working in an organization and we had a big meeting, saying, "What are we going to do?" First of all what we did was to have a big delegation that would go from one family to another for those families with someone who was killed. I am talking about the Arabs. And we are going to go and say that we are really, really sorry; as Israelis we are really, really sorry. We were about 10 people who visited a family, and we went one day to the north. And we visited some families. And one of the families was a really respectable family from Nazareth, and the other one was Professor Brada from Haifa University. And the last family we came to were the nicest, warmest, common family in the area, I think. First of all the brother of the guy who died was afraid of me because I was Israeli and

Jewish. And it was the first time I had any interaction with someone who thought that I was the enemy. It was the first time, and I was shocked and couldn't speak for an hour or something because I heard he was really afraid of me.

But then the whole family accepted us and were really, really nice and so kind. And I didn't know what to say. And when I sat down there and I saw the family talking to me I knew if I could bring all of Israel through to that family and have a discussion with them, then everything would be okay. Then they could see eye-to-eye. And this is the point where I decided that in my organization that this was going to be the new—no, not the new—but the main issue and the main policy. And ever since then we started all these kind of groups. And we had several good projects that succeeded. They were successful because we understood that we have to see eye-to-eye and not patronize them. Because usually what we do as Israelis is that we patronize the Arabs, and we assume that we know better. We tell them to do this.

At that moment in that family we were simply so warm, I just realized that we should work together.

ROTAN
Israel

Interviewed by Christine Velure-Roholt

The youth I have been working with for the last year-and-a-half are young conscientious objectors, 17 or 18-year-olds, or people who are thinking about going back out of the Army. The experience that got me to this place was my own [experience of] objection. I was conscripted, like other Israelis, at age 18, to go to the Army. I spent my first six months in a unit that does liaisons with foreign countries in the south of Israel, on the border with Egypt. I spent my first six months there, and then I moved to another unit that teaches soldiers in schools. And I spent another year there, and then I refused to serve.

I didn't have a specific moment or memory when I refused my Army service. It was a specific moment when it happened, but there were a barrage of things that kept piling up, and I think for me my specific moment was when I realized that what I was doing was irresponsible. And it was irresponsible because I had never really been a soldier wholeheartedly. And I never really believed in the reasoning that led me to be a soldier, which in Israel could be various things. It could be that there's an external threat--you're under threat from the enemy. It could be to show you're strong. It could be that it's good for your career and it's good for your work. It could be that everyone is doing it, so why aren't you doing it? All kinds of reasons.

You don't want to be seen as a traitor or weak. And all those reason just stopped working for me very early on. And I kept being a soldier. And so my moment of clarity was when I realized that it wasn't the Army's fault I was in the Army, it wasn't my parent's fault, it wasn't society's, it wasn't anybody's fault. It was my own choice and I need to choose differently, being where I am and the beliefs and thoughts that I had about the military and about human beings.

And so the work I do with young people comes out of a real need for alternative education in Israel. There's a different set of values, different set of rules, and a whole different lifestyle that we need to adopt if we want a life that is free of conflict. It's not just a different political platform. It's not just a different political thinking. It's not just an intervention by a foreign army. It is not cosmetic like that. It's a real commitment to a life that is completely different in context than it is now, because the life we are living now as Israelis is a life of conflict. We look for conflict.

It's not just with Palestinians. It's with each other. People walk down the street and they look like they are ready for war. It's a whole mindset and a whole education. So I got involved to help change that mindset, not just politically but spiritually and emotionally, changing the way we look at ourselves in our communities and the way we view our world. I think it sort of springs out of my being a conscientious objector and seeing how beneficial and how easy it is to live a different life if you commit to it and how much harder it is to live a life that is full of hatred and violence and confusion. It was very important when I found this out to make it available to other people.

Technically what I do is I work on a couple different levels. Most of my work is sort of politically oriented. I work with an organization called New Profile. It is a feminist organization for the civilization of Israeli society. How do we create a civil society as opposed to the militaristic society? It is feminist because the outlook of it has to do with a way of equality and with alternative values to the ones we have now. Of course, Israel being a militarized society, it's a very chauvinist society. It is very male-orientated both in practice--a male kind of control of the resources in the nation--and also in thinking.

I had an opportunity last year to lead three seminars for young people. These are two-day seminars where we really get to look deeply into more of the context from which we stem as Israelis. So the military is really an excuse to look deeply at our identity. We bring different speakers and activities from a wide sphere. We speak about the 1948 war from the Palestinian perspective. We speak about Israel as a Jewish society and what that means. We bring people from the Army and outside the Army, people who have refused and people who are currently serving. The idea is just to give young people a good, clear, and clean space so that they can get really good information. They can talk with each other and raise it as an issue, because conscription is considered a non-issue by many people. There is an army, and you go to it if you are Jewish. And our idea is not to say that there is an army and you don't go to it. It's to say there is an army and it's a question. It's your life, and it's our society, and it's your responsibility to really look deep into this to decide and to choose out of knowledge and out of a commitment. Like, what is your life about? If it's about that, then you go to the Army. If it's not about that, you have the responsibility to refuse and go be active about it. That is one thing that dawned on me.

Last year we had 55 Israelis take the seminar. So it has been very successful. Out of these seminars we have had young people who have decided to refuse. I am currently guiding eight young men who have decided to refuse their Army service, which is a very tough ordeal for young Israelis socially, because you are very much putting yourself on the outside of Israeli society, since the Army is a unifying sort of experience for young Israelis or all Israelis. But it is also a very different experience of society as well. It also usually means prison time. Or a visit to the shrink, sort of going through a psychological process of getting released, which can be very tough. It's tough with your family, it's tough with your friends, and it's tough with yourself. It can be physically very trying because some of the people have been in prison for three years now for refusing to serve. It's very politically trying. Having to think about political alternatives is not very easy for a 17-year-old.

ANYA FRIARS
Northern Ireland

Interviewed by Christine Velure-Roholt

So my name is Anya Friars. I was born, raised, and still live in the Catholic/Nationalist/Republican areas of West Belfast. The area that I come from is called the Younger Springfield area. And in that area is Battle Murphy and Turf Lodge and Newbarnsey. So when I was growing up the area was a close-knit community. When I was growing up there was a lot of conflict going on. One of my earliest memories, when I was three years old, was being lifted out of bed at 3 o'clock in the morning by my mommy, and there was a British soldier standing behind her in the bedroom. That was, like, my first memory of the British raids. Our house was raided on a regular basis until I was, like, 16.

My daddy was and is a member of the Republican Army, the IRA, and I didn't know this growing up. All I knew was that British soldiers were coming into our house every few months, ripping up floorboards and lifting us out of bed. So I just hated them, hated them with a passion. Because they were taking my daddy of out the house, taking him to jail, and I didn't know why or what was going on. Plus there was the outside thing where, do you know, when you are growing up on the street and you are listening to all the things that your friends are telling you about what is going on. Then I was getting mixed messages from my friends saying that the IRA was bad because of the punishment beating and punishment shootings. And then I was getting other messages from other kids in the street because they were protecting the area. And all I knew was that somewhere in it all was the IRA and somehow it all it had something to do with our house.

There was a youth club around the corner from us where my mommy worked called Newhill. She was a youthworker there. And when there was no one to mind me I was always brought round to Newhill for the nights out. Because my daddy was in the IRA, there was a sense of protecting the community, and there was my mommy who was a youthworker who was protecting the young people in the community from the riots and getting them off the streets and basic diversionary work.

But when I was 16 my daddy was arrested and sent to prison for 25 years. And I was very shocked. I sort of had an idea he was involved in something but didn't really know. So I was very shocked and very confused about everything. I sort of went on a bit of a bender, taking drugs and drinking. "Fuck round, and fuck you, and fuck this." Just basically, rebelling against everything until a youthworker brought me in and actually sat me down and talked to me about what was going on in my head. And why it was all going on? Cause I hadn't talked. And actually this is the first time I have told this story as well. So that's not very good.

So she sat down with me and talked to me. It was the first time that anyone had sat down and listened to what was going on in my head. There were big conflicts going on in my head that I didn't even understand. So she sat down with me and we talked through what was going on in my head and where I wanted to go. So she directed me into a youth program--a peer education program. And this gave me the opportunity to gain access to information about health and social issues and, you know, personal development stuff. Basically I was able to start focusing on my life and learning a whole lot of of things I hadn't even heard about before then.

So this really really turned my life right round to the point that I thought, "Yeah, I want to do this, because I wanted to put back into this area what these youthworkers had put into me." Because I knew there were other kids out there going through the same thing and had no one there, you know, to bring them in and say, "Look, what's going on with you? What's the *craic*? Let's sit down and talk about this. Tell me what's going on." So I did, I started to volunteer and I trained to be a peer educator. Which is what I am still doing now and it's, like, 11 years later. I was also introduced to a group called Tarnell, which is a Republican's ex-prisoners project, and they work with ex-prisoners, prisoners, and their families. And they helped me with a lot of stuff. You know, they helped me understand that there are also focus groups for kids whose fathers or mothers or both parents are in jail or were in jail. So I met with them a few times as well. And decided that I would like to do some stuff with them as well. I have all that stuff going on in my head.

PETER
Northern Ireland

Interviewed by Christine Velure-Rohol

My name is Peter, and I was born here in Northern Ireland, in 1967, and I grew up here in Northern Ireland. I am from the Protestant, Unionist, Loyalist, and British community. And that community would have seen it as nearly a duty to serve in the British Armed services. So all the male members of my family for generations would have served in the British army. I was born in 1967 when the conflict was just starting to begin again. So, this was a time of a lot of civil disturbance on the streets where police would be attacked by rioters. A lot of the male members of my family, including my father, would be coming home injured from the rioting. And I would have seen this as a child. A lot of friends of our family have been murdered in the conflict by the terrorists on the other side of the conflict in the other community, which had a very deep impact on me.

I grew up in a city called Londonderry. It's called Londonderry from people in my community. It is called Derry by the people in the Catholic community. Everything in that city was divided, and we were very conscious of the conflict happening around us. There were gun battles, street disturbances, and bombs going off. My younger sister was injured in a bomb when she was two years old. You would have heard people in our house discussing the troubles and saying, "We should be allowed to deal with these people the way we want to. The British government isn't allowing us to deal with this situation the way we want to." I would have processed all this in my head. And, at a very early age, I was thinking that when I grow up, I'll do it. I'll get involved.

So I got involved in the conflict when I was about 15, in the Loyalist part of the terrorist organization. I later joined the British Army when I was 16. When I was in the British Army I was still involved with Loyalist paramilitaries, and they discovered this fact and I was put out of the British Army. When I got out of the British Army, I got involved fully in the conflict. I have spent a lot of time in prison. I have been arrested more times than I can remember, probably in excess of 100 times. The conflict was my whole identity, and so I envisioned it lasting forever. So I was quite shocked when we had a peace process that seemed to be working and then we had a ceasefire. I wouldn't have been for a ceasefire; I would have wanted the conflict to continue. And it was during the negotiations when we were talking to people in our own community about what we should do that I realized that the game was up. The people wanted the conflict to come to an end.

Now, what has happened lately is in a lot of the books people talk about how the prisoners or paramilitary groups brought the conflict to an end. It's complete nonsense. Anybody that I knew, on all sides, wished the conflict to continue. It was the ordinary people who didn't support it anymore. And we had to bring it to an end. So it left people like me with a huge problem, because we have very large organizations with a lot of young people involved and a lot more young people wanted to get involved, and what were we going to do with them? So we decided we needed to initiate some sort of program that would redirect people away from violence and into politics and community development, because we were trying to build our community and we were trying to take over the community development sector.

We started to deliver history and political projects. This happened gradually—I mean, I didn't have a Road to Damascus experience. I wasn't one day a bad person and then the next day a good person. But then, gradually, there was a process within me that happened, because at that time I sort of lived in hope that the conflict would break out again. But it was a gradual sort of realization that the conflict was over and a gradual sort of realization that we had left an awful legacy behind us with the conflict. And that it was time for people in a leadership position to address this. At that time I was looking back on what had happened, and for the first time I realized that all the close friends that I had were either dead or serving prison sentences. I thought of, really, the waste of human life.

What was happening in the paramilitaries at that time is they were getting more and more involved in organized crime. And the young people were being recruited in the organizations and used as cannon fodder and used to bring in money for paramilitary bosses. And I couldn't: I couldn't sort of square that with what I believed and the past. With a number of others we decided to try and help address this; we could try and help deal with the legacy of the trouble that we were a part of creating. A number of us who were ex-prisoners formed an organization that delivers politics and history education classes that then developed into community development and community leadership.

We got bigger and we started delivering more programs and we started getting more professional about it. That led me then into going to university to study youth and community work and community development. And so the work that we do now is with young people who are in paramilitary groups or on the fringes of paramilitary groups or involved in violence. The object, the aim, is to get them out of the paramilitary groups or to get them away. We don't tell them that at the start. But that's the aim at the end of it.

It's hard work to evaluate. You don't know how successful you've been or not in each case. You only see very small goals. We have only one or two people who leave. So it is very hard to evaluate. That said, my experience of young people here in N.I. is that they want to learn; young people here want to be challenged. Young people here want to meet their peers on the other side. They really wanted to do it. It was the older people that didn't. It was the adults in our community who didn't want it to happen. I think one of the biggest problems that we face in our work is old leadership. Not in the paramilitary sense but within the politics, within the church, within the community. And young people were crying out for it.

That would have been one of my greatest experiences. Young people actually do want to do this work. You don't have to force them. What you have to do is create a space that is safe enough for them to do it. Officially we say our work is about giving young people enough information to make their own decisions and then to support them when they do. There is a tendency in Northern Ireland and other places, for any social problem, to blame it all on young people.

I am very hopeful about the situation here in N.I. We have had 800 years of conflict, and it was never going to be put right with one Good Friday agreement- -one piece is never going to put it right. And we'll have to live and other generations after us will have to live with the consequences of Irish history. And I mean never see us regressing to where we were. I never see that happening. But neither do I see us erasing sectarianism, racism, or violence completely from this country. People have to be realistic about that when they talk about the peace processes.

A PERSONAL STORY ABOUT THE WORK AND GROWING UP IN NORTHERN IRELAND

Matt Milliken

It is not possible to divorce the process of learning from its source in the lives of the learners themselves.
Paulo Freire, 1978

On a cold and lonely spot atop a drumlin in the Castlereagh hills stands a church, and beneath that church lies a graveyard. Within that graveyard stands a heavily weathered granite slab bearing the legend, *"This Stone Belongs To Samuel Milliken of Cregagh 1779."* Samuel Milliken was my grandfather's grandfather's grandfather; his last resting place will probably also be mine. I come from a long, unbroken line of rustic, smallholding Presbyterians, with the minor amendments that I grew up in the town, own no land, and do not follow any system of established beliefs.

Such family traditions were imprinted on my sense of identity early on in life. I was born during a brief period of peace on this troubled island, in the early 1960s, the second child of a constable in the Royal Ulster Constabulary and his young wife. Two other people had, arguably, a stronger influence on my life: my grandmothers.

My maternal gran was a gentle country lass who had moved from Maghera, County Derry, to Lisburn, County Antrim, in her late teens to take up an appointment as housekeeper to a local minister and his family. Here she met a local farmer, married, and raised her family (and, by all accounts, half of the local community as well). I spent many happy childhood hours in the company of this very special lady.

My father's mother was a very different proposition. A co-op shoe salesgirl from Belfast's Shore Road, she considered herself to have made a real catch by attracting and wooing a university educated civil engineer, my grandfather. In my teenage years I developed a close relationship with this charismatic *townie*. Both grandmothers were great storytellers, and I recall two tales that had a profound impact on my understanding and interpretation of the conflict, which seemed to me at the time to be a natural way of life in the province.

Gran Mercer's Story

It was a tradition in rural Derry to whitewash all the houses in the village in the days and weeks leading up to the Twelfth of July commemorations, irrespective of religion or political perspective. One eleventh night, the pre-procession revelries got out of hand and a bunch of youth threw a bucket of pitch-tar over the pristine gable end of a local Catholic family's home. The family were frightened that, if they raised the issue, they risked upsetting the local status quo at this most sensitive of seasons.

My gran's father was incensed and, although he was not a member of the Orange Order, confronted the grandmaster of the local lodge. My great-grandfather was an elder at the local kirk and was held in esteem by the community. His intervention was critical. Immediate action was taken to identify the culprits and to have them rectify the damage prior to the commencement of the parade. To borrow a term from Lederach (1995), my great grandfather had acted as the "strategic who" in this peace building exercise.

Gran Milliken's Story

My grandmother Milliken's father was a riveter who worked in the shipyards of Glasgow and Belfast, moving between the two according to the available work. He was a Quaker, a pacifist, and a socialist. He worked on the Titanic and helped found one of the first unions in Haarland and Wolff. He was encouraged to stand for election in North Belfast as a Labour candidate. Shortly before the election the standing member for the constituency visited the family home. He was a capitalist Unionist. He brought with him his henchmen. Paddy Black (my great grandfather) was threatened. Although the seat was not a marginal, a Labour candidate ran the risk of splitting the Protestant vote, thereby letting a Nationalist in. Under threat of violence Paddy Black withdrew his candidature and shortly afterwards left for Glasgow, disillusioned. He never returned to Belfast.

For most of my childhood my father was a distant figure, frequently away from home for prolonged periods, working unsociable hours. I knew him to possess great joviality, generosity, and warmth but that, at times of extreme stress, he was capable of arrogance, callousness, and brutality. Unfortunately for me, growing up in the late sixties and seventies at the height of the troubles, this was the side of my father that I was most frequently exposed to.

The need for safety combined with my father's career path meant that we moved house several times during my primary school years. We feared assassination attempts. Every knock on the door could be an IRA man, every car journey commenced with a quick check under the wheel arches; we never took the same route twice going anywhere. My father slept with a pistol under his pillow and I with a penknife under mine.

A consequence of this actual or imagined, ever-present threat was that, until my middle teenage years, I had no contact whatsoever with any Catholics. Even a local newsagents, Maggie Brady's, was avoided because Maggie *kicked with the wrong foot*.

At the age of twelve I transferred to a middle-class grammar school. I was the only pupil there from my former primary school. I knew no one and the cliques, particularly those that had their origins in the institution's preparatory department, seemed impenetrable. My life experiences up to this point had combined to unusual effect. I was sensitive yet stubborn, I had a deep-seated resentment of authority, and was a champion of lost causes. I was a perfect recruit to the cohort of disaffected youth who became Punks.

> Don't believe them,
> Question every thing you're told.
> Just take a look around you at the bitterness and strife,
> Why can't we take over and try to put it right.
> --(Suspect Device, Stiff Little Fingers, 1978)

I took pride in waving two fingers at every form of established society: parents, school, religion and, particularly, at the Protestant/Roman Catholic conflict. For me the issue was the struggle between the powerful and the powerless, the rich and the poor, the young and the old, and not the ongoing battle between the Orange and the Green.

In the summer that bridged my sixth form years I needed to finance a hitchhiking expedition to Europe. I applied for a job with Voluntary Services Belfast, lied about my age, and was appointed as a summerscheme worker in "The Village," a hard-line Protestant enclave in south Belfast.

Carrie's Story

It was the marching season and the inevitable annual tension was raised yet higher by the hunger strike. We were working out of a double *portakabin* on the waste-ground beside Windsor Park with a daily attendance of over 80 kids. One morning the eager throngs that usually awaited our arrival were absent from the spiked gate that protected our place of work. We sat outside in the warmth of the July sun and waited. Then Carrie came into view. Carrie was too young to attend the scheme; she had not yet reached school age. Nevertheless she hung around day after day in the forlorn hope that we might turn a blind eye and let her in, in spite of her age. Carrie was inching towards us bent over double, her back was arched, and her legs were splayed. Her arms stretched to her ankles as she struggled to carry the immense weight of a half-brick. I called out a greeting: "Where do you think you are you going with that?" Carrie let her burden drop, with not little relief. She wiped her hands on her pinafore and smiled at me with pride. "I'm going to fight the Fenians with the Big-uns."

On that day I became aware of the depth of sectarianism in our society. An infant, barely capable of rational thought, had already been infected with the virulent cancer of hate. As a child I had sung songs of hate about bloody Sunday, in art class I had drawn pictures of tricolours crashing in flames, all my gangs had had paramilitary overtones. But on that day something in me changed.

267

I returned to school that September with motivation for the first time since I had entered its portals six years earlier. To become a youthworker I needed to go to college, to go to college I needed A-levels, and to pass those exams I needed to study.

Tertiary education was a revelation to me; for the first time I actually actively enjoyed learning and working. Many of the ideas that I had been struggling with had already been written about! And, to my surprise, the lecturers actually encouraged the sort of challenge and questioning that had brought me into conflict with teachers at school. More importantly, college brought me into contact, for the first time, with people whose life experiences were almost diametrically opposed to my own, such as the fellow student whose brother was in the Republican wing of Long Kesh for the murder of a policeman. I had a four-year opportunity to focus my energy and ideas at the state's expense.

An important aspect of the Youth and Community Work course was the strong emphasis on practical work, affording me opportunities to work and learn in places outside of the parameters of my familiar world. I had placements in Nationalist areas of Belfast, in the Irish Republic, and in London. As a teenager I had chosen to be an outsider along with other outsiders, but these opportunities for learning in the field facilitated the experience of facing exclusion on my own, without the support of peers. It fostered in me a strong sense of my own (changing) identity, an independence of thought, and a consistency of action in accordance with these.

The Polytechnic also offered opportunities for international exchanges, one of which led me into emigration to Berlin where I lived for five years, an intense and active period of learning. For the first few years I made extensive efforts to assimilate myself into my adopted home, learning the language, and adapting to German social and cultural mores.

> The Germans are a cruel race; their operas last for six hours and they have no word for fluffy.
> --"Blackadder Goes Forth," Richard Curtis and Ben Elton, 1990

Typically, Germans are stereotyped in N.I. as being abrupt, rude, and abrasive. I found this not to be the case. The characteristics seen as typifying this supposed arrogance are misinterpretations of the honesty and assertiveness that are regarded as *de rigueur* in Germany. If, in this country, a friend purchases a new shirt that you feel does not suit him, our code of politeness insists that, not only do we refrain from being critical, we actually pay our unfortunate pal a compliment! German cultural etiquette demands that if you respect the wearer of the hideous garb, it is your duty to point out their folly clearly and honestly. That which is for us *politeness* seems, to German attitudes, to be downright *dishonesty*.

This philosophy of open, honest assertiveness is a frame of mind that I have applied as an underpinning value when dealing with controversial issues. Without such assertiveness and clarity, difficult topics can remain untouched and thus unresolved, allowing mistakes not only to be repeated but also built upon. Without correction our friend may buy a ghastly pair of trousers to match his repulsive shirt! And so it is when dealing with issues of diversity and conflict.

268

Following the fall of the Berlin Wall in November, 1989, I was for the first time in my life confronted by genuine hatred on the grounds of my nationality. When I stood on the Wall at the Brandenburg Gate on that Thursday morning, I was intensely aware that this was not my party; I was a gatecrasher. Later that year the vitriol grew from what were to become the New German States. In the cosmopolitan oasis of western liberalism, being a foreigner had been no big deal. Some of my friends from Africa and Asia were more obvious targets for racism, marked out by their skin colour. My identity was hidden until I spoke, and my flawed command of the language and my residual Belfast accent became apparent. Housing shortages, broken political promises, and mass unemployment in the East created frustration and xenophobia in the hangover that followed *die Wende*. In spite of the anxiety that the situation produced for me, I felt a degree of empathy with the Easterners. Capitalism promised so much from a distance, but the reality was not quite so simple or so pleasant.

On my return to Northern Ireland in 1990 I found employment as an Area Youth Worker with an Education and Library Board. My willingness to engage in work on controversial issues was initially viewed with some suspicion, but my employers' wariness began to ease as the projects I developed showed success. At the same time, the curriculum area *Cross-Community Work* was being afforded a higher profile in the youth service generally (Bell et al 1992; Mawhinney, 1987).

The crucial importance of such work was never so horribly emphasised for me as by the sectarian murder of six Catholics watching football in O'Toole's bar, Loughinisland on 18 June, 1994. Loughinisland lay in my patch; I had endeavoured for many months prior to the atrocity to engage with the local Protestant churches to set up programmes between the two communities. My efforts drew a blank. The representatives of one church told me that they would not engage in such work because they risked losing their congregation to the local Free Presbyterian Church. Such a massacre of innocents is only possible when those responsible see their victims as *the enemy* and not as real people. Such an attitude is only possible if one has no contact across the divide.

The successes and failures of my work with young people in the field of community relations and other sensitive issues led me to draw up a set of guiding principles which underpin any project I am responsible for developing.

- Participants must want to take part; results cannot be obtained by coercion.
- All elements of the practice should be open and honest.
- Confidences within the programme should not be revealed but those outside the immediate process must have trust in it.
- An atmosphere of assertiveness and honesty needs to be established. Group members must feel valued and there must be a strong bond of trust.
- The programme must be enjoyable and rewarding; otherwise participants will vote with their feet.
- Goals need to be set within a timetable. The process is important, but progress is difficult to judge without a baseline.

- Establish where the common ground lies and where shared interests exist. The differences will already be in the air without trying to raise them.
- Once commonality is established and trust is beginning to be built, raise the issues of difference. You are not trying to create a melting pot but a tapestry where diversity is appreciated and its appreciation is fun.
- Engage the group in the planning process; someone else may have initiated the group, but if they are to develop it needs to be on their terms, to their agenda. They must *own* the project.
- At the conclusion of the project evaluate its outcomes with *all* stakeholders.
- A static project will swiftly die; it requires movement, momentum, and dynamism.

It has been my experience that the facilitator needs not only to possess the skills of group work, facilitation, and mediation; she or he also needs, above all, confidence and belief in the value and importance of the work that s/he is engaging in.

Matt's Story

I was having dinner with my (now retired) father. We were talking about my work, because I happened to be working in an area where my father had been stationed for many years. We talked about the local characters, and then my father told a tale of how one evening IRA snipers had taken up position on the roof of the local chapel. He told how he feared for his life as the bullets flew past his head and ricocheted off the tarmac. The very next day I had a meeting in the community centre beside that same chapel. I was leading a project that was taking a group of young people drawn from both communities to London. Across the table from me, drinking tea and working on practical arrangements, sat the local Sinn Fein representative. With a shiver I realised that this respected community activist had, in all probability, had my father in the cross hairs of his rifle-sights on the evening that my dad had vividly described to me over Sunday dinner. I froze as he spoke. An icy chill ran the length of my spine. *You tried to kill my dad.* In a matter of seconds I went through myriad emotions: Anger, hatred, and loathing turned to fear as I realised that his intelligence sources had almost certainly already identified who I was. That he was entertaining the son of a man who had probably raided his house, arrested his brother, intimidated his children. My frozen spine thawed. *Isn't it better that we two are sitting here building bridges than that your son has me in his sights?*

> Peace building may not always make the impact that we hope for. But is it not better to try and to fail than to fail by never having tried in the first place?
> All that is required for evil to flourish is for good men to do nothing.
> −Edmund Burke

Matt Milliken, Northern Ireland

REFERENCES

Bell, G. et al (1992). *Community relations guidelines: Youth work curriculum*. Belfast: Youth Council for Northern Ireland.

Curtis, R., & Elton, B. (1990). *Blackadder goes forth*. British Broadcasting Corporation.

Freire, P. (1970). *Pedagogy of the oppressed*. London: Penguin.

Lederach, J. P. (1995). *Preparing for peace: Conflict transformation across cultures*. Syracuse, NY: Syracuse University Press.

Mawhinney, B. (1987) *A Policy for the youth service in Northern Ireland*. Bangor, NI: DENI.

Stiff Little Fingers & Ogilvie, B. (1978). *Suspect device*. Rigid Digits Music, Belfast.

PAUL LEGRANGE
South Africa

Interviewed by Christine Velure-Roholt

I read a poem called, I think, "Five Ways to Kill a Man." The simplest way to kill a man is to place him in the 20th century and leave him there. But I have a different one. I think the simplest way to kill a person is to place him or her in the middle of a township and leave him. Because something happens to us when people do that. Certainly in South Africa apartheid did that–divided us, placed us into categories, and simply left us in separate communities. Left us to fend for ourselves and find our own way through to the light. That was certainly the experience of a lot of young people. And from my own experience, I didn't know what was happening to me for a very long time. I think the windows of our townships are so high that we can't see through them. There are a lot of things happening on the outside, and we don't understand.

What we experience is the pain and the irritation. And nobody seems to offer us solutions or explanations so that we can understand. For a very long time I didn't understand. I grew up in a township that was extremely violent. Every significant person I knew belonged to a gang or had an experience of violence. My own experience of violence started at the age of six. We lived in flats that were basically housing estates. And there were four blocks of flats where I grew up. But we knew that the boys in the other flats were our enemies and that we needed to to wage war against them. So we started by meeting between the flats and, initially, we played soccer.

But soccer didn't have the thrill we were looking for. So we decided we would play a game called "Kati Kati." And the way we played it was that we rolled up newspaper and we used it to beat each other. And you come back and, I guess, look at your wounds and share stories about how exciting and adventurous it was. And in a short space of time Kati Kati wasn't exciting any more for us, so we decided to become more inventive, so we took cardboard boxes and we rolled it up. What that meant is that it was harder than newspaper and you would get hurt even more. So we would play this game of going to the battlefield and fighting with the cardboard. But still it wasn't enough so we decided that if you use shorter cardboard, it even hurts more. And that's what we did. Until one day when my mother stopped my brother and I at the door and said, "Where are you going with those knives?" The windows were too high and we didn't know how we got there. But at one point at age six, I had a knife in my hand and we were very prepared to use it. Every weekend in my community we couldn't wait for the weekend to end, because every Monday morning we would run down to a small river close to our flat to see which body was in the river. And we would walk to school from there and we would describe or try to investigate what possibly could have happened to the person who had died. And then 1976 happened and all hell broke loose. But we weren't surprised by the violence, with people running all over in the presence of the police. At the age of 6, 7, 8, if you have not seen someone personally being murdered on the street, then you were living in another community and not in our block.

And I remember high school when I was 15. We were in our classes and there was nothing to do that day, and two rival gangs came and used the school as a battlefield and we were unaware that this battle was going on. And when they were finished they decided they would go into the classrooms and rob us and take as much as they could possibly take from everybody. And one of the gangsters came into our classroom, and I was sitting on the table because some of my friends were gambling. We were throwing the dice and gambling. And they went up to them and they started robbing them. And then he came up to me and I was just sitting there. And he said, "What do you have to offer?" And I said, "I have nothing to offer you." And he got upset and he hit me so hard and I thought that was unnecessary. And after he left I realized that I was bleeding, but I had not yet realized he had stabbed me. I then investigated and realized I had been stabbed and thought this was uncalled for.

Within less than three minutes he was lying on the ground, and I had stabbed him about six times. And I walked away remembering not feeling any remorse, not any pain, that I had done anything wrong. But I also remember walking back home with this blood, because I needed to explain now what had happened to me. And on my way I asked myself, "How did you get here?" I remember asking myself, "How did you get here?" And I didn't know. I never thought it was possible for a 15-year-old who had grown up in a home where the mother was strict, who was raised with all the positive values that you could be raised with, how that person could have stabbed someone six times, and I wasn't aware of how I had done it.

So I came home and I said to my mom, " I just stabbed somebody, and I may be arrested." And she obviously didn't know what to say. I wasn't arrested, but I fast forward to the day when I found myself at 1:00 a.m. in the morning with a knife over my dad. I was that close to killing my father. And at that moment I asked myself again, "How did I get here?" I cannot retrace all the events that led to that moment. But I guess it comes from growing up in the middle of the township where, from the age of five, every weekend you get beaten. Where every weekend before my father gets home, we pack our bags, my mom and I, and we are ready to run. Where every weekend you have to walk from this block to the other block without being robbed, without being hurt. It comes from every time you take to the street as a form of protest and action against a form of injustice, then a young white policeman is beating you. And every time they hit you, you recall all those previous moments they beat you. You recall all the pain that growing up in the middle of the township has done to you. And every time he hits, you hate. And sometimes you invite him to hit, because the more he hits, the more you can hate: The more you can feel the comfort of and the pleasure of having to lash back because one is so angry.

I am telling you these snippets, because sometimes the window is so high that you can't see what's happening, you don't know what's happening. You just find yourself doing things. And that in a nutshell is what happens. It makes you afraid to listen. Growing up in the middle of a township, growing up in the middle of South Africa where people are waging a war for peace outside, to ensure that this kind of thing doesn't happen. But if you don't see, if you don't understand it, if you don't know why it is happening, you inevitably find yourself becoming fatalistic. You think, "I'm not going to see tomorrow, I am not going to make it to the next street, into the next day. So why do I care?"

And that beyond that there is a reality, but we need to drop the windows so that people can see that. That people can get a sense of hope. That what's happening outside is just for now and that it can change. People then become fatalistic. Then we must ask why is it is that people place themselves in so much risk with something that is short-term and unsustainable. There are no real benefits. I do not blame them, because the windows are too high. They cannot see what is happening outside. And maybe it is important that they go outside and get a sense of what is happening. So many young people have that experience. So many of us don't know what is happening outside, so many of us don't know what's happening inside. So we act out and live out our lives in a world that is painful and fatalistic.

Why do I do what I do? Because I want to place myself at risk. Because I believe in the benefits of what I am doing. Why do I go into prisons and work with young people who the world has given up? Why do I go and work with young people who are fatalistic and tell me I am probably not going to see tomorrow, because somebody might shoot me? I do it because I think I know it can change the experiences in my own life. I do it because there's a long term and sustainable benefit out there. And young people are not prepared to wait. If you take too long with helping us to understand what's happening to us, then we invent our own solution. It may sometimes be risky and dangerous and damaging to us, but we create our own solutions.

So maybe that is the other reason I got involved. Because I don't want them to become so inventive they become destructive. I did. It made me very inventive. And I guess it's a blessing that I didn't end up in prison, because my whole attitude would have been different. But we need to get involved because some of them like myself may be experiencing the same thing. They are not understanding. They don't understand why, one day, you wake up and you have a knife in your hand and you've stabbed somebody six times. You don't understand why you are prepared to stand and face the barrel of a gun and not be afraid.

Yes, there is some form of fear. There is so much fatalism this fear is not real any more. They don't understand why we do that. We do it because we can't leave young people in the middle of the communities. Try to look through the window.

SABULALA
South Africa

Interviewed by Christine Velure-Roholt

I am a participant in the Youth Service Program in South Africa. I will try and explain the feeling of young people in South Africa: How we feel, our expectations, and all of our needs, etc. It is not always [the case] that youthworkers will know or understand young people. As young persons we gather together to listen to different stories. And there's a time when we talk, and you will see that it is a very emotional situation, because as a young person you are so frustrated and expectations are high because, as a young person, you want a life. You want to live, to have a good living.

And now there is nothing to do: The only thing that is looking you in the eye is drugs to keep you busy, crime to keep you busy, or going to prison. And I want to say that most young people in South Africa would rather choose to go to prison than live in their homes, because you will find that circumstances even in prison are much better than at home. Not being able to be who you are, to do what you are able to do. Sometimes it is not okay.

We understand that government cannot provide each young person with a job and know what their needs are. But, you know, sometimes as a young person you are like, "Okay, I am in South Africa. I want to have a job and to start a family like a normal human being." But now you tend to think about things. You want to do that but it is impossible because there are no resources. You can't go to work. You can't go anywhere. You can't go to study because what you need is money. And you are unable to do all of this. So these are all the feelings that young people in South Africa feel. It will be the most difficult for youthworkers and people who work with youth, to really understand them. And the most important thing is always to try and get people who can understand and recognize the needs of young people so that they can know what to try and give them. Because sometimes they take it all and sometimes they don't make any difference in your life whatsoever.

In the meanwhile, you must understand the difference between youthworkers and young people. Sometimes it is difficult to be a young person in South Africa because of the situation. We understand apartheid issues as they come out. You know what we are looking for: to better our living situation and the circumstances around us.

LINZI THOMAS: MY LIFE PROJECT
Cape Town, South Africa

Interviewed by Tanja Bosch

Thousands of children live on the streets of South Africa, with around 800 on the streets of the city of Cape Town. The majority of children on the streets of South Africa were not born there but have moved away from a place where their reality is worse than the idea of living on the streets. Their choice is thus not driven by a desire to live on the street but from the desire to escape from a life of difficulties. The children on the streets are at high risk of contracting disease, including HIV/AIDS, and being exploited by gangs. Their association with crime impacts adversely on tourism and economic development and they are vulnerable to the commercial sex industry.

Linzi Thomas is the executive director of the My Life project, a Cape Town based non-governmental organization working with the street children of Cape Town. Together with two street children, she started the project in June, 2002, and has spent seven years working on the streets with children and youth. What immediately stands out about My Life is their belief that the young people on the street are the solution to the problem, even though they have never been included in policy decisions regarding their lives.

My Life's vision is to create opportunities for marginalized youth, to fill in the service delivery gaps on the streets to deal with HIV/AIDS and substance abuse, to develop leaders from young people who have lived on the street who, in turn, become mentors to others, to provide leadership and direction in respect of resolving the problem of street children, to promote responsible media coverage that educates and informs rather than perpetuates negative stereotypes, and to consistently lobby to keep the matter on government's agenda.

The project started with 20 youth who first attended a healing phase that deals with drug addiction, after which they are placed in accommodation, backpacker style, in or on the outskirts of the city. My Life then works with the youth one-on-one to develop employment-related skills in an area of interest to them. For Linzi, it's important to help youth identify their passion in life and to help them to realize these passions through skills training.

> So many kids say to me, when I ask what they want to do, "I want to weld" or "I want to be a carpenter," because those are the only skills they know. And I say go and sleep on it, I'm not interested in that, and they come back and say, "Linzi, I just really want to work in a hotel making beds," you know, and that's fine. So then I get them that opportunity and start working with them.

And when she speaks about realizing passions as a means of changing one's situation, she speaks from her personal experience as a street child. "I know that I got out of my situation when I was 14 because I was passionate about swimming. That's what drove me. I had the opportunity to go into prostitution, whatever, but I never did, because every single morning I was in my passion."

These 20 youth who completed the first phase were all leaders of various street gangs. The idea is that they can now return to the streets and their communities and bring back more recruits for another round.

> Linzi explains where the name of the project comes from.

> The reason it's called My Life is that I realized in my life that, unless I sorted out me, stop working in a microcosm, because we were in a little microcosm on the city centre streets, started looking at the global trends, started looking at other projects around the world that haven't been successful, I went down the whole road with my life and it was absolutely unbelievable that we realized that all of us had to change to be able to help the kids.

But it hasn't been an easy road. "One day one of the kids slapped me and another spat at me," Linzi says.

> It unleashed an anger that they weren't able to express, and we got to the nitty gritty of why that person was doing that. I'd say that one of the terrible things that we face, and I say it's terrible because it's accepted by society as a prototype in some way, is love. I mean these kids suddenly started getting love and acceptance, and they didn't know how to handle it. And it turned into anger.

Linzi's unmistakable passion stands out, perhaps stemming from her own experiences. She was born in Hillbrow, Johannesburg, and spent the first two years of her life living with a gangster father and a mother who was intimidated by her husband. At this early age she witnessed her mother being abused and was physically and sexually abused by her father and his friends. As a result she moved in and out of orphanages and the homes of extended family. When her mother remarried she was adopted by her stepfather at the age of three. But when their marriage failed, she was kicked out of the home at the age of 14. Linzi's own father was murdered when she was 17, and she never got to know or even see a picture of him.

> The most important realization for her was that although she went onto the streets to heal the children, this was a time of healing for her as well. She says that the street children mirrored her pain and helped her to work through her problems, and for that she will never give up her work with them. During her years on the street she has identified two key factors to rehabilitation, which the My Life project utilizes: healing and finding a way for children to exit the programme without returning to the streets. "There're two main missing links globally, in the street children sector," she says.

> You can't work with a child when they're addicted to a drug on the street. That drug is not an addiction, it's just blocking the pain. The other thing is. . . . a kid reaches a certain stage, and then suddenly he's told he must fly and he doesn't know how to fly. So that's what we've taken on. My passion lies with the little children and I see the millions of kids that are in

> danger of becoming street children. And I've realized that if we don't build capacity and leadership and mentorship and parenting in the youth, then we don't have a way forward in this country.

There are many success stories of the project. Wiseman Dinizulu and Sifiso Jezile spent 12 years on the streets but have been working for two years, under mentorship, as technicians in the film industry with international casts and crews. They now rent their own accommodation and are self-sufficient. Sifiso is a director of the My Life project. Another participant, 21-year-old Leon Kapa says,

> I left home for the streets of Claremont after the death of my brother in 1994. My path took me into shelters and children's homes and eventually my mother found me and I was back home. My father died a year later and I ran away again, feeling absolutely empty. I survived many years in this system; I even managed to get far in my schooling and then the poverty that my mother was living in drove me to find a job. I am now a father and work as a chef at a city restaurant.

Mkhanyisele will be travelling to the UK in 2005 to work for a month as an apprentice in internationally acclaimed chef Jamie Oliver's kitchen. Aspiring singer, Freda Darvel, lived on the streets for seven years and has been out of the cycle for two-and-a-half years. Her struggle was captured on film in 2002 in a documentary, "Beneath the Stars," and she will be releasing her first single in South Africa in 2005.

> Linzi is inspired by the fact that today the project will go on without her if necessary. "If I were to close the project down now these guys would carry it on and run out there and make it happen."

MOHAMMAD
Iraq

Interviewed by Christine Velure-Roholt

I want to tell you about one thing. We have learned one thing as intellectuals: That each of us sees the world from our point of view, but the good point is to see the world from other angles. Maybe the angles that you are seeing from are not the right angles. The question is, "How will you write a book about the youth participation and democracy and you live in America, Europe, whatever?" And you don't know the story I am telling and the relative concept. How will the picture become a real picture when you are not experiencing the relative concept?

NOOR
Iraq

Interviewed by Christine Velure-Roholt and Tareq AlBakri

I used to think only of being a doctor just as soon as I graduated, and I wanted to travel away, because I don't have a future in Iraq. The regime has no future or possibilities. I won't work with the government; I'll just go and travel and have experience there and not try to go back to my country. But after the war we all stopped to think and find reasons why are we staying there. Like we had to think about our country as ours. Like the feeling of belonging, we started to think we are not alone, we need to feel connected there. There are people being killed, and they are our people. There are big cars and tanks in our street. It's my country and I am facing something in MY country and I had the feeling like, "It's ours! It's our buildings being destroyed. The things we like are being destroyed."

So why do you stay?
[Noor cries for a moment]

It's just that we thought of reasons that we stay there. Like when you live in your house and you have feeling for your home. And you feel connected to the place where you live and areas that you live in and streets where you used to go. For that reason you cannot just be indifferent to these, for all the connections that you have. After all, we're human and we're not just machines. We want to graduate and we want to get degrees and we want work and that is also an idea of my plan.

But the challenges we are facing in our world are bigger then just your profession. Disease is spreading more. War is creating more harm, the harm bigger than just your field. Someone needs to think of action towards all. Most beneficial, let's say. I don't need to be making lots of projects.... I do have my degree. I do have my career. Yet at the same time if I am seeing something negative I can change it. That's the simplest idea. If you are seeing someone doing something harmful to himself or to the community around you, that is your world. That's the good thing. It's our world. It is not any more my home and finished. It's not any more just me. It's ours and all. And we are all being affected.

MOHAMMED
Gaza

Interviewed by Christine Velure-Roholt

I became involved in the nonviolence movement in Bethlehem. That was during and after the church nativity siege in Bethlehem, in the beginning of 2003. We were under curfew so we used to gather and think and [plan] something, nonviolent events. So I remember we announced a boycott from the beginning of the war on Iraq. We faxed the American Embassy, the British Embassy, the Spanish Embassy, and started a boycott. We told them, you are not welcome to come to Bethlehem since you are participating in the war on Iraq. And after that, in about a month, we had an inauguration of a museum in Bethlehem. And the mayor asked the British Ambassador and American Ambassador to come, but they didn't come because of the boycott, and we collected 50 young people--males and females--and we were gathered in the Manger Square in the middle of Bethlehem downtown. And they didn't come...

So after that I was asked by an NGO in Bethlehem to develop a manual for training in nonviolence. Each module deals with a different problem like communication skills, nonviolence skills from the international, national, and Arab worlds, leadership skills--all those things. And I developed the manual and I became very much involved. Then I became a trainer. The first training I gave was at an Arabic university in Jenin. I trained 25 students from the university with three other colleagues. But I was the main trainer since I was the one who edited and collected the materials.

As Palestinians we have a lot of stories and examples. For example, sometimes accidents change your life subconsciously. You don't know that this exactly would change your life. I still remember once I was in Spain and there was the siege of the nativity, the siege of the Church of the Nativity in Bethlehem. And I was watching Al-Jazeera channels. I was watching those Israeli soldiers stop the girl, and they were hitting her and began searching her in a very bad and vulgar way. I was very close to crying. I felt like the tears would go out of my eyes. Because when you're brought up in such a community, a patriarchal community, the male has no right to cry, otherwise he will be weak, and, I don't know, whatever--all those stupid things. But in that moment I felt that a volcano in my heart was just going up. And I wanted to do something but I didn't know what.

So when I went back to Palestine I was thinking, "How can we do something and benefit [from this]? How can we benefit our people?" Since the propaganda is very much strong and biased toward the Israeli side. Since they are dominating all those broadcasting channels like CNN, BBC, or whatever. They put a stigma on the Palestinian community, saying that they are a terrorist people, and they are saying this is an armed uprising, despite the fact that, according to our statistical bureau, only 2% of the Palestinians are really participating in the armed resistance. So we have 98% of the people who are not. So why don't we benefit from those people? Because if we want to end the occupation, two percent of the people cannot end the occupation. They cannot achieve aspirations for the rest of the population. So I was thinking about a way that would be legitimate and legal in some way that all people could participate: all people, male and female. I can't carry a gun, but I could do a boycott. You could go for a walk and say, "End the occupation." You could write in a journal. You could do many things. From that point I began thinking in such a way that we don't have to give the other side the pretext to attack us and to curse us with the stigma that we are terrorist....

So when I worked I had a slogan. All the time I say that I want to plant the hope in the hopeless souls, in the hopeless hearts. Those people get dejected and frustrated. They have nothing to do in this world. I want to reassure them that they are still alive and have a dream. Like Martin Luther King said, "I have a dream." We have a dream. And we want to live just like other people. We want to study. We want to love. We want to live our life. We don't want anyone to hinder or inhibit our life by those inhumane people.

And after that, I forgot to tell you something. Once I was in my house. I was reading in my room and then the shelling came. It comes to the camp. Because when they used to shell during 2003, they were shooting randomly, without interrogating anything. Just shooting randomly. The bullet will come. The same thing in the camps. Once I was in my room and they shelled it and a board fell down on me. I was lying down on the floor. My parents left and escaped downstairs. I don't know what they were doing. When I went down after 15 minutes, they were shouting and screaming because they thought I was dead. But I was still alive. So this was 2001--I can't remember the month.

Do you think it is possible that people, Palestinians, will ever be able to forgive the Israelis?
It is not a matter of forgiving or not. It's bigger than that. Actually I have been asked almost the same question by the Intelligence Captain, the Israeli Intelligence Captain. Because they caught me two months ago, and they arrested me for the whole day. I was going to give a lecture, give a course about nonviolence. And they caught me at the checkpoint between Ramallah and Bethlehem.

So why did they ask that question?
They took me first and, of course, they cuffed my hands and blindfolded my eyes, and they put my pull over my head. And they let me stand in the Jeep, which is very hard. They let your backside up and your head down. And we arrived at the headquarters. Then they released my hands.
The Intelligence Captain came and said, "You are Mohamed Azzila?" And I said, "Yes."
"What are you doing, man? Where are you? We have been looking for you for a long time, why you don't come?"
I said (laughing), "Do I know you want me?"

He said, "Okay, tell me what you are doing." I said, "What am I doing? Nothing. I am here."

He said, "We know you are working with those peace things."

I said, "Yes."

He asked, "Why do you work on peace things?"

"Because I love peace."

"But," he said, "We live in war. All your people, thousands and hundreds of your people, are dead every day, and you are working with peace. Are you stupid?"

I said, "No, I am not stupid, but we still believe in peace."

He said, "Why don't you live just like other people, like other persons, who live in a war like this. Do you understand English?" And I said "Yes."

He said, "Okay, all those things you do is bullshit. Do you understand what that means?" I said "Yes," and I translated literally, just to insult him.

He said, "So what do you think? How can we achieve the peace?"

"Okay, it is easy: Just apply all those resolutions from the Security Council and the United Nations and laws for the rightful return for the refugees."

So he said, "WHAT? You are stupid; you don't understand politics. You are an idiot. You can't do anything," and he got pissed off and insulted me. And I was very happy. I was very happy; do you want to know why? Because when you get inside an interrogation and your interrogator gets pissed off, that means you won. That means you won. Especially because I behaved in a way and acted in a way to piss him off. He was asking me questions, and I answered in the same form of the questions.

So once he said, "So what do you think will happen?" I said, "Okay, what do you think?" He said, "I asked first." I said, "Okay, I asked you, so what do you think?"

"LISTEN, MOHAMMED, I AM THE CAPTAIN, NOT YOU. DON'T CONVERT OUR RULES!"

Do you think you are making a change? Is the occupation going to go away because of what you are doing?

Actually if you asked me, it is not working exactly to end the occupation. I'm working on the domestic issues within Palestine. Because you cannot work something out unless you have a calm and peaceful and safe community. So when we have our problems inside, how can we solve our problems outside? For this I am working to build my community from inside. And other people are working, probably, from outside. But, I mean, my work, most of my work with children, teachers, and people on domestic issues like domestic violence, how can we create good links between each other? How can we think and brainstorm to do creative things? Those things will not end the occupation in the meantime, but it will when we raise awareness about such an issue. Like nonviolence.

AMAL SABAWI
Gaza

Interviewed by Christine Velure-Roholt

So we started doing something to assist in this situation. We thought that education is the only thing. From my work with youth.... it's given new opportunities that youth can use in the future or while they are living this space to have the power to change things....

We started working with the Public Achievement program. For me I had lots of questions before I started this program. I have to be aware of to what extent this program is different than other programs. I have to be aware of how we can provide things in the way that people can perceive and people can find issues not provided and not accessible by others, so people can take it and can handle it. I was afraid that with all these pressures, circumstances, and restrictions, how we can manage and, for the first time for me, work with youth directly. And work with them, and work with them with the leaders on the backstage, not on the front stage. So we started doing the first training, training people to lead the program and to run the work with young people.

The first group was 24 years old, and there were 23 participants in the first training. I couldn't tell you about my feeling at that time. I discovered that I didn't know youth. All my fears about youth and how, to what extent, I committed to do things, was new for me. I discovered that the way youth learn is different than what I thought. I saw people who are willing, who have will about everything, have commitment, they want to do things, they are very anxious to get the opportunity. This gave me lots of hope.

We finished the first experimental period in three months and learned about the issues in the community. One of the issues that I can tell you about is in a village located in the south of the Gaza strip and between the border of the Palestinians and Israelis. The students or participants felt that we have to focus on the health issues, and they did many things like interviews with youth and health service providers. And they discovered that the area doesn't have an ambulance or an AIDS car to take people to the hospital, because it is so far. So they decided they could work on getting one ambulance for the village, which was really, extremely difficult, you couldn't believe. They said we will do it and we have to know how to handle it.

I know I couldn't imagine that in this age they have all this power to do things and this way. And again, I thought to myself, I have to be really more aware about how we can remove these things that still remain in our minds about how we handle youth as people. We need to be asking, as youthworkers, whether we can be doing things better.

NOURA TEEJANI
Palestine

Interviewed by Christine Velure-Roholt

My story begins when I was thirteen years old. I was working in the kitchen and searching for the sugar to make Nestle Café. Suddenly, I saw the baking powder and, I thought, I want to make a cake. Such a thing needed permission from my mother. I went to my mother and asked her to do this cake. And she said to me, "How can you do this cake? You are too young to do this. You are going to cause a big mess in the kitchen and you are going to not be clean enough. And you are not going to do the cake very well. It will be spoiled."

I felt very miserable and frustrated at that time, and I felt that I could not do this cake. I felt that some people were looking at me as a child, while I am an adult. I sat in my room, and I was looking from the window. I saw my neighbor passing by. And he was wearing a vest and written on it was PRCS (Palestine Red Crescent Society). I linked this scene with the cake story, and I thought, "How can I change this society's view about me?" Probably I can do the same thing that my neighbor does: Be a part of this organization that is volunteering in order to make something, to be in a society, to be exposed, to explore it, and to feel that I exist here.

So that was the first time that I visited the PRCS department for youth and voluntary department.

I wanted to work away from this violence. I just want to be away from this violence, because I will lose my humanity, and I feel that when I get used to it I will just lose my humanitarian sense. That is why I decided to do community service but away from violence. So I joined the Howard Ehrlich Institution for Conflict Resolution. It's an institution that gives the chance for youth to serve their society, to participate in decisions, leadership, and many things. And one of the projects I worked on through the Quakers is Public Achievement. I accomplished something very good at that time. I was able to create a group of Debka dancers, and they were asked to perform on television and in festivals. I felt that it was really a good achievement. I don't like to have an ending for my story because from here I start.

THUKAN QISHAW
Palestine

Interviewed by Christine Velure-Roholt

My name is Thukan. This story takes us back 18 years ago, to the mid-1980s, when I was about 16 or 17. At that time, when the *intifada* started, a chief entered my village and said that this coming night there would be a curfew. No one was allowed to go out of his home. After two or three days, we discovered that the Israelis damaged five houses. I felt energized to do something to help these people who were newly homeless and had to live in tents. So I gathered with my friends, and we decided to fight for the young.

We went inside Israel to a small town. At the time we didn't pray, but this time we went to the mosque on a Friday. We prayed with the spirit of ourselves and we told our story to the Imam, and we collected the money for the people who became homeless. Without any planning, it was the first action on our part. Really, I appreciate that it gave me power in the future. I find in myself the power just to give assistance to the students who were not able to go to the universities since the closures. So I started to gather them in my house in some communities and give them physics courses, English courses for a small fee, and serving them.

Then my dad forced me to leave Palestine because I used to go to demonstrations against the Israelis. He was afraid that maybe one day I would be killed. So he told me that I should go to the American University in Cairo. I listened to him since he was my dad. At the American University, I used to write in a local newspaper sponsored by the students' union, called the *Caravan*. I wrote many things about Palestine. And I worked as a volunteer with a school for orphans.

After graduation in 1994 came the start of the peace process. So it was a dream for me just to return to Palestine. So I went to Ramala and opened an information technology business, an IT center. And it was very good. There was a demand for internet courses from youth who attend these courses, and they asked me to start an internet café. I studied the market and then created my internet café. I used to have 27 computers, and they cost me a lot. But it was good for youth, because I used to give them free hours to talk and chat to others all over the world.

During the second *intifada*, in 2001, the Israelis invaded Ramala, and they damaged the building where my office is located. My office is located in the building in the center of Ramala on the 4th floor. The 5th floor was for the Palestinian Council offices, and the 3rd floor was for Palestinian Radio. So they fired two rockets into that building. I lost the computers, and I lost more than $50,000. I don't care for the money, but I still feel the anguish just to lose things.

286

At that time there was a friend there in Ramala, a Christian named George. We used to have many things in common, and we wondered, "Why are we not allowed just to go to Jerusalem and be there? Why are we not allowed just to go inside a place where we can go swimming?" During the curfew I started with him building our new NGO. We built it under the curfew, and we called it the Caravan Association for Supporting Palestinian Children. During the curfew, we used to go around the Israeli forces to other homes to collect some food and bring it to children who needed it.

It was something. You feel that you are under attack. You feel one minute you can be killed, but you really feel that you are happy you are helping these people. I can feel that something talking about these stories.

After that I went to work with United States Aid for International Development (USAID) on a project called IT youth. IT Youth is sponsored by USAID, the International Youth Foundation, and also the Welfare Association. It is located in the north of Palestine. I like this project very much. It discusses IT and how we can use IT for peace-building in the future, how we can use IT for building forums just to talk across the boundaries of the world and to talk to the Israelis. And so we try to make forums for chatting between the Palestinian and the Israelis.

I used to be responsible for an employment program, because during the *intifada* more than 75 percent were unemployed. So, for example, we find there is a huge need for executive secretary courses. We tried to invite students who were about 18-20 years old to help them find a job.

And then something very important happened to me during that curfew. This was a debate that happened between me and a soldier. When they invaded our home during that *intifada,* 21 soldiers came, and they destroyed it completely, because it was in front of the Ministry of Education, and they destroyed the Ministry as well. We stayed under a curfew, and they stayed in my house for three days and two nights. So 21 soldiers lived in my house. What are they doing? I have a daughter. So I tried just to break the barrier between me and one soldier. He was a guy 21 or 22 years old. I asked him whether I could go to the kitchen to get something for my daughter. He said okay, and I entered the kitchen and I told him I have nothing, nothing. So we started to make a debate. It was a fruitful debate. He's from the reserve army, and some of them don't know why they are coming. After the debate, we exchanged email addresses, and we became friends.

We became friends in this moment. Really, I advise all the soldiers to invade my home and we will make friends with all the Israelis. So now I am working with the American Friends Committee. We can make the peace in the future, we can invest in the youth. Our country doesn't have any natural resources, but we are rich in human character and human resources.

RUSSIA
Syria

Interviewed by Christine Velure-Roholt

.... I think if we would organize this power to the youth, I think we will reach to a good achievement.

Is there an experience that you can think of in your work that typifies this?
Yeah, when we were first working it was so difficult to gather. As I told you we faced so many problems. It is difficult to gather about things that government didn't approve of. So first we gathered in secret; we gathered around ourselves people who are interested in this. We tried to gather more young people with us. This thing was very difficult, because we don't want anyone to know. We find these young people who can really help us at the beginning. It was a little bit difficult. Then, later, not a lot, but some young people came. We did this in every city. So youth can express their opinions, and we just didn't lecture the youth about the future. We asked them, "What if we make this organization? What do you want? What things do you want? What stuff do you like?"

You said earlier, you didn't want the wrong people to find out. So how did you let the "right" people know about your work? How did you figure out who to talk to?
First friends, and then friends of friends, and then relatives, like this.

You mean word of mouth.
Then the government learns about this thing. So, firstly, the government was afraid that things like this can be political, but we said this thing was just for youth and it is difficult to get this approval. But now I am looking for a way to have this approval from the government.

TALA SWEISS

Interviewed by Christine-Velure-Roholt

I am 26 years old, and I have been working with the American Friends Community, Quaker Service, as a youth program officer. I joined them in May, 2004.

I had a passion for working with youth. Because I do believe that it is hard to work with grown-ups or adults, because the culture has formed them in a way they have their own beliefs. But the youth are still fresh. And they don't have limitations to their ideas. And still, sometimes, as grown-ups and adults you would see a problem and start exaggerating the whole thing, but the solutions lie across and you can't see it because you are just framed by how you are raised: The way that the culture is moving you--the beliefs you had acquired.

But the youth are still fresh; they can see opportunities. They are creative. They have a potential or inner strength. I don't know how to explain it. And they can drive you to take action and help you to do that. So even when I worked with the women sector and the local communities, I have to say that I learned a lot from these experiences. Especially the one where I visited the villages to get to know the real needs of the people all over. But still the driving force of working with youth is something. So when I had this opportunity of working with the Quaker Service as a youth program officer, I just grabbed this opportunity.

What is failing and succeeding when working with youth?

You have to know how to grab their attention because, unlike the other kids, you have to know the entry points: How to talk to them; you have to understand that you have to give them something that they do not know about so they start listening to you and not start telling them about the things they already know. You have to throw out an idea, get their attention, and then start building on the information they know. But you have to be smart enough to know how to get them onto your side and how to listen to them. At first when I would go into the class, it was empty because they were outside on the playground. The teacher would go and start screaming through the window to come into the class or something. So I told her not to scream. I went down to the playground and played with them. And afterwards they went up to the class on their own. But it's not that you have to scream at them or something like that. You have to be with them and then they will join you.

Now when I am thinking I don't think about this spoiled kid in Amman having a PlayStation and a computer and he can go to McDonalds and Burger King any time he wants. I am thinking of the kid who lived in a village. I still remember this area. I always share this story. A kid, the youth living in a village, a very, very, very, very poor area. They don't even have clean water or something like that. When we met the people there it was the most clean village I visited. It was the most organized. Because they didn't have anything to do, they just got the stones from the street and made fences to make the village beautiful. When we used to meet with the people, we used to ask them what they needed. They said, "We want a computer, a computer system." I was shocked. "You want a computer? A whole village and you don't have a computer? "No-no-no. There's someone who's well off in the village, and he has a computer in his home."I was asking them why they consider this family well off if they get 300 Jordanian dinars (JD) a month. Some kids in Amman just take 1500 JD from their parents and go spend it on what they want. They can buy Nike shoes. And these people are considered well off with 300 JDs. So now when I am thinking about the youth, I don't just consider the spoiled youth in Amman.

When I was in the tenth grade, I used to go to a church or a youth ministry, you know. So I always had this auntie, Auntie Vivian. She always told me that you have to work with kids, you have to have a ministry in your church. So basically she encouraged us. So I used to work with younger ages, when I was in tenth grade, I used to work with younger ages in the Sunday school, in the fifth grade or something like that. And when I graduated from the *jiihee,* which is the high school in Jordan, I went into University. She said, "Now you have to have a ministry if you want with other ages—*addadhi*—between 7th, 8th and 9th grades." At this point I had been working with them since 1996. We used to do summer camps. Every year we had a summer camp. And when I was in the university we had summer camps for the university students. We used to get ourselves connected.

At that point I didn't know that this would be called youthwork. I didn't know that there was something that existed called youthwork or something called the participatory approach. You know, these definitions, they were not in my mind. We used to do that because we loved the thing we were doing. First, the driving force was that we loved God, and we wanted to do something to help in this context. And another thing: We loved our country, and we wanted to do something to benefit our country. And we loved each other and enjoyed our work. But we didn't have definitions of youthwork and these big concepts. They were built in us without knowing that there were people outside doing this work. For us it was something there built in.

Do you think that "something built in" is still valued?
Yeah, I'm telling you that it's built in. It's there, and we practice it, because we have this belief deep inside us. We have this deep motivation inside us. I don't know what you would call it in the youthwork world. Maybe they would put it under ethics or values of the work. I don't know what would be the definition, but it's something deep inside about doing this kind of work. Others can categorize it and give you a science about it. But its deep inside and you're just practicing it because you believe in it.

Youthwork is not a cookbook that can be applied. You have to grab the moment and see how you learn from that moment and how you help others learn from within that moment. There are certain basics that can be applied, but the approaches you use have to be fitted to the moment.

So what are the basics of youthwork?

Love. Love is something that should be there. You have to love the kids whatever their background. You have to feel loved in order to feel that you are productive. Teamwork is something basic. Yeah, but I think the core thing is love. I think that the basic ingredient to all the work is love and faith and your belief in what you are doing: The value of doing and having it. You want to share the experience. It's not territorial. It's not being possessive of the young people. You worked with them, now let them go and spread the good news. Let them share what they learned, and they will help others. Teach them and they learn from others.

I want to tell you that in Jordan, youthwork is generally a new thing. The youthwork in Jordan is relatively new. Maybe two or three years maximum. Most of the people doing this kind of work are learning from their work experience or from their own lives. We don't have youthwork accreditation training programs. I told you I hate big definitions, but I do believe in the importance of having a theoretical background for youthwork in this region.

LILJANNA KARANOV

Humanitarian organization Mati Tatjana,
Monastery Gračanica, Kosovo

Interviewed by Christine Velure-Roholt

This is a story about one of the most beautiful towns in Kosovo. Today in this town only Albanians and Turkish people live. Serbs are not there any more. My aim was to take people from the north who have been away from their homes more than five years because of war. There was no contact for those five years with their relatives or their neighbours. And we didn't have any idea what would come out of it. It was a "go and see" visit.

Because we were warned about street fights when we came there. And they told us that there are a lot of mine fields around houses. And maybe there is some kind of set up when we put the key in the lock that maybe the houses would explode. NATO has a duty to protect us, to give us personal protection. But when we arrived in the jeep, no one was waiting for us. The UN said that we were not allowed to proceed. UNHCO told us that they didn't want to escort us to the houses. They say it's dangerous, even though they previously gave permission.

Everyone was afraid of a strong incident in that situation. Because in our group there are a lot of old people. We were going in order not to come back. We were waiting two-by-two in the group; if there was an incident it was a way to escape, because we didn't know what kind of situation would develop. There were no police, no one.

We stepped into our street and approached the house of one of the members of our group. And two young Albanians were running across, they were shouting in the Albanian language, and we didn't understand them. They tried to stop us. In that moment the group felt a very great fear and we were expecting an incident. Then a few women showed up in that street and they were shouting at us. One woman stepped into one of these houses and came out with her arms like this, holding something. We thought it was a bomb and she wants to throw it to us. But the woman opened her arms and she showed us a present—a traditional Albanian gift. It is a very old one, from an old shop. And she said, "You are very welcome here."

EDIN VELJOVIČ
Youth Initiative for Human Rights,
Belgrade, Serbia

Interviewed by Christine Velure-Roholt

I am from Belgrade. It is the capital of Serbia and the state of Serbia-Montenegro. It is a big city of about 3 million people. In that city you can have every kind of fun. Some parts of Belgrade are in the 21st century, and some parts of Belgrade are deeply in the past. It was March 17th of this year when there was violence in Kosovo and this time against the Serbs. Albanians are mostly Muslims. But you have Catholics and Arabs as well. People in Serbia have the perception that all Albanians are Muslims and all Albanians and Bosniacs think those people are the Turkish people who were in Serbia during the 6th century when it was the Ottoman Empire. As a kind of revenge, as a stupid revenge for the violence in Kosovo, some young people in Belgrade Niche and Novi Sad were doing some actions which are not civil.

On that March 17th I was sitting in a very fancy street in Belgrade, with three friends, on a fancy street with a lot of restaurants in a fancy café. The reason we were going in that place is because I went home to see one of these friends-- Serbs. They were very angry because of violence in Priština against the Serbs. And I wanted to make them feel better or to focus their minds on some other stories. And I was afraid I would hear some stories that I did not want to hear from some friends of mine.

Around us were other tables with laptops, good phones, they were wearing some fancy clothes. In front of that café there were very expensive cars that cost more than $100,000--Mercedes, Porsches, etc. It was some kind of normal atmosphere in Belgrade, sitting in that kind of place and you are talking about who knows what. In that moment my mobile phone rang and my friend asked me where I was. And I said I was there having a drink with the friends. In that atmosphere, there is nothing that reminds us of what is happening in Kosovo. And he said, "Okay, be careful and take a taxi and go home." And I said, "Why?" He said, "Just go and when you come home immediately call me back." And I said, "Please tell me what is happening." He said some youth are going to burn the mosque in Belgrade. The mosque was two streets above the street where I was so I said I was going there. My friend was begging me, "Please don't go there. It's dangerous." I said, "I am a human rights activist and I want to see what is happening."

I went there and I saw about 100 young people, very beautiful young people. People like you meet on buses, in cafes, in discos, in schools, in universities. Ordinary people. Their eyes were full of some kind of revenge, a fire in their hearts, and they were burning all around the mosque. There were police, there were ambulances, and a lot of what we call peaceful citizens who didn't do anything to stop them. And there were even politicians there and they did nothing to stop it. As my religion is Muslim, I felt very lonely and I was very upset. I didn't know what to do. I thought, "I am only alone in the world. What am I doing in life? I am fighting for human rights and look at this." In two streets, you come from the 21st century to the 13th century. You come from very expensive restaurants and a café with a lot of very high technology to a place where people destroy their mosque, their religion, their objectives. I was really, really upset.

And those friends who I mentioned at the beginning of the story, they were really angry about things that were happening in Kosovo, but at that moment they saw me, they saw my face and saw that I was very sad. "We are not going to apologize to you because these people are not our friends, you are our friend. We like you as you are. Now look at this, I feel sorry that these people are not really good people." So in that moment I cannot describe to you my happiness because of those Serbian friends. That I can count on them in a very difficult situation.

I WAS THERE
Goran
Pančevo, Serbia

Interviewed and translated by Marko Gashi

It was winter 1996/97, right after the elections. At that time I was working on a project for reconciliation of young people in Serbia and Croatia. We were just a group of people trying get as many youth as possible to think with their own head and not to listen to state propaganda and to not lose hope. Fortunately, we were not alone. There were not many, but the number was not insignificant. It was 1996, but that was five years ago when we started to stand against Milosevic's politics and war propaganda in our Serbia. Our country at that time was a country with, so to speak, malignant processes of metathesis in its society. Youth were confused but determined to work for a change.

I was there in the square, like many times during opposition meetings. It was a crowd, a positive crowd with people, young and old, gathering for one more "swallow" of democratic thoughts, one more dose for a healthy, good night. We didn't want to acknowledge that he won again. It didn't make sense. I saw one more confused and negative year behind me with no real light at the end of the tunnel. The foreign press still reported on Milosevic and his actions and not really mentioning me, my friends, us there as "healthy cells" of Serbian metathesis. It seemed they didn't care.

And there was I, in the square, shouting, singing, and celebrating that I still have peace in my head and that I am not alone in rejecting state policy and craziness, rejecting the prison of my soul. I was happy, really happy; I didn't care about what the foreign television reporters say about my country−I knew they say what they want to say. First, I was scared of why they didn't report me being on the square, but later I didn't care about that either. Later that night, as we were walking down the streets in a crowd, whistling, hitting provisional drums, hitting kitchen dishes in the rhythm of liberty−it was our way. It was that night and many nights after, it was winter 1996/1997. The streets were full, the police were hitting us, and there was shooting. I was there.

YOUTH WORKER'S REALITY

Gordana

Novi Sad, Serbia

Interviewed and translated by Marko Gashi and Snežana Kresoja

On the 27th of February, 1996, I was coming back home from my work. I was organizing roundtables about multicultural society, democracy, and human rights in several places in Vojvodina, an area that was always so interesting to me to live in, and many times I felt privileged to live there.

That evening, an old woman came to the meeting. First she sat to one side, but later she was very well accepted in the group of young people. Although at first she looked like she was a bit embarrassed, soon she started to actively join the discussion. She saw information about the workshop while coming back from the market. I asked her why she was attracted to the title, and she said that it was interesting for her to hear why people talk so much about democracy. She was puzzled and wanted to learn that once and for all.

I started a discussion in which there were many opinions. Several students quoted famous philosophers, some had clear liberal phrases, and some were reading extracts from newspaper articles and quoting politicians who say many different definitions of democracy. There were many attempts to define it that evening. I felt very good; it was my way of doing things. I like to talk and especially to hear and question what others have to say about democracy.

While we were talking the old lady briefly told us that the house of her sister in Croatia was burned and that the word "democracy" was on the burned walls of the house. She wanted an explanation. I let the discussion continue, without my active leadership. Although I heard thousands of stories like this, I did not think of involving myself more in it for the moment. Soon we finished the meeting and planned for our next discussion.

That evening meeting caused strange feelings: I am here talking about democracy and some old lady, just several kilometers from my town, is there trying to survive with no home left. I was disgusted. I could not explain the thoughts at the time. All that I was doing stopped somehow in my head. And I remembered all the stories, all my personal tragedies and tragedies of my dear ones. For so many years I am here, working with kids--young boys and girls--teaching them and telling them that there is better world out there.

But what did I do? Where are the results of my work? Whom did I really help? Am I a coward who cannot go and help an old lady but can just talk and discuss with youth about democracy and human rights? Who gets anything from my talking? Where am I? Who am I fooling?

CHURCH FIGHT

Ivan, 29
Belgrade, Serbia

Interviewed and translated by Marko Gashi

I am a member of a youth group from an evangelical church in Belgrade. Since I was a kid I was active in church life, mainly organizing different activities, seminars, conferences, and summer camps. Through our group there were many group leaders that we grew up with who helped make our teenage lives more interesting and keeping it on track with good values, especially when our surroundings were very morally challenged. Soon after the war in Bosnia I was in a team to organize a conference with young people from all over the former Yugoslavia. It was a challenging job for me at the time, and I was seeing it as a possibility to meet again with old friends but, also, now that I was older, to see about our voice and possible influence on politicians and politics.

I was working in a welcome team, and I was thinking of how the conference would flow. Since we are all from different places and different things were happening to us during the war years, some participants even had family members lost in war and, as I heard, it was extremely difficult for them even to come to Belgrade. It actually turned out that we were all in a war with each other during recent years, and when one tries to understand what happened it becomes chaotic; it is even sometimes like that in our heads as well.

I was pleasantly surprised with the guests and all went well. We were sitting and talking about school, about God, our travels, and participated in different sessions. Generally it seemed to me it was going well. The only thing that I was surprised about was when I saw two boys from Belgrade arguing about whose group would give their report first and on what day. There were several groups, and these two boys were leaders of their groups, and each of them wanted to have their groups' presentations during the most visited part of the day.

I tried to involve myself in solving the problem and tell them that it is not important for them to present it in some special part of the day. Immediately I had a flashback in my mind about the years of conflict and wars: Those two boys seemed to me like the politicians who started the wars, behaving the same way. I was shocked, even more when I realized that those two boys were members of my church. Vanity and stubbornness: Human imperfections that can lead to great sins toward other people and those who have them.

What it indicated for me was this possibility of arguing in church. I didn't experience before such stubbornness in church and lack of tolerance. I was there from my childhood and always experienced freedom, warmth, and friendships. But that day I saw that even in church it is possible that we have such manifestations of bad habits, even hatred. Is it possible we forget why we go to church? Is it possible we are able to forget and not see that we are not "church" anymore when we fight?

THE CIRCLE IN LIFE
Marijana, age 25
Belgrade/Kosovska Mitrovica, Serbia

Interviewed and translated by Marko Gashi

I was born and lived in Kosovska Mitrovica, a town in Kosovo province, until I was 19. I was living there with my mother, father, and two brothers, with a house and all that comes with it. During the wars in Croatia and Bosnia, we used to have lot of refugees in our town and, as a secondary school student, I applied as a volunteer to distribute humanitarian help from western countries. During that time I used to see many different cases of what is left when families are destroyed in wars. I tried to help by being a volunteer of the Red Cross of Serbia when refugees need help with necessities and helping them adapt better into our community. All that was hard but I felt I was useful and can share some of myself with these poor people.

There were people who came with almost nothing and they could not bring anything with them. Many claimed that they were wealthy where they come from. But all that does not matter in wars. I saw how property is so relative when you have to escape and save your life. I listened to the stories when they were telling me how they lost their loved ones: mother, father, brother, sister, son, daughter.

In 1998 I enrolled in Belgrade University, and there I rented an accommodation. Very soon, in the spring of 1999, serious unrest began in Kosovo and the bombing of Yugoslavia. I didn't hear from my parents for more than two weeks. One morning I heard from my parents that they escaped from Kosovo, and they left our house and our land and had only a few things with them. They came to our relatives in Nis.

As soon as I heard I went to Nis to see them, and when I met them I was so happy that we were still alive and healthy, but I noticed my brother was not there. They told me he is officially missing. He never came back from his work. These days after were very hard for me. I loved my brother so much, but soon I realized he would not come back. As time passed I stopped believing and accepted the reality: He was gone.

My mother, father, brother, and me became refugees. This was an irony because, just few years ago, I was helping refugees while I still had a normal life. This experience helped me to understand more the real needs of refugees. There is much more than property. There are lives of people you care for, there are so many questions in your head you have to deal with, and there are so many answers that are not enough to explain your situation. My parents started to receive humanitarian help from different organizations and also myself. During my university years I felt the need to help those in need, and I was active, like in my school years, in many organizations that distributed humanitarian help, this time to my home place. It was a circle in my life.

YOUTHWORKERS' THOUGHTS
Danijela, age 38
Niš, Serbia

Interviewed and translated by Marko Gashi and Snežana Kresoja

I was asking myself several times what it is to be a good youthworker. Is there some formula to be followed, or is it good experience, or is it just something you are gifted for, or is it circumstances that make you a better or very good youthworker? I still have no answer to these questions, but I could watch and evaluate myself several times, and I tried to see it as objectively as possible.

Someone once said, "You are going to see how good you are by your results." I was always feeling great responsibility for what I do and how I work with young people, especially with young refugees and homeless from war. I asked myself many times about my competence. So far, I was working in different organizations or professional groups of special trainers or educational trainers, and always I was leading myself according to my sense of what should I do or where and when I should put more attention.

Now when I look back it seems a little chaotic how much I was like a bee going from a flower to another flower, making sense of my drive to help young people find stability in their lives and with their lives. Several times I asked myself, "Am I a good role model? Do I actually have to be a role model to these young people?" Several times I was faced with the issue of being a model to some girls I was taking care of during the Kosovo crisis in the late 1990s. They really started to be dependent on me and what I said or did.

I am not a psychologist or some specialist; I am just a medical nurse who happened to be in such situations that led me to work with youth in conflict places. I was also comparing myself with colleagues and other specialists. But no matter how hard I was trying to find some model of good youthwork, I came to the same conclusion: Each youthworker is really unique with a special way of communicating and developing relationships with young people. And although it was a little scary for me, because it seemed that there is no real formula for a good youthworker, it also freed me from expecting to be a good youthworker, because I realized that it is very individual and that it is good that it is individual.

Now I can say I am more relaxed about this and seeing myself much more driven by situation. I see youthwork more holistically and am more open to different possibilities. I guess I am seeing my work now much more extended and with different possibilities that I haven't seen before. And it is a very good feeling. Somehow in developing such thoughts I faced different and very nice ideas of young people, and I started to be open to different suggestions and ideas, and I am not bothered that much about competence anymore. Because I think that not only experience but being open and, especially, introspective, being open to explore myself with my own eyes, not so much worried about comparisons with others is what brings confidence, creativity, and more love and joy to my work.

LITTLE JOURNALIST

Snježana, age 26
Sarajevo, Bosnia

Interviewed and translated by Marko Gashi

As a girl I volunteered on a Sarajevo children's television programme and wanted to become a journalist when I grew up. I will never forget one of events that happened to me when the conflict started to spread in Sarajevo and the whole of Bosnia.

I was with my friends preparing for making a report on children's playgrounds in Sarajevo. When we finished I called my mother to pick me up and go home. I waited for my mom some time and started to ask myself what was happening, because it had already been an hour, and she was still not there. Even two hours passed and, finally, she came. She was so serious in her face, I never saw her like that. She said to us, "There is some shooting outside, some lunatics are shooting and I couldn't make it that fast, sorry sweety."

I didn't say anything, just put my jacket on and asked her whether we were going home. She said that we should stay here a little and tried to make a phone call. My father was in town, and he was worried because he also heard some guns but was not sure about it. Soon my mother told me we could leave, and we came safely home.

Several days passed and I almost forgot what happened. But then again I saw on television that on one street there were some people wearing guns, and the reporter said that it is not so unusual now for Sarajevo. My father said, "This is totally stupid. What are those people doing?" It was strange to me; it reminded me of some war or some movies I watched on television. The image of those men was so difficult to understand. What is the meaning of carrying guns?

It was annoying to me to watch it, and I got nervous. I told this to my friends on television and asked an editor if we could make some special report or some broadcast for kids about being against guns and wars. And we started to work on that. Some of our grown-up friends helped us, and soon we had some celebrities for guests and also some people from abroad talking about wars and telling us how we should prevent it.

Our main ammunition, as we thought then, was music and making people sing. At one time my grandmother said to me: "Who sings never thinks bad things." And I was led by this sentence. In several broadcasts we asked children for poems to make some songs against the war, and some of them were very beautiful. Our broadcast lasted for six weeks more. Then a war started. It ended four years later.

Although I wanted to be a journalist when I was a kid, I couldn't help but not to become a youthworker as well. I think this early engagement in media and being able to see all the abusurdity of war is something that led me to be a youthworker. Even now I remember myself at that time, all the disappointment, seeing that it is not in my hands to make people stop fighting and killing. My experience as a kid and ideas and my frustrations at the same time I see as a source of my energy to work with youth.

DIFFERENCE IS BURNING!

Vuk, age 28
Belgrade, Serbia

Interviewed and translated by Marko Gashi

Living in Belgrade, the capital of Serbia, I always considered myself a citizen of the world. After one day I thought of myself more as a citizen of Belgrade than a citizen of the world.

When nationalism knocks on your door you have to make a decision. It is a test that lasted in this country for 15 years and still lasts. It is a never-ending, explicit, and hidden message that you have to deal with at a conscious level and extract it from your unconsciousness. You have to deal with it and destroy it if you want to preserve yourself as a democrat and pacifist. The thing is that you are sometimes more or less aware of your surroundings where you are living.

That was also the case with me. Much of reality one is not aware of, because of living among people who think the same as you. And, naturally, I was always going around with people who think the same and have positive values of my nation and who fight nationalism and its chameleonic forms.

As a former member of "Otpor,"-an organization that became a movement helping organize people against Milosevic's rule in the 1990s throughout Serbia, many times today I think with my friends about founding a new organization to fight nationalism and offer a new perspective on possible dialogue and reevaluating different nationalities who live in Serbia.

Still, it seems that it is not so organized an idea as it was against the Milosevic dictatorship. It seems in Serbia people need much time to pass from experiencing bad feelings and thoughts of hatred in order to organize better and fight against things that slow progress. That is what I think about my people here and, possibly, it is the same everywhere.

Pride is again one obstacle that makes it all worse, such as being over-emotional about things from the past and holding it close as one would sainthood. Many youth here do not understand its importance. So it is a constant question of how much we should preserve of such patriotic feelings and how much we can sacrifice our time in order to keep our past and traditions and, at the same time, keep our progress on pace.

It was one more test in the spring of 2004 when Albanians in Kosovo, which is still part of Serbia at the moment, started violence against Serbians who remained in Kosovo. The majority of Albanians want Kosovo to be independent, having had a bad experience under Serbian rule. That spring they started to burn churches, monasteries, monuments, houses, and villages that were Serbian. And international peacekeepers did nothing much to prevent it: They were not well prepared for it.

305

It was a typically nice spring day in Belgrade, and its restaurant gardens started to open. I was with my friends downtown for an evening drink, reviewing the past week and taking a walk. My friends were different nationalities. Usually I don't care, but for this story I will explain: There were three Serbians, a Bosniak-Muslim, and a Macedonian. While walking, I noticed how winter slowly passes, and I noticed one burned paper rolling along the street. Soon I noticed another burned paper with traces of fire still on it, and soon more and more such papers started to fly on us.

I thought that maybe there was a fire nearby, and I was right. I started to walk with friends toward a place where these papers were coming from and looked behind the corner. The biggest mosque in Belgrade was burning. The fire was huge. It was just 100 meters from the restaurant on a parallel street. We could hear the noise of young men yelling and cursing and enjoying what they had done. Hundreds of young men shouted nationalistic phrases that they grew up with, all the repertoire of the Milosevic vocabulary just spread on the streets of that quarter in the city centre.

It was like a flashback to the dark 1990s. And I saw that they still live in us, they contaminated us, and each of us is more or less immunized to it. But it was a place for one to be aware that there are still many of us who are slaves of nationalistic decadence. Police were there doing nothing. Molotov cocktails were constantly in the air. Reporters watched. I felt so much responsibility and very ashamed. In a few seconds I realized that my friend is a Muslim, and I saw him just looking at it, watching without words. I thought of doing something to stop, but there were so many people and no organized force to stop the destruction.

I turned to my friend and I wanted to say to him that we are not guilty because some hooligans are destroying his mosque. I wanted to tell him that he should not worry because of that because there are always such people. But really, are we not guilty? Does he need not worry? I didn't tell him anything. When I saw his face and tears started to fill his eyes, I didn't tell him anything but just hugged him.

In this case education and information is what we need as a next step toward democratic society. It is obvious that, four years after the end of Milosevic's rule, we are still living in an information gap with lots of unsolved things in our heads. The only thing is to take a responsible strategy for educating people, especially the young, about what it is to love difference. It is sad that even Christian values in Serbia started to be associated with nationalism because of the church's involvement in politics.

But it is a Christian value that we should start to love our neighbors in a significantly different way than we used to. Tolerance is one bad word that tells us nothing. It seems to me like a bomb ready to explode: It solves nothing. It just points out how different we are and we cannot do anything about it. It is a negative perspective. We need more readiness and more youth actions, which, I am happy to say, I see more and more in recent time in Serbia and look into the future with more responsibility.

FACING THE SERVANTS OF THE PEOPLE
Goran, age 24
Zemun, Serbia

Interviewed and translated by Marko Gashi and Snežana Kresoja

I was an activist in the organization Otpor during 1998-2000. I was 16 when I entered into this organization and was fascinated with so many young people there. I was totally ready to join and give myself to fight the oppression of Milosevic and his police. I was always there to distribute materials and talk to young people on streets while giving them brochures and flyers.

It was a night in Belgrade, the summer of 2000, a summer time in my city that never sleeps. Five of my friends and I were on the streets of Zemun, an old part of Belgrade, full of rolls of posters from Otpor's new campaign. We gave our best to make these posters and financed it from our own pockets. We also had a few car color spray paints to write anti-regime graffiti on "free places." We always carried such sprays to write at night to shake up people's heads to start to think with their own mind and not to listen to lying television.

Although we were going mainly at night putting posters and writing graffiti, we also were choosing places that are visible and that people see everyday. Many times we were escaping police and many times police were hunting us but with no success: We were faster and smarter. But that night we got into a trap, because the police were hunting us and we didn't know it. We didn't expect them, although we were always prepared.

This time we wanted to put posters on some well-known buildings, and when we did it we started with some side streets as well. The police came with several cars, and they pointed guns at us. They had never pointed guns at us before; this time we saw it was more serious. We immediately stopped what we were doing, and they approached us and handcuffed us.

One of the policemen burned our posters, making a big fire. We were put into a police vehicle and, after 20 minutes, we were in prison in a room, all six of us with three policemen. They were yelling at us, like animals, that we are traitors, foreign spies, we are brainwashed, and our parents are retarded in their heads, stupid to sacrifice their children in such a way. They were cursing our families and our names. They were promising that they will make our lives hell if we didn't stop with activities in Otpor.

Two of my friends were hit hard in their stomachs and one of them fell on the ground. A policeman slammed me [into the wall] and spit on me. One of my friends was lying down on the floor while a policman hit him with his boot in his knees. I remembered some movies about prison torture in communist countries like North Korea or China, and I saw that it is actually the same here in my own country. I thought that something like this was not possible, but actually I was seeing it with my own eyes. I thought they would never let us go or that maybe we would die here.

It was like an eternity to me being there in that room. I started to think about my mom and dad and hoped they will not be too sad when they find out I was dead. But then one of the policmen said, "That's enough," and all three of them brought us to another room where we had to sign some papers, and they let us go. We didn't know where we were. Some of us had bleeding noses, some bleeding knees and arms, and one had a serious eye injury. We were just trying to follow the lights suggesting the way back to town. Luckily we were back to our homes later that night.

In some independent media this event was covered with lots of publicity, and I was hoping this would again show people what madness we were living in. I was just hoping this would open people's eyes to fight the regime and oppression and craziness and lies we were living in.

Later, during 2000, we were celebrating!

THE BOY WITH BIG BLUE EYES
Nataša, age 32
Vranje, Serbia

Interviewed and translated by Marko Gashi

I was working in a youth center that we opened within the primary school in the suburbs of Nis. We wanted to call it a youth center, but it was actually two rooms that we used for additional educational programs for kids who experienced war trauma. We had a group of young psychologists and volunteers who were identifying such kids in classes and, along with their friends, invited them to come to our place and participate in our activities.

Our activities were mainly formed as workshops where we went through different psychological topics such as emotions, difficulties growing up, problems in school, and problems at home. We also talked about things that are happening in our time and all the daily events and news that affected us some way. Young people there were from 9 to 17 years of age. Many of them experienced life as a refugee, some escaped with their parents, some were without one parent, and some lived in highly dangerous places during the wars in Bosnia and Croatia.

I was working as a psychologist in a group with my colleagues. We had rotating schedules, so we all got to know all the children. In one group there was a boy who was coming to my class regularly, whom I noticed had a special appearance and was very much different from others. His name was Bojan, aged 12 years. He had a father, but his mother died from cancer years ago. Actually, maybe he was like the other boys, but I noticed something much more behind those big blue eyes.

He was very often in all our activities but a little distant and not always prepared to talk. Later, we started to visit different places of interest to children and also took excursions in the countryside. He also attended these trips but prefered to be alone and not in a group of other children. Once we went to Vlasinsko Jezero: It is a lake with nice surroundings for hiking and biking. Bojan wanted to sit by the lake, and it seemed he was quite satisfied with it. I came to him and asked him why he did not come with us for a walk. He replied, "It's okay, I am fine here."

I felt this was maybe a good moment to try to spend some more time with him and see what is the mystery with this boy and to try somehow to integrate him more with others. I told my colleague to go without me, and I decided to stay by the lake and watch birds. The group went and soon we were alone, not hearing children's voices. I started a conversation about how much I liked to watch birds when I was small and that sometimes I still do it, when I want to relax. He told me he likes to watch stones sinking in water, disappearing to the bottom of the lake. I told him it can be quite meditative and relaxing too, especialy when you have different sizes and colors of stones. We were talking about birds and then were silent for couple of minutes.

Suddenly he said to me: "It reminds me of life." At first I did not understand, so I asked him to explain to me what he meant. He sighed and told me quietly, "My grandma was like this." He was not looking me in the eyes and continued explaining, but with a very silent voice, difficult to understand.

My grandma was like this; she went to a well and when she came back people came and started shooting. I was in the house and hid myself in an old chest. I waited for some time and came out...I saw my grandma lying in front of the doors with open eyes looking for me...she saw me and I was looking at her eyes and then they became so distant...like a stone sinking in the water.

I had no reply. It was quite upsetting for me, because I did not expect such a story, and I was suprised how suddenly this boy opened his heart and started talking. I was sure that I would need some time to get him talking, since he was so distant and quiet in our activities. But, obviously, I was wrong. It seemed it was a perfect time to talk.

He continued his story. He told me that when that happened he had gone to visit his grandma in Bosnia. It was like any other summer when he spent a lot of time in the countryside. Soon this conversation became much more open and we talked about many things: schools, nature, different occupations. I never saw him so talkative. It looked like he overcame some big barrier. We had a great communication until he went to secondary school and had to move to another town.

It seemed to me like an amazing afternoon. That day I was just a person, being there, sitting with this boy and talking with him. It was interesting to me later and now when I think about it: Sometimes you do not need many extra activities to work with youth...[you need to] just be there, show your true interest about their lives, and offer them company. They recognize it, and it goes so well after that. Young people are so sensitive to honesty and true care and interest. They really can reward you, and great things can happen.

LOVE FOR OUR NEIGHBORS
Ivana, age 29
Loznica, Serbia

Interviewed and translated by Marko Gashi

I live in the southwest of Serbia. I am Serbian and mostly Serbian people live here. During the war, in the former Yugoslavia, a lot of refugees came to us from all the places that were affected by wars. Since they came they had no job, so it was difficult for them to adapt in this sense as well. Since Serbia at that time was under international economic sanctions, it was very hard for an ordinary citizen of Serbia to find a proper job, not to mention refugees who were coming by the thousands. At that time I was facing huge difficulties with the local people who were beginning to be angry with refugees, because they started to get jobs that locals intended for themselves.

So it was quite a strange conflict inside of me. I realized our community had a phenomenon of helping refugees and, at the same time, hating them, wishing them to be out of our public life and excluding them from socialization. I was a member of one music youth group that established an orchestra, and we formed an organization that had nothing to do with politics or anything that might be similar to politics, although we had a drive to discuss such issues. We also had a mission to teach children to play different instruments. We were playing in local venues, in schools, and we went to competitions. There were, at first, 12 of us, and later 28, from 18 to 30 years of age.

At that time, while we were playing, we had a rule that someone is always conducting the orchestra, since there was no professional conductor in our group. At each rehearsal we rotated several people who took turns conducting. We wanted to see who was the best for this position. So we were judging the candidates.

One day a guy who was a refugee came to conduct the orchestra. He actually wanted to play violin, but somebody asked him if he would like to try conducting. It was clear that he had music knowledge but, like many other refugees, with no diploma to prove it. So he started with exercises and, later, we would play a piece that will help us judge his performance and our marks.

But then I noticed the rehearsal was very inconsistent, and the orchestra sounded unusually bad. I thought, "It is just one of our bad days," but later on I noticed that this is just too bad! I also noticed several of the people in different sections of the orchestra made unusual mistakes and, somehow, it started to be very strange.

Then I came up with an idea with my friends around me: These people actually made intentional mistakes. I could not believe it at first, but later it became obvious. Then it all started to come back to me, the whole problem that we had as a society at the time. We were an isolated country, threatened by war, and just 15 kilometers from us there was a front, and we could sometimes hear bombs and noise. And here we were having an orchestra, trying to make all our surroundings bearable.

But it simply was not possible to be unaffected in different levels, not only physically, but psychologically. We started to behave like those who were in war, like those who kill each other physically, only we were doing it psychologically. It was a horrifying explanation, but it was very logical to me and it proved to be true.

Later on, while we were practicing, I realized that even the refugee was better at conducting than many of us, although few would like to admit it. I started to remember many of the occasions when people were talking about refugees who "came to steal what was ours." But the question was what was ours, really, in all this poor time. We couldn't control frustrations, and we even started to lose our common sense.

Several days passed after that bad rehearsal, and the man continued to be a member of our orchestra. He was really enjoying playing, although he didn't have many friends. I treated him with respect like some of the others, but I think he was most happy when he actually returned his real home--to the place he had to leave. I was feeling very bad about it. I didn't have knowledge about politics, although I was a witness of how it was in Serbia at the time, with poor people everywhere and the crash of the economy and devastation.

I started to talk to people about the problem of refugees who experience such poor attitudes from locals. I was just trying to make my surroundings more tolerant of different behaviors and needs of refugees. I can just hope I reached some of the people I was talking to and tried to make them think. Later we formed a small, unofficial group of young people who were meeting once a week and talking about what we were experiencing with refugees, and some of us were helping them accommodate in our community. We don't know how successful we were, but since some of our refugees stayed after the war and made a family, we hope we contributed at least something. After the war we never heard again about the violin player, but he was the inspiration for our later work and to start changing our minds. I suppose he is enjoying his music at his place, and maybe conducting too.

CLEAR DIRECTION

Marijana, age 30
Belgrade, Serbia

Interviewed and translated by Marko Gashi and Snežana Kresoja

I live in Belgrade. It was a time when my generation was finishing high school in 1991. In our school, I was involved in a special project, "Youth for Kids," a joint project of several high schools in Serbia. We were involved in many activities to help children without parents socialize better and prevent delinquency and street gangs.

I formed a group of us who were involved with one group of suburban kids who were having problems with drugs: glue sniffing, smoking, stealing from supermarkets, and hanging out not going to school. Our intention was to offer them our company and be pals to them, trying to give them some other point of view about the society instead of the negative one that most of them had. It was a simple activity for us, but I see now one that was very important as an alternative to the official rigid policy of the government at that time.

Usually at the end of high school students go on a trip or excursion to celebrate. We went to Split, a Croatian coastal town, known for archaeological sites and famous ruins. At the same time it was a nice possibility to enjoy the good weather and the sea. There were 30 of us on that trip. I shared a room with my best friend. One evening I heard that there are many things happening in town. We just had a nice long walk by the sea and heard from the receptionist that there were some clashes and demonstrations.

We didn't pay much attention to it, since we wanted to have a good time, although we were aware of the tense situation in Yugoslavia. But we were optimist that politicians would resolve this situation. Now, from this distance in time, I can say that it was actually the beginning of war in Croatia. I heard that there were fights started in the city centre between our boys and some local boys who were telling them that they are Croats. They were saying: Croatia to Croats, Serbians get out of Croatia.

Our excursion trip turned out to be a trip of bloody heads, cut clothes, and tears, something we didn't expect at all. After all, Split was a place many of us visited several times with our parents as a holiday destination. I simply couldn't believe what was happening and the whole reality of it. But it was real.

Soon after we heard about the fight, a group of young men came into our hotel and started to go into rooms, hitting doors, and yelling. I started to hear screams and broken glasses. There were three young men who entered my room with baseball bats, and I knew they came to hurt us, because we were from Serbia. With my friend in the room, we got very scared and went to the corner.

One guy came closer to Jelena, my friend, and slammed her face and tore her t-shirt with the Yugoslav flag. He also hit her several times more in her face and cursed. She fell down and cried. The other one came closer to me and I thought instantly that the same thing would happen to me. But he hugged me and greeted me like a sister and said to me, "Hey sister."

At the first moment, I didn't realized what was happening and what he was up to, but later I knew. Since I had a t-shirt with the Croatian seal and with "Croatia" printed on it, they didn't touch me. I bought that flag two days before in Split as a souvenir, not so much thinking about the situation in the country in general and not realizing the seriousness of all this: Croatia, Yugoslavia, independence.

They left the room, and I started to cry when I saw my friend. Later on, many people from the hotel came to help us, apologizing and talking to us and affirming to us that there are such gangs in recent times that are becoming more powerful, and they could do nothing to prevent them from breaking into the hotel, because they would be hurt.

The next day we were all on our way back home. Our high school excursion ended. It was supposed to mark the end of one time in our life and give us nice memories for our new university life. On our way back I was thinking about the recent two years spent with kids with behavioural problems and the seriousness of the situation and responsibility for such kids. Actually I was preoccupied with these thoughts later on too, in a sense that I entered into university starting to study pedagogy. The thing is that I realized how much we do without really knowing the necessity of it. I was working with kids because, generally, I thought it was important to prevent criminality among children, but from my perspective now I see how major a role we all have in education, how much we can actually channel children's behavior, how much we can really do by giving a good example, and how much we can manipulate young people with our thoughts, behaviors, and emotions. It was a clear example for me at the time, clear enough to continue working with children in a much more aware and responsible way.

SOON IT WILL BE OVER

Anonymous, age 36
Belgrade, Serbia

Interviewed and translated by Marko Gashi

My father is an artist and raised me to enjoy life and people's diversities. I guess this is why I chose to work with young people. When you work with young people, there are such great differences in opinions, attitudes, and views on life that you cannot grow old, you are always updated.

My work includes youth with behavioural and family problems. During the 1990s in Serbia, it seemed that there are many more youth with such problems and, additionally, there were youth who, because of the economic situation, started to get involved in different gangs, stealing, taking drugs, and abusing people. Many times I found it hard to explain to them that there are good stories and good people and that it is worthy to keep going with school and that it is good to get a proper job--all that in the situation as it was in Serbia in the 1990s.

In 1993, when I arrived at home, usually I thought how it could be that the military didn't get me yet. But they had their system. At that time it was usual that everybody, all males over 18, received a paper [ordering them] to go to the army and, although it was not officially declared, all were going to fight in the war. Every day I was hearing that somebody was killed, either my professor or my colleague or a friend from high school. It seemed horrible to me at the beginning, but later I got used to it.

One day some armed people from the military came to my house and demanded to see my father, because he avoided going to the military headquarters for mobilisation. They came suddenly and started to interrogate me and my sister and mother and threatened us with guns. I couldn't believe what was happening; actually I thought it is like some movie and could not see guns as real. I thought they were toys; they looked like rubber toys. And all that forcing was like in the movie.

Actually up to that time I was not fully aware of the seriousness of the situation I was living in. I said to myself, "Okay, it is bad economically, and there are some bad things happening there, but it will soon be over and there will be peace again." But then I realized that this "soon" had lasted for three years already and that it is becoming worse.

One afternoon, when the military came, I started to realize faster the situation around me. It was real. The soldiers who came into my house left a very bad taste in my mouth and some broken teeth as well, but I was scared to talk about it and, believe it or not, I still am, because I don't see any real change of human rights in my country.

Tomorrow, I go back to the guys and girls who waited for me for another day of friendship.

EARLY WAR LOGICS

Zoltan , age 32
Novi Sad, Serbia

Interviewed and translated by Marko Gashi and Snežana Kresoja

It was a time when the war in Bosnia was starting. Still, there were people who were not aware how serious it all was, and I was one of them, along with my friends. We were from Sombor, a place in the north of Serbia that is multiethnic, and we wished to visit our friends in Bosnia very near to the Serbian border. At the time I was a teacher in primary school, just finished with my studies, and fortunate to have a job, unlike my friends.

Since we were listening to the radio and television, we were informed about the conflict in Bosnia, but since it was so minor at the time, we thought it was okay to go, so we went to meet our friends. But our parents were very worried; they wanted us to invite these friends to our place, but we were determined to go there and see them. Our reply to our parents' worries was that the conflict was in the central part of Bosnia--not on the border--where we were supposed to meet our friends.

And so it was. We phoned our friends and agreed to meet them and made arrangements about where to stay and what to do. We made gifts and went on the road. There were four of us: two of my friends who were working in a church organization and were teachers of catechesis and were active in the region north of Vojvodina organizing activities for young people, mainly friendship camps, competitions, football matches, and that sort of event.

We were travelling with one old car, full of confidence. Two of us were Serbians and two were Hungarian, including me. So we thought we wouldn't have problems, since we were coming from Serbia and entering into a part of Bosnia mainly inhabited with Serbians. We thought that nothing bad could happen to us and that we had no reason to worry.

We passed the border quite easily, but we saw many things there: guns, soldiers--just too many of them--some boxes of food mixed with guns. It was confusing, but we didn't pay so much attention to it, and we were still convinced we were going to a place where all was normal. After three years our company and friendships would be restored.

We finally arrived. They were so happy to see us and we were so warmly welcomed. Their fathers, however, were not there: They were mobilized by the military. They were near but were guards of the area. Although we were warmly welcomed, after smiles and the usual laughs we were told about the situation and the tensions. It was unpleasant to hear all that, how it started, and what is happening.

317

Later, we went to some café, and there were people who were meeting there; it was a popular place for socializing. While we were talking to our friends, a man came into the café.

He had guns and some bombs around his waist, and all of a sudden he yelled: "Are there any Croats here?"

There was no answer. "Are there any Muslims here? Hungarians or others?"

He had a strong voice and so powerful. And people just kept quiet.

One of them asked: "Why do you need them?"

And he said, "To suck their blood…" and he cursed. After some time he left.

I was cold as ice; I remember not thinking about anything. I didn't have anything [in my experience] to refer to in this kind of situation…and such people and this way of thinking about who is what [ethnic group] and what nation. I didn't care about it. In a sense I didn't make a big deal out of it.

The next day we went home, and I had my experience with me. Although my friends told me not to worry, I was remembering that man. I was thinking how it is almost impossible to predict such things and that there is so much irrationality I cannot explain. I just knew that place was not the place for me to be safe. This place was already a war zone, with special logics. And today our company still meets. We remember sometimes what happened.

During these war years we were all somehow more or less connected with peacekeeping. My friends were in a church organization. I was working with several non-governmental organizations with schoolchildren on projects concerning mental health and civil education, and two of my friends escaped from the war zone abroad and never came back.

JERRY STEIN AND MIKE BAIZERMAN

BEING ADDRESSED AND OBSESSED BY QUESTIONS: CALLS AND CRIES FROM THE MEETINGS OF YOUTHWORK IN CONTESTED SPACES

ABSTRACT

The second and third annual meetings on Youthwork in Contested Spaces (YWCS) were held in September, 2004, and October, 2005, at the Corrymeela retreat center on the coast of Northern Ireland. Delegates came from five continents, almost all of whom worked directly or indirectly (policy, program development or management) with young people in violent, post-violent, conflict, post-conflict societies. Many of the delegates also grew up in these societies. Together, we listened and engaged the many issues and voices.

In many countries there are bounded spaces of violence and places of conflicts; neighborhoods and geographical communities in which young people live that are "war zones." We who hosted the meeting made a working assumption about youthwork in these zones: Youthwork in contested and violent places would be both similar to and, at the same time, very different from regular youthwork. But how? We listened to stories and conversation and questions from youth and youthworkers who had lived in conflict situations, sometimes for many years. We hoped that these stories would begin to illuminate the lives of youth and the qualities of the youthworkers who worked with them.

In this chapter we bring these haunting and daunting conversations, and those dialogues, as interrogatives: as the questions heard and engaged over the four days at the two meetings. The questions belong to all of us who are doing, thinking about, and studying this courageous work with young people. The answers too can become ours; that depends on our ways of answering, our responses and, specifically, whether and how these questions and answers bring us to a model of youthwork in contested spaces. These questions open and sustain the spaces for thought, youthwork, and scholarship about young people and our own work with them and on their behalf.

In addition, our concluding discussion includes some speculations regarding tentative understandings of youth in conflict that emerged at these meetings. These differences and speculations emerged in conversations with youthworkers well after the meetings at Corrymeela.

The following questions are organized into two families: young people and youthwork. Since we could not be everywhere at the meetings, this is only a sample of the queries asked, reflected on and engaged.

Doug Magnuson and Michael Baizerman (eds), Work with Youth in Divided and Contested Societies, 319–323.

YOUNG PEOPLE

1. *How do young people do their everyday lives in such conditions, and to what effect on them, their friends, families, and communities?*

    Here is where psychology meets sociology and politics: me, my life, the world I'm in, and what it is like to be me, here, now. How do young people make sense? How do they keep going? And what happens when their lives become too much?

2. *How do young people respond to the realities of ongoing conflict situations?*

    When and why do some young people become passive or submissive? When do they join political factions? Why do some search for civic roles or seek resistance to violence? How do young people's reactions spread across a range of resistance, from non-violence to extreme violence? Another cousin in this family of questions illuminates everyday life in such circumstances:

3. *How do the young people who stay in their communities deal with the loss and their sense of abandonment by their friends and family who leave?*

    Not all in violent and/or contested spaces are stuck there; many try to leave and some do go by luck, connections, bribe. What does their leaving do to those young people who choose to stay? What compels those who want to leave and go and those who want to leave and cannot?

4. *What is normal in such conditions and what is known about its shapes?*

    Many of the stories were about schoolwork, dates, and conflicts with friends and family. They could have been told of any youth and any youthworkers. But these stories were juxtaposed with police break-ins, deaths, and resistance. So what is normality?

Youthwork

A second family of questions concern youthwork as an occupation, profession, and practice or praxis.

5. *What indeed is youthwork?*

Is it a family of practices, a (semi)profession, or simply the "work" done with young people? Does it have to be formalized, organized, and certified training? Is it a vocation, a calling, or is it "just a job?" What then is a "youthworker?" Who then is a youthworker? And, of course, what then is the "work" of youthwork: Personal counseling? Draft resistance? Recreation? Contesting paramilitary groups for the allegiance of your young people? Are there boundaries to this work, or working definitions? Does any of this matter when the context is contested, even violent? Do these young people "need" or want us, whatever we are called, however we are trained, whomever we work for or with, or not? What is youthwork's value nexus, its knowledge base, its skills? Is youthwork art, craft, and science applied? Is it "approach," method, or technology? On what ground do each of these rest? Is there a more or less identifiable philosophical (theological, political, psychological or other) anthropology basic to "the work?" What are the images of young people that guide youthworkers? What are the scientific and folk theories that are the sources of youthwork? These are some of the *big questions* under, in, and around the questions asked at Correymeela. Among the latter:

6. *How do you (re)construct a youthwork field when the socio-historical and socio-cultural knowledge of this work has been erased, lost, gone?*

What happens when the people who can tell you how to work with young people, who have the memories of previous organizational and youthwork experiences, are all gone or dead? How do you respond when libraries with curriculum have been destroyed? If you ask, "Do you need chairs to open a youth club?" and no one can answer you, because no one remembers, then what?

7. *What are the pathways (we could co-construct) along which young people in violent/contested spaces can themselves become youthworkers?*

8. *What is known about whether and how violent youth organizations move to become nonviolent and "constructive" groups, in effect, workers for peace and justice with young people and their community?*

9. *What are the roles of youthworkers in guiding youth away from violence towards living peace(fully)? Does this ever include the judicious application of violence. i.e. do you as a youthworker agree to organize your young people as a fighting force in order to gain the respect and safety necessary to continue your band or other clubs?*

10. *Is youthwork possible in places where no meetings are permitted?*

11. *How can (and should) youthworkers develop the necessary political skills to maneuver the shoals of public ideologies that thwart youthwork, political incidents that inflame communities, and outside organizations that appear with money and resources to "help?"*

12. *Can "peace" be as exciting to young people as violence?*

There were more in a series of practical, everyday, difficult questions that we group together below:

321

13. *Is it ethical to support young people in activities which can (are likely to) lead to their arrest, injury, even death? How can and do youthworkers encourage (lure, seduce, pull...) young people away from the violent groups and organizations from which they get respect and other needed/wanted recognitions and statuses? (e.g. belonging, protection, sense of safety). Who or what "protects" youthworkers in violent/contested spaces? Who hires, pays, supervises, and supports them in this work? And always: What can I do in my everyday life as young person, adult, citizen, youthworker to "make a difference?" What is my responsibility? What should I do in this situation?*

Woven through these questions about practice and the field of youthwork are the existential questions:

14. *Why am I doing this? Why can't I remember/feel how I did when I started this work? Is my work meaningful? Is this the me I truly want to be? Am I capable, able, ready, skilled enough to do this work well (enough)? What is the place of violence in all of this? And living and working everyday in spaces contested politically, socially, culturally, psychologically, spiritually: How is all of this affecting me, my work, the young people? How come so few of us are murdered while many are threatened by the "call to lynch?" Is it because our work is so little known, recognized, respected, feared?*

Finally we pose the questions that are always present:

15. *Why do I stay and continue to do this work? How do I "hang in there," persist in the light of all that is going on?*

Martin Luther, a Protestant theologian said: "Here I stand. I can do no other." Martin Buber, a Jewish theologian, tells the story of a person wondering what questions will be asked to gain entry into heaven: Had he/she been enough like Moses? But instead they are asked: "How come you were not yourself?"
Young people address us and in our response we are (or are not) youthworkers (however contested that term). We are or are not who we must be. Over and over and over, movement after movement: That is the me I choose to be.

DISCUSSION

These questions invite endless analysis and reflection, as well as focused, goal-driven responses: They are universal and local, timeless and time-bound, theoretical and practical. And they are above all necessary, for to respond to, even to "answer" them, is the act of defining the family of youthwork practice in divided, contested, and violent places: In answer we say who we are, what we do, and how we do it. These questions address us and in response we name the youthworker as we are and do. Since questions like these so powerfully invite us to craft our field, needed are more, even better queries. From you! And since most of these questions must outlast our answers, we must engage and reengage these in the unending dialogues that will serve to help ourselves and others understand our everyday work on the ground that this must be our courage and our responsibility. If you are to continue to be a vital, vibrant, and responsive praxis in the levels of young people in conditions of conflict: We can do no other!

Jerry Stein
Michael Baizerman
University of Minnesota, United States

MICHAEL BAIZERMAN

WHAT HAVE WE LEARNED?

ABSTRACT

Herein are presented the generalizations, aphorisms, provisional truths, and possible principles of practice extracted from three international meetings on Youth Work in Contested Spaces, the papers in this text, and the larger literature. Included are the same topics used to order the questions in the Introduction: Contested Spaces, doing youthwork, teaching and training, youth policy, research and evaluation, and youthworkers as persons and worker.

Themes presented in this chapter have three sources: The readings of this text, other literature, and notes and observations from the three international meetings, Youthwork in Contested Spaces, held in Northern Ireland in the early fall of 2003, 2004, and 2005.

There is no one size fits all when it comes to direct practice in contested spaces: Obviously, each violent space is violent in its own way, and specific measures have to be crafted to fit local particulars. Yet generalizations are also crucial as a guide, with each to be tested in the unique situation, each specific, concrete, and particular context and space: It is unreasonable and poor practice to reject generalizations because they are, by definition, abstract: calling these theory or academic is a try to devalue and marginalize the idea, leaving room only for specific practices and "my way." Both are needed! Needed too are the truly theoretical in the scientific sense: It was said that, "nothing is so practical as a good theory" because it has "predictive potency." Indeed this is still a viable aphorism in some areas of practice, such as medical and health work. Even post-modernist social constructionists with heart troubles want a physician who knows theoretical and applied cardiology and is up on pharmacology!

There are valid and useful generalizations that can be made about youthwork in contested spaces. Some of these follow next but omitted is practice on child soldiers, because this still growing literature is solid and filled with policy and program suggestions, many tested in and/or derived from practice (Boyden & de Berry, 2004; McConnan & Uppard, 2001).

Doug Magnuson and Michael Baizerman (eds), Work with Youth in Divided and Contested Societies, 325–333.

I am not sure how to categorize what was learned, indeed even if it were learned. I am confident that an expanded conception of learning will help. Much of what is presented is known to the field. By this I mean it was written or spoken about and is part of the working knowledge of several schools of youthwork practice. Bringing it to these pages serves to make it available as learning, available to be learned anew by both more and less experienced practitioners. In a phenomenological sense, this is like bringing to awareness one's taken for granted, hence invisible and typically unexamined practices, and the assumptions on which they were founded, sustained, and lived. Now about how to categorize the content.

Are these "principles of practice" aphorisms about practice simply generalizations? This is more than simply a problem of classification and its consequences. To place something in the category "practice principle" is to make an epistemological claim, i.e. to say that it has a certain knowledge/truth-power. I simply do not know the knowledge power of these learnings. True to what follows in the next paragraph, I stand on the notion that these general learnings were gleaned from the three sets of sources and that *for the practitioner* the truth-status of each lies in the concrete, specific, particular and unique context of the work; it is there that each must be tested for efficacy. All youthwork and youthwork knowledge in that sense is *always* provisional, partial, situational, ever necessary to be tested in the next concrete, specific moment. A different order of knowledge, perhaps "principles of practice," work to guide the test made in the concrete-specific.

Again, I simply do not know the knowledge-power for practice of these generalizations. My sense is that each is a valid, ethical, non-violent, just, equitable, and right guide. Will each work to guide practice that is morally good and technically competent? Not likely. But that, as we argue next, is your work!

South Africa had a Truth and Reconciliation Commission and, according to Albie Sachs, it worked with a practical and expanded conception of knowledge and truth. There is scientific truth, juridical truth, moral truth, and the narrative experiential truths of victims (and perpetrators) – each a different type or level, each with a different notion of truth (Walker & Unterhalter, 2004). There is young people's narrative truth, as it were, and youthworker truth, too. The *practical value* of each is what matters here and that is judged in one's *everyday practice* of work with young people and on their behalf.

YOUTHWORK PRACTICE

Youthwork is a family of practices, a large and extended family composed of smaller family groups. In another metaphor, youthwork is a big tent within which there are many groupings and groups.

Child and youth care, therapeutic group work, recreation, school counseling, social work, employment advising, sports coaching, and health advocacy are examples of direct, "hands on" youthwork. Indirect work on behalf of young people is done by policy makers, journalists, managers of youth services, program evaluators, and scholars of young people.

Here we do not claim that in the abstract one family of practice is more relevant or more effective than another in contested spaces in general. Rather, some *practices* may be both more relevant and effective in contested spaces. Will that be true in your space? Our perspective argues for ongoing evaluation of practice and ongoing "action-research:" youthwork as the intentional testing in practice of an idea, using information (data) to modify (or discontinue) the practice. In the North and West, this is called "data-based" or "empirically based practice." This approach may seem (and may be) a luxury in a context of violence, especially if it is seen as "academic" and unreal. Yet remember that your very survival as a person, youthworker, and project is in part precisely because you can read the text (the information and data) of your space and that is what you use to make the decisions which taken together add up to your survival.

All of this means that the youthworker is responsible for knowing about, modifying, testing, carrying-out, and evaluating (in practical, quick, low cost, and defensible ways) generalizations about working with young people directly and on their behalf. Put differently, your actual practice depends upon what *you* do with the generalizations presented here: You are indeed responsible.

Given the wide range of direct and indirect work with young people (only some of it called youthwork), the wide range of practitioner backgrounds and training, the range of program and project auspices, and the wide array of relevant and useful theories, concepts, and practices about what to do and how to do it, what we present may seem too little, too simplistic, too obvious. Indeed it may be all three! Our preference is that you read what follows as suggestions of how to go about finding and testing general practices in your world.

What would this section look like if we knew what you and others knew? Practitioners tell stories to each other about what they do and what they know far, far more often than they write about these. This book is an exception; our hope is that *you* will contribute to building practice expertise ("practice knowledge," "practice wisdom," "rules of thumb," and the like.

What have we learned in general about youthwork practice in contested spaces?
> *Contested space is treated as real.*
>> Youthworkers are intently aware of the violent space and plan and work accordingly.

> *Each contested space has its own ways of being present and influential.*
>> Youthwork is place/time-specific, with context-specific practices developed in response to local realities, e.g. armed, youth-recruiting/kidnapping paramilitaries and neighborhoods open only to those belonging to a particular family/clan, religion, race/ethnicity or political group.

> *There are general themes (if not principles) across sites.*
>> −Youthwork begins in the realities of one's society and community.
>> −The work team authors the work and the fingerprint is theirs.

–There are multiple project/program ethos; a newly emergent one is youth civic engagement with emphasis on projects co-designed, co-led and co-evaluated by young people.

–Contested spaces challenge critical thinking that pushes thought toward the reactive and ideological and to the absolute and inflexible.

–Networkers of youthworkers, programs/projects, and young people may have a time-limited lifespan and are difficult to organize, sustain, and fund. As it becomes older and larger, such networks tend towards greater complexity and bureaucracy and become harder to manage--internally and externally. To survive the network must generate its own funds. A network cannot be sustained by volunteers, and funders too easily become powerful, often controlling the work and workers. A network is never developed "once and for all" and must be renewed continuously over and over. In contested spaces, with its own power dynamics, including clear power distinctions, it may be particularly difficult to build and sustain a network of equals. In the end, networks are political instruments and must be understood and worked with as such; this holds for networks of youth projects and programs.

–Youthwork in contested spaces serves to teach the communities about the talents, competencies, and contributions of young people while showing the limitations of current sociocultural and political conceptions of youth, especially when these are simply chronological or simplistically developmental.

–To enhance the continuity of volunteer-led and staffed programs, the work should continue to serve youth already affiliated with community-based groups and encourage their involvement as volunteers (i.e. doing public work; citizens).

ETHICS

–Youthwork ethics show themselves constantly (and inevitably) around issues of trust, confidentiality, and disclosure, and all of these have real consequences for young people and workers. Ethical space is primordial for civil society, youthwork, and young people. Ethical standards for youthwork must be explicit, known, lived, and monitored.

–Information about young people, projects, funds, and the contested space per se is power and thus is never neutral, with its uses always contingent, tactical, and/or strategic.

–Youthwork as such serves to legitimate certain ways of working with all people.

–Youthwork becomes and is seen as political work.

–Your personal and professional integrity is most crucial in these contexts.

–Youthwork must begin in recognition and acknowledgement of the rights of both sides.

–The youthworker must be aware of their own and young people's everyday worlds and must try to grasp the Other's (young person, adult, etc.) realities and their meanings.

–Youthworkers are obligated to inform others about their work: the youth they are concerned about and work with and the young people's realities.

A Participatory Ethos:

–Youthwork begins with what the specific young people *want*, not with what the worker thinks they want or what she thinks they *need*.

–Youthwork can begin with "problems," with "possibilities," and/or "opportunities."

–Youthwork must cocreate with young people and others the spaces where they can struggle with issues real to them.

–Youthworkers, young people, and others must try to separate the "political" from the "valuational" and from core personal and social values so that non-violent, on-going conversations among contesting groups of young people can begin and be sustained.

–Youthworkers must embody patience and tolerance, along with contradiction and paradox: life-conditions in contested spaces.

–Young people are never expendable for any purpose: Youthwork witnesses this. Yet there are always and everywhere stories about workers using and abusing young people for their personal and/or political ends.

–Youth civic engagement – youth participation in decision-making about community and self – is emerging as a powerful practice ethos as well as an alternative or as complementary to intense clinical work with individual young people who were intimately touched by violence. Nonviolent adjustment and reintegration into civic society may be enhanced by meaningful involvement in civic life about issues of concern to them as youth and as citizens. This could be read as a vocational call to serve their community.

–Youthwork is often within existing local and international "discourse(s) of trauma and victimization" (Newman, 2004), and these serve to both legitimize certain practices and limit other types of intervention, such as youth participation, which are outside typical clinical therapeutic frames of practice.

–Youthwork practice may have to challenge the exclusive--and even the common use--of such discourses which serve to transform young people into objects, not actors with agency and meaning, capable of acting competently in civil society.

—Youthworkers in contested spaces witness for young people, embodying their promise as individuals and as citizens of their community and of civil society.

Teaching Youthwork

—Youthwork is a family of multiple occupations including semi-professions, paid and volunteer youthwork and is itself a contested space.

—This is true across the distinction between paid work and volunteer (public work), and varies within and across nations and within and across areas of practice and by youth populations.

—There are many authoritative communities of youthwork practice, each with its own practice theory, philosophy, and skills, and these too vary by country, areas of practice, and youth populations.

—There is education in and training for direct and indirect work with youth, the former most typically university-based and, because of that, linked more closely to research (empirically-based practice) and to world-wide academic and practice communities (e.g. professional groups). Training often is local, closer to the practice community, based in institutes, not necessarily university affiliated, and using local texts in local languages. In contrast, university-based learning more often uses international texts in both local languages and English.

—A consequence of this multiplicity and pluralism is that there is no single world-wide acceptable curriculum of teaching youthwork practice, direct and indirect. Practice is always local and unique, situational and contextual – especially so in divided and contested spaces.

—Practitioners of direct work with young people typically teach and train each other; the extent to which this occurs depends in contested spaces on local customs, politics and danger.

—A cross-national, cross-sectional, and cross-professional curriculum is needed, and should be written and used to build local skills for context-specific practice.

—Practitioners from contested spaces should lead such courses in conjunction with institute and university faculty, when conditions permit, thereby linking practice to concepts and in turn to principles and theory.

—All education and training should be grounded in analysis of the nature and work of contested spaces as such, i.e. how they perform and shape as context the life-realities of community, groups, individuals, and youthwork.

—Needed still are rich and grounded "thick" narratives of practice for use as exemplars and as subjects of analysis.

   −A curriculum with multiple core subjects, e.g. contested spaces,
   violent realities, young people's life-worlds, practice guidelines for
   working with youth in such environments are possible, and these
   could be used to draw-out, particularize, and enrich local narratives
   (told in local languages), which then could be shared for use,
   including examining them for cross-local patterns.
   −Simple program evaluation approaches and methods should be taught.
   So too should evaluation capacity building (Compton, Baizerman, &
   Hueftle, 2002).
   −So too should be the basics of social research, especially practical,
   low-cost, defensible, and action research.

Policy

   −There is public policy on the national and local levels, and policy on
   the level of organizations. All may be important for young people,
   depending on sociopolitical context, type, and degree of violence.
   −There can be public policy about contested spaces, about violence,
   about young people, about everyday life, and about the life-course in
   conditions of violently contested spaces. All may be important.
   −Policy can also drive programs and it is programs that employ
   youthworkers.
   −Policy may be the engine of funding.
   −Some policy is law and some policy may have no statutory base,
   especially in conditions of war.
   −Policy decision-structures are a focus for active monitoring and, often,
   change to help communities and young people. These must be joined
   to structures and resources, not a simple connection under conditions
   of violence.
   −Guides on how to understand what policy is and how it can be useful
   are found in Lorey (2001) on child soldiers.

Research and Evaluation

   −There is virtually no program evaluation of youthwork in contested
   spaces.
   −Evaluation of model and specific programs over time is needed,
   across programs of the same type (e.g. youth civic engagement, in
   one locale and also across locales), and within and especially across
   youth populations.
   −Young people must be co-evaluators with adults and co-researchers.
   −While formal research can be done in violently contested space (as
   work in Northern Ireland, Palestine, Uganda, and South Africa
   show), such work is difficult and too often dangerous.

331

−What is done on young people and other immediately relevant questions may not be given to youthworkers for use in their practice. Better synaptic connections are needed to name and urge study of immediate practical questions, and similar communication channels are needed to bring to youthworkers research findings and their practice implications.

Youthworkers

−Youthworkers in conditions of violently divided and contested space suffer psychosocial (e.g. exhaustion) and existential "burn-out" (i.e. the loss of meaning in one's work). Prevention of both is necessary, while therapeutic responses to both are a moral necessity.

−Youthworkers name their person, their role, and their work variously, and this naming follows local naming practices and may not travel well across geographies, functional programs, or occupational areas.

−Those who self-define as youthworkers and in what terms this self-designation is made should not be restructured *a priori* by others using strict naming rules: An open tent that invites all fellow travelers might be best (e.g. teacher, physicians, employment advisors, community organizers, youth program managers).

−Youthwork is a contextualized and situational practice in divided and contested spaces, and youthworkers must be judged by their grasp of the immediate, the practical, the safe, and the just.

−Youthwork practice itself must be non-violent, and youthworkers must hold to the values of justice, fairness, inclusiveness, and nonviolence.

−Since youthwork in divided and contested spaces is often dangerous, issues of worker and youth safety must be acknowledged and actively responded to. Romantic notions of violence and exceptional risk-taking have no moral or other legitimacy or place in youthwork on the ground, and workers in their roles must be supervised closely, even dismissed from their jobs.

−Youthworkers in these spaces always exist and work as moral embodiments doing moral interventions.

−Youthwork in such spaces and under such conditions is always political.

CONCLUSIONS

Are these principles of practice? I'm still not sure. At minimum, these are generalizations about youthwork in divided and contested spaces, many derived

from practitioner common sense and practice wisdom. What is their epistemological truth status? Likely most are valid, if not profound, reasonable, partial, incomplete, and still contestable.
The utility of these will be proven by those who take them up and try them in day-to-day practice, in research, and in programevaluation.

Michael Baizerman
University of Minnesota

REFERENCES

Boyden, J., & de Berry, J., (Eds.). (2004). *Children and youth on the front line: Ethnography, armed conflict, and displacement.* New York: Berghahn Books.
Compton, D., Baizerman, M., & Hueftle, S., (Eds.). (2002). The art, craft, and science of evaluation capacity building. *New Directions for Program Evaluation* (No. 93). San Francisco: Jossey-Bass.
McConnan, I., & Uppard, S. (2001). *Children, not soldiers: Guidelines for working with child soldiers and children associated with fighting forces.* London: Save The Children.
Lorey, M. (2001). *Child soldiers. Care and protection of children in emergencies: A field guide.* NP: Save the Children.
Walker, M., & Unterhalter, E. (2004). Knowledge, narrative and national reconciliation: Stored reflections on the South Africa Truth and Reconciliation Commission. *Discourse, 25*(2), 279-297.

LIST OF CONTRIBUTORS

Michael Baizerman
University of Minnesota
School of Social Work
105 Peters Hall, 1404 Gortner Ave.
St. Paul, MN 55108 USA
Email: mbaizerm@umn.edu

Doug Magnuson
University of Victoria
School of Child & Youth Care
Box 1700 STN CSC
Victoria, BC V8W 2Y2
Canada
email: dougm@uvic.ca

Phil Lancaster
University of Victoria
School of Child & Youth Care
Box 1700 STN CSC
Victoria, BC V8W 2Y2
Canada
email: philiplancaster123@hotmail.com

Yvonne Kemper
Berghof Research Center for Constructive Conflict Management
email: ybkemper@yahoo.de

Paul Smyth
Public Achievement N.I.
87 Wellington Park
Belfast, N.I. BT9 6DP
email: paul@publicachievement.com

Steve Mokwena
28 Arundel Rd.
Johannesburg, South Africa
email: steve@modjadjiworks.com

Sanja Spanja
Hrvatskog Zrakoplovsta 14/13
Vukovar, Croatia
email: marko.spanja@vk.htnet.hr

LIST OF CONTRIBUTORS

Siobhan McEvoy-Levy
Butler University
Political Science
4600 Sunset Ave.
Indianapolis, IN 46208 USA
email: smcevoy@butler.edu

Women's Commission for Refugee Women and Children
122 East 42nd St., 12th Floor
New York 10168 USA
www.womenscomission.org

Katy Radford
Irish School of Ecumenics
Trinity College Dublin
683, Antrim Road
Belfast BT15 4EG
email: radfordk@tcd.ie

Tony Morgan
University of Ulster
Room 21C10
Jordanstown, Newtownabbey
Co. Antrim BT37 OQB Northern Ireland
email: tmorgan@ulster.ac.uk

Alan Grattan
Department of Youth Work
Faculty of Law, ARts, and Social Sciences
University of Southampton, England
U.K.
email: a.grattan@soton.ac.uk

Ken Harlan
Room 21CO1
Dalraida
University of Ulster
Northern Ireland BT37 OQB
email: k.harland@ulster.ac.uk

Vesna Ognjenovic
HI Neighbour
Kapetan Misina 23/1
11000 Belgrade, Serbia
email: zdravo@eunet.yu

Suzanne Hammad, Tareq AlBakri
email: talbakri@qub.ac.uk

Rebecca Manski
Baladna Association
Hertzlia St. 12
Haifa Israel
email: reefcah@yahoo.com

Snežana Kresoja
Helsinki Committee for Human Rights in Serbia
Novi Sad Branch Office
Rudjera Boskovica 2c
Serbia
email: kresojas@neobee.net

Tanja E. Bosch
Journalism
Stellenbosch University
South Africa
email: drbosch@sun.ac.za

Stephanie Griffin
University of Victoria
School of Child & Youth Care
Box 1700 STN CSC
Victoria, BC V8W 2Y2
Canada
email: stephg@uvic.ca

Marko Gashi
External Associate of Helsinki Committee for Human Rights
Novi Sad Branch Office
Rudjera Boskovica 2c
Serbia
email: lmg@neobee.net

Jerry Stein
University of Minnesota
School of Social Work
1404 Gortner Ave.
St. Paul, MN 55108 USA
email: stein035@umn.edu

Lightning Source UK Ltd.
Milton Keynes UK
UKOW04f2301260614

234117UK00008B/90/A